OVIDIAN TRANSVERSIONS

Conversions
Series Editors: Paul Yachnin and Bronwen Wilson

Available titles
Ovidian Transversions: 'Iphis and Ianthe', 1300–1650
Edited by Valerie Traub, Patricia Badir and Peggy McCracken

Visit our website at: www.edinburghuniversitypress.com/series/CONV

OVIDIAN TRANSVERSIONS
'IPHIS AND IANTHE', 1300–1650

Edited by Valerie Traub, Patricia Badir and
Peggy McCracken

EDINBURGH
University Press

Edinburgh University Press is one of the leading university presses in the UK. We publish academic books and journals in our selected subject areas across the humanities and social sciences, combining cutting-edge scholarship with high editorial and production values to produce academic works of lasting importance. For more information visit our website: edinburghuniversitypress.com

© editorial matter and organisation Valerie Traub, Patricia Badir and Peggy McCracken, 2019, 2020
© the chapters their several authors, 2019, 2020

Edinburgh University Press Ltd
The Tun – Holyrood Road, 12(2f) Jackson's Entry, Edinburgh EH8 8PJ

First published in hardback by Edinburgh University Press 2019

Typeset in 10/12.5 Sabon by
Servis Filmsetting Ltd, Stockport, Cheshire

A CIP record for this book is available from the British Library

ISBN 978 1 4744 4890 1 (hardback)
ISBN 978 1 4744 4891 8 (paperback)
ISBN 978 1 4744 4892 5 (webready PDF)
ISBN 978 1 4744 4893 2 (epub)

The right of Valerie Traub, Patricia Badir and Peggy McCracken to be identified as the editors of this work has been asserted in accordance with the Copyright, Designs and Patents Act 1988, and the Copyright and Related Rights Regulations 2003 (SI No. 2498).

CONTENTS

List of Figures vii
Acknowledgements xi
Contributors xiii

Introduction: Transversions of 'Iphis and Ianthe' 1
Valerie Traub

1 Metamorphosis as Supplement: Sexuality and History in the *Ovide moralisé* 43
   Peggy McCracken

2 The Trans* Temporality of Lament: 'Foolish' Hope and Trans* Survival in the *Ovide moralisé*'s 'Iphis and Ianthe' 60
   Laurel Billings

3 Gower's Riddles in 'Iphis and Iante' 80
   Karma Lochrie

4 Fortune's Touch: Reading Transformation in Christine de Pizan's *Mutacion de Fortune* 99
   Miranda Griffin

5   Becoming Scattered: The Case of Iphis's Trans*version and the
     Archipelogic of John Florio's *Worlde of Wordes*   118
     Marjorie Rubright

6   Alchemy, Humanism and the Uses of Disknowledge in John
     Lyly's *Galatea*   150
     Katherine Eggert

7   The Problem with Love: Untoward Engagement and Humanist
     Pedagogy in *Galatea*   172
     Elizabeth Mathie

8   Coastal Squeeze: Environmental Metamorphosis and Lyly's
     Lincolnshire   191
     Patricia Badir

9   Illegible Bodies: Reading Intersex and Transgender in Early
     Modern France (the Case of Isaac de Benserade's *Iphis et Ianthe*)   213
     Kathleen Perry Long

10   Lesbianism in Benserade's *Iphis et Ianthe* (1634): Gallantry and
     the Making of Heterosexuality in Seventeenth-Century France   241
     Matthieu Dupas

11   Changing the Ways of the World: Sex, Youth and Modernity in
     Benserade's *Iphis et Iante*   261
     Susan S. Lanser

Appendices: Translations and Images of 'Iphis and Ianthe'   279
A   'Iphis and Ianthe' in the *Ovide moralisé*, trans. Miranda Griffin,
     Blake Gutt and Peggy McCracken   279
B   'Iphis and Ianthe' in John Gower's *Confessio amantis*, trans.
     Karma Lochrie   286
C   'Iphis and Ianthe' in Christine de Pizan's *La Mutacion de Fortune*,
     trans. Miranda Griffin   288
D   'Iphis and Ianthe' in Arthur Golding's *Metamorphosis* (1567)   289
E   'Iphis and Ianthe' in George Sandys' *Ovid's Metamorphosis*
     (1632)   293
F   Select Images of 'Iphis and Ianthe' to 1700   297

Index   321

LIST OF FIGURES

3.1	John Gower, *Confessio Amantis* (*c.*1393). Oxford Bodleian Library, MS Fairfax 3, folio 8r.	87
5.1	John Rider, *Riders dictionarie corrected* (1612). RB 302497. The Huntington Library, San Marino, California.	120
5.2	John Florio, *A Worlde of Wordes* (1598). RB 59838. The Huntington Library, San Marino, California.	122
5.3	Cristoforo Buondelmonti, *Liber insularum archipelagi* (*c.*1420). Mich. MS. 162. Special Collections Research Center, University of Michigan, Ann Arbor, Michigan.	135
5.4	Bartolomeo dalli Sonetti, *Isolario* (1484). RB 84726. The Huntington Library, San Marino, California.	136
5.5	Bartolomeo dalli Sonetti, *Isolario* (1484). RB 84726. The Huntington Library, San Marino, California.	139
8.1	Lincolnshire banks from the Humber Bridge (between Barton-upon-Humber and Hull). Author's photograph.	193
8.2	Christopher Saxton's Map of Lincolnshire (1576). Royal MS 18.D.lll. no. 5. © The British Library.	193
8.3	Christopher Saxton's Map of Lincolnshire (detail, 1576). Royal MS 18.D.lll. no. 5. © The British Library.	194
8.4	The Humber river from the Lincolnshire banks (at Barton-Upon-Humber). Author's photograph.	195

8.5	Humberside fields and pastures. Barton-Upon-Humber. Author's photograph.	200
8.6	'Tide Facts: The Humber Estuary'. TIDE Project. http://www.tide-project.eu/index.php5?node_id=Reports-and-Publications;83&lang_id=1.	202
8.7	St Peter's Church, Barton-Upon-Humber. Author's photograph.	206
F.1	'Birth of Iphis' (detail). *Ovide moralisé* (14c.). Rouen Bibliothèque Municipale ms. 04, fol. 243.	298
F.2	'Telethusa and Iphis Pray to Isis' (detail). *Ovide moralisé* (14c.). Rouen Bibliothèque Municipale ms. 04, fol. 244v.	299
F.3	Marriage of Iphis and Ianthe' (detail). *Ovide moralisé* (14c.). Rouen Bibliothèque Municipale ms. 04, fol. 244v.	300
F.4	'Birth of Iphis' (detail). *Ovide moralisé* (14c.). Bibliothèque Nationale de France. Bibliothèque de l'Arsenal, ms. 5069, fol. 131.	301
F.5	Bernard Salomon. 'Lygde & Teletuse'. *La métamorphose d'Ovide figureé* (Lyon, 1557), 60r. Bibliothèque Nationale de France.	302
F.6	Bernard Salomon. 'La fille Iphis en fils'. *La métamorphose d'Ovide figureé* (Lyon, 1557), 60v. Bibliothèque Nationale de France.	303
F.7	Bernard Salomon. 'Teletusa fa credere al marito che la sua figliuola è maschio'. Gabriele Simeoni, *Del Metamorphoseo abbreviato, con la rinovatione d'alcune stanze, libro decimoquinto, con figurator* (Lyon, 1559), p. 132, plate 120. Warburg Institute.	304
F.8	Bernard Salomon. 'La figliuola di Lyddo conuertita in maschio'. Gabriele Simeoni, *Del Metamorphoseo abbreviato, con la rinovatione d'alcune stanze, libro decimoquinto, con figurator* (Lyon, 1559), p. 133, plate 121. Warburg Institute.	305
F.9	Virgil Solis. 'Lyctus & Telethusa uxor'. Johan Spreng, *Metamorphoses Ovidii, argumentis quidem soluta oration . . . una cum singularum transformationum Iconibus, a Vergilio Solis, eximo picture, delineates* (1570), p. 115. Bibliothèque Nationale de France.	306
F.10	Virgil Solis. 'Iphis puella in marem'. Johan Spreng, *Metamorphoses Ovidii, argumentis quidem soluta oration . . . una cum singularum transformationum Iconibus, a Vergilio Solis, eximo picture, delineates* (1570), p. 116. Bibliothèque Nationale de France.	307
F.11	Anonymous (after Virgil Solis). 'Telethusa and Isis'. *Pub. Ovidii Nasonis Metamorphoseon libri XV, ex postrema Jocobi Micylli recognitione, et recensione nova Gregorii Bersmarni, cum*	

LIST OF FIGURES

	eiusdem notationibus . . . (Leipzig: Joannes Steinman, 1582), p. 383. Warburg Institute.	308
F. 12	Anonymous (after Virgil Solis). 'Iphis Disguised as a Youth Prays to Become a Youth'. *Pub. Ovidii Nasonis Metamorphoseon libri XV, ex postrema Jocobi Micylli recognitione, et recensione nova Gregorii Bersmarni, cum eiusdem notationibus* ... (Leipzig: Joannes Steinman, 1582), p. 386. Warburg Institute.	309
F.13	Petrus Vander Borcht. 'Lyctus et Telethusa Uxor. IX'. Lactantius Placidus, *P. Ovidii Nasonis Metamorphoses: argumentis brevioribus / ex Luctatio Grammatico [i.e. Lactantius Placidus] collecti expositae; una cum vivis singularum transformationum iconibus in aes incisis* (Antwerp: Ex Officina Plantiniana apud viduam & J. Moretum, 1591), p. 235. Warburg Institute.	310
F.14	Petrus Vander Borcht. 'Iphis Puella in Marem. X'. Lactantius Placidus, *P. Ovidii Nasonis Metamorphoses: argumentis brevioribus / ex Luctatio Grammatico [i.e. Lactantius Placidus] collecti expositae; una cum vivis singularum transformationum iconibus in aes incisis* (Antwerp: Ex Officina Plantiniana apud viduam & J. Moretum, 1591), p. 237. Warburg Institute.	311
F.15	Pietrus de Jode. 'The order of Lyctus to Telethusa about the child'. Antonio Tempesta. *Metamorphoseon sive Transformationum Ovidianarum libri quindecim, aeneis formis ab Antonio Tempesta Florentino incise* . . . (Antwerp, 1606), plate 89. Warburg Institute.	312
F.16	Pietrus de Jode. 'Telethusa Praying to Change Iphis to a Man'. Antonio Tempesta. *Metamorphoseon sive Transformationum Ovidianarum libri quindecim, aeneis formis ab Antonio Tempesta Florentino incise* . . . (Antwerp, 1606), plate 90. Warburg Institute.	313
F.17	Crispijn van de Pass, the Elder. 'Lyctus, Telethusa, Iphis'. *P. Ovid Nasonis XV Metamorphoseon librorum figurae elegantissime a Crispiano Passaeo Iaminis aeneis incisae* (Cologne: Passaeus; Arnhemiae: Janssonius, 1607), plate 84. Herzog August Bibliothek, Wolfenbüttel.	314
F.18	Francis Clein (engraved by P. Lombart and S. Savery). George Sandys. *Ovids Metamorphosis: Englished, mythologiz'd, and represented in figures* (Oxford, 1632), p. 301. University of British Columbia.	315
F.19	Unidentified Dutch or Flemish. 'Fable Douzième', executed before 1677. Pierre Du-Ryer. *Les Metamorphoses d'Ovide en latin et francois*. Amsterdam, 1702. p. 302. Warburg Institute.	316
F.20	Johann Wilhelm Baur. 'Iphis Puella in Marem'. *Bellissimum*	

ix

Ovidii theatrum . . . (Nuremberg: P. Fürstii, 1687; first published in Vienna in 1641). Warburg Institute. 317

F.21 Melchior Küsel I (after Johann Wilhelm Baur). 'Lyctus and Telethusa uxor'. *Metamorphosis oder Ovidii der Poeten Wunderliche Verenderung* (Augsburg, 1681), p. 89. Warburg Institute. 318

F.22 Melchior Küsel I (after Johann Wilhelm Baur). 'Iphis puella in marem'. *Metamorphosis oder Ovidii der Poeten Wunderliche Verenderung* (Augsburg, 1681), p. 90. Warburg Institute. 319

F.23 Johann Ulrich Kraus. 'Iphis Changed from a Girl into a Youth by the Grace of Isis'. *Die Verwandlungen des Ovidii in zweyhundert und sechs und zwanzig Kupffern* (Augsburg: Kraus, 1694), p. 82, plate 159. Warburg Institute. 320

ACKNOWLEDGMENTS

As described more fully in the Introduction, this volume is the result of collaborative thinking and the work of many hands. Our indebtedness is, first and foremost, to the indomitable Paul Yachnin, whose entrepreneurial energy, intellectual generosity and curiosity about all things convertible have provided our *sine qua non*. Beyond his unstinting leadership of the Early Modern Conversions project, Paul's capacious embrace of this volume has offered just one more proof of his open mind, heart and hands. We thank, as well, Bronwen Wilson for her enthusiasm for this volume, as well as for the warmth of her insights and thoughtful editorial oversight. Kathleen Perry Long's vision of a 'Transforming Bodies' conference was itself transformed into an opportunity for our contributors to workshop their papers at Cornell University; we appreciate her flexibility and care, as well as the help of her colleagues at Cornell. For many logistical acts of forethought and attentiveness, a big call out is due to Stephen Wittek, who expertly managed the Early Modern Conversions project at McGill University during the years of this volume's inception. Since his departure, Marie-Claude Felton has picked up the logistical reins without a hitch. In addition to underwriting the positions of these dedicated personnel, the support of the Social Sciences and Humanities Research Council of Canada for the Early Modern Conversions project has been crucial; among other things, SSHRC provided extraordinary opportunities for us to collaborate in person, not only at annual team meetings but also in Ann Arbor and Vancouver. For their varied contributions to the symposium on metamorphosis hosted by the University of Michigan Institute for the Humanities in 2016 – without which this volume would not have happened – we thank Sidonie Smith, Patrick Tonks, Doretha Coval, Stephanie Harrell, Nina Barraco, Steven Mullaney, Doug Trevor and George Hoffmann. Jade Standing provided excellent research assistance on numerous aspects of preparing the manuscript. At Edinburgh University Press, Michelle Houston and Ersev Ersoy have skilfully shepherded the manuscript through production. In our diverse and ever-changing interlocutors in the Early Modern Conversions project, we have been enormously fortunate; even when offering intellectual friction, their intellectual vitality and good will have never flagged. And each of the contributors to this volume has been not only smart, but responsible and responsive; we thank them for making our editorial labour so easy.

Finally, because little good in academia ever happens without kindness and such kindness rarely receives sufficient acknowledgment, Valerie wishes to thank Patsy and Peggy: Patsy for greeting my reluctance to embark on another editing project – despite the publication worthiness of wonderful symposia papers – with a simple and unbidden 'I'll help you'; and Peggy for replying, without a moment's hesitation, 'yes' to our subsequent request to join the editorial team. In such acts, kindness lives and friendship grows.

CONTRIBUTORS

Patricia Badir is Professor of English at the University of British Columbia. She is the author of *The Maudlin Impression: English Literary Images of Mary Magdalene, 1550–1700* (University of Notre Dame Press, 2009) and her most recent set of articles studies the archival remains of early twentieth-century productions of medieval and Renaissance drama. She is currently working on a series of articles that explores what it means to study the early modern past 'from here' as well as a book on the early twentieth-century director, Roy Mitchell, and the matter of the theatrical archive.

Laurel Billings is a PhD student in English and Women's Studies at the University of Michigan. Her research interests include gender, empire and environment in late medieval and early modern literature.

Matthieu Dupas is Assistant Professor of French at Northwestern University. He holds a PhD in French Literature from the Université de Paris III-Sorbonne Nouvelle and a PhD in French from the University of Michigan. His research reads French literary texts written before and after modernity from the viewpoint of the history of sexuality and queer theory. His forthcoming book *Corneille Galant: Genre et sexualité dans la comédie cornélienne* (Classiques Garnier) shows how seventeenth-century gallantry reconfigured gender relationships and erotic subjectivities on the threshold of modernity and paved the way for modern heterosexuality.

Katherine Eggert is Professor of English at the University of Colorado Boulder. She is the author of two books, *Showing Like a Queen: Female Authority and Literary Experiment in Spenser, Shakespeare, and Milton* (2000) and *Disknowledge: Literature, Alchemy, and the End of Humanism in Renaissance England* (2015), and of articles on Spenser, Shakespeare, Jonson, Donne, early modern literature and science, and Shakespeare on film. She is currently writing a book entitled *Renaissance Happiness*.

Miranda Griffin is the Dawson Lecturer in Modern and Medieval Languages at St Catharine's College, University of Cambridge. Her first book, *The Object and the Cause in the Vulgate Cycle*, was published by Legenda in 2005; her second book, *Transforming Tales: Rewriting Metamorphosis in Medieval French Literature*, was published by Oxford University Press in 2015. She has published articles on the medieval French lai, verse and prose romance, and the *Ovide moralisé*.

Susan S. Lanser is Professor Emerita of Comparative Literature, English, and Women's, Gender, and Sexuality Studies at Brandeis University. Her most recent monograph, *The Sexuality of History: Modernity and the Sapphic, 1565–1830* (University of Chicago Press), won the Joan Kelly Prize for the American Historical Association's best book in women's history/feminist theory, received honourable mention for the Louis D. Gottschalk Prize of the American Society for Eighteenth-Century Studies and was a finalist for the Lamda Literary Award in LGBT Studies.

Karma Lochrie is a Provost Professor of English at Indiana University who specialises in Middle English Literature. She has written extensively on gender and sexuality in medieval texts, including her book, *Heterosyncrasies: Female Sexuality When Normal Wasn't* (University of Minnesota Press, 2005). Her most recent book is *Nowhere in the Middle Ages* (University of Pennsylvania Press, 2016).

Kathleen Perry Long is Professor of French in the Department of Romance Studies at Cornell University. She is the author of two books, *Another Reality: Metamorphosis and the Imagination in the Poetry of Ovid, Petrarch, and Ronsard* and *Hermaphrodites in Renaissance Europe*, and editor of volumes on *High Anxiety: Masculinity in Crisis in Early Modern France*, *Religious Differences in France* and *Gender and Scientific Discourse in Early Modern Europe*. She has written numerous articles on the work of Théodore Agrippa d'Aubigné, on gender in early modern Europe and on monsters. She is preparing a translation into English of *The Island of Hermaphrodites (L'isle des hermaphrodites)*, a book-length study of the works of Agrippa d'Aubigné, and another on the relationship between early modern discourses of monstrosity and modern discourses of disability.

Peggy McCracken is the Mary Fair Croushore Collegiate Professor of the Humanities and Professor of French, Comparative Literature and Women's Studies at the University of Michigan. She is the author or co-author of six books, including most recently *In the Skin of a Beast: Sovereignty and Animality in Medieval France* (2017), and translator of Gui de Cambrai's *Barlaam and Josaphat: A Christian Tale of the Buddha* (2014).

Elizabeth Mathie is a Postdoctoral Research Fellow in the Tsinghua-Michigan Society of Fellows and a member of the international faculty in the Department of Foreign Languages and Literatures at Tsinghua University in Beijing. Her current work focuses on representations of training (of both animals and humans) in early modern England, especially in instructional manuals and on the stage. She has interests in early modern English drama and poetry, contemporaneous prescriptive literature, humanist pedagogy, early English colonialism and animal studies.

Marjorie Rubright is Associate Professor of English and Director of the Arthur F. Kinney Center for Interdisciplinary Renaissance Studies at the University of Massachusetts Amherst. She is author of *Doppelgänger Dilemmas: Anglo-Dutch Relations in Early Modern English Literature and Culture* (University of Pennsylvania Press, 2014) and co-author of *'So Long Lives This': Celebrating Shakespeare's Life and Works 1616–2016* (Thomas Fisher Rare Book Library, Toronto), which was awarded the 2017 Katharine Kyes Leab and Daniel J. Leab Award. She is currently writing a book entitled *A World of Words: Language and Earth in the Renaissance*.

Valerie Traub is the Adrienne Rich Distinguished University Professor and Frederick G. L. Huetwell Professor of English and Women's Studies at the University of Michigan. Working across the disciplines of literature and history, she is a specialist in the study of gender and sexuality in sixteenth- and seventeenth-century England. She is the author of three monographs: *Thinking Sex with the Early Moderns* (2015), *The Renaissance of Lesbianism in Early Modern England* (2002) and *Desire & Anxiety: Circulations of Sexuality in Shakespearean Drama* (1992, 2014). Her most recent collection is *The Oxford Handbook of Shakespeare and Embodiment* (2016).

INTRODUCTION:
TRANSVERSIONS OF 'IPHIS AND IANTHE'

Valerie Traub

It's an old story. A father issues a decree: because of his family's poverty and the burdens that girls bring, if his wife gives birth to a girl, the infant must be killed. His distraught wife sees, as if in a dream, the goddess Isis, who tells her to disobey her husband; if the child is female, Isis will protect her. The female infant is given the non-gendered name Iphis and is raised by her mother and nurse as a boy. At the age of thirteen, Iphis is betrothed by her unsuspecting father to the maiden Ianthe. Both girls, who are depicted as alike in all ways but their gender, are deeply in love. While Ianthe eagerly longs for the wedding, Iphis despairs, giving voice to a long lament about her 'strange' and 'prodigious' predicament, contrasting her fate to that of cows, sheep, deer and birds, whose females never seek to mate with other females. On the day before the wedding, her mother fervently prays to Isis and, as mother and daughter walk from the temple, Iphis's body is transformed: her hair shortens, her complexion darkens, her limbs gain strength, her stride lengthens. Venus, Juno and Hymen join to bless the marriage, made possible by an apparent change of sex. That, in brief synopsis, is Publius Ovidius Naso's story of 'Iphis and Ianthe' from Book 9 of his Latin *Metamorphoses* (666–797).[1]

If this story doesn't sound familiar, that is not surprising. The tale of 'Iphis and Ianthe' is one that few people today know. Compared to the stories of Venus and Adonis, Narcissus and Echo, Philomela, Pygmalion, Orpheus and Ganymede, the plight of Iphis and Ianthe has not attracted the broad critical interest of scholars seeking to understand Ovid's influence on literary history – particularly in the medieval and early modern periods when that influence was at its height. This is true, despite the considerable interest in the tale shown by medieval and early modern translators, commentators and adapters. *Ovidian Transversions:'Iphis and Ianthe', 1300–1650* aims to redress that critical neglect by exploring a range of issues to which this tale was made to speak in pre-modern France and England.

No full manuscripts of Ovid's *Metamorphoses* survive from antiquity and the earliest manuscript fragments date from the ninth century.[2] The earliest extant witnesses to the complete poem date from the eleventh century.[3] Between then and the fourteenth century, the *Metamorphoses* circulated in concert with Latin commentaries that provided several approaches to the text. Commentators glossed words and meanings, explicating the literal sense of the poem and providing a framework that would be exploited by subsequent authors intent on appropriating the poem for Christian allegory. Around 1170, Arnulf of Orléans provided an *accessus* (introduction), philological and grammatical glosses, a list of transformations included in each book and allegorical interpretations for each 'fable'.[4] Building on Arnulf's allegories, John of Garland composed a verse moralisation, the *Integumenta Ovidii*, around 1234, claiming 'to untie knotty secrets, to open closed matters, to clarify cloudy matters and to proclaim hidden things'.[5] Prose paraphrases, introductions and interlinear and marginal glosses multiplied over time as commentaries sought to impart philological, grammatical, historical, mythological, geographical, ethical and/or literary instruction.[6] As early as the late eleventh century, the presence of an 'Ovidian subculture' in monastic and cathedral schools encouraged ways of reading and imitating Ovid that exceeded his use for instruction; the members of this subculture 'responded playfully and immediately to his literary techniques and to his amatory teasings'.[7]

By the thirteenth century, the *Metamorphoses* was a centrepiece of the school curriculum,[8] and Ovid was being approached simultaneously as a moralist, natural theologian and scientist, as well as a versatile poet showcasing a variety of literary techniques. These variable approaches mean that the *Metamorphoses* was 'marked by inherent instability of meaning' and 'was interpreted and augmented by medieval scholars and writers in ways which often accentuated that instability'.[9] In the fourteenth century, the capacious medieval commentary tradition was itself metamorphosed quite dramatically into the *Ovide moralisé*, a poem of 72,000 lines of octosyllabic verse translations, accompanied by euhemerist (historical) interpretations and Christian moralisations.[10] Composed by an anonymous Franciscan between 1316 and 1328, the *Ovide moralisé* translated all the stories into French, supplementing the narrative with earlier mythographical texts and commentaries, adding interpretations identifying natural phenomena and historical events as the sources of the stories, and recasting lustful gods, tyrannical fathers and suffering maidens as allegories of Christian truth.[11]

Versions of the *Ovide moralisé* circulated as well in two fifteenth-century vernacular prose abridgements, a prose version published by Collard Mansion and an independent Latin prose text by Benedictine Pierre Bersuire, the *Ovidius moralizatus*.[12] In both the *Ovide moralisé* and the *Ovidius moralizatus* the aim of revealing universal truths led to surprisingly flexible modes of allegoresis.[13] In fact, Bersuire's text, which was ultimately banned by the Catholic church in 1559, offered multiple and often self-contradictory interpretations, imparting what has been called an 'unpoliceable self-generating polysemousness'.[14] It may be in this invitation to habits of thought – rather than in their invitation to embrace divine revelation – that medieval moralised Ovids registered their greatest cultural impact:

> To regard a classical fable as veiled truth, necessarily open to interpretation on different levels, and to keep simultaneously in one's head several equally valid but self-contradictory 'meanings' for a single text and make the equations between them, is an attitude of mind which remained with sixteenth-century writers and with their public long after the moralized Ovids themselves were forgotten.[15]

Latin editions with and without commentary continued to be published throughout the sixteenth century, often as grammar school textbooks, and the allegorical mode of interpretation remained relevant well into the seventeenth century.[16] The *Metamorphoses* was also translated, largely without religious commentary, into other vernacular languages relatively early. A full Italian translation appeared in the first half of the fourteenth century, with an allegorical reworking appearing around 1375 and many subsequent translations.[17] By 1600 there were two German, one Dutch, and five English editions. Appearing in England were William Caxton's complete prose translation of 1480, and several verse translations, the most influential being that of Arthur Golding (composed of fourteeners) of 1567 and George Sandys (of couplets and commentary) in 1632. Despite the Latin text's popularity as a grammar school resource, during the Elizabethan era many more editions appeared in English than in Latin.[18] Equally popular in France, at least four French translations of the *Metamorphoses* appeared between 1539 and 1617.[19] Translations, commentaries and adaptations provided humanists, students and authors with a capacious template that could accommodate a variety of purposes: instilling lessons in Latin grammar, argument and rhetoric; teaching mythology, mythography and morals; providing models of vernacular oratory, emotional affect and cross-gender voicing;[20] and inviting a variety of responses to the literary and erotic pleasures of this heterogeneous text.[21]

'Iphis and Ianthe' was included in all of these Latin and vernacular texts but its cultural uptake was not limited to them. Traces or analogues of the story are found as well in a variety of medieval texts: the anonymous thirteenth-century *Chanson d'Yde et Olive* and its later adaptations in French and English;[22] John Gower's Middle English *Confessio Amantis* (1390); the fourteenth-century *Cantari della Reina d'Oriente* by Antonio Pucci and *Bella Camilla* by Piero da Siena; and Christine de Pizan's allegorical *Le livre de la mutacion de Fortune* (1403). Beginning with the influential canto 25 of Ludovico Ariosto's *Orlando Furioso* (1516), the Renaissance witnessed an escalation of references, anecdotes and citations: for instance, in Austin Saker's *Narbonus: The Laberynth of Libertie* (1580) and the 'Of Phylotus and Emelia' episode of Barnabe Riche's *His Farewell to Militarie Profession* (written in the 1570s, published in 1581), which itself became the source for the anonymous Scottish play, *Philotus* (1603). Charles Estienne also included an entry on Iphis in his *Dictionarium historicum, geographicum, poeticum* (1595).

More extended treatments, including wholesale adaptations, were developed in John Lyly's stageplay *Galatea* (1584); Sir Philip Sidney's prose epic the *New Arcadia* (1590); a neo-Latin play of 1,152 lines, *Iphis*, by the Oxford undergraduate Henry Bellamy (c.1622–5);[23] and Issac de Benserade's stage play, *Iphis et Iante* (1637). In addition, Alfred Harbage's authoritative *Annals of English Drama* records a lost play of uncertain origin, written between 1591 and 1615, entitled *Iphis and Iantha; or A Marriage Without a Man*.[24] Across the period, visual images illustrating the tale appear as well: in the *Ovide moralisé*,[25] in the illustration of Book 9 of George Sandys' 1632 translation and in other manuscripts and printed texts (see Appendix F). Furthermore, a number of medical writers, including the influential medical compiler Jacques Ferrand, included references to the tale as they struggled to comprehend ambiguous signs of gender and hermaphroditism alongside legal charges of gender 'fraud'.[26]

Opportunistic engagements with the story typically focus on Iphis as an emblematic referent of virtue (or vice), or they draw on isolated aspects of her narrative (her lament, her moment of transformation, the results of her change of sex) to support a specific argument. Iphis's lament as she prays to Isis became a particularly popular literary topos. A few treatments highlight the two lovers' predicament (which is, incidentally, the only form of exposition that enables the portrayal of Ianthe's situation). Whatever the focus, the intended uses for which 'Iphis and Ianthe' has been employed are surprisingly diverse. The tale has been harnessed to affirm the special interest that God takes in his creatures, the veracity (and doubtfulness) of miracles, the creative power of the imagination, the historical truth (or falsehood) of transformations in sex and the possibility of surmounting obstacles to love, including that between men and women, imposed by family and convention.

The tale regularly appears in lists and examples of miracles, both to affirm and discount their possibility. The first dedication in Saker's *Narbonus*, for instance, mentions Iphis in a list of approved metamorphoses,[27] while her story attests to 'thinges woonderfull and straunge unto nature' in *The Pilgrimage of princes, penned out of Sundry Greeke and Latine aucthours*, by Lodovvicke Loid (1573).[28] In contrast, in the middle of a double cross-dressing plot, Riche's *His Farewell to Militarie Profession* puts Iphis's story in the mouth of Philerno, as he, disguised as his look-alike sister, Emelia, attempts to convince the unwitting Brisilla of the possibility of changing his sex to stave off the women's intended marriages to two old men. In reply to Brisilla's opinion that 'suche wishes are but waste, and unpossible it is, that any suche thing should happen', he asserts that 'there is nothing impossible'; after listing the transformations of Pygmalion, Acteon, Narcissus and Arachne, he offers a robust narration of Iphis's story as 'moste meete and fitting to our purpose', concluding that a similar miracle could be granted them by 'the Goddesse' if approached with sufficient 'zeale and faith'.[29]

Riche's allusion to Iphis not only furthers the twists and turns of a heteroerotic plot but also plays on the gullibility of Brisilla who, upon experiencing Philerno's intimate embrace (and presumably erect penis), thinks that '*Emelia* was perfectly metamorphosed'. In making Brisilla a dupe, this episode has something in common with those medical texts and treatises of natural philosophy that increasingly posed the observations of 'science' against the wish-fulfilments of 'fable', and that interpreted transformations such as that undergone by Iphis as instances, not of the power of God, desire or the imagination, but of deception and credulity. By the early seventeenth century, the idea of spontaneous sex change had been put under considerable pressure by anatomical investigations, which countered stories of women's transformation into men (both past and present) with arguments regarding the presence of an enlarged clitoris, a small penis or genuine hermaphroditism.[30]

We sometimes can glimpse contradictory intentions within a single author as he struggles to reconcile the meanings of the tale with his beliefs. Note, for instance, the complexity of the commentary that accompanies Sandys' English translation. On the one hand, Sandys proposes the tale's allegory as the transformation of the soul, reiterating a consistent theme of earlier moralised Ovids: 'By this the Ancient declared, that men should despaire of nothing; since althings were in the power of the Gods to give; and give they would what was justly implored.' But like those medieval predecessors who offered euhemerist interpretations, Sandys also drew on secular writing, both ancient and modern, to assert that women had, in fact, been changed into men. Contrasting female sex transformation to the lack of similar stories about men being transformed into women, he drew this moral from authorities both ancient and modern, 'that as it is preposterous in Nature, which ever aimes at perfection, when men degenerate into effeminacy; so contarily commendable, when women aspire to manly wisdom and fortitude.'[31] Bringing together religion and science, the transformation of the soul and the medicalisation of sex – and routing all of this through early modern gender asymmetries – Sandys's treatment suggests the flexibility and utility that many writers and readers found in this story of miraculous change.

Even very brief cultural references to 'Iphis' indicate a broad range of interpretative engagements. For instance, entries on 'Iphis' occur in four early modern English lexicons between 1584 and 1676, three of which emphasise that her sex change comes about not to enable heterosexual marriage but, in the words of Edward Phillips, 'least Lygdus [Iphis's father] finding himself deceived should be incensed'.[32] Whereas concerns with fraud had long been present in medical commentaries that invoke the tale in discussions of sex change, here the concern about the patriarch's response to such deception begins to suggest the extent to which Iphis's story admitted interpretative leeway. Nonetheless, this leeway would slowly ebb away: in 1778, the shorthand diary entry by Hester Thrale Piozzi that 'Ovid's Iphis & Ianthe no longer seems out of Possibility' attests to the primary erotic currency that the tale possessed by the late eighteenth century.[33]

By far the most extended, publicly available and popular versions of the story during this period are those provided by two early modern stageplays, one published in England, and one in France: Lyly's *Galatea* and Benserade's *Iphis et Iante*. Lyly was perhaps the most famous Elizabethan writer of his time. Since the nineteenth century, he has more often been celebrated (or derided) for the stylistic innovations of his prose fiction *Euphues: The Anatomy of Wit* than the eight plays he wrote for the boy players of St Paul's Cathedral.[34] Yet his plays not only dominated the repertoire of the boys' companies, but were 'the most famous theatrical events of the 1580s', helping to stoke popular appetite for commercial drama performed in permanent playhouses and helping, as well, to inaugurate a market for printed plays.[35] Just as Golding infused the *Metamorphoses* with English referents, Lyly transposed Ovid's love plot and the antics of the gods to the early modern marshes of Lincolnshire.[36] First performed at Queen Elizabeth's court in 1588 and published in 1592, the play begins with an attempt to deceive Neptune, who has demanded a sacrifice of the area's most beautiful virgin every five years to keep the land from being flooded by the Humber river. Two fathers independently disguise their adolescent daughters, Galatea and Phillida, as boys to prevent their being chosen as the sacrificial victim.[37] The two cross-dressed girls fall in love, leading to mutual delight as well as confusion and consternation. Their predicament is dramatically resolved only when Venus asserts her authority against Neptune and promises to change the sex of one of the girls.[38]

Benserade's comedy, *Iphis et Iante*, first performed at the Hôtel de Bourgogne in Paris in 1634 and published in 1637, is focused more squarely on Ovid's plot than is *Galatea*, of which the 'Iphis and Ianthe' story comprises just one subplot among three. Benserade increases Iphis's age to twenty, presents her as longing for her marriage rather than fearing it (much to her mother's dismay) and delays her metamorphosis until after the wedding night.[39] Iphis's eagerness and the delay of the marriage allow Benserade to portray her erotic desire in vividly physical terms. In each of these plays, the plight of Iphis and her beloved, as well as the meanings of the sexed body, are connected to foundational social relations: divine and patriarchal authority, the status of women and girls, the question of erotic knowledge and the relationship of erotic desire to the social polity.

* * *

A steady stream of publishing since the 1970s about Ovid's influence on medieval and early modern literature has offered a range of analyses on the consequences of metamorphic figures, tropes and themes. Ovid's impact on the literary production of Francesco Petrarch, Geoffrey Chaucer, Louise Labé, Pierre de Ronsard, Ludovico Ariosto, Edmund Spenser, Christopher Marlowe, John Lyly, William Shakespeare, John Donne and John Milton – across the genres of epic verse, lyric, erotic epyllia and drama – has been comprehensively surveyed, along with analyses of translations and adaptations of Ovid's *Metamorphoses*. We thus now enjoy detailed analyses of Ovidian-inspired treatments of humanism, identity, nationhood, patronage, pastoral, sexual violence, trauma, poetic voice, rhetoric, irony, authorship, *galanterie*, modernity and artistic creation and imitation in medieval and early modern literature.[40] Within studies of sexuality, Ovidianism as a source for representing male homoerotic desire has been particularly well explored.[41] With a few, mostly brief, exceptions, however, the tale of 'Iphis and Ianthe' goes absolutely unremarked in this extensive body of work.[42] Moreover, despite the existence of a number of visual illustrations (see Appendix F), no entry on Iphis appears in *The Oxford Guide to Classical Mythology in the Arts*.[43]

Although the reasons for this indifference are no doubt complex, they most likely include the following:

- *The unwieldy, episodic and segmented form of the* Metamorphoses. Exigencies of form appear to have influenced both medieval and early modern engagements with Ovid's epic, as well as the parameters of scholarship concerned with it. With over 250 loosely linked narratives marked by conflicting narrative tones and inconsistent narrative personae, Ovid's poem is often read as an unrelated set of extracts rather than a continuous narrative. The dissociation of one strand of plot from another was embraced by medieval commentators supplying *tituli* directing readers to specific tales,[44] by allegorists who parsed each fable's personae into Christian personifications and by humanists who used specific tales to enumerate exempla and *sententiae*.[45] When medieval and early modern writers take up Ovid, they appear to mimic his strategy of segmentation, leading to a selective focus on certain stories to the exclusion of others.[46] Scholars likewise tend to focus on individual stories, often separating, for instance, Echo from Narcissus, or the rape of Calisto from the larger story of Diana and her nymphs.

- *Scholarly expectations regarding Ovid's influence on particular literary genres, themes and concepts of poetic authority.* When not focused on amorous love or the basic tenor of metamorphosis, scholarship on Ovidian reception has concentrated particularly on literary form, especially Renaissance *elecutio* and *imitatio* (of poetic tropes, allusions, dramatic characters and plots). Poetic origins and authorial self-fashioning, sometimes modelled on Ovid's own career, have also been an influential focus. So too have the epic themes of heroism, nationhood, republicanism, empire and exile, as well as the phenomenon of 'galant' literary culture.[47] 'Iphis and Ianthe', it has been assumed, contributes nothing to this intertextual, citational matrix. Moreover, the dramatic monologue at the core of the tale does not seem to have inspired any verse epyllia, which was a major mode of English Ovidianism during its heyday in the 1580s and 1590s.[48] That 'Iphis and Ianthe' seems to have directly inspired the plots of at least four dramas, however, leads one to wonder how Iphis's complaint may have existed 'behind the scenes' of dramatic monologues voiced by other literary figures.

- *The story's lack of etiological consequence.* Many treatments of medieval and Renaissance Ovidianism begin with the assumption that the *Metamorphoses* is, above all, a series of origin stories: the rape of Calisto explains the origin of the constellation Ursa Major, the union of Salmacis with Hermaphroditus is the cause of a fountain's effeminising waters, and so on. Such etiologies often segue into tales of distinctively human consequence: the tale of Hermaphroditus explains the existence of intersex individuals (with the fusion of boy with nymph answering the proleptic riddle of his name: child of Hermes and Aphrodite). Narcissus, meanwhile, is regularly believed to explain the existence of 'passive' male homosexuality. More generally, metamorphosis is assumed to be the *cause* of novel effects. The transformation of Iphis, in contrast, offers no broader etiological explanation, no remarkable consequence, other than the effects it has on the story's unhappy protagonists.

- *The separation of sex transformation from other scholarly concerns.* One might be inclined to think that the topic of sex transformation was off-putting to Ovid's imitators, as well as to contemporary scholars. It is not, however, as though the topic of sex change is itself taboo: there are a number of medieval narratives about miraculous sex changes, and Ovid's narrative of Tiresias's temporary sex change (*Met.* 3: 316–38) was as popular in the early modern period as it is today. At the same time, very few readers are familiar with Mestra, daughter of Erysichthon – who implores Neptune to save her from slavery by changing her shape and is given the power to shift gender and species at will (*Met.* 8: 847–74) – or with Caenis, daughter of Elatus, who, raped by Neptune, asks in recompense to 'cease to be a woman' so that she need not suffer penetration again and pursues life thereafter as a man, Caeneus, invulnerable to weapons (*Met.* 12: 168–209). The abbreviated reference to Sithon in *Met.* 4: 274 – 'Nor shall I say how by a strange quirk of nature, Sithon's sex once became uncertain, and he was now a man and then a woman' – remains mysterious.[49] Why, we might ask, are these tales not better known?[50]
- *Scholarly expectations regarding Ovidian eroticism.* While 'alternate desires' are increasingly recognised as a vital aspect of Ovid's corpus, many scholars would agree with Cora Fox that 'Renaissance English Ovidianism is ... generally characterized by the narrative of desire based on the subject-object binary model of the hunt, [and] its repetitions of the rape/abduction narrative.'[51] 'Iphis and Ianthe' fulfils neither of these expectations. Indeed, when readers come to Ovidian-inspired texts, we often think we know what we are going to encounter: male desire of whatever sort (hetero, homo, cross-species) and vulnerable female victims. As Heather James puts it: 'Ovid's repertoire of precepts, plots, and visual scenarios tends, after all, to frame women as pictures for a male viewer's delectation and, too often, as objects of his violence.'[52] 'Iphis and Ianthe' doesn't fit this scenario. Contrariwise, critics who uphold the dubious view that 'faithful mutual love is the highest value of the *Metamorphoses*' have yet to cite the devotion of Iphis or Ianthe as an obvious example.[53]

Whatever the reasons for the neglect of 'Iphis and Ianthe' in treatments of the *Metamorphoses*, it was not until literary critics began to offer lesbian and queer interpretations of 'Iphis and Ianthe' – as well as of its translations, analogues and adaptations written between the thirteenth and the seventeenth centuries – that this tale entered a wider scholarly conversation.[54] And it did so as a story of cross-dressing and lesbianism.[55] Often exploring the differences between Ovid's tale and the treatment of his translators or adaptors, a growing number of scholars have analysed whether gender and sexuality in these texts are tied to biological sex (and thus are essentialised or are presented as socially constructed or performative), whether patriarchal institutions such as marriage and paternal authority are affirmed or challenged and whether lesbian desire (and sometimes lesbian identity) is accepted, tolerated, celebrated or condemned.[56]

In an attempt to shift the terms of debate from a subversion/containment framework of endorsement or indictment of female-female desire, I proposed in 2002 that 'Iphis and Ianthe' was not only the *locus classicus* of 'lesbian' desire in the early modern period, but that its rhetorical strategies could clue us into the early modern terms of intelligibility for such desire, as well as to an unacknowledged literary tradition of female homoerotic lament – its terms explicitly rearticulated, for instance, by Fiordispina in Ariosto's *Orlando Furioso* as she mourns the impossibility of her passion for Bradamante,[57] as well as by Philoclea as she describes the torment of her love for Zelmane in Sidney's *New Arcadia*.[58] Erotic desire in the absence of gender difference is rendered legible in Ovid and many of its intertexts, but often only as *amor impossibilis*. As the tale was reworked in Lyly's *Galatea*, I argued, this tension between possibility and impossibility simultaneously upholds the unnaturalness of female-female sex acts while articulating the terms of potential satisfaction in the masculinised body. Erotic desire, in this cultural logic, is not the problem; the problem is the body, its perceived incapacities, and its social function as a marker of gender within a patriarchal system.

The topos of (im)possibility present in 'Iphis and Ianthe' set the terms for subsequent literary negotiations of the viability of female erotic bonds.[59] By the eighteenth century, the story of Iphis and Ianthe referenced explicit sexual meanings that could not be safely projected onto the distant classical past; rather, it evoked the increasingly public nature of sapphism. In her own development and nuancing of this argument, Susan Lanser maintains that 'Iphis and Ianthe', *Galatea* and *Iphis et Ianthe* all represent the 'metamorphic' scenario that dominates sapphic discourse in Western Europe around 1600. Metamorphic plots attempt to 'resolve homoerotic relations through a logic of substitution' by erasing 'the "same" in same-sex relations' – a strategy, she argues, that comes under epistemological stress by the time of Benserade's play, where 'the problem is not homoeroticism as such but its public accommodation'.[60] The effect of Benserade's changes to Ovid's plot is a shift in 'the discursive emphasis from the private preservation of a secret to the public resolution of an impasse'.[61] As Lanser's broader analysis reveals, the impasses produced by such metamorphic plots eventually give rise to a 'sapphic episteme' in which 'the *logic* of woman + woman' is increasingly made socially available, in both its celebratory and phobic formulations.[62]

Even as scholars have analysed the tale's impact on concepts of lesbianism in increasingly complex ways, others have begun to employ transgender theory to approach its depiction of sex change. Focused on 'Iphis and Ianthe' in the moralised Ovids of the fourteenth and fifteenth centuries, Robert Mills mobilises transgender 'as a prism for understanding medieval encounters with sex change and other modes of gender variance, as well as interrogating the category's associations (or not) with homoerotic behavior'.[63] Simone Chess reads *Galatea*'s double MTFTM (male to female to male) cross-dressing in terms of the gender labour involved in trans* relationships, including the erotic partner's 'labor of forgetting' and 'labor of alliance' by which gender for both partners is co-created as relational rather than the property of an individual.[64] We might note that the play's conclusion, which defers the change of sex, correlates with more recent calls for a less teleological understanding of trans* which suspends the sequential logic that underpins the concepts of MTF and FTM. Additional archival and interpretative work on apprentice boy actors has implicitly strengthened recognition of *Galatea*'s erotics – an eroticism complexly layered and circulated through the multiply cross-dressed, youthful male body – while reminding us that plays written for child companies can lose some of their queerness when these roles are played by adult actors.[65]

* * *

Ovidian Transversions: 'Iphis and Ianthe', 1300–1650 builds on this prior body of scholarship with essays that advance our understanding of these texts' investments in the body, intersexuality, gender, transgender, youth and homoeroticism. In the aggregate, the essays published here make clear that the tale should be considered a key text for feminist criticism, queer studies and the history of sexuality – as central as are the stories of Arachne, Philomela, Narcissus and Ganymede.[66] What would early modern literary histories of sexuality look like, we might ask, if, rather than viewing the amorous, homoerotic Neptune of Marlowe's *Hero and Leander* as the privileged, 'quintessentially' Ovidian figure of the 1590s in England,[67] readers were also directed to the beautiful, sapphic and potentially transgender Galatea and Phyllida?

In light of the uptake of Ovid's tale for later representations of female homoeroticism and transgender, it is worth reconsidering the specific terms of Iphis's lament, which has long been read, by classicists, medievalists and early modernists, as a wholesale condemnation of the unnaturalness of her love.[68] In *Queer Philologies*, Jeffrey Masten argues that 'even as scholarship in the history of sexuality has begun to make its way into the introductory materials in editions [of literary texts], editors must work harder to think about the broader ramifications of research into the history of sexuality for editing the text "itself".'[69] In particular, Masten calls for renewed, sex-sensitive attention to the textual gloss – which, in this instance, I propose to treat as a corollary to textual translation. '"[Q]uis me manet exitus", inquit, / "cognita quam nulli, quam prodigiosa novaeque / cura tenet Veneris?"' The authoritative Loeb edition by Frank Justus Miller translates these lines as '"Oh, what will be the end of me", she said, / "whom a love possess that no one ever heard of, a strange and monstrous love?"' This concluding phrase, which has understandably informed many English readings of Iphis's self-description of her love as 'strange and monstrous', is derived from parsing the capacious term 'prodigiosus', which the *Oxford Latin Dictionary* defines as 'monstrous' and 'unnatural' – but also as 'marvelous'.[70] Ovid appears to have been the first Latin author to use 'prodigiosa', which he employs twice in the *Metamorphoses*: here in Iphis's lament and in reference to what the Loeb edition translates as the 'wondrous court' of Circe (*Met.* 13: 968). What is it, the queer philologist might ask, that renders Iphis's plight monstrous and strange, whereas the residence of Circe, where men are involuntarily turned into animals, is considered merely wondrous? This question only becomes more pressing when we recall that the final sentence of Byblis's story of incestuous love for her brother that precedes and provides a segue to the story of Iphis refers to both monstrosity and miraculous things. In the translation provided by Diane Pintabone: 'Fame of this new *monstrosity* (*monstri*) would perhaps have filled the hundred Cretan cities, / if Crete had not recently borne its own *miraculous things* (*miracula*), / with Iphis having been changed' (*Met.* 9: 666–8, emphases mine). Implicit in Ovid's juxtaposition of these stories is the idea that Iphis's transformation is not monstrous (*monstri*), but miraculous (*miracula*). Economically synthesising both approaches, Arthur Golding's sixteenth-century translation condenses *monstri* and *miracula* into the category of wonder, using it to implicitly describe both phenomena: 'The fame of this same *wondrous thing* perhaps had fillèd all / The hundred towns of Candy, had a greater not befall / More nearer home by Iphis's means, transformèd late before' (emphasis mine).[71]

Given this choice, the fact that Golding translates Iphis's lament as 'How strange a love, how uncouth, how prodigious reigns in me!'[72] – reiterating the sense of 'strange' but foregoing 'monstrous' – seems all the more provocative. According to the *Oxford English Dictionary*, from the late fifteenth century the meanings of 'prodigious' included '1) Of the nature of an omen; portentous; 2) That causes wonder or amazement; marvellous, astonishing. Also in an unfavourable sense: appalling'. It appears that only after the publication of Golding's edition, however, did 'prodigious' take on the meaning of 'unnatural, abnormal; freakish'. Also instructive is that 'prodigious' is as often paired with 'wonderful' and 'miraculous' as it is with 'monstrous' in sixteenth- and seventeenth-century English lexicons. John Florio's *Worlde of Words* (1598) defines 'prodigioso' as 'prodigious, monstrous, unnaturall, woondrous, that giveth a strange signe or token, woonderfull, contrarie to the common course of nature'. Robert Cawdry's *A Table Alphabetical* (1604) defines 'prodigious' as 'wonderfull, giving an ill signe'. Randle Cotgrave's *A Dictionary of the French and English Tongues* (1611) defines 'prodigiuex/euse' as 'prodigious; wonderous, monstrous, most unnaturall or out of course'. John Bullokar's *An English Expositor* (1616) and Henry Cockeram's *English Dictionary* (1623) define 'prodigious' as 'strange, wonderfull to see'. That prodigious is just as easily collocated with wondrous and wonderful as monstrous and unnatural leads me to ask (taking my cue not only from Masten but also from Karma Lochrie's essay in this volume): could the meaning of 'prodigiosa' in this tale function, perhaps, not only as a textual crux, but as a riddle? At the very least, the multiple meanings of 'prodigiosa' might encourage scholars to resist imputing wholesale negativity to Iphis in the midst of her own self-doubt – in other words, to resist following Iphis's anxious anticipation of impending shame as the only possible story. To pick up on the terms of Laurel Billings's essay included here, we might find in Iphis's articulation of her 'prodigiosa' love not only the fear of social death, but also the possibility of queer survival.

In addition to challenging the critical consensus about dominant modes of Ovidian eroticism, the terms of Iphis's complaint should give us cause to rethink a host of other issues. We might ask, for instance, whether medieval and early modern representations of nature, in which Ovid and other metamorphic texts played an influential role,[73] might productively be approached in terms of her lament, which decries the prohibitions of nature by articulating a bestiary of sex. How might Iphis's human exceptionalism in regards to sex and gender – an exceptionalism bewailed rather than exalted – enable scholars to think anew about the relations between queerness and the natural world? If nature enforces gender difference as a precondition for desire's fulfilment, how queer is it? And does nature get the last word? Second, if, as Lynn Enterline has persuasively argued, grammar school boys cut their emotional teeth on imitating, in writing and speech, Ovid's heroines, and if the tales of two of the most commonly offered of those models – Niobe and Hecuba – end, like Iphis's, in metamorphosis, might it be that such practices of *ethopoeia* (character making) utilised Iphis's complaint as well?[74]

More startling, perhaps, is the extent to which common wisdom regarding the role of Ovid in literary history, and in particular the history of English Renaissance drama, is challenged by 'Iphis and Ianthe'. Maggie Kilgour voices a settled tradition of criticism when she writes that 'While Shakespeare is familiar with the range of Ovid's work, he seems most drawn to the *Metamorphoses*, and in particular *Metamorphoses* 2–4 (Phaeton, Acteon, Narcissus, Hermaphroditus, Pyramus and Thisbe), *Metamorphoses* 10 (the stories told by Orpheus, most notably those of Pygmalion, and Venus and Adonis), and *Metamorphoses* 15 (Pythagoras' vision of external flux as well as the poet's final claim of immortality in art)'.[75] What is it that authorises recognition of Pyramus and Thisbe or Pygmalion – who appear as intertexts, albeit crucial ones, only in single plays – and the elision of Iphis and Ianthe, who arguably influenced an entire subgenre of romantic comedy, of which Shakespeare is a supreme, but not the only, progenitor?

In 1987 Phyllis Rackin proposed that 'Lyly, writing in the 1580s for Queen Elizabeth's court, was the most influential comic playwright of his age ... and of all his plays, *Gallathea* seems to have exerted the greatest influence on Shakespeare.'[76] Since then it has been widely recognised that *Galatea* inaugurated the vogue for cross-dressing plays on the English stage. The full contours and import of this Ovidian genealogy, however, are only beginning to be credited. Heather James has recently shown that Ovid's influence on Shakespeare established Juliet as his 'first major heroine in any genre' by linking her to four other transgressive Ovidian girls in the *Metamorphoses* Books 7 to 10 who reflect 'on the unstable nature of passion, the arbitrary force of custom and law, and the tyranny of the name of the father'.[77] In pursuit of this argument, James provides a fresh reading of Iphis's dramatic monologue (which, she argues, 'issues a powerful series of negative examples from nature that ironically make the case for the opposing truth'), posits a possible means for managing the girls' sexual satisfaction (given what Daedalus does for Pasiphaë, James remarks, he 'could invent the world's best dildo') and offers a perceptive observation about Iphis's metamorphosis: 'The scene of metamorphosis is more impressive for what it ignores (the penis) than for what it describes (secondary sex characteristics): if Iphis undergoes a genital change, it is apparently not worth mentioning.'[78] Insofar as Iphis may be passing as male as much as experiencing a change of genital sex, she can be seen as 'the original of Shakespeare's boy heroines'.[79] To put this even more strongly: knowing, as we do, that 'Ovid was Shakespeare's favorite poet',[80] it is to 'Iphis and Ianthe' that we should give thanks for the creation of Rosalind/Ganymede, Viola/Cesario and even, perhaps, the gender-bending fantasies of Cleopatra.[81] Moreover, while we cannot know for certain the authorship of *Iphis and Iantha, or A Marriage without a Man*, given what we know of the homoerotics of Shakespearean comedy, it's worth reconsidering Alfred Harbage's attribution of this lost play to Shakespeare.

While discussions of gender, sexuality and the body thus loom large in this volume – and our contributors would agree that such concerns are closely linked to the issues they consider – the import of 'Iphis and Ianthe' is not limited to these matters.[82] Our contributors' investigation of the array of topics engaged by this tale extends the analytic purview to discourses of religious conversion, climate change, humanist pedagogy, apprenticeship, scientific and medical treatises, alchemical texts, geography, lexicography and practices of reading – and thus to such fields as the history of religion, environmental criticism, the history of education, the history of science, the history of material texts and the history of language. By demonstrating the uptake of 'Iphis and Ianthe' for this extended set of considerations, our contributors reveal the extent to which medieval and early modern writers found in Ovid's story a productive space within which to dwell, a theme to riff upon, a suggestion of an idea that teases them to do something more (or different) with it. Like the 'artificial' member that appears in several of the essays that follow, 'Iphis and Ianthe' is itself a *supplement* that enables new and untoward combinations of ideas, concepts and concerns to arise. Given the multiplicity of treatments, it becomes clear that there is not one medieval or early modern 'Iphis and Ianthe' but many.

This capacity for invention is of a piece with the hermeneutic uncertainty and epistemological opacity analysed by many of our contributors, particularly in regard to the presumed intelligibility of Iphis's body. As their essays attest, this tale raises important questions not only of subjectivity, desire and embodiment, but also of temporality (the status of past, present and future), ontology (the origins of gendered being and erotic desire) and epistemology (how embodied, desiring subjects know and are known). Questions of scepticism and doubt occur repeatedly across these pages. In the aggregate, the essays in this volume suggest the importance of questioning the 'before and after' syntax of metamorphosis routinely adopted by its readers and critics: What *exactly* has been transformed? On what grounds do we *know* that a transformation has occurred? What is the basis of our certainty? Is her transformation an externalisation of essential, internal character? Is this metamorphosis an example of change-within-continuity or continuity-within-change? Is Iphis always, already, *really* a man – and what would it mean to assert that she is or isn't? What is at stake – hermeneutically, ethically, politically – in our answers to these questions?

* * *

Such questions motivate our offering of the term 'transversion' as an overarching rubric for the translations, commentaries, appropriations, analogues, intertexts and afterlives inspired by this tale, as well as an analytic for rethinking the concept of transformation itself. As a Latin prefix, 'trans' means 'across, through, over, to or on the other side of, beyond, outside of, from one place, person, thing or state to another' (*OED*, 1). The multivalent signification of 'trans' informs this collection in several important ways. The very idea of 'trans' is implicit in the poetics and rhetoric of metamorphosis and thus is central to any Ovidian project. We thus highlight, as a first principle, the meaning of transformation itself, and the questions, such as those above, that it carries in its wake – about which more will be said at the end of this introduction.

Second is the act of translation, the manner in which 'Iphis and Ianthe' circulates by way of 'carrying over' from one language to another. Focused on the medieval and early modern versions of Ovid's tale in Latin, French and English, issues of translation crop up throughout this volume. Informed by theories in which, in the words of Miranda Griffin, translation poses an 'impossible relationship between language and truth',[83] raising questions of fidelity and transparency that can never fully be resolved, the essays included here approach translation as a transformation, accomplished not only through the (never unproblematic) transit from one language to another, but by incorporating and addressing the social concerns of different times and places. If, as Karen Newman and Jane Tylus maintain, there would have been no Renaissance without translation, this volume affirms the value, as their collection does, of the 'borrowings' and 'generative misprisions' involved in acts of cultural and literary mediation.[84]

If translation is itself metamorphosis, a change into a new form, then there is no reason to analytically separate the *Ovide moralisé* from non-moralising translations, or any of these works from later literary adaptations. Such generic levelling of text, translation and intertext has paid off in the work of Raphael Lyne, who reads the translations of Arthur Golding and George Sandys alongside the poetry of Edmund Spenser and Samuel Drayton, of Liz Oakley-Brown, who examines the cultural and sexual politics of Ovidian translation from '*translatio* to *allusio*', as well as of Susan Wiseman, who reads metamorphosis across different kinds of writing in order to historicise and challenge disciplinary divides.[85] We promote this levelling strategy here as one way to more fully recover and appreciate the literary and social import of 'Iphis and Ianthe'. Further, in order to make some of the versions produced in England and France more readily available, we have included in the book's appendices modern English translations of 'Iphis and Ianthe' from the *Ovide moralisé*, John Gower's *Confessio Amantis* and Christine de Pizan's *Le livre de la mutacion de Fortune*, along with excerpts from Arthur Golding's and George Sandys's early modern English translations of the *Metamorphoses*.

The concept of 'trans' also informs our approach in terms of the temporal and spatial registers across which this volume traverses. Exploring texts produced over three centuries in France and England, this volume seeks not to collapse time into an undifferentiated transhistoricity but to demonstrate both change and continuity in approaches to Ovid's tale. The various and sometimes quite extraordinary alterations to the text between 1300 and 1650 are analysed by several contributors. In geography as well as time, this volume transits 'across, through, over, to or on the other side of' the Channel – La Manche that separates France from England.[86] The inclusion of essays on the French moralised Ovids as well as on Christine de Pizan's 'autobiography' next to an essay on Gower's English poem and John Florio's bilingual dictionary offers an implicit dialogue among several traditions, as do the cluster of essays on Lyly's and Benserade's plays. Across differences of time and place, what is remarkable in the texts analysed here is the nature of what is preserved: namely, the fact of cross-dressing, the erotic nature of the girls' desire and the transformation of the material body to enable a socially acceptable resolution. No author, whatever his or her intentions in adopting or alluding to Ovid, elides the couple's passion: their desire may be roundly condemned, but it is not hidden from history or forced into a closet.

In light of this commitment to candid portrayals of desire (however roundly it is sometimes condemned), it is notable that early modern dictionaries include a surprising number of terms referring to the kind of transformation at issue in this tale. Sir Thomas Blount in his *Glossographia* (1656) and Elisha Coles in *An English Dictionary* (1676) include the words *transection* ('a turning or passing from one sex to another'), *transfeminate* ('to turn from woman to man, or from one sex to another') as well as *transpeciate* ('to change kind or form').[87] It is thus with awareness of both alterity and resemblance across time that we affirm, as theoretical and thematic motivations, the resonance to our project of the contemporary terms *trans* (a stand-alone category referring to a spectrum of non-normative genders, the disarticulation of sexed bodies from gender as well as gender transition), *trans-* (the hyphen signifying a prefix connecting trans to a specific set of referents) as well as *trans** (the asterisk referring to as-yet-unknown sex and gender possibilities).[88] Several of the essays included here are motivated by the concepts of 'trans' and 'trans-', as they shift the focus from Iphis's and Ianthe's homoerotic desires to the tale's emphasis on gendered embodiment.[89] The concept of trans*, in contrast, 'foregrounds and intensifies the prehensile, prefixial nature of *trans-* and implies a suffixial space of attachment'[90] rather than a category, object or specific location. Trans* thus attempts to bring into being 'binary-resistant ontologies that exist within and beyond our grasp',[91] and its political and conceptual work is therefore always potentially unfinished. Two of the essays here deliberately mobilise 'trans*' to explore the prepositional quality, the instability and open-endedness, of sexed and gendered modes of identification.[92] The broader theoretical questions and investments activated by each of these different concepts – anatomised especially in Rubright's essay – inform the volume as a whole. Rather than promote any particular version of trans, trans- or trans*,[93] this volume perceives the issue at stake – *as they work as analytic concepts* – as the way they signify a conceptually productive tension between identity and non-identity, positionality and prepositionality.[94]

Important as well is that these terms are not mutually exclusive. Both 'the prefix dash and the asterisk', according to A. Finn Enke, 'force us to know *trans* as modification and motion across time and space'.[95] This sense of temporal and spatial change and movement reverberates all the more when placed in close proximity to the noun 'version'. The textual twists and turns that are implied by the word 'version' mirror the complexity of bodily processes indexed by trans/trans-/trans*; whether as a manifestation of embodied experience or as an interpretative mode, *transversion* signals a forward-and-backward movement across space and/or time. Thus, while the plots and themes of different versions of the story are themselves of considerable interest to us, our curiosity extends to the question of what makes a version, historically and theoretically, a version. Sometimes, as in the case of *Yde et Olive*, the relationship to the reputed Ovidian source has been contested or minimised.[96] This approach, bound as it is by concerns of originality, authenticity, fidelity and direct transmission, is to our mind less productive than thinking in terms of intertexts and a broadly construed adaptational field. Adaptation of early modern authors is increasingly being theorised as a rhizomatic network of relays, citations and transmediations;[97] as is true for this body of work, our aim is to explore which questions and concerns the act of constellating related texts and terms – however they may be related – can bring to the fore. Doing so does not wholly dispense with the concept of fidelity (to an author or a text) but, rather than construe value in terms of degrees of fidelity, we are more interested in tracking the intensities and types of resemblance and difference among texts.[98]

Our use of transversion is historically as well as theoretically motivated. The *OED*'s first definition for the noun 'version', which first appears in 1582, doubles down on the word's relevance for our project by emphasising its relationship to translation. 'Version' is 'a rendering of some text or work, or of a single word, passage, etc., from one language into another; a translation; also (rarely), the action or process of translating' (*OED*, 1.a). (This meaning is preserved in the French pedagogical practice of *thème et version*.) In addition to this sense of translation, the *OED*'s third definition of 'version', first recorded in Sir Francis Bacon's use in 1625, is also salient: 'a turning about; a change of direction'. Version, in other words, involves a translation, a turning, a reorientation both linguistic and directional.[99] But the conceptual connections do not stop there. The first *OED* definition of the noun 'transversion' (*transversio*), appearing in Blount's *Glossographia*, is 'a turning away or crosse, a traversing, or going athwart', to which the *OED* adds: 'the action of turning across or athwart; intersection, a turning into something else, conversion, perversion, transformation, transposition'.[100] (No less interesting, it turns out, are some modern derivations: in molecular biology, for instance, a genetic transversion is a *sport of nature* – a phrase that might well have been applied to Iphis in the medieval and early modern eras.) Without venturing further down the rabbit hole of early modern etymology, we can see that 'trans', 'version', 'transversion', 'translation', 'conversion' and 'perversion' are all linked conceptually by the seventeenth century in a chain of association that most likely pre-dates the recorded etymology and usefully extends into our critical practices. Comprising a constellation of interdependent terms, their analytic purchase for 'Iphis and Ianthe', we hope, will spark a diverse range of future investigations.

* * *

The creation of this volume has been, from the start, a collaborative process – a fact we emphasise because we advocate it as an important future direction for modes of literary critical work.[101] Indeed, we see a collaborative ethos as itself a transformation of business as usual in the humanities. Our collaboration arose out of a symposium at the University of Michigan in 2016,[102] which was in turn inspired by two events: a graduate course that I co-taught with Peggy McCracken several years prior entitled 'Woman, Animal, Human', and my, Peggy's and Patsy Badir's involvement in the Early Modern Conversions project housed at McGill University. Insofar as Peggy's and my course compared medieval and early modern French and English materials in light of poststructuralist and posthumanist theories of embodiment, the syllabus included several medieval and early modern translations of 'Iphis and Ianthe' and *Galatea* alongside renditions of 'Narcissus and Echo'. The approaches that Peggy and I took to these materials quickly evolved into a mode of hermeneutic counterpoint. Inspired by Deleuze, Peggy tended to focus, both historically and theoretically, on the fundamental instability of concepts, categories and practices, while I, attempting to channel Foucault, tended to stress the historical and theoretical consequences of the culture's emergent attraction to fixity, classification and regulation. To draw the contrast more specifically: a deconstructive approach to medieval renderings of 'Narcissus and Echo', in Peggy's view, demonstrates how language and desire can exceed the organisation and moralisations of myth, while propelling analysis towards Deleuzian lines of flight. Narcissus and Echo are not just figures of instability and excess but of becoming: becoming voice, becoming shadow, becoming reflection, becoming lover.[103] Beyond the dictates of gendered bodies and sex, new and untoward assemblages of self-other arise through specific becomings manifest in relation to certain objects – for instance a fountain or pool.[104] When the class discussion turned to 'Iphis and Ianthe', I emphasised that for all the manifest attractions of becoming and assemblage, the performance of gender in both Ovid's tale and its medieval and early modern transversions is insistently tethered to material embodiment. Both 'Iphis and Ianthe' and *Galatea* return lines of flight to the workings of power, manifested in the (nascently biopolitical) drive to order, stabilise and classify. Erotic desire and the body are not just subject to flux and transformation but are delimited by social desire and its material manifestations in the form of patriarchal authority and sacrificial femicide.[105]

The point, of course, is that both critical emphases are productive – and potentially dialogic. For the irresolvable stand-off between the intellectual traditions represented here by Foucault and Deleuze seems to broadly characterise the tension between fixity and becoming, classification and transformation, that in both historical and conceptual terms provides a crucial organising logic of medieval and early modern cultures. Not incidentally, this is also an organising logic present in the history of sexuality – for instance, in the tension between minoritising and universalising approaches toward 'modern' homosexuality.[106] This tension also might be said to describe a faultline within contemporary trans/trans-/trans* discourses which can, on the one hand, insist that trans marks a transition from one clear state to another and, on the other, deliberately refuse such clarity on behalf of the genderqueer. This volume demonstrates that such faultlines have a centuries-long genealogy. It therefore is of considerable interest that early modernists have approached similar tensions in light of Ovidian metamorphosis. As Leonard Barkan notes: 'For all its emphasis upon the blurring of clear categories, metamorphosis is as much concerned with reduction and fixity as with variability or complexity.'[107] Alternatively, in her analysis of the sapphic discourse she terms 'metamorphic', Susan Lanser notes that while 'the appeal of sex-change resolutions lies in the attempt to stabilize flux and restore fixity . . . these metamorphic scenarios leave considerable residue.' By residue (what she elsewhere calls 'sapphic remainder') Lanser gestures toward what the plot cannot logically solve by means of its resolution – which is why, in the main, metamorphic stories resort to a 'literal or discursive deus ex machina'.[108] Likewise, in an essay on Ovid's influence on Shakespeare's *The Winter's Tale*, Lori Humphrey Newcomb identifies a tension between 'monumentalizing' and 'spectacularizing' impulses,[109] indexing them to gender in ways that prove salient to 'Iphis and Ianthe' and its transversions. Monumentalising is a materialising mode whose tendency is 'to shape and fix texts, to demand singular control of the art object, to memorialize the body in an exact duplicate, to contain women in immobility'. Spectacularising, in contrast, is a performative mode that 'leave[s] texts behind . . . embrace[s] collaboration and proliferation . . . [and] celebrate[s] the changefulness of the human body, even the female body'.[110] Emphasising that these two impulses cannot be reconciled, Newcomb traces their complex interplay within both Shakespeare's play and the dialectic between page and stage.[111]

The tensions between monumentalising and spectacularising, fixity and flux, biopolitics and becoming, that Peggy and I engaged pedagogically were given a new set of terms, coordinates and interlocutors by way of the Early Modern Conversions project. The noun 'conversion' means 'turning in position, direction, destination' (*OED*, 1), as well as 'change in character, nature, form, or function' – both of which have obvious affinities with the constellation of terms related to 'trans' noted above. We thus hope that new questions and approaches will arise when conversion is approached through 'Iphis and Ianthe' and its transversions, and transversion is approached by means of the intellectual repertoire involved in rethinking conversion. In particular, we hope to bring more exactitude to our understanding of the historical and theoretical implications of certain concepts that have organised the study of medieval and early modern religion, politics, social hierarchy, race, gender and sexuality. Based on our evolving appreciation of transversion as an analytic, we propose that this concept offers a resource for moving beyond tried and true categories of experience and identity that have governed analysis of both conversion and metamorphosis. This is in no small part because at the heart of these concepts reside two basic ontological and epistemological questions: What *is* metamorphosis, conversion or transformation? And how do we know when it has occurred? Is the change an expression of the radical replacement of one thing by another or the unfolding or development of an essence that endures?[112] These were certainly questions that medievals and early moderns worried about in regard to the professions of Christian faith by Jews and Muslims who claimed to have converted, as well as in regard to the confessional differences tearing Christianity apart.[113] Furthermore, differences of opinion about how to address these questions have created impasses within the Early Modern Conversions project itself. Whether participants were analysing autobiographical narratives of the voluntary, aspirational conversion of one's own faith (modelled on Augustine's *Confessions*) or the coerced, mass conversions of religious and ethnic others (whose touchstones are the Spanish Inquisition and conversion in the New World), whether we were trying to define the global politics of conversion or its subjective phenomenology, we often seemed to be at conceptual loggerheads, forced to choose between knowledge and uncertainty, fixity and flux, classification and change, being and becoming.

Rather than gloss over these tensions, we ask: How might the analytic of transversion address this impasse? Much criticism of metamorphosis, for instance, upholds the 'clarification' of an essential identity as its central, governing function.[114] Our contributors suggest, instead, that the bodies depicted in 'Iphis and Ianthe' and its transversions might best be considered as the manifestation of a *process* of embodiment, rather than a readily legible and already achieved representation of bodies. If one thinks of embodiment as a process, the transit from one ontological state to another is not necessarily arrested by reaching what, at any discrete moment in time, seems a terminal point, nor is it necessarily unidirectional. But neither, we would insist, is this process as open-ended as the overused trope of 'fluidity' – often used to describe changes in gender, subjectivity or desire – might suggest.[115] Further, any movement entailed by embodiment-as-process involves not only a spatial reorientation but temporal duration as well. Several essays dwell on the temporality of transition, showing it to be less a moment than a process, eventuating less in a terminal result than in a movement *in between* that undermines the neat sequence of past to present to future. If we deliberately and patiently track each moment of change *across*, then new understandings of what is at stake emerge.

The moment that Iphis walks from the temple, starting off female and ending (maybe) as a (kind of) male; the lack of mention of a penis in the tale's scene of metamorphosis;[116] the arbitrary nature of whose sex will be transformed, Galatea's or Phyllida's, and the deferral of this change beyond the frame of Lyly's play; the fact that Benserade's drama starts near the end of the story, slows down the plot and emphasises resistance to marriage and postponement of the transformation and the truth[117] – each of these matters command our attention for its dilation and deferral of the meaning of metamorphosis, as well as of the transformation implied by the all-too-simple, shorthand concept of 'sex change'. Indeed, they offer a mandate for considering transversion, metamorphosis and conversion *in slow motion*, insisting that we ask: Is the change of sex a trans*fixion*? Or does it always leave some *version* of something (else, other, prior) behind?[118]

Beyond suggesting the interpretative payoff of slowing down our analyses to account for minute processes of change – as well as the sometimes recalcitrant resistance to it – a number of ontological and epistemological challenges ensue from the methodological application of transversion. First, in terms of ontology: it is often said that metamorphic dynamics entail a psychologically enabling loss of the self – and this insight has become a staple of criticism of Ovidian-influenced comedies such as *The Comedy of Errors*, *A Midsummer Night's Dream* and *Twelfth Night*. Others, conversely, have argued that Ovid's fleeing nymphs, in particular, are 'saved' by a metamorphosis that paradoxically allows them to retain their essential identity – albeit in altered form.[119] Each of these positions, while theoretically attractive, encounters a problem of ethical discernment: who is losing one's self, who can experience that loss as enabling, and whose self is saved? We suggest that rethinking metamorphoses in terms of transversion enables interpretative acts that do not hinge on absolute or universalised conceptions of loss or gain, which themselves tend toward ethical positions that fail to account for social hierarchy and privilege.

Second, in terms of epistemology: the fact that knowledge is withheld from many of the actors in these texts (the father as well as the beloved); the fact that Galatea and Phyllida literally do not know what to make of one another's bodies and even after they go off into the forest to 'make much of one another' still do not seem to know;[120] the fact that scholars routinely profess opinions of whose sex will be changed in Lyly's play based on presumptive knowledge of a character's 'essential' masculinity[121] – each of these issues translates an ontological question into an epistemological one, that is, a problem of knowledge. Such a shift also underlies medieval euhemerist and Christian interpretations of the *Metamorphoses* as the revelation of divine truths. Because one of the central anxieties about religious conversion was the inability to *know* if someone's conversion was authentic, attention to the problems that conversion presents to knowledge relations has ramifications for those whose interests lie primarily in the history and politics of religion as well as those interested in the history and politics of embodiment.

Indeed, transversion might provide further analytic purchase in terms of the effort to balance awareness of the historical specificity of conversion as a phenomenon indicatively formed in the realm of religion with awareness of the concept's capacious salience for a variety of transformations. Within the Early Modern Conversions project, the challenge has been to accomplish this balancing act without evacuating conversion's historical and conceptual specificity or rendering conversion simply a synonym for all change. This volume thus offers transversion as a potential lever to press conversion and metamorphosis against one another. For instance, it has become a cliché in scholarship on Ovid that his *Metamorphoses* is itself always undergoing metamorphosis.[122] It has yet to be fully appreciated, however, that conversion is also always a converting – not a settled state but an ongoing process. Conversely, the tethering of conversion to the high-stakes realm of religion may tend to elicit more scholarly exactitude than the generally fuzzier (and often purely phenomenological) concept of metamorphosis. For instance, scholars of conversion necessarily wonder whether it is a turning away or a turning toward – or both. Conversion may follow (or impart) a different structural logic than metamorphosis, insisting on specific material entailments of temporal moment and geography, training the eye on *when* and *where* change happens. The virtue of transversion is that it asks us to scrutinise such dynamics of location and temporality, to watch movements as they transit forward and back, and to attend to the play of difference as well as similarity.

* * *

The transversions that motivate this collection are visually represented in the bronze statue sculpted by Auguste Rodin for his *Gates of Hell* that adorns this book's cover. Part of the amortisement of the right-hand pilaster of the *Gates*, these entwined lovers are known in that context, as well as in stand-alone versions, as *Ovid's Metamorphoses*. Because the sculpture is placed vertically in the *Gates*, the figure lying on her back is almost completely hidden by the body of her partner. (This hidden figure appears in several of Rodin's compositions, including 'Young Girl with a Serpent'.) The pair have enjoyed a number of names over the course of Rodin's career. They were described as 'Castor and Pollux', even as Rodin affirmed to Carl Jacobsen on 18 October 1907 that the pair depicts 'the episode where the nymph Salmacis falls in love with a hermaphrodite'.[123] The statue was also known as 'Les Amies' (the friends) and, with reference to Baudelaire, as 'Voluptuousness (Les Fleurs du Mal)'. A photograph annotated in Rodin's hand names it 'Desire'. Currently, it is advertised as 'Iphis and Ianthe' by the on-line image service Artnet. How it received this attribution, we do not know. We do know that the models were two dancers from the Opéra, known as 'priestesses of the isle of Lesbos' recommended by Degas to Rodin.[124]

Such conundrums of attribution need not trouble us. The flexibility of names for this loving pair, not to mention their feminised if ambiguous embodiment, are altogether fitting emblems of transversion, suggesting just how transferable its conceptual logic may be as we seek to understand the variability and complexity of bodies coming together – as female, as male and as uncircumscribed by gender – over the centuries.

Acknowledgments

I thank Peggy McCracken, Patsy Badir, Susan Lanser, Marjorie Rubright, Miranda Griffin, Heather James, Lynn Enterline, Joseph Gamble, and Charisse Willis for sharing their various forms of expertise, Laurel Billings for her timely bibliographic assistance, and Jade Standing for preparing the manuscript for publication.

Notes

1. See the Loeb translation of Ovid's *Metamorphoses* by Frank Justus Miller. Although there is some debate, the apparent source for the story of 'Iphis and Ianthe' is that of Leucippus in Book 2 of Nicander's lost *Heteroeumena*, the probable prose summary of which is preserved in the transformation tales compiled by Antonius Liberalis; see Wheeler, 'Changing Names'.
2. These manuscript copies of the Latin *Metamorphoses* include subtitles (*tituli*) to help readers orient themselves in the text and prose paraphrases (*argumenta*) to help readers understand it. See Hexter, 'Medieval Articulations of Ovid's *Metamorphoses*'.
3. Tarrant, 'The *Narrationes* of "Lactantius" and the Transmission of Ovid's *Metamorphoses*'.
4. Gillespie, 'From the Twelfth Century to *c*.1450'. See also the introduction in Gura, *A Critical Edition and Study of Arnulf of Orléans' Philological Commentary to Ovid's 'Metamorphoses'*.
5. Gillespie, 'From the Twelfth Century to *c*.1450', p. 194. See also the introduction in Born, *The Integumenta on the Metamorphoses of Ovid by John of Garland*. *Integumentum* refers to the veiling of a hidden truth.
6. Coulson, 'Ovid's *Metamorphoses* in the School Tradition of France', and 'Ovid's Transformations in Medieval France'.
7. Gillespie, 'From the Twelfth Century to *c*.1450', p. 189.
8. Hexter, 'Medieval Articulations of Ovid's *Metamorphoses*', p. 76. Gillespie argues, however, that 'none of the surviving school collections of *accessus* from the twelfth and thirteenth centuries treats the *Metamorphoses*', suggesting that many pedagogues 'felt strongly that this was not a suitable work to put into the hands or minds of impressionable students', p. 193.
9. Minnis, *Magister amoris*, p. 12.
10. Gillespie, 'From the Twelfth Century to *c*.1450'.
11. The author of this text 'assumes variously', in the words of Copeland, 'the posture of moral expositor, biblical exegete, allegorist, and translator', roles that also extend to the compilation and incorporation of 'existing vernacular versions of some Ovidian material'; *Rhetoric, Hermeneutics and Translation in the Middle*

Ages, p. 117. Copeland further argues that its 'vernacular system of exegesis replaces its Latin precedent; and in a radical move of appropriation, a vernacular translation substitutes itself for the Latin original as the object of exegetical interest', p. 114.
12. In addition to Coulson, 'Ovid's *Metamorphoses* in the School Tradition of France', and Gillespie, 'From the Twelfth Century to c.1450', for the complicated history of these interrelated works, see Dimmick, 'Ovid in the Middle Ages', and Mills, *Seeing Sodomy in the Middle Ages*, p. 100.
13. According to Moss, *Ovid in Renaissance France*, in the medieval moralised Ovids, 'Poetic language is essentially figurative language, and poetic fable is the pleasant telling of truth disguised, an extended metaphor or allegory, to be read rather as riddle than as narrative', p. 24.
14. Gillespie, 'From the Twelfth Century to *c*.1450', p. 206.
15. Moss, 'Ovid in Renaissance France', p. 26.
16. In addition to Moss, 'Ovid in Renaissance France', see Blair, 'Ovidius Methodizatus', and Green, *Humanism and Protestantism in Early Modern English Education*, pp. 222–3, who notes that a new edition of the *Metamorphoses* was published in England 'every three or four years from the 1580s to the 1740s', p. 223.
17. Cornish, *Vernacular Translation in Dante's Italy*.
18. Green, *Humanism and Protestantism*, p. 318.
19. These include *Les XV livres de la Metamorphose D'ovide* (1539); *Olympe, ou Metamorphose d'Ovide* (1597); *Les métamorphoses d'Ovide traduites en prose françoise*, trans. Nicolas Renouard (Paris: M. Guillemot, 1606); and *Les métamorphoses d'Ovide* (1617). Over the next few decades, Renouard's translation was reprinted over twenty times; see Taylor, *The Lives of Ovid*, p. 50. In addition, two parodic 'burlesque' versions of the *Metamorphoses* were published in France in 1650; see Taylor, *The Lives of Ovid*, pp. 55–69.
20. The *Metamorphoses* was widely disseminated through humanist pedagogy, alongside the *Ars Amatoria* and *Heroides*, for lessons in prosopopoeia (imitation) and ethopoeia (character-making); see James, 'Shakespeare, the Classics, and the Forms of Authorship'; Enterline, *Shakespeare's Schoolroom* and 'Rhetoric and Gender in Early Modern British Literature'.
21. For gendered readings of some of the commentaries and translations, see McKinley, *Reading the Ovidian Heroine*.
22. These include a late fourteenth-century drama, *Miracle de la fille d'un roy*, a fifteenth-century French prose epic adaptation in *Les processes et faicts du trespreux noble et vaillant Huon de Bordeaux, pair de France et Duc de Guyenne*, and an English prose epic from the 1530s.
23. Freyman et al., *Iphis*. For a hypertext, Latin–English version, with critical notes correlating lines from Bellamy's *Iphis* to the *Metamorphoses* and discussion of how Bellamy amplifies the lesbian plot, see Sutton, www.philological.bham.ac.uk/iphis/.
24. Harbage, *Annals of English Drama*, pp. 106–7.
25. These images, and the movements between text and image, have been surprisingly under-read. For pertinent analysis of some of them, see Mills, *Seeing Sodomy in the Middle Ages*, pp. 116–21.
26. See Ferrand, *De la maladie d'amour ou mélancholie érotique* (1610). In tracing the history of some of these citations, Beecher, 'Concerning Sex Changes', p. 997, notes that Pliny the Elder's source for his 'case study' of the change from male to female of Lucius Cossitius in his *Natural History* 'is so close to [the] Ovidian tale that we may wonder whether it is not displaced from an underlying mythological tradition.' Whereas Beecher finds it 'strange to think that by a process of citation,

even the myths of the ancients became the substance of scientific analysis', it is the intent of our volume to suggest the extent of this form of intertextuality.
27. Saker matter of factly states '& that young *Iphis* retayning till her mariage day the shape of a Maide, though attyred in the habite of a man, was then made a husband, for which he long wished, and enioyed the company of his beloued wife', n.p.
28. Loid, *The Pilgrimage of princes*, p. 107.
29. Riche, *His Farewell to Militarie Profession*, n.p. For a modern translation, see Beecher, *Barnabe Riche*, pp. 303–4. In the anonymous Scots play *Philotus* (1603) which closely follows Riche's plot, this exchange is much reduced, with the reference to Iphis accorded only four short lines (stanza 107).
30. Traub, *The Renaissance of Lesbianism*; Beecher, 'Concerning Sex Changes'; Long, in this volume.
31. Sandys, *Ovid's Metamorphosis Englished*, p. 450.
32. Phillips, *The New World of English Words*, accessed on-line through *Lexicons of Early Modern English*. According to *LEME*, the two other lexicons that emphasise paternal displeasure are Thomas Cooper, *Thesaurus Linguae Romanae et Britannicae* (1584) – 'Then Telethusa percetuing the matter coulde no lonnger be hid, and fearing hir husbandes displeasure, called to the Gods for helpe' – and Elisha Coles, *An English Dictionary* (1676) – 'Iphis, a Cretan Virgin turn'd into a man on her wedding day (at the prayers of her Mother) to avoid the anger of her husband Lygdus.' Henry Cockeram's *English Dictionary* (1623) notes only that 'her Mother seeing the matter could be no longer hid, praied to the gods'. Interestingly, Phillips' lexicon, the only of the four to include an entry for Ianthe, mistakenly describes her as 'a certain Virgin, the daughter of Telessa, who the first day of her marriage was transformed into a man'.
33. Piozzi, *Thraliana*, Vol 1, p. 356.
34. For more scholarship on *Galatea*, see Lunney, 'Recent Studies in John Lyly'.
35. Kesson, *John Lyly*, p. 4. 'Lyly was the first Elizabethan to see a series of his plays go into print, and the first writer to see his plays reprinted', p. 4. 'Having opened up a new market for single-story fiction books in the late 1570s, Lyly's authorship then helped to open up the market for play books in the 1580s and early 1590s', Kesson, p. 167.
36. Golding's translation refers to such English phenomena as fruits and flowers; see Badir in this volume.
37. Interestingly, in the probable source for Ovid's tale, Nicander's *Heteroeumena*, the name of the Iphis figure's mother is Galataea; see Raval, 'Cross-Dressing and "Gender Trouble" in the Ovidian Corpus', and Wheeler, 'Changing Names'.
38. Critical fashion has long viewed Lyly's plays as stilted and, in essence, non-theatrical, a view that recent university productions and theatre-based staged readings have refuted. That this criticism has gone hand in hand with allegations of his stylistic 'effeminacy' and aesthetic 'impotence' is broached by Kesson but worth additional analysis.
39. There is no translation of this play into English.
40. See Lanham, *The Motives of Eloquence*; Fyler, *Chaucer and Ovid*; Pearcy, *The Mediated Muse*; Loewenstein, *Responsive Readings*; Rubin, *Ovid's 'Metamorphosis English'*; Harvey, *Ventriloquized Voices*; Taylor (ed.), *Shakespeare's Ovid*; Enterline, *The Rhetoric of the Body from Ovid to Shakespeare*; Lyne, *Ovid's Changing Worlds*; James, 'Ovid in English Renaissance Literature'; Pugh, *Spenser and Ovid*; Kilgour, *Milton and the Metamorphosis of Ovid*; Taylor, *The Lives of Ovid*; Wiseman, *Writing Metamorphosis in the English Renaissance*; and Casali, 'Ovidian Intertextuality in Ariosto's *Orlando Furioso*'.

41. Barkan, *Transuming Passion*; Smith, *Homosexual Desire in Shakespeare's England*; DiGangi, 'The Homoerotics of Marriage in Ovidian Comedy'; Stanivukovic, *Ovid and the Renaissance Body*; Ferguson, *Queer (Re)Readings in the French Renaissance*; Carter, *Ovidian Myth and Sexual Deviance*; and Nardizzi et al. (eds), *Queer Renaissance Historiography*.
42. The exceptions include Chess, 'Queer Gender Informants in Ovid and Shakespeare'; Scragg, *The Metamorphosis of Gallathea*; Barkan, *The Gods Made Flesh*; Perry, *Another Reality*; Bate, *Shakespeare and Ovid*; Braden, 'Ovid and Shakespeare'; Keith and Rupp (eds), *Metamorphosis: The Changing Face of Ovid*; Oakley-Brown, *Ovid and the Cultural Politics of Translation*; Ferguson, *Queer (Re)Readings in the French Renaissance*; Carter, *Ovidian Myth and Sexual Deviance*; Starks-Estes, *Violence, Trauma, and* Virtus *in Shakespeare's Roman Plays and Poems*; and James, 'Shakespeare's Learned Heroines in Ovid's Schoolroom' and 'The Ovidian Girlhood of Shakespeare's Boy Actors'. Earlier work on this tale is testament to a change in scholarly understandings of gender and sexuality. Fairly typical of the earlier brief mention is the casual treatment of Burrow, 'Original Fictions: Metamorphoses in *The Faerie Queen*': 'Is the world populated by people produced from the rapes of the gods? From Iphis-like lesbianism? From Pygmalian [sic] union with stones? The poem is an extraordinarily tense mixture of the generative and the perverse. And Ovid is not interested in reconciling them', p. 100.
43. Reid, *The Oxford Guide to Classical Mythology in the Arts*.
44. This method was also evident in the popular twelfth-century phenomenon of creating *florilegia*, or selected extracts, of the *Metamorphoses*. See Gura, *A Critical Edition and Study of Arnulf of Orléans' Philological Commentary*.
45. Hexter, 'Medieval Articulations of Ovid's *Metamorphoses*', notes that for medieval interpreters of the poem, 'segmentation is a precondition for interpretation', p. 63. Halpern, *The Poetics of Primitive Accumulation*, however, distinguishes between the *Ovide moralisé*, which 'overcoded the text with an officially sanctioned (Christian) narrative', whereas later humanist pedagogues privileged 'copia' which 'decoded the [Ovidian] text into rhetorical and discursive components. The older method subsumed dangerous contents within a larger ideological unity; the newer method decomposed this same material into harmless, inert atoms', p. 47. Crane, *Framing Authority: Sayings, Self, and Society*, argues that humanists and their students treated Latin texts such as Ovid's *Metamorphoses* as 'containers of extractable fragments of wisdom and eloquence', p. 87.
46. Even translators of the full work seem to have been challenged in this regard; according to Oakley-Brown, even as 'they aspire to the unity they thought they saw in Ovid's text', they 'were unavoidably trapped by the fragmentation which was at the heart of Ovid's narrative method', *Ovid and the Cultural Politics of Translation*, p. 192.
47. See, in addition to work cited in note 40, Greene, *Light in Troy*; James, *Shakespeare's Troy*; and Cheney, *Marlowe's Counterfeit Profession*. See also Dupas in this volume.
48. Hulse, *Metamorphic Verse*; Keach, *Elizabethan Erotic Narratives*; Ellis, *Sexuality and Citizenship*.
49. Compare Groves' more trans-positive translation: 'Nor do I tell the story of how once Sithon lived as both sexes, now man, now woman, through an innovation of natural law', in 'From Statue to Story', p. 322.
50. There are two ways of thinking of 'Iphis and Ianthe' in relationship to intertextuality: as related to themes, texts, and intellectual projects *beyond* Ovid's original Latin poem, and as internally, laterally, connected to other stories within

the Ovidian corpus. Whereas our volume explores the former, readers may well be interested in the latter. An earlier tradition of scholarship tended to associate Iphis with the stories of 'unnatural love' in Book 9, including the incest tales of Byblis and Myrrha, and/or the male homoerotic tales of Orpheus, Ganymede and Hyacinthus. Surprisingly few scholars read 'Iphis and Ianthe' in terms of other Ovidian tales of sex change (e.g. Tiresias, Caenis/Caeneus, Mestra, Sithon, and Salmacis and Hermaphroditus).

For a sense of classicists' readings of the tale, see Hallett, 'Female Homoeroticism and the Denial of Roman Reality in Latin Literature'; Pintabone, 'Ovid's Iphis and Ianthe: When Girls Won't be Girls'; Raval, 'Cross-Dressing and "Gender Trouble" in the Ovidian Corpus'; Kamen, 'Naturalized Desires and the Metamorphosis of Iphis'; Ormand, 'Impossible Lesbians in Ovid's *Metamorphoses*'; and Walker, 'Before the Name'. Sharrock's overview, 'Gender and Sexuality', leads with the story of Iphis. See also Alison (trans.), *Change Me: Stories of Sexual Transformation from Ovid*.

A few scholars who have analysed 'Iphis and Ianthe' briefly consider other Ovidian tales of cross-dressing, androgyny and sex change: see, for instance, Barkan, *The Gods Made Flesh*, who discusses Tiresias and 'Salmacis and Hermaphroditus'. Mestra and Sithon have received little comment. Regarding Tiresias, see Carp, '"Venus Utraque"'; Liveley, 'Tiresias/Teresa'; and Brisson and Lloyd, *Sexual Ambivalence*. For 'Salmacis and Hermaphroditus', see Nugent, '"This Sex Which Is Not One"'; Robinson, 'Salmacis and Hermaphroditus'; Nagle, '"Amor, Ira," and Sexual Identity in Ovid's "Metamorphosis"'; Zajko, '"Listening With" Ovid'; Groves, 'From Statue to Story'; Keith, 'Versions of Epic Masculinity in Ovid's *Metamorphoses*' and, briefly, 'Gender and Sexuality'. In 'Versions of Epic Masculinity' Keith also briefly addresses Caenis/Caenus, as does Brisson; see also Papaioannou, *Redesigning Achilles*.

51. Fox, 'Sexuality and Desire', p. 162; 'alternate desires' is her phrase, p. 167. See also Curran, 'Rape and Rape Victims in the "Metamorphoses"'.
52. James, 'Shakespeare's Learned Heroines in Ovid's Schoolroom', p. 68.
53. Pugh, *Spenser and Ovid*, p. 57.
54. My impression is that classicists' revisionary work on this story (see note 50) has also largely been initiated by feminist scholars, and that their trajectories of interpretation have, with due deference to historical and linguistic differences, paralleled that of medieval and early modern scholarship. In this regard, the lack of mention of 'Iphis and Ianthe' in Rimmel's *Ovid's Lovers* is especially a lost opportunity, as she positions her book as an intervention in the binary rubric whereby literary critics analyse '*either* female *or* male figures, *either* constructions of femininity or masculinity', proposing instead to explore 'relationality', particularly 'the desiring subject in Ovidian poetry as a being-in-relation', pp. 3–4.
55. See also Smith's novel, *Girl Meets Boy*, which turns its titular phrase on its head with its multiple challenges to gender binaries in the matter of love and sex; and Charles Martin's poem, 'Iphis and Ianthe'.
56. Most of the medieval and Renaissance scholarship on 'Iphis and Ianthe' offers a reading of Ovid's tale in relation to one of its transversions. Among these, 'Yde et Olive', *Galatea* and *Iphis et Iante* have been most frequently analysed. On 'Yde et Olive', see Watt, 'Behaving Like a Man? Incest, Lesbian Desire, and Gender Play'; Kłosowska, *Queer Love in the Middle Ages*, pp. 81–7; Weisl, 'How to Be a Man, Though Female'; and Robins, 'Three Tales of Female Same-Sex Marriage'. Amer, *Crossing Borders*, pp. 50–87, traces the genealogy of this tale to the Arabic 'The Story of Qamar al-Zaman and the Princess Boudour', from *Alf layla wa layla* (*One Thousand and One Nights*). Using trans and disability theory, Chess,

'Queer Gender Informants in Ovid and Shakespeare', reads Iphis in terms of Shakespeare's (non-faithful) adaptation of her into Viola/Cesario: both are non-binary gender informants who instigate a 'queer gain' in the form of 'utopian possibility' for themselves and other characters.

On *Galatea*, scholarship has focused largely on cross-dressing, chastity, lesbianism, the Elizabethan court and the (erotic) role of the boy player. Rackin's essay on the androgyny of Lyly's boy heroine was an important precursor for early modern scholarship; see 'Androgyny, Mimesis, and the Marriage of the Boy Heroine on the English Renaissance Stage'. See also Bruster, 'Female-Female Eroticism and the Early Modern Stage'; Jankowski, '"Where there can be no cause of affection": Redefining Virgins, Their Desires, and Their Pleasures', and *Pure Resistance: Queer Virginity*; Pincombe, *The Plays of John Lyly: Eros and Eliza*; Franceschina, *Homosexualities in the English Theater*; Shannon, 'Nature's Bias: Renaissance Homonormativity and Elizabethan Comic Likeness'; Dooley, 'Inversion, Metamorphosis and Sexual Difference'; Wixson, 'Cross-Dressing and John Lyly's *Gallathea*'; Robinson, 'The Metamorphosis of Sex(uality)' and *Closeted Writing and Lesbian and Gay Literature*; Walen, *Constructions of Female Homoeroticism*; Drouin, 'Diana's Band: Safe Spaces, Publics, and Early Modern Lesbianism'; Carter, *Ovidian Myth and Sexual Deviance*; and Lanser, *The Sexuality of History*. In *Masculinity, Corporality and the English Stage*, Billing proffers a male homoerotic reading based on the 'stable' phenomenology of the boy actor's erotic body, and in *Male to Female Crossdressing in Early Modern English Literature*, Chess reads *Galatea* through a trans* analytic.

On *Iphis et Iante*, in addition to Lanser, *The Sexuality of History*, and Robinson, *Closeted Writing and Lesbian and Gay Literature*, see Leibacher-Ouvrard, 'Speculum de l'Autre Femme'; Legault, 'De-Sexing the Lesbian'; and Row, 'Queer Time on the Early Modern Stage: France and the Drama of Biopower'.
57. On Fiordispina and Bradamante, see DeCoste, *Hopeless Love*; and Casali, 'Ovidian Intertextuality in Ariosto's *Orlando Furioso*'. *Orlando Furioso* was translated into English by Sir John Harington in 1591, and the story of Fiordispina was mined for the episode of Britomart and Malecasta in Sir Edmund Spenser's *The Fairie Queene*.
58. Traub, *The Renaissance of Lesbianism*.
59. Another Ovidian tale, that of Jupiter's rape of Calisto while in the guise of Diana, is another crucial model for female-female homoeroticism; see Traub, *The Renaissance of Lesbianism*.
60. Lanser, *The Sexuality of History*, pp. 25 and 57.
61. Lanser, *The Sexuality of History*, p. 80.
62. Lanser, *The Sexuality of History*, p. 29, emphasis in original.
63. Mills, *Seeing Sodomy*, p. 132. His focus on 'things' intersects with the concerns of Lochrie and McCracken in this volume.
64. Chess, *Male to Female Crossdressing*, p. 141. Gower's version also has been read through a trans perspective focused on gender dysphoria by Bychowski, 'Unconfessing Transgender'.
65. See Bryan, *In the Company of Boys*, and Munro, 'Queering Gender, Age, and Status in Early Modern Children's Drama'.
66. On Arachne, see Miller, 'Arachnologies: The Woman, the Text, and the Critic'. On Philomela, see Enterline, *The Rhetoric of the Body*; Carter, *Ovidian Myth and Sexual Deviance*; Lamb, 'Singing with the (Tongue) of the Nightingale'; Newman, '"And Let Mild Women to Him Lose Their Mildness": Philomela, Female Violence, and Shakespeare's *The Rape of Lucrece*'; and Starks-Estes, *Violence, Trauma, and Virtus in Shakespeare's Roman Poems and Plays*. On Narcissus, see

DiGangi, 'Male Deformities'. On Ganymede, see Barkan, *Transuming Passion*, and Saslow, *Ganymede in the Renaissance*. A similar case might be made for the story of Calisto, most often viewed as simply Diana's nymph, but who engaged in a dalliance with Jove while he impersonated Diana; see Traub, *The Renaissance of Lesbianism*.
67. This is the assessment of Burrow, 'Re-Embodying Ovid', p. 305.
68. We might take Makowski's 1996 summary for the consensus that has reigned until recently:

> The centerpiece of the Iphis story is the monologue on the pathology of homoerotic love ... a speech remarkable both for its rhetorical display and for its insistence on the unnaturalness of homosexual passion ... The word *prodigiosa* is significant as it connotes a type of love not wondrous but rather monstrous in the same sense that freaks of nature are monstrous. ('Bisexual Orpheus', p. 31)

69. Masten, *Queer Philologies*, p. 214.
70. *Oxford Latin Dictionary*. In 'Impossible Lesbians in Ovid's *Metamorphoses*', Ormand translates 'prodigiosa novaeque cura Veneris' as 'a monstrous heartache of novel love', p. 98.
71. The fungibility of terms can be seen in comparing Miller's Loeb translation, 'The story of this *unnatural passion* would, perhaps, have been the talk of Crete's hundred towns, if Crete had not lately had a *wonder* of its own in the changed form of Iphis', to that of Melville, *Ovid's Metamorphoses*: 'The tale of this *strange miracle* might well / have been the talk of all the hundred towns / Of Crete, had not that island lately known / In Iphis's change a *marvel* nearer home' (emphases mine).
72. See Forey, *Ovid's Metamorphoses, Translated by Arthur Golding*.
73. See Wiseman, *Writing Metamorphosis in the English Renaissance*; Salisbury, *The Beast Within*; Crane, *Animal Encounters*; Shannon, *The Accommodated Animal*; and Nardizzi and Feerick, *The Indistinct Human in Renaissance Literature*.
74. With thanks to Lynn Enterline.
75. Kilgour, 'Virgil and Ovid', p. 528.
76. Rackin, 'Androgyny, Mimesis, and the Marriage of the Boy Heroine', p. 29.
77. James, 'The Ovidian Girlhood of Shakespeare's Boy Actors', p. 111, p. 112. See also Lanser in this volume.
78. James, 'The Ovidian Girlhood of Shakespeare's Boy Actors', pp. 116 and 117.
79. James, 'The Ovidian Girlhood of Shakespeare's Boy Actors', p. 117.
80. James, 'The Ovidian Girlhood of Shakespeare's Boy Actors', p. 106.
81. In 'Ovid and Shakespeare', Braden notes in an offhand remark that the cross-dressing comedies do 'in play what Ovid's Iphis does for real', p. 449. In 'Shakespeare's Learned Heroines in Ovid's Schoolroom', James distinguishes between the Ovidian genealogy of Rosalind, whose linguistic prowess derives from the *Ars Amatoria* and *Amores*, and that of Viola, whose plight 'recalls Ovid's story of Iphis', who 'views herself as a 'monster' (*Met.* 9.736) and her love as a hopeless and strange prodigy' (*Met.* 9.727–8), p. 75. See also Chess, 'Queer Gender Informants', on the relationship between Cesario and the eunuch Mardian, who has an impact on Cleopatra's erotic imaginings.
82. In this, they follow in the footsteps of queer studies scholars who have expanded the purview, both historical and theoretical, of sexuality in culture, most prominently Bray, *The Friend*, which established that male homoerotic bonds were embedded in a nexus of social relations – not only the patriarchal household but education, patronage and service.

83. Griffin, 'Translation and Transformation in the *Ovide moralisé*', p. 42. Griffin argues that the 'practice of reading into an original an eternal truth which was not originally written into it has the effect of unsettling the role and identity of exactly what is "original" in this transaction of translation and transformation: any hierarchy of pre-existing text and its translation is troubled', p. 47.
84. Newman and Tylus, *Early Modern Cultures of Translation*, pp. 1–2.
85. Lyne, *Ovid's Changing Worlds*; Oakley-Brown, *Ovid and the Cultural Politics of Translation*; Wiseman, *Writing Metamorphosis in the English Renaissance*.
86. We are aware of the importance of the Ovidian tradition elsewhere, particularly in Italy, Germany and the Netherlands, and look forward to others' engagement with this literary history.
87. With thanks to Joseph Gamble, who alerted to me to material from the online *Lexicons of Early Modern English* as part of his work on early modern lexical connections among trans- and con-version.
88. For a range of articulations of transgender and a survey of the field, see Stryker and Aizura (eds), *The Transgender Studies Reader 2*. Enke, 'Introduction: Transfeminist Perspectives', notes that 'the asterisk in *trans** functions as a truncation symbol the way that putting an asterisk after a word or fragment works in many library search systems', p. 7.
89. See Lochrie, Griffin and Long in this volume.
90. Hayward and Weinstein, 'Tranimalities in the Age of Trans* Life', p. 196.
91. Enke, 'Introduction', p. 7.
92. See Billings and Rubright in this volume.
93. Although they place different emphases on the import of identity, none of our contributors countenance a use of 'trans' that fails to do justice to the lived experience of individuals or to their right to self-identify in whatever way makes most sense for them.
94. Such issues have come to the fore in online debates about the term trans*, which has proven over time to be controversial, particularly in activist circles, and has sometimes been seen as a sign of invalidation rather than inclusivity. At stake in the use of language and typography are such issues as reproducing or disrupting binarisms, allegations of transmisogyny, attachments or disattachments to identity, and the value and function of historical memory. Our aim is not to resolve such issues, but to acknowledge the tensions they enact.
95. Enke, 'Introduction', pp. 7–8.
96. See, for instance, Durling, 'Rewriting Gender', as well as Amer, *Crossing Borders*.
97. See Douglas Lanier, 'Shakespearean Rhizomatics', and 'Shakespeare / Not Shakespeare: Afterword', and Lisa Starks-Estes, *Ovid and Adaptation in Early Modern English Theater*. Like Lanier, Bryan Reynolds (and his several co-writers) employs Deleuzean concepts to explore how Shakespeare's texts, particularly when adapted or remediated, create modes of becoming rather than static identities. Reynolds dubs this quality 'transversalism'; see *Performing Transversally*.
98. The circularity of influence between the Latin original, its translation and its intertexts is especially clear in the Italian tradition: upon the sixteenth-century publication of two major translations of the *Metamorphoses* – the *Transformationi* of Ludovico Dolce (1553) and the *Metamorfosi* of Giovanni dell'Anguillara (1561) – 'The *Metamorphoses* became an Ariostesque poem', insofar as the translator followed 'Ariosto's imitation rather than the Latin original'; see Casali, 'Ovidian Intertextuality in Ariosto's *Orlando Furioso*', p. 307.
99. In 'Version, Con-, Per-, and In- (Thoughts on Djuna Barnes's Novel, *Nightwood*)', Burke briefly considers how conversion, perversion, inversion and aversion all share the root 'vert', meaning 'to turn'.

100. For analysis of the early modern meanings of 'perversion', see Dollimore, *Sexual Dissidence*.
101. The Early Modern Conversions project, which collected an international team of scholars to study conversion as a social, political, religious and aesthetic phenomenon, has provided crucial support for the kinds of creative collaboration that are, in their own way, transforming work in the academy. A University of Michigan symposium brought together nine of the volume's contributors, and the editors were enabled to twice work face to face with the help of Conversions funding, provided by SSHRC. I, in particular, benefited from the opportunity to discuss conceptual frameworks for this introduction. In addition, all of the contributors participated in a workshop underwritten by the Early Modern Conversions project as well as the generosity of Cornell University. This volume would not have developed without the support of the University of Michigan, Cornell, SSHRC and Paul Yachnin, director of the Early Modern Conversions Project. See the Early Modern Conversions project: http://earlymodernconversions.com/.
102. The symposium took place at the University of Michigan in January 2016 under the auspices of the Institute for the Humanities and the Institute for Research on Women and Gender. Hearty thanks to Paul Yachnin, Steven Mullaney, Stephen Wittek, Sidonie Smith, Patrick Tonks, Doretha Coval, Stephanie Harrell, Nina Barraco, Doug Trevor and George Hoffmann for their help.
103. Deleuze and Guattari, *A Thousand Plateaus: Capitalism and Schizophrenia*.
104. For McCracken's analysis of becoming-animal, becoming-human and becoming-sovereign in medieval French literature, see *In the Skin of a Beast*.
105. Recognition of this might challenge the truism within criticism of the *Metamorphoses* that, as Charles Segal, 'Ovid's Metamorphic Bodies', puts it, 'it is not the body that leads the narrator to the story, but the story that is forced to end in something that happens to the body', p. 14. The threat of infanticide begins with the fact of Iphis's female body, which in turn leads to her story.
106. See Sedgwick, *Epistemology of the Closet*.
107. Barkan, *The Gods Made Flesh*, p. 66. Barkan reads the tale in terms of 'a manifest destiny of masculinity within Iphis', indicated by the child's androgynous name and her 'quite masculine love for Ianthe', p. 71.
108. Lanser, *The Sexuality of History*, pp. 58, 79, 57.
109. Newcomb, '"If that which is lost be not found"', pp. 239–59.
110. Newcomb, '"If that which is lost be not found"', p. 240.
111. See also Feldherr's contention in 'Metamorphosis in the *Metamorphoses*' regarding Ovid's portrayal 'of participation in the creation of the structured world we know' and his 'exposure of the flux, change, and victimization that underlines it' that 'an interpretation that privileges one tendency at the expense of the other remains fundamentally incomplete', p. 177.
112. See Bynam's discussion of two medieval models of change, 'replacement-change' and 'evolution-change', in *Metamorphosis and Identity*, pp. 20–5.
113. See Kruger, 'Conversion and Medieval Sexual, Religious, and Racial Categories'; Britton, *Becoming Christian*; and Shoulson, *Fictions of Conversion*.
114. See Feldherr, 'Metamorphosis in the *Metamorphoses*', p. 170.
115. For the concept of embodiment-as-process from another associate of the EMC project, see Spiess, 'Puzzling Embodiment'.
116. James, 'The Ovidian Girlhood of Shakespeare's Boy Actors', notes that 'in Ovid's Latin, there is no need to choose between masculine and feminine pronouns. Iphis may be a boy or she may pass for a boy, and in either case Iphis may still enjoy the love of '*sua . . . Ianthe*'. The feminine possessive adjective, *sua*, attaches

to the direct object (Ianthe) regardless of the gender of the subject (Iphis) of the sentence', p. 117. In contrast, in Golding's translation, Iphis 'Did take Iänthe to his wife, and so her love enjoy'.
117. See Row, 'Queer Time on the Early Modern Stage', who reads the play in terms of *retardement* or delay. See also Billings in this volume.
118. Lanser, *The Sexuality of History*, observes that: 'In an epoch [the sixteenth and seventeenth centuries] preoccupied with alteration, appearance, and movement, it seems to be necessary not simply to demand a change from same-sex to cross-sex affiliation but to show change as it is happening, even if – or because – that process is often covering a sleight-of-hand', p. 56.
119. See, for instance, Britton, *Becoming Christian*, pp. 76–7.
120. *Galatea*, ed. Scragg (III, ii, 65). See Mathie in this volume. Kesson, '"It is a pity you are not a woman"', alludes to a Globe Theatre staged reading in which 'the girls' surprise at discovering one another's real identities at the end' of the play is staged as 'a performance for the benefit of those around them', 43.
121. See Cartwright's thoughtful discussion of the play's deferral of such knowledge in *Theatre and Humanism*, pp. 182–4. See also Eggert, Rubright, Long, Lochrie and McCracken in this volume.
122. See Lyne, *Ovid's Changing Worlds*, and Feldherr, 'Metamorphosis in the *Metamorphoses*'.
123. Le Normand-Romain, *Rodin*, p. 74. There are overlaps between the story of 'Iphis and Ianthe' and that of 'Salmacis and Hermaphroditus', including the extent to which the force of a frustrated female desire instigates the process of transformation.
124. Le Normand-Romain, *Rodin*, p. 74.

References

Alison, Jane (trans.), *Change Me: Stories of Sexual Transformation from Ovid* (Oxford: Oxford University Press, 2014).
Amer, Sahar, *Crossing Borders: Love Between Women in Medieval French and Arabic Literature* (Philadelphia: University of Pennsylvania Press, 2008).
Anonymous, *Philotus: a comedy: reprinted from the edition of Robert Charteris* (Edinburgh: Ballantyne, 1835).
Barkan, Leonard, *The Gods Made Flesh: Metamorphosis and the Pursuit of Paganism* (New Haven, CT: Yale University Press, 1986).
Barkan, Leonard, *Transuming Passion: Ganymede and the Erotics of Humanism* (Stanford: Stanford University Press, 1991).
Bate, Jonathan, *Shakespeare and Ovid* (Oxford: Oxford University Press, 1994).
Beecher, Donald (ed.), *Barnabe Riche His Farewell to Military Profession* (Ottawa: Dovehouse Editions, 1992).
Beecher, Donald, 'Concerning Sex Changes: The Cultural Significance of a Renaissance Medical Polemic', *Sixteenth Century Journal* 36: 4, 2005, pp. 991–1016.
Billing, Christian M., *Masculinity, Corporality and the English Stage 1580–1635* (Burlington, VT: Ashgate, 2008).
Blair, Ann, 'Ovidius Methodizatus: The *Metamorphoses* of Ovid in a Sixteenth-Century Paris College', *History of Universities* 9, 1990, pp. 73–118.
Born, Lester Kruger, *The Integumenta on the Metamorphoses of Ovid by John of Garland*, Dissertation (University of Chicago, 1929).
Braden, Gordon, 'Ovid and Shakespeare', in Peter E. Knox (ed.), *A Companion to Ovid* (Chichester, West Sussex: Wiley-Blackwell, 2009), pp. 442–54.
Bray, Alan, *The Friend* (Chicago: University of Chicago Press, 2003).

Brisson, Luc and Lloyd, Janet (trans.), *Sexual Ambivalence: Androgyny and Hermaphroditism in Graeco-Roman Antiquity* (Oakland, CA: University of California Press, 2002).
Britton, Dennis, *Becoming Christian: Race, Reformation, and Early Modern English Romance* (New York: Fordham University Press, 2014).
Bruster, Douglas, 'Female-Female Eroticism and the Early Modern Stage', *Renaissance Drama* 24, 1993, pp. 1–32.
Bryan, Emily, D., *In the Company of Boys: The Place of the Boy Actor in Early Modern English Culture* (Northwestern University, Dissertation, 2005).
Burke, Kenneth, 'Version, Con-, Per-, and In- (Thoughts on Djuna Barnes's Novel, *Nightwood*)', *Southern Review* 2: 2, 1966, pp. 329–46.
Burrow, Colin, 'Original Fictions: Metamorphoses in *The Faerie Queen*', in Charles Martindale (ed.), *Ovid Renewed: Ovidian Influences on Literature and Art from the Middle Ages to the Twentieth Century* (Cambridge: Cambridge University Press, 1988), pp. 99–119.
Burrow, Colin, 'Re-embodying Ovid: Renaissance Afterlives', in Philip Hardie (ed.), *The Cambridge Companion to Ovid* (Cambridge: Cambridge University Press, 2002), pp. 301–19.
Bychowski, M. W., 'Unconfessing Transgender: Dysphoric Youths and the Medicalization of Madness in John Gower's "Tale of Iphis and Ianthe"', *Accessus* 3: 1, Article 3 [no date], pp. 1–38.
Bynam, Caroline Walker, *Metamorphosis and Identity* (New York: Zone Books, 2005).
Carp, Teresa, '"Venus Utraque": A Typology of Seerhood', *Classical World*, 76: 5, 1983, pp. 275–85.
Carter, Sarah, *Ovidian Myth and Sexual Deviance in Early Modern English Literature* (New York: Palgrave Macmillan, 2011).
Cartwright, Kent, *Theatre and Humanism: English Drama in the Sixteenth Century* (Cambridge: Cambridge University Press, 1999).
Casali, Sergio, 'Ovidian Intertextuality in Ariosto's *Orlando Furioso*', in John F. Miller and Carole E. Newlands (eds), *A Handbook to the Reception of Ovid* (Oxford: John Wiley & Sons, 2014), pp. 306–23.
Cheney, Patrick, *Marlowe's Counterfeit Profession: Ovid, Spenser, Counter-Nationhood* (Toronto: University of Toronto Press, 2011).
Chess, Simone, 'Queer Gender Informants in Ovid and Shakespeare', in Lisa Starks-Estes (ed.), *Ovid and Adaptation in Early Modern English Theater* (Edinburgh: Edinburgh University Press, forthcoming).
Chess, Simone, *Male to Female Crossdressing in Early Modern English Literature: Gender, Performance, and Queer Relations* (New York and London: Routledge, 2016).
Cockeram, Henry, *English Dictionary* (London: Eliot's Court Press, 1623).
Coles, Elisha, *An English Dictionary* (London, 1676).
Cooper, Thomas, *Thesaurus Linguae Romanae et Britannicae* (London, 1584).
Copeland, Rita, *Rhetoric, Hermeneutics and Translation in the Middle Ages: Academic Traditions and Vernacular Texts* (Cambridge: Cambridge University Press, 1991).
Cornish, Alison, *Vernacular Translation in Dante's Italy: Illiterate Literature* (Cambridge: Cambridge University Press, 2011).
Coulson, Frank T., 'Ovid's *Metamorphoses* in the School Tradition of France, 1180–1400: Texts, Manuscript Traditions, Manuscript Settings', in James G. Clark, Frank T. Coulson and Kathryn L. McKinley (eds), *Ovid in the Middle Ages* (Cambridge: Cambridge University Press, 2011), pp. 48–82.
Coulson, Frank T., 'Ovid's Transformations in Medieval France (ca.1100–1350)', in Alison Keith and Stephen Rupp (eds), *Metamorphosis: The Changing Face of Ovid*

in Medieval and Early Modern Europe (Toronto: University of Toronto Press, 2007), pp. 33–60.
Crane, Mary Thomas, *Framing Authority: Sayings, Self, and Society in Sixteenth-Century England* (Princeton: Princeton University Press, 1993).
Crane, Susan, *Animal Encounters: Contacts and Concepts in Medieval Britain* (Philadelphia: University of Pennsylvania Press, 2013).
Curran, Leo C., 'Rape and Rape Victims in the "Metamorphoses"', *Arethusa* 11: 1, 1978, pp. 213–41.
DeCoste, Mary-Michelle, *Hopeless Love: Boiardo, Ariosto, and Narratives of Queer Female Desire* (Toronto: University of Toronto Press, 2009).
Deleuze, Gilles and Guattari, Félix, *A Thousand Plateaus: Capitalism and Schizophrenia*, trans. Brian Massumi (Minneapolis: University of Minnesota Press, 1987).
DiGangi, Mario, 'Male Deformities: Narcissus and the Reformation of Courtly Manners in "Cynthia's Revels"', in Goran V. Stanivukovic (ed.), *Ovid and the Renaissance Body* (Toronto: University of Toronto Press, 2001), pp. 94–110.
DiGangi, Mario, 'The Homoerotics of Marriage in Ovidian Comedy', *The Homoerotics of Early Modern Drama* (Cambridge: Cambridge University Press, 1997), pp. 29–63.
Dimmick, Jeremy, 'Ovid in the Middle Ages: Authority and Poetry', in Philip Hardie (ed.), *The Cambridge Companion to Ovid* (Cambridge: Cambridge University Press, 2002), pp. 264–87.
Dollimore, Jonathan, *Sexual Dissidence: Augustine to Wilde, Freud to Foucault* (Oxford: Clarendon Press, 1991).
Dooley, Mark, 'Inversion, Metamorphosis and Sexual Difference: Female Same-Sex Desire in Ovid and Lyly', in Goran V. Sanivukovic (ed.), *Ovid and the Renaissance Body* (Toronto: University of Toronto Press, 2001), pp. 59–76.
Drouin, Jennifer, 'Diana's Band: Safe Spaces, Publics, and Early Modern Lesbianism', in Vin Nardizzi, Stephen Guy-Bray and Will Stockton (eds), *Queer Renaissance Historiography: Backward Gaze* (Farnham, England: Ashgate, 2009), pp. 85–110.
Durling, Nancy Vine, 'Rewriting Gender: *Yde et Olive* and Ovidian Myth', *Romance Languages Annual* 1, 1989, pp. 256–62.
Ellis, Jim, *Sexuality and Citizenship: Metamorphosis in Elizabethan Erotic Verse* (Toronto: University of Toronto Press, 2003).
Enke, A. Finn (ed.), 'Introduction: Transfeminist Perspectives', *Transfeminist Perspectives in and Beyond Transgender and Gender Studies* (Philadelphia: Temple University Press, 2012), pp. 1–15.
Enterline, Lynn, 'Rhetoric and Gender in British Literature', in Michael J. MacDonald (ed.), *The Oxford Handbook of Rhetorical Studies* (Oxford: Oxford University Press, 2017), pp. 489–504.
Enterline, Lynn, *Shakespeare's Schoolroom: Rhetoric, Discipline, Emotion* (Philadelphia: University of Pennsylvania Press, 2012).
Enterline, Lynn, *The Rhetoric of the Body from Ovid to Shakespeare* (Cambridge: Cambridge University Press, 2000).
Feldherr, Andrew, 'Metamorphosis in the *Metamorphoses*', in Philip Hardie (ed.), *The Cambridge Companion to Ovid* (Cambridge: Cambridge University Press, 2002), pp. 163-79.
Ferguson, Gary, *Queer (Re)Readings in the French Renaissance: Homosexuality, Gender, Culture* (Aldershot and Burlington, VT: Ashgate, 2008).
Ferrand, Jaques, *De la maladie d'amour ou mélancholie érotique* (Paris, 1610).
Forey, Madeleine (ed.), *Ovid's Metamorphoses, Translated by Arthur Golding* (Baltimore: Johns Hopkins University Press, 2001).

Fox, Cora, 'Sexuality and Desire', in Patrick Cheney and Philip Hardie (eds), *The Oxford History of Classical Reception in English Literature*, Vol. 2, 1558–1660 (Oxford: Oxford University Press, 2015), pp. 159–71.

Franceschina, John, *Homosexualities in the English Theater: From Lyly to Wilde* (Westport, CT: Greenwood, 1997).

Freyman, Jay M., Mahaney, William E. and Sherwin, Walter K. (eds), *Iphis: Text, Translation, Notes* [c.1625], in *Salzburg Studies in English Literature, Elizabethan and Renaissance Studies* 107: 1 (Salzburg: Institut für Anglistik and Amerikanistik Universität Salzburg, 1986).

Fyler, John M., *Chaucer and Ovid* (New Haven, CT: Yale University Press, 1979).

Gillespie, Vincent, 'From the Twelfth Century to *c*.1450', in Alastair Minnis and Ian Johnson (eds), *The Cambridge History of Literary Criticism*, Vol. 2, The Middle Ages (Cambridge: Cambridge University Press, 2005), pp. 145–235.

Glare, P. G. W. and Christopher Stray, *Oxford Latin Dictionary*, 2nd edn (Oxford University Press, 2012).

Green, Ian, *Humanism and Protestantism in Early Modern English Education* (Farnham: Ashgate, 2009).

Greene, Thomas M., *Light in Troy: Imitation and Discovery in Renaissance Poetry* (New Haven, CT: Yale University Press, 1982).

Griffin, Miranda, 'Translation and Transformation in the *Ovide moralisé*', in E. Campbell and R. Mills (eds), *Rethinking Medieval Translation: Ethics, Politics, Theory* (Cambridge: Brewer, 2012), pp. 41–60.

Groves, Robert, 'From Statue to Story: Ovid's Metamorphosis of Hermaphroditus', *Classical World*, 109: 3, 2016, pp. 321–56.

Gura, David Turco, *A Critical Edition and Study of Arnulf of Orléans' Philological Commentary to Ovid's 'Metamorphoses'* (Ohio State University, Dissertation, 2010).

Hallett, Judith, 'Female Homoeroticism and the Denial of Roman Reality in Latin Literature', *Yale Journal of Criticism* 3: 1, 1989, pp. 209–27.

Halpern, Richard, *The Poetics of Primitive Accumulation: English Renaissance Culture and the Genealogy of Capital* (Ithaca, NY: Cornell University Press, 1991).

Harbage, Alfred, *Annals of English Drama, 975–1700*, 3rd edn, rev. Silvia Stoler Wagonheim (London and New York: Routledge, 1989).

Harvey, Elizabeth, *Ventriloquized Voices: Feminist Theory and English Renaissance Texts* (London and New York: Routledge, 1992).

Hayward, Eva and Weinstein, Jami, 'Tranimalities in the Age of Trans* Life', *TSQ: Transgender Studies Quarterly* 2: 2, 2015, pp. 195–208.

Hexter, Ralph, 'Medieval Articulations of Ovid's *Metamorphoses*: From Lactantian Segmentation to Arnulfian Allegory', *Medievalia* 13: 1, 1987, pp. 63–82.

Hulse, Clark, *Metamorphic Verse: The Elizabethan Minor Epic* (Princeton: Princeton University Press, 1981).

James, Heather, 'Ovid in English Renaissance Literature', in Peter E. Knox (ed.), *A Companion to Ovid* (Chichester, West Sussex: Wiley-Blackwell, 2009), pp. 423–41.

James, Heather, 'Shakespeare, the Classics, and the Forms of Authorship', *Shakespeare Studies* 36, 2008, pp. 80–9.

James, Heather, 'Shakespeare's Learned Heroines in Ovid's Schoolroom', in Charles Martindale and A. B. Taylor (eds), *Shakespeare and the Classics* (Cambridge: Cambridge University Press, 2004), pp. 66–85.

James, Heather, 'The Ovidian Girlhood of Shakespeare's Boy Actors: Q2 Juliet', *Shakespeare Survey* 69, 2016, pp. 106–22.

James, Heather, *Shakespeare's Troy: Drama, Politics, and the Translation of Empire* (Cambridge: Cambridge University Press, 2007).
Jankowski, Theodora, '"Where there can be no cause of affection": Redefining Virgins, Their Desires, and Their Pleasures in John Lyly's *Gallathea*', in Valerie Traub, M. Lindsey Kaplan, and Dympna Callaghan (eds), *Feminist Readings of Early Modern Culture: Emerging Subjects* (Cambridge: Cambridge University Press, 1996), pp. 253–74.
Jankowski, Theodora, *Pure Resistance: Queer Virginity in Early Modern English Drama* (Philadelphia: University of Pennsylvania Press, 2000).
Kamen, Deborah, 'Naturalized Desires and the Metamorphosis of Iphis', *Helios* 39: 1, 2012, pp. 21–36.
Keach, William, *Elizabethan Erotic Narratives: Irony and Pathos in the Ovidian Poetry of Shakespeare, Marlowe, and Their Contemporaries* (New Brunswick, NJ: Rutgers University Press, 1986).
Keith, Alison, 'Gender and Sexuality', in Peter Knox (ed.), *A Companion to Ovid* (Chichester, West Sussex: Wiley-Blackwell, 2009), pp. 355–69.
Keith, Alison, 'Versions of Epic Masculinity in Ovid's *Metamorphoses*', in Stephen Hinds et al. (eds), *Ovidian Transformations: Essays on the Metamorphoses and Its Reception* (Cambridge: Cambridge Philological Society, 1999), pp. 214–39.
Keith, Alison and Rupp, Stephen (eds), *Metamorphosis: The Changing Face of Ovid* (Toronto: Centre for Reformation and Renaissance Studies, 2007).
Kesson, Andy, '"It is a pity you are not a woman": John Lyly and the Creation of Woman', *Shakespeare Bulletin* 33: 1, 2015, pp. 33–47.
Kesson, Andy, *John Lyly and Early Modern Authorship* (Manchester: Manchester University Press, 2014).
Kilgour, Maggie, 'Virgil and Ovid', in Patrick Cheney and Philip Hardie (eds), *The Oxford History of Classical Reception in English Literature*, Vol. 2, 1558–1660 (Oxford: Oxford University Press, 2015), pp. 518–38.
Kilgour, Maggie, *Milton and the Metamorphosis of Ovid* (Oxford: Oxford University Press, 2012).
Kłosowska, Anna, *Queer Love in the Middle Ages* (New York: Palgrave Macmillan, 2005).
Kruger, Steven F., 'Conversion and Medieval Sexual, Religious, and Racial Categories', in Karma Lochrie, Peggy McCracken and James A. Schultz (eds), *Constructing Medieval Sexuality* (Minneapolis and London: University of Minnesota Press), pp. 158–79.
Lamb, Mary Ellen, 'Singing with the (Tongue) of the Nightingale', in *Gender and Authorship in the Sydney Circle* (Madison, WI: University of Wisconsin Press, 1990).
Lanham, Richard A., *The Motives of Eloquence: Literary Rhetoric in the Renaissance* (New Haven, CT and London: Yale University Press, 1976).
Lanier, Douglas, 'Shakespeare / Not Shakespeare: Afterword', in Christy Desmet, Natalie Loper and Jim Casey (eds), *Shakespeare / Not Shakespeare (Reproducing Shakespeare)* (New York: Palgrave Macmillan, 2017), pp. 293–306.
Lanier, Douglas, 'Shakespearean Rhizomatics: Adaptation, Ethics, Value', in Alexa Huang and Elizabeth Rivlin (eds), *Shakespeare and the Ethics of Adaptation* (New York: Palgrave Macmillan, 2014), pp. 21–40.
Lanser, Susan, *The Sexuality of History: Modernity and the Sapphic, 1565–1830* (Chicago: University of Chicago Press, 2014).
Le Normand-Romain, Antoinette, *Rodin: The Gates of Hell* (Paris: Musée Rodin, 1999).
Legault, Marianne, 'De-Sexing the Lesbian: Issac de Benserade's Narrative Quest', in Chris Mounsey (ed.), *Developments in the Histories of Sexualities: In Search of*

the Normal, 1600–1800 (Lewisburg, PA: Bucknell University Press, 2013), pp. 71–89.
Leibacher-Ouvrard, Lise 'Speculum de l'Autre Femme: Les avatars d'*Iphis et Ianthe* (Ovide) au XVIIe Siècle', *PFSCL* 30: 59, 2003, pp. 365–77.
Liveley, Genevieve, 'Tiresias/Teresa: A "Man-Made-Woman" in Ovid's Metamorphoses 3.318-38', *Helios* 30: 2, 2003, pp. 147–62.
Loewenstein, Joseph, *Responsive Readings: Versions of Echo in Pastoral, Epic, and the Jonsonian Masque* (New Haven, CT: Yale University Press, 1984).
Loid, Lodovvicke, *The Pilgrimage of princes, penned out of Sundry Greeke and Latine aucthours* (London, 1573).
Lunney, Ruth, 'Recent Studies in John Lyly (1990–2010)', *English Literary Renaissance* 41: 3, 2011, pp. 529–54.
Lyly, John, *Galatea* [1592], ed. Leah Scragg (Oxford: Oxford University Press, 2012).
Lyne, Raphael, *Ovid's Changing Worlds: English Metamorphoses, 1567–1532* (Oxford: Oxford University Press, 2001).
McCracken, Peggy, *In the Skin of a Beast: Sovereignty and Animality in Medieval France* (Chicago and London: University of Chicago Press, 2017).
McKinley, Kathryn L., *Reading the Ovidian Heroine: 'Metamorphoses' Commentaries 1100–1618* (Leiden, Boston and Cologne: Brill, 2001).
Makowski, John, 'Bisexual Orpheus: Pederasty and Parody in Ovid', *Classical Journal* 92: 1, 1996, pp. 25–38.
Martin, Charles, 'Iphis and Ianthe', *Arion: A Journal of Humanities and the Classics* 23. 3, 2016, pp. 117–22.
Masten, Jeffrey, *Queer Philologies: Sex, Language, and Affect in Shakespeare's Time* (Philadelphia: University of Pennsylvania Press, 2016).
Melville, A. D., *Ovid's Metamorphoses* (Oxford: Oxford University Press, 1986).
Michalopoulos, Charilaos, 'Tiresias Between Texts and Sex', *EuGeSTa: Journal on Gender Studies in Antiquity* 2, 2012, pp. 221–39.
Miller, Nancy K., 'Arachnologies: The Woman, the Text, and the Critic', in *The Poetics of Gender* (New York: Columbia University, 1986).
Mills, Robert, *Seeing Sodomy in the Middle Ages* (Chicago: Chicago University Press, 2014).
Minnis, Alastair, *Magister amoris: The Roman de la Rose and Vernacular Hermeneutics* (Oxford: Oxford University Press, 2001).
Moss, Ann, *Ovid in Renaissance France: A Survey of the Latin Editions of Ovid and Commentaries Printed in France Before 1600* (London: Warburg Institute, 1982).
Munro, Lucy, 'Queering Gender, Age, and Status in Early Modern Children's Drama', in Jennifer Higginbotham and Mark Albert Johnston (eds), *Queering Childhood in Early Modern English Drama and Culture* (New York: Palgrave Macmillan, forthcoming 2018).
Nagle, Betty Rose, '"Amor, Ira," and Sexual Identity in Ovid's *Metamorphoses*', *Classical Antiquity* 3. 2, 1984, pp. 236–55.
Nardizzi, Vin and Jean Feerick (eds), *The Indistinct Human in Renaissance Literature* (New York: Palgrave Macmillan, 2012).
Nardizzi, Vin, Guy-Bray, Stephen and Stockton, Will (eds), *Queer Renaissance Historiography: Backward Gaze* (Farnham, England: Ashgate, 2009).
Newcomb, Lori Humphrey, '"If that which is lost be not found": Monumental Bodies, Spectacular Bodies in *The Winter's Tale*', in Goran V. Stanivukovic (ed.), *Ovid and the Renaissance Body* (Toronto: University of Toronto Press, 2001), pp. 239–59.
Newman, Jane O., '"And Let Mild Women to Him Lose Their Mildness": Philomela, Female Violence, and Shakespeare's *The Rape of Lucrece*', *Shakespeare Quarterly* 45: 3, 1994, pp. 304–26.

Newman, Karen and Tylus, Jane (eds), *Early Modern Cultures of Translation* (Philadelphia: University of Pennsylvania Press, 2015).
Nugent, Georgia, 'This Sex Which Is Not One: De-Constructing Ovid's Hermaphrodite', *differences* 2: 1, 1990, pp. 160–85.
Oakley-Brown, Liz, *Ovid and the Cultural Politics of Translation in Early Modern England* (Aldershot: Ashgate, 2006).
Ormand, Kirk, 'Impossible Lesbians in Ovid's *Metamorphoses*', in R. Ancona and E. Greene (eds), *Gendered Dynamics in Latin Love Poetry* (Baltimore: Johns Hopkins University Press, 2005), pp. 79–110.
Ovid, *Les métamorphoses d'Ovide, mises en vers françois, par Raimond et Charles de Massac, père et fils* (Paris: F. Pomeray et P. Rocolet, 1617).
Ovid, *Les métamorphoses d'Ovide; traduites en prose françoise, et de nouueau soigneusement reueuës, corrigees en infins endroits, et enrichies de figures à chacune fable*, trans. Nicolas Renouard (Paris: Chez la veufue Langelier, 1606).
Ovid, *Les XV livres de la Metamorphose D'ovide: (poëte treselegát) contenans L'olympe des histoires poetiques traduictz de Latin en Francoys, le tout figures & hystoires* (Paris: Denys Janot, 1539).
Ovid, *Metamorphoses Books IX–XV*, ed. and trans Frank Justus Miller, 3rd edn, rev. G. P. Goold, vol. 2, Loeb Classical Library 43 (Cambridge, MA: Harvard University Press, 1984).
Ovid, *Olympe, ou Metamorphose d'Ovide. Traduction nouvelle, conferée avec le latin, et enrichie de plusieurs figures* (Geneva: Jean II de Tourmes, 1597).
Papaioannou, Sophia, *Redesigning Achilles: 'Recycling' the Epic Cycle in the 'Little Iliad' (Ovid, Metamorphoses 12.1–13.622)* (Berlin: Walter De Gruyter, 2007).
Pearcy, Lee T., *The Mediated Muse: English Translations of Ovid, 1560–1700* (Hamden, CT: Archon Books, 1984).
Perry, Kathleen Anne, *Another Reality: Metamorphosis and the Imagination in the Poetry of Ovid, Petrarch, and Ronsard* (New York and Bern: Peter Lang, 1989).
Phillips, Edward, *The New World of English Words* (London, 1658).
Pincombe, Michael, *The Plays of John Lyly: Eros and Eliza* (Manchester and New York: Manchester University Press, 1996).
Pintabone, Diane T., 'Ovid's Iphis and Ianthe: When Girls Won't be Girls', in Nancy Sorkin Rabinowitz and Lisa Auanger (eds), *Among Women: From the Homosocial to the Homoerotic in the Ancient World* (Austin: University of Texas Press, 2002), pp. 256–85.
Piozzi, Hester Lynch Thrale, *Thraliana: The Diary of Mrs. Hester Lynch Thrale (Later Mrs. Piozzi), 1776–1809*, ed. Katharine C. Balderston, 2 vols (Oxford: Clarendon Press, 1942).
Pugh, Syrithe, *Spenser and Ovid* (Aldershot: Ashgate, 2005).
Rackin, Phyllis, 'Androgyny, Mimesis, and the Marriage of the Boy Heroine on the English Renaissance Stage', *PMLA* 102: 1, 1987, pp. 29–41.
Raval, Shilpa, 'Cross-Dressing and "Gender Trouble" in the Ovidian Corpus', *Helios* 29, 2002, pp. 149–72.
Reid, Jane Davidson, *The Oxford Guide to Classical Mythology in the Arts* (Oxford: Oxford University Press, 1993).
Reynolds, Bryan, *Performing Transversally: Reimagining Shakespeare and the Critical Future* (New York: Palgrave, 2003).
Rimell, Victoria, *Ovid's Lovers: Desire, Difference and the Poetic Imagination* (Cambridge: Cambridge University Press, 2006).
Robins, William, 'Three Tales of Female Same-Sex Marriage: Ovid's "Iphis and Ianthe", the Old French *Yde et Olive*, and Antonio Pucci's *Reina d'Oriente*', *Exemplaria* 21: 1, 2009, pp. 43–62.

Robinson, David, 'The Metamorphosis of Sex(uality): Ovid's "Iphis and Ianthe" in the Seventeenth and Eighteenth Centuries', in Chris Mounsey (ed.), *Presenting Gender: Changing Sex in Early Modern Culture* (London: Associated University Presses, 2001).

Robinson, David, *Closeted Writing and Lesbian and Gay Literature: Classical, Early Modern, Eighteenth-Century* (Aldershot: Ashgate, 2006).

Robinson, Matthew, 'Salmacis and Hermaphroditus: When Two Become One (Ovid, Met. 4.285–388)', *Classical Quarterly* 49: 1, 1999, pp. 212–23.

Row, Jennifer E., 'Queer Time on the Early Modern Stage: France and the Drama of Biopower', *Exemplaria* 29: 1, 2017, pp. 1–24.

Rubin, Deborah, *Ovid's 'Metamorphosis English': George Sandys as Translator and Mythographer* (New York: Garland, 1985).

Salisbury, Joyce, *The Beast Within: Animals in the Middle Ages*, 2nd edn (New York: Routledge, 2010).

Sandys, George, *Ovid's Metamorphosis Englished, Mythologized, and Represented in Figures* (1632), eds Karl K. Hulley and Stanley T. Vandersall (Lincoln: University of Nebraska Press, 1970).

Saslow, James, *Ganymede in the Renaissance: Homosexuality in Art and Society* (New Haven, CT: Yale University Press, 1986).

Scragg, Leah, *The Metamorphosis of Gallathea: A Study in Creative Adaptation* (Washington, DC: University Press of America, 1982).

Sedgwick, Eve Kosofsky, *Epistemology of the Closet* (Berkeley: University of California Press, 1990).

Segal, Charles, 'Ovid's Metamorphic Bodies: Art, Gender, and Violence in the *Metamorphoses*', *Arion: A Journal of Humanities and the Classics*, 5: 3, 1998, pp. 9–41.

Shannon, Laurie, 'Nature's Bias: Renaissance Homonormativity and Elizabethan Comic Likeness', *Modern Philology* 98, 2000, pp. 183–210.

Shannon, Laurie, *The Accommodated Animal: Cosmopolity in Shakespearean Locales* (Chicago and London: University of Chicago Press, 2013).

Sharrock, Alison, 'Gender and Sexuality', in Philip Hardie (ed.), *The Cambridge Companion to Ovid* (Cambridge: Cambridge University Press, 2002), pp. 95–107.

Shoulson, Jeffrey, *Fictions of Conversion: Jews, Christians and Cultures of Change in Early Modern England* (Philadelphia: University of Pennsylvania Press, 2013).

Smith, Ali, *Girl Meets Boy: The Myth of Iphis* (Edinburgh, New York and Melbourne: Canongate, 2007).

Smith, Bruce, *Homosexual Desire in Shakespeare's England: A Cultural Poetics* (Chicago: University of Chicago Press, 1991).

Spiess, Stephen, 'Puzzling Embodiment: Proclamation, *La Pucelle*, and *The First Part of Henry VI*', in Valerie Traub (ed.), *Oxford Handbook of Shakespeare and Embodiment* (Oxford: Oxford University Press, 2016), pp. 93–111.

Stanivukovic, Goran V. (ed.), *Ovid and the Renaissance Body* (Toronto: University of Toronto Press, 2001).

Starks-Estes, Lisa S. (ed.), *Ovid and Adaptation in Early Modern English Theater* (Edinburgh: Edinburgh University Press, forthcoming).

Starks-Estes, Lisa S., *Violence, Trauma, and* Virtus *in Shakespeare's Roman Poems and Plays: Transforming Ovid* (New York: Palgrave Macmillan, 2014).

Stryker, Susan and Aizura, Aren (eds), *The Transgender Studies Reader 2* (London: Routledge, 2013).

Sutton, Dana F. (ed.), *Henry Bellamy: Iphis (ca.1625)*, www.philological.bham.ac.uk/iphis/.

Tarrant, Richard J., 'The *Narrationes* of "Lactantius" and the Transmission of Ovid's *Metamorphoses*', in Oronzo Pecere and Michael D. Reeve (eds), *Formative Stages of Classical Traditions: Latin Texts from Antiquity to the Renaissance* (Spoleto: Centro italiano di studi sull'Alto medioevo, 1995), pp. 83–115.
Taylor, A. B. (ed.), *Shakespeare's Ovid: The Metamorphoses in the Plays and Poems* (Cambridge: Cambridge University Press, 2000).
Taylor, Helena, *The Lives of Ovid in Seventeenth-Century French Culture* (Oxford: Oxford University Press, 2017).
Traub, Valerie, *The Renaissance of Lesbianism in Early Modern England* (Cambridge: Cambridge University Press, 2002).
Walen, Denise A., *Constructions of Female Homoeroticism in Early Modern Drama* (New York: Palgrave Macmillan, 2005).
Walker, Jonathan, 'Before the Name: Ovid's Deformulated Lesbianism', *Comparative Literature* 58, 2006, pp. 205–22.
Watt, Diane, 'Behaving Like a Man? Incest, Lesbian Desire, and Gender Play in *Yde et Olive* and Its Adaptations', *Comparative Literature* 50: 4, 1998, pp. 265–85.
Weisl, Angela Jane, 'How to Be a Man, Though Female: Changing Sex in Medieval Romance', *Medieval Feminist Forum* 45: 1, 2009, pp. 110–37.
Wheeler, Stephen M, 'Changing Names: The Miracle of Iphis in Ovid's *Metamorphoses* 9', *Phoenix* 51: 2, 1997, pp. 190–202.
Wiseman, Susan, *Writing Metamorphosis in the English Renaissance, 1550–1700* (Cambridge: Cambridge University Press, 2014).
Wixson, Christopher, 'Cross-Dressing and John Lyly's *Gallathea*', *SEL* 41, 2001, pp. 241–56.
Zajko, Vanda, '"Listening With" Ovid: Intersexuality, Queer Theory, and the Myth of Hermaphroditus and Salmacis', *Helios* 36: 2, 2009, pp. 175–202.

I

METAMORPHOSIS AS SUPPLEMENT: SEXUALITY AND HISTORY IN THE *OVIDE MORALISÉ*

Peggy McCracken

The stories in Ovid's *Metamorphoses* describe divine interventions in the world of humans: the gods dwell among people, they covet sexual relations with them, and they use their powers to protect some and abuse others. The human body is a primary object of divine action in the *Metamorphoses*, as the gods transform people into animals, plants, objects or, as in the Iphis story, into a different human form. Perhaps because Ovid's stories dwell so extensively on the consequences of divine action in human worlds, they seem to have had great appeal for medieval clerics who devoted imaginative intellectual effort to explaining the pagan stories as allegories of Christian truth. The fourteenth-century *Ovide moralisé* is one of the most elaborate of such interpretive reworkings, and it is also the first full translation of the *Metamorphoses* into French. As the narrator translates the stories, he supplements Ovid's account using other mythographical texts and commentaries, and he adds moralising interpretations to the stories. Euhemerist explanations identify the natural phenomena or historical events that inspired the narratives, and allegorical readings demonstrate the Christian truths that inhere in them.[1] For the narrator of the *Ovide moralisé*, Ovidian stories about bodies and bodily transformations figure Christian conversion: the pagan gods' many interventions in the human world are analogous to the Christian God's supreme act of mercy in the sacrifice of his son to save humanity, and in the Christian interpretations of the Ovidian stories, the specific bodily changes enacted by the pagan gods are most often interpreted as figural representations of the soul's transformation when it embraces salvation.

Such interpretations require seeing the Ovidian text from a particular angle, a perspectival logic that Sarah Kay has described as anamorphosis. 'Metamorphosis becomes the vehicle of anamorphosis', she claims, 'as every transformation – whether wrought by Ovid on his characters or by the moralist on Ovid – provides a means of seeing Christ incarnate in the very letter of the pagan text.' Relationships characterised by the text as 'unnatural' lend themselves especially well to this move, she suggests, given that the Incarnation and the virgin birth also flout natural law.[2] Accordingly, by the time we get to Iphis and Ianthe in the ninth book of the *Ovide moralisé*, it comes as no surprise when Iphis's love for Ianthe is explained as the desire of the soul for forgiveness and mercy, and the transformation of a girl into a boy is interpreted as an allegory of the soul transformed by the grace of salvation. The *Ovide moralisé* explicitly aligns bodily and spiritual transformations: the embodied metamorphosis of the Ovidian story is redefined as the redemption of the penitent soul in the Christian allegory that supplements the Ovidian story and its historical explanation. Yet the tidy Christian allegorisation cannot entirely contain the meanings and things introduced in the Ovidian story and in the *Ovide moralisé*'s account of its historical source. The allegory supplements the two versions of the Iphis story that precede it, adding another layer of truth, in the narrator's view, but also revealing the complex work of supplementarity in the narrative nexus of Ovidian story, historical explanation and allegorical interpretation. The *Ovide moralisé* is itself a metamorphosis of Ovid's *Metamorphoses*, as many critics have noted; metamorphosis is both the subject of the translated stories, and a figure for what happens to them as they are translated, moralised, historicised and allegorised.[3] Less noticed is the extent to which the critical metamorphoses of the text that operate through translation and moralisation are also supplements, additions to the Ovidian story that extend and reshape its meanings. Just as metamorphosis is both the subject of the Ovidian stories and a figure for the transformation they undergo in their Christian interpretations, so too, the interpretations supplement the meaning of the Ovidian tale and – in the Iphis story, in particular – figures of supplementarity are also represented in the interpretations. Here supplementarity is explicitly associated with sexual desire and gendered bodies and shapes an understanding of both sexuality and history.

The *Ovide moralisé*'s euhemerist and allegorical readings make the Ovidian story itself into an interpretation; the Ovidian *fable*, as the French translator consistently calls it, puts a historical or Christian truth into narrative form.[4] The euhemerist interpretations that accompany many of the stories read them in terms of past events or present social relations, and all of the Ovidian stories receive at least one allegorising interpretation. Interpretations may be inspired by specific words or events recounted in the stories, or they may be based on loose associations, and it is impossible to pin the sequences of story and interpretations into any kind of pattern. As Renate Blumenfeld-Kosinski puts it with wry accuracy: 'What the poet was seeking was undoubtedly variety, and although reading some of the endless allegorizations, mostly those on sin and redemption, can plunge the reader into a kind of stupor, the large variety of interpretive methods is a testimony to the poet's inventiveness.'[5] In the Iphis story, a notable feature of the narrator's inventiveness is the specificity of the historical interpretation that intervenes between the account of Iphis's metamorphosis and the explanation of its allegorical meaning. The narrator's 'historical explanation' ('historial sentence', 9: 3115) identifies the events that inspired the story of gender metamorphosis: it could be that some time in the past, a woman disguised herself as a man and seduced another woman. This is a speculative history ('it could be . . .'; 'estre pot . . .', 9: 3116) that imagines a same-sex erotic relationship even as it condemns it. The alignment of history and sexuality is not unique to the Iphis story in the *Ovide moralisé*, but the specificity of the account – which involves an unusually detailed explanation of the technology of sex – suggests that this history is contingent on the articulation of a particular sexual relationship or act. In other words, without the same-sex seduction, the Iphis story would have no history at all. Here sexuality shapes historical understanding and is an instance of what Susan Lanser defines as the sexuality of history. In Lanser's words, 'just as the historical constructs the sexual, so too does the sexual construct the historical, shaping the social imaginary and providing a site for reading it.' History is rendered intelligible through understandings of the sexual, and in the Iphis story, a sexual relationship explains how the story could be true.

By adopting Lanser's notion of the sexuality of history, I do not mean to suggest that medieval representations of sexuality are like the early modern European discourses that Lanser studies, nor do I mean to suggest that sexuality itself is transhistorical. The way that the *Ovide moralisé* puzzles through what constitutes sex and what constitutes sex between women is historically specific, grounded in the clerical origins of the text, in a long tradition of commentary on Ovid's *Metamorphoses*, and in a long history of Christian teachings that condemn same-sex desire. Nonetheless, as a text that repeatedly identifies history as both an explanation of the Ovidian story and a basis for moralising commentary, the *Ovide moralisé* invites a consideration of the relationship between history and fiction, and of the ways in which that relationship is figured through representations of sexual desire and sexual practice. The medieval narrator's interpretation of Ovid's 'Iphis and Ianthe' using a speculative fiction about the past is not unusual since it follows a tradition of euhemerist readings of Classical literature, nor is this clerical narrator's condemnation of same-sex erotic attraction surprising since it corresponds to conventional Christian morality. Worth noting, however, is that the narrator's invention of a historical interpretation brings together figures of artifice, amendment and supplementarity in a representation of sexuality, and that such figures subtend the narrator's trajectory from the Ovidian *fable* to a historical explanation and then to an allegorical interpretation. Ultimately, the historical fiction inflects the allegorical project, and, through the logic of the supplement represented in the stories and articulated by the succession of interpretations, the narrative suggests the sexuality of sacred history.

Translating Ovid

The *Ovide moralisé* is a massive compilation of about 72,000 lines, composed in rhyming octosyllabic couplets. Translations of the *Metamorphoses* make up roughly half the text; about 8,000 lines are additions to the stories drawn from other mythographical sources, glosses and commentaries, and the narrator's historical and allegorical interpretations occupy around 28,000 lines. The translation appears to have been commissioned by Joan of Burgundy, wife of Philip VI of France, and we assume that the translator-narrator-commentator was a cleric. The *Ovide moralisé* circulated widely in medieval Europe: it was twice abridged in prose adaptations, one of which was printed by Collard Mansion in 1484; it influenced Pierre Bersuire's mid-fourteenth-century Latin moralisation of Ovid; and it is one of Gower's sources for the story of Iphis and Ianthe in the *Confessio amantis*.[6]

We do not know what Latin text the anonymous French translator worked from to adapt the *Metamorphoses* into French verse, but a comparison with modern editions of Ovid's works reveals a number of changes and additions. For example, when Iphis laments what she calls the 'insanity' of her love ('fole rage', 9: 2931) and she reproaches the gods for not directing her desire toward a 'more fitting beloved' ('convenable amour', 9: 2933), she turns to the natural world to reason that the female should love only the male. In Ovid's version, Iphis claims that 'Cows do not love cows, nor mares, mares; but the ram desires the sheep, and his own doe follows the stag. So also birds mate, and in the whole animal world, there is no female smitten with love for female.'[7] The sexual habits of animals are taken as models for human sexuality; here animals represent the natural world and 'natural' sexual desire. This notion of orderly desire is undercut again and again in the *Metamorphoses*, as Laurie Shannon points out, but in Iphis's lament, animal exemplars of sexual desire form unambiguously cross-sexual couples.[8]

When the *Ovide moralisé* narrator translates this passage, he preserves the turn to nature in the cross-dressed woman's discourse, but modifies the list slightly in Iphis's lament:

> Why couldn't I have directed my desires towards a more fitting beloved? What cow seeks another cow; what mare approaches another mare? Ewes desire rams, and the cow's affection is for the bull. Thus each female seeks a male of her own kind.
>
> ... que n'oi je mon corage
> En convenable amour aquerre?
> Quel vache seult vache requerre,
> Ne quel eque autre eque atoucher?
> Les brebis ont le moton cher,
> Et la vache dou tor s'acointe.
> Ensi veult à male estre jointe
> Chasque femele en son endroit.[9]

The translation of Iphis's lament follows Ovid's Latin very closely; the changes in the French are small but significant, here as elsewhere in the *Ovide moralisé*.[10] First, the translator lists only domestic animals; he eliminates the wild animals, the deer and the birds that Iphis names in the Latin text. The 'nature' invoked in the French text is a nature shaped by human industry and human culture. Second, when the translator lists the male and female animals that join together, he replaces the wild doe and stag that we find in Ovid's version with the cow and the bull. So he doubly domesticates the list. These small changes are significant in light of Iphis's comparison of her plight with that of another figure of 'unnatural' desire: Pasiphaë, who loved a bull.

> Pasiphaë loved more in accordance with her own kind than I do. As I understand it, she loved the bull, joining a female to a male. She cunningly deceived him with fraud and ingenuity, but nothing can make two women a fitting pair.
>
> Cele ama miex en son endroit
> Que je, folle, n'aim orendroit.
> Le tor ama, ce m'est vis, cele.
> Au malle se joint la femele,
> Si le deçut soutivement
> Par fraude et par engignement.
> Mes il n'est riens qui peüst faire
> De feme à feme avenant paire.
>   (9: 2953–60)

The comparison follows immediately after the enumeration of animal examples, as it does in Ovid's story. Pasiphaë's heart burned for a bull, but Iphis says that her own love is more outrageous because at least the bull was male. In this taxonomy of unnatural desires, bestiality is cross-sexual and therefore not as bad as Iphis's desire for another woman.

Iphis's comparison of her own passion to Pasiphaë's love for a bull is found in Ovid, but the comparison resonates differently in the Old French text because the narrator has earlier expanded the Latin text's brief account of Pasiphaë into a full story followed by an allegorisation.[11] The *Ovide moralisé*'s Pasiphaë narrative opens with a long, repetitive elaboration of just how foolish, evil and corrupt Pasiphaë was, followed by a justification of the translator's decision to recount this awful story, ending in a single line in which he finally reveals what makes Pasiphaë so repugnant: 'Against nature, she loved the bull' ('Le buef contre nature ama', 8: 718).[12] Then he questions whether love for a bull can even be called love, and, finally, he tells the story, moralising as he goes. Pasiphaë's foolish love for the bull is another example, in his account, of a woman's 'unnatural' desire.[13] As in the Iphis story, 'natural' desire is represented by the animal; the *Ovide moralisé* narrator insists that the bull did not respond to Pasiphaë's attentions because 'it was not in his nature to do what she required' ('Qu'à sa nature pas n'affiert / De ce faire qu'ele requiert', 8: 813–14). Nature requires same-species unions, both Iphis and the narrator insist, but the 'naturalness' of same-species, different-sex desire is troubled in the two accounts of loving a bull. The Pasiphaë account condemns a woman's passion for a bull, but in Iphis's lament, the cow's love for the bull is cited as exemplary of 'natural' desire. To be sure, there's a big difference between a cow loving a bull and a woman loving a bull, but even so, the enumeration of amorous animal pairs in the *Ovide moralisé* naturalises love for a bull even as the Pasiphaë story characterises such love as 'against nature' ('contre nature').[14] The question of what is natural and what is 'against nature' can take a wide range of sometimes contradictory meanings in medieval texts. In the *Ovide moralisé* the 'natural' aligns closely with what is permitted in Christian morality, but the two versions of women's 'unnatural' desire, brought together by Iphis in her discourse on comparative depravity, work against each other and unsettle sure definitions of what is 'natural' about desire. The stories are further united, as the historical interpretation will make clear, by the association of unnatural desire with instruments of trickery and artifice.

When Iphis makes her long lament about the impossibility of her desire for Ianthe in the *Ovide moralisé*, she does not explicitly refer to Daedalus, as she does in the Latin original ('Though all the ingenity in the world should be collected here, though Daedalus himself should fly back on waxen wings, what could he do? With all his learned arts could he make me into a boy from a girl?').[15] As Heather James points out with reference to Golding's translation of the *Metamorphoses*, it would be apparent to readers, if not to the tortured heroine, 'that Daedalus could invent the world's best dildo, if required: he constructed a wooden cow, illustrating his genius for sex toys, so why not a phallic counterpart to the far more difficult proposition of a wooden cow?'[16] And in fact, the medieval translator of Ovid seems to have recognised this very possibility. Although the reference to Daedalus is omitted from Iphis's lament, the material apparatus that Daedalus built so that Pasiphaë might couple with the bull is implicitly invoked: 'she deceived him with fraud and ingenuity', Iphis says ('Si le deçut soutivement / Par fraude et par engignement', 9: 2957–8). Here *par engignement* describes the way in which Pasiphaë manoeuvred: with ingenuity, or with trickery, to deceive the bull. But *engignement* may also name a device, or a machine, and it recalls not just the deception but the instrument of deception. In fact, in the Pasiphaë section of the *Ovide moralisé*, the wooden cow is called an *enging*, that is a deception or an artifice (8: 910).[17] Iphis's lament about the way Pasiphaë acts ('par engignement') recalls the device, the artificial instrument that enabled her to realise a desire judged as both unnatural because bestial and natural because cross-sexual. And the artificial instrument comes back in the historical interpretation of the story of Iphis and Ianthe in the *Ovide moralisé*, suggesting, in Robert Mills's words, that 'erotic life is never simply a matter of bodies in 'nature'; it is also fundamentally a matter of things.'[18] A thing may supplement the body, the *Ovide moralisé* narrator explains, and a thing supplements his imagination of sex between women in an identification of the historical event that inspired Ovid's story.

Historicising Ovid

The *Ovide moralisé* narrator introduces his first interpretation of the Iphis story as a speculative history: the story 'could be true', he tells us, but then he immediately corrects his conditional statement to attest historical certainty: 'indeed it was the case without doubt' ('Estre pot, ains fu sans doutance . . .', 9: 3114). This initial uncertainty about what exactly happened – it could be true, it was true – pervades the account of the historical woman who inspired the fictional story of Iphis's gender metamorphosis.

> Now I wish to tell you the historical explanation of this fable, which could be true according to a historical reading. It could be – and indeed it was the case without doubt – that long ago a woman seemed to be a man in her clothing and behaviour. Everyone who saw her in this clothing believed her to be a man, and her mother encouraged this belief, testifying to its truth. There may have been some maiden who saw her looking noble, attractive, and fine in her men's clothing, and truly believed that she was a man. She hungered to have her in love and marriage.

> Or vueil espondre par estoire
> Ceste fable, qui puet estre voire
> Selonc historial sentence.
> Estre pot, ains fu sans doutance
> C'une feme ancienement
> D'abit et de cultivement

> Sambloit home, et cil le cuidoient
> Qui en tel habit la veoient,
> Et sa mere le fesoit croire,
> Qui tesmoignoit la chose à voire,
> Si pot estre aucune pucele
> Qui la vit gente et bone et bele
> En habit d'home, et crut de voir
> Que fust homs, s'ot fain de l'avoir
> Par amours et par mariage.
> (9: 3113–27)

Here as elsewhere, the narrator describes the Ovidian story as a fable ('une fable', 9: 3114), that is a fabulous, fictional story, but also a story that calls for explanation and ultimately for a moral that transforms it into a lesson. But unlike most fables – we think most readily of beast fables, where animal behaviour is interpreted in moral lessons for humans – Ovid's fables can be explained by history, or at least this is the narrator's perspective as he locates the origin of Ovid's fable about Iphis and Ianthe in a historical anecdote. We learn that long ago ('ancienement') there was a woman who cross-dressed and everybody thought she was a man, and her mother encouraged this belief. The narrator does not explain the mother's complicity in her daughter's disguise, nor does he seem to recognise the alignment of his own position with the mother's: both testify to the efficacy of the disguise, and both are instrumental in promoting the truth of a successful gender performance, one from outside the story and one from inside.

Although he argues that the cross-dressed woman's appearance is convincing, the narrator also inadvertently acknowledges that gender may appear differently to different viewers. Those who saw her in men's clothing would have believed she was a man, as the mother's testimony confirms, the narrator claims. Then he speculates that there may have been some maiden who saw the cross-dressed woman and found her 'noble, attractive, and fine'. The use of feminine adjectives, 'gente et bone et bele', agrees with the antecedent 'une feme' (9: 3117). Presumably the feminine adjectives are meant to insist on the deception. Yet these gendered adjectives also open the possibility that the maiden who looks at the cross-dressed woman is not deceived, but recognises a 'noble, attractive, and fine' woman in masculine dress. In other words, the feminine adjectives may suggest the maiden's perspective, what she saw: another woman. Even as the text insists on deception – the maiden 'truly believed' that the person she loved was a man ('crut de voir / Que fust homs', 9: 3125–6) – at the same time it opens the possibility that the maiden seduced by the cross-dressed woman fully recognised her beloved as a woman in masculine dress.

The narrator attempts to foreclose any suggestion of reciprocal desire between the two women by insisting on the foolish and depraved nature of a relationship that does not conform to his view of 'natural', cross-sexual carnal fulfilment.

> That other foolish and silly woman agreed to take her as wife, even though she had nothing like a penis or any other member to serve this purpose. Nevertheless she desired, against all that is right and natural, to fulfil her affection and lust in a carnal way, despite this impediment about which the other, her beloved wife and true lover, knew nothing.

> Cele, qui fu de fol corage
> Et nice, à feme la plevit
> Tout n'eüst elle point de vit
> Ne de membre à ce convenable,
> Non pourquant el fu desirrable,
> Contre droit et contre nature,
> De s'amour et de sa luxure
> Acomplir en li charnelment,
> Tout eüst elle impediment
> Tel que l'autre ne savoit mie,
> Qui ert s'espouse et vraie amie.
> (9: 3129–38)

The judgment that the cross-dressed woman lacks a 'suitable member' ('membre à ce convenable') with which to carnally fulfil her desire recalls Iphis's earlier lament about the gods' failure to inspire in her a 'suitable love' ('un convenable amour', 9: 2933). Suitability here corresponds to what is 'right and natural', that which the woman who desires another woman does not possess. The narrator insists on this lack, and uses repetition to align what the cross-dressed woman doesn't have (a penis) with what she does have (an impediment): 'Tout n'eüst elle point de vit . . . Tout eüst elle impediment'. This 'impediment' leads not to frustrated desire, as in the Iphis story, but to an ingenious solution, an anatomical supplement with which the woman seduces the maiden she loves. Instead of praying to the gods for their help in consummating her desire, as Iphis does in the Ovidian story, this woman who long ago dressed as a man and married another woman seeks a technical solution to her 'impediment'. She accomplishes what the narrator calls her 'evil desire' ('le mal desirrer', 9: 3145) through 'the cunning art and advice of a hideous old crone' ('par l'art et par la mestrie . . . d'une orde vilz maquerele', 9: 3141–3). The narrator recounts that the cross-dressed woman marries another woman and to render the marriage debt, she uses 'a false member' ('un membre apostis') that the 'hideous old crone' helped her to fashion.

> She married the woman whom the laws of marriage forbade her from having. In order to fulfil her duty to her wife, she deceived her with a false member.

> Cele espousa qu'el ne devoit
> Par loy de mariage avoir,
> Et pour lui rendre son devoir
> Par member apostis la deçut.
>   (9: 3146–9)

This short passage foregrounds the verb of obligation 'devoir': she should not have married another woman ('Cele espousa qu'el ne devoit'); she owes the marriage debt ('pour lui rendre son devoir'). What the cross-dressed woman should not do (marry another woman) is indexed to what she should do (have sex with her wife), and yet the narrator also indicates that she does have sex with her wife, and it's as though he can see that his explanation of the historical meaning of the Iphis story has got out of hand because he ends it quite abruptly. When the maiden perceived it, he says – not specifying whether she perceives the 'false member', the *membre apostis*, or whether she perceives that she is being deceived about the sex of her partner – when the maiden perceived it, he says, the thing is no longer hidden but openly revealed ('Ne fu la chose plus celee, / Ains fu en apert revelee', 9: 3151–2). This revelation ends the story for the *Ovide moralisé* narrator, who concludes with an endorsement of the social condemnation of the cross-dressed woman. Once 'the thing' is revealed, he explains, 'everyone talked about it, and the woman was thoroughly shamed, as she so richly deserved' ('Si en tenoit chascuns son conte, / Et la fole en fu mise à honte, / Qui bien ot honte desservie', 9: 3153–5). Again, 'the thing' could be the false member or the gender deception; the text conflates the artificial instrument and the gender identity of the cross-dressed woman. But the notion of supplementarity troubles this conflation as well as the narrator's insistence on the alignment of 'natural' gender and 'natural' sexuality that subtends Christian marriage and Christian morality.

This 'thing' compensates a lack, and in the narrator's view, it is a sorry substitute, a prosthetic artifice that stands in the place of a 'natural' member. As Mills has stressed in his reading of John Gower's Iphis story, 'things may have queer effects when conjoined with bodies', and Mills further suggests that Ovid's medieval moralisers were 'exercised by the capacity of things to render intelligible the otherwise unintelligible and unknown possibilities for sex between women'.[19] If the thing – here, a particular thing, the 'artificial member' – joins with bodies to represent sexual practices and identities that remain otherwise unimagined, it also supplements the gendered body. In the narrator's view, the prosthesis is unnatural, and its use is 'damnable and vile' ('damnable et vis'). Yet any notion of prior or natural integrity or sufficiency is subverted by the prosthesis, as David Wills has explained: 'What is at stake in prosthesis ... is the discovery of an artificiality there where the natural founds its priority.'[20] Wills alludes to the Derridian logic of the supplement, that is the claim that the supplement exposes incompleteness in the original; the very fact that the original can be supplemented demonstrates an incompleteness that was not earlier apparent. The supplement adds to and replaces, it completes – and in completing, it exposes a prior incompleteness.[21] The *Ovide moralisé* narrator would probably not dispute this claim, since in many medieval discourses, women are described as imperfect or incomplete men. Yet Wills brings into view the opposition between nature and artifice disrupted by supplementarity, emphasising that the prosthesis denaturalises the body itself as a site of plenitude and completion, and insisting on 'the non-originary status of the body, on the nonintegrality of its origin'.[22] In the Iphis story, the artificial member, as a prosthetic supplement, suggests that no body is 'naturally' sufficient to the desires that move it, and that any notion of the body's integrity or completeness is disputed by the additions, embellishments and amendments that supplement it. In the *Ovide moralisé*'s euhemerist interpretation of the Iphis story, the event that the Ovidian story mythologises is imagined through the narrator's description of a false member, an artifice or a trick that allows a woman to seduce a woman. Here, the historical event is a sex act, and historical truth depends on a recognition of sexuality, articulated through a logic of the supplement. But the narrator, so intent on moving on to the spiritual meaning of the Iphis story, cannot fully leave behind the supplemental logic introduced in the Ovidian story's invocation of Pasiphaë and in his own historical explanation of how a cross-dressed woman once had sex with her wife. As the supplement traverses the Iphis narratives it amends notions that appear more secure when located in Christian belief and morality.

Once he has thoroughly condemned the cross-dressed woman and her use of the 'artificial member', the *membre apostis*, the narrator returns to this 'thing' and declares that 'Nobody desires such a thing [*tele oeuvre*], for it is vile and damnable' (9: 3156–7). The narrator concludes in a rush to judgment that avoids any more technical information about sex, or about the 'artificial member', and that precludes any expression of desire or pleasure on the part of the maiden so vilely deceived by her cross-dressed spouse, in the narrator's view. There's a flustered quality to the resolution of this story, as though the narrator just wants to get out of this historical interpretation as fast as he can and by turning to ground on which he is much more secure, the Christian allegory. A better meaning (*meilloir sentence*) of Ovid's story is the allegorical one, he says, and returning to *devoir*, his favourite verb of obligation, he asserts that this reading should be more pleasing ('doit ceste estre miex amee', 9: 3161) –

or, in a more literal translation, this reading should be better loved. The *Ovide moralisé* narrator has a lot of opinions about what should be loved and to what degree. His opinions are pretty conventional – he's a cleric, after all – but in order to make a claim for a true account behind the story of Iphis's transformation into a man, he has to imagine a woman who dresses as a man and falls in love with another woman. Again, this historical reading is a short, descriptive, third-person account. We have no insight into the cross-dressed woman's perspective, and although the narrator clearly describes the passionate desire of one woman for another, he can only conceive of such desire in terms of artifice and deception. Mostly, though, this narrator just wants to move on, and move toward the goal that motivates his recounting of the Ovidian story in the first place, its meaning as Christian allegory. And in the allegorical interpretation of the sex-change story, supplementarity also structures understandings of transformation, of metamorphosis, of conversion.

Ovidian Allegory

The allegorical reading of the story of Iphis is ten times longer than the historical interpretation, so we see where the narrator's primary interest lies. He will tell us the truth, he claims ('Or vous dirai la verité', 9: 3190): Iphis's father represents God the Father, her mother is the Holy Church. When the father demands his daughter's death, he acts as a loyal judge who gives a harsh sentence to feminine nature, that is, the sinful soul that constantly seeks worldly pleasures and is condemned to die. The Holy Church, mother to us all, takes pity on the sinful soul and nourishes her in the hope that she will come to repentance. Isis and her entourage represent confession and penitence, the narrator tells us, and he then launches into a long description of the repentance of the soul: she ardently desires salvation, the narrator tells us, but feels that she can never atone for all her sins.

> Then [the soul] weeps and laments and humbles herself, repenting of her foolishness, seized by fear and trembling. This intensifies and redoubles her love, for joy which seems a little hopeless is desired all the more.
>
> Lors plore et plaint et s'umelie
> Et se repent de sa folie,
> Si est en doute et en cremour.
> Ce fet croistre et doubler l'amour.
> Quar assez plus est desirree
> La joie un poi desesperee,
> Et quant plus l'ame en est douteuse,
> Plus est ardans et desirreuse
> Pour qu'esperance ne li faille.
>   (9: 3381–9)

The soul's experience of hopeless desire for eternal joy translates Iphis's complaint about the impossible love of a woman for another woman; Iphis did not think she could ever be united with her beloved Ianthe, and this impossiblity 'intensified and redoubled the love which inflamed the maiden Iphis for fair Ianthe' ('Ce fet l'ardour croistre et doubler, / Qui plus embrase la pucele / Hyphis pour Hienté la bele', 9: 2916–18). The notion that hopelessness or impossibility intensifies desire – explicitly stated for both the allegorical soul and the Ovidian heroine – is a conventional trope in the representation of same-sex desire, here extended to describe the sinful soul's desire for salvation.[23] The allegory translates the descriptions of the Ovidian story into Christian meaning, but the translation works both ways: just as same-sex desire is subsumed into the soul's desire for salvation, so too the soul's desire for salvation recalls same-sex desire. But as the narrator's historical interpretation has taught us, this desire is not as impossible as it might seem; a prosthetic thing supplements the desiring body, demonstrating not just that things can make visible apparently impossible sexual relationships, as Mills notes, but also that desires and the bodies that act to fulfil them are never fully 'natural'. Artifice, supplement and amendment are integral to desire, and this is also true for the allegorical soul that so ardently longs for salvation.

> And the more the soul is fearful, the more she is ardent and desiring because she hasn't completely abandoned hope. So she suffers, works, undergoes fasts and privations, afflictions and penitence, and prays for divine grace, that she should be given time and space to live in an altered state.
>
> Pour qu'esperance ne li faille,
> Se se paine, si se travaille,
> Si fet jeüne et abstinence,
> Affliction et penitence,
> Et prie la divine grace
> Que li doinst terme et espace
> De vivre par amendement.
>   (9: 3389–95)

The last line of this passage emphasises the narrator's focus on repentance and penitence; by living in atonement, living 'in an altered state' ('vivre par amendement'), the soul compensates for sin. But the noun 'amendement' may also recall the amended body, the transformed body of the Ovidian story or the supplemental body of the historical interpretation. To the extent that it invokes change in terms of addition, of adding on, this *amendement* also calls on the logic of the supplement, and thereby recalls the *membre apostis*, the supplemental artificial member of the story's historical meaning. Both are compensations, in the narrator's view: the miraculous gift of a penis figures the miraculous gift of salvation, though of course the narrator does not say it this way. Yet even as the allegorical interpretation of the Iphis story insists on the spiritual meaning of amendment, the historical representation of sexual supplementarity persists and underscores not just the logic of the supplement that structures all three versions of the Iphis story, but also the extent to which history – whether in the literary story, the euhemerist explanation or the allegory of salvation – is shaped by sexuality, by understandings of the ways in which bodies enact desire.

Narration is inflected by judgment throughout the *Ovide moralisé*. Whether in the translation of Ovid's *Metamorphoses*, in the euhemerist account of the event that inspired the story or in its allegorical explanation, narration includes moralisation, most often articulated in chastisements and condemnations of those who desire worldly pleasures more than spiritual rewards. In the allegorical interpretation of the Iphis story, the conflation of explanation and judgment comes to the fore in the use of the noun *sentence*, used five times in the first eighty lines. The narrator will explain the story's spiritual meaning or *sentence* (l. 3158), he tells us, and this meaning includes the verdict or sentence (*sentence*, ll. 3201, 3217, 3231, 3266) pronounced against the sinful soul. *Sentence* recalls the narrator's historical explanation or *historial sentence*, which is also a verdict, a condemnation of a woman who used a prosthetic device to make love to another woman. The repetition of *sentence* emphasises the supplementarity of the *Ovide moralisé* itself, the series of narrative moralisations that recount, judge and interpret Ovid's stories. The narrator's efforts to explain and then explain away the sexual dynamics of the Ovidian story remain in dialogue with each other, supplementing each other and demonstrating the persistence of the sexuality of history.

We should praise God, the narrator tells us, because he took human form to save us. Spirit becomes flesh in the incarnation, but in the allegorical explanation of the Iphis story, the body becomes spirit: both the female and the male Iphis are figures for the soul, the female is sinful human nature, and the male is the repentant soul that lives in atonement, *par amendement*, amended by repentance. The amended soul is the spiritual interpretation of the transformed body, and the narrator moves with confidence from the Ovidian story to the Christian allegory: the changed body represents the changed soul. Yet the narrator's effort to establish the historical truth of Ovid's story troubles this symmetry by characterising the desire for change in terms of supplementarity. His development of the story of Pasiphaë introduces the prosthetic in the *engin*, the apparatus Pasiphaë uses to seduce the bull, a prosthetic strategy more fully described in the narrator's identification of the *membre apostis*, the artificial member used long ago by a cross-dressed woman to realise her desire. The narrator's *historial sentence*, his claim for the historical truth of the story, suggests the inventive ways in which sexual practices and gendered bodies define each other, as Mills has shown. But the historical thing also disrupts the interpretive logic of the moralisation by exposing the supplementarity of the allegorisation itself, which is revealed as a kind of *membre apostis*: an artificial member added to the Ovidian story to secure the conversion of the body as a figure for the conversion of the soul, and a literary prosthesis that remains rhetorically and conceptually tied to a history of a woman's desire for another woman.

Notes

1. For a thorough overview of Ovid's medieval fortunes, see Gillespie, 'From the Twelfth Century to *c*.1450', pp. 186–206.
2. Kay, *The Place of Thought*, 51. Other studies that use anamorphosis to read the *Ovide moralisé* include Griffin, *Transforming Tales*; Simpson, *Fantasy, Identity and Misrecognition*; Croizy-Naquet, 'L'*Ovide moralisé*'; Pairet, *Les formes*. Blumenfeld-Kosinski points out that the instances of what the narrator sees as problematic sexuality also generate moments of hermeneutic reflection, as the spiritual interpretation is explicitly identified as better than the historical interpretation (*Reading Myth*, pp. 120–1).
3. On the *Ovide moralisé* as a metamorphosis of Ovid's *Metamorphoses*, see Possamaï-Pérez, 'L'*Ovide moralisé*, monument de l'âge gothique'. On metamorphosis and translation, see Griffin, 'Translation and Transformation' and *Transforming Tales*, esp. pp. 18–21. The segmentation of the text into a translated story followed by various interpretations is a form found in the earliest commentaries – see Hexter, 'Medieval Articulations'.
4. Hult, 'Allégories de la sexualité', p. 61. On the use of 'fable', see Blumenfeld-Kosinski, *Reading Myth*, pp. 101–6.
5. Blumenfeld-Kosinski, *Reading Myth*, p. 119.
6. For an overview of the Latin Ovidian tradition, see Viarre, 'Une survie multiforme'.
7. 'Nec vaccam vaccae, nec equas amor urit equarum: / urit oves aries, sequitur sua femina cervum. / Sic et aves coeunt, interque animalia cuncta / femina femineo conrepta cupidine nulla est' – *Metamorphoses*, 9: 731–4; trans. pp. 55–7.
8. Shannon, 'Nature's Bias', p. 198.
9. *L'Ovide moralisé*, 9: 2932–9. All references are to the DeBoer edition; all translations are from Griffin et al., trans. in Appendix A.
10. For a reading of the way that subtle, slight changes to the Old French translation shape the story in view of its Christian moralisation, see Possamaï-Pérez, 'Comment Acteon devint le Christ'.
11. On Iphis and Pasiphaë in Ovid, see Pintabone, 'Ovid's Iphis and Ianthe'. In the *Ovide moralisé* the story does not receive a historical interpretation. On the sources of the *Ovide Moralisé* account (primarily the *Ars amatoria*), see Blumenfeld-Kosinski, 'The Scandal of Pasiphaë'.
12. Translations of the Pasiphaë story from the *Ovide moralisé* are mine.
13. See Blumenfeld-Kosinski, 'The Scandal of Pasiphaë'; Mills, *Seeing Sodomy*, p. 112.
14. See Blumenfeld-Kosinski's discussion of bestiality in 'The Scandal of Pasiphaë'.
15. 'huc licet ex toto sollertia confluat orbe, / ipse licet revolet ceratis Daedalus alis, / quod faciet? Num me puerum de virgine doctis / artibus efficiet?' (*Metamorphoses*, 9: 741–4).

16. James, 'The Ovidian Girlhood', p. 116. See also Pintabone, 'Ovid's Iphis and Ianthe', pp. 265-7.
17. Mills also makes this point in *Seeing Sodomy*, p. 113.
18. Mills, *Seeing Sodomy*, p. 108.
19. Mills, *Seeing Sodomy*, pp. 109, 111. In his study of the text, Mills explores the filtering of so-called sodomitical acts through gender and he shows that the medieval moralisations of Ovid both imagine and contain transgender bodies.
20. Wills, *Prosthesis*, p. 16.
21. Derrida, *Of Grammatology*, pp. 141-64.
22. Wills, *Prosthesis*, p. 137.
23. For the trope of impossibility intensifying desire in early modern representations, see Traub, *Renaissance of Lesbianism*, 286.

BIBLIOGRAPHY

Blumenfeld-Kosinski, Renate, 'The Scandal of Pasiphaë: Narration and Interpretation in the *Ovide moralisé*', *Modern Philology* 93: 3, 1996, pp. 307-26.

Blumenfeld-Kosinski, Renate, *Reading Myth: Classical Mythology and Its Interpretations in Medieval French Literature* (Stanford: Stanford University Press, 1997).

Croizy-Naquet, Catherine, 'L'*Ovide moralisé* ou Ovide revisité: de métamorphose en anamorphose', *Cahiers de recherches médiévales* 9, 2002, pp. 39-51.

Demats, Paule, *Fabula: Trois études de mythographie antique et médiévale* (Geneva: Droz, 1973).

Derrida, Jacques. *Of Grammatology*, trans. Gayatri Chakravorty Spivak (Baltimore: Johns Hopkins University Press, 1976 [1967]).

Gillespie, Vincent. 'From the Twelfth Century to *c*.1450', in Alastair Minnis and Ian Johnson (eds), *The Cambridge History of Literary Criticism*, Vol. 2, *The Middle Ages* (Cambridge: Cambridge University Press, 2009), pp. 145-235.

Griffin, Miranda, 'Translation and Transformation in the *Ovide moralisé*', in Emma Campbell and Robert Mills (eds), *Rethinking Medieval Translation: Ethics, Politics, Theory* (Cambridge: D. S. Brewer, 2012), pp. 41-60.

Griffin, Miranda, *Transforming Tales: Rewriting Metamorphosis in Medieval French Literature* (Oxford: Oxford University Press, 2015).

Hexter, Ralph, 'Medieval Articulations of Ovid's *Metamorphoses*: From Lactantian Segmentation to Arnulfian Allegory', *Medievalia* 13: 1, 1987, pp. 63-82.

Hult, David F., 'Allégories de la sexualité dans l'*Ovide moralisé*', *Cahiers de recherches médiévales et humanistes* 9, 2002, pp. 53-70.

James, Heather, 'The Ovidian Girlhood of Shakespeare's Boy Actors: Q2 Juliet', in *Shakespeare Survey* 69, 2016, pp. 106-22.

Jung, Marc-René, 'L'*Ovide moralisé*: de l'expérience de mes lectures à quelques propositions actuelles', in Laurence Harf-Lancner, Laurence Mathey-Maille and Michelle Szkilnik (eds), *Ovide métamorphosé: Les lecteurs médiévaux d'Ovide* (Paris: Presses Sorbonne nouvelle, 2009), pp. 107-22.

Kay, Sarah, *The Place of Thought: The Complexity of One in Late Medieval French Didactic Poetry* (Philadelphia: University of Pennsylvania Press, 2007).

Mills, Robert, *Seeing Sodomy in the Middle Ages* (Chicago: University of Chicago Press, 2015).

Ovid, *Metamorphoses*, ed. Frank Justus Miller, rev. G. P. Goold, Loeb Classical Library (Cambridge, MA: Harvard University Press, 1976).

L'Ovide moralisé. Poème du commencement du quatorzième siècle, publié d'après tous les manuscrits connus, eds Cornelius de Boer, Martina G. de Boer and Jeannette Th. M. van't Sant, Vol. 3 (Books 7-9) (Amsterdam: J. Müller, 1931).

Pairet, Ana, '*Les formes qui muees furent*: Figures et enjeux de la *mutacion* dans l'*Ovide moralisé*', in Marylène Possamaï-Pérez (ed.), *Nouvelles études sur l'Ovide moralisé* (Paris: Champion, 2009), pp. 19–34.
Pintabone, Diane T., 'Ovid's Iphis and Ianthe: When Girls Won't Be Girls', in Nancy Sorkin Rabinowitz and Lisa Auanger (eds), *Among Women: From the Homosocial to the Homoerotic in the Ancient World* (Austin: University of Texas Press, 2002), pp. 256–85.
Possamaï-Pérez, Marylène, 'Comment Actéon devint le Christ', in *Textes et cultures: réception, modèles, interférences* (Besançon: Presses universitaires de Franche-Comté, 2004), pp. 187–210.
Possamaï-Pérez, Marylène, 'L'*Ovide moralisé*, monument de l'âge gothique', in Laurence Harf-Lancner, Laurence Mathey-Maille and Michelle Szkilnik (eds), *Ovide métamorphosé: Les lecteurs médiévaux d'Ovide* (Paris: Presses Sorbonne nouvelle, 2009), pp. 123–37.
Shannon, Laurie, 'Nature's Bias: Renaissance Heteronormativity and Elizabethan Comic Likeness', *Modern Philology* 98: 2, 2000, pp. 183–210.
Simpson, James R., *Fantasy, Identity, and Misrecognition in Medieval French Narrative* (New York: P. Lang, 2000).
Traub, Valerie, *The Renaissance of Lesbianism in Early Modern England* (Cambridge: Cambridge University Press, 2002).
Viarre, Simone, 'Une survie multiforme: Ovide de l'Antiquité à l'*aetas ovidiana*', in Laurence Harf-Lancner, Laurence Mathey-Maille and Michelle Szkilnik (eds), *Ovide métamorphosé: Les lecteurs médiévaux d'Ovide* (Paris: Presses Sorbonne nouvelle, 2009), pp. 21–32.
Wills, David, *Prosthesis* (Stanford: Stanford University Press, 1995).

2

THE TRANS* TEMPORALITY OF LAMENT: 'FOOLISH' HOPE AND TRANS* SURVIVAL IN THE *OVIDE MORALISÉ*'S 'IPHIS AND IANTHE'

Laurel Billings

I. THE TALE

'Iphis and Ianthe' is a story of trans* survival in an environment where the central figure's femininity operates as a death sentence. In the medieval French translation known as the *Ovide moralisé*, the tale begins just before Iphis's birth, when her father, Ligdis, orders her pregnant mother, Telethusa, to kill the child if it is born a girl. The distraught Telethusa prays to Isis, the two-horned goddess of childbirth and motherhood, who advises her to defy her husband and let the child live regardless of its sex. When Iphis is born female, Telethusa and the nurse dress the child as a boy and present her to Ligdis as male. It is therefore not until Iphis falls in love with Ianthe, another girl, and both fathers encourage the marriage that the crisis re-emerges. Although Iphis passes easily as boy in her everyday life, she and Telethusa worry that she will not be able to carry this deception onward into the marriage chamber. The 'truth' of her deadly femininity will be revealed by her inability to consummate the marriage, an eventuality that drives the mother and daughter to exercise what limited agency they possess in the forms of delay and prayer. While the two defer the wedding with various excuses, Telethusa once again prays to Isis until, at last, Iphis becomes a man. This transformation in identity and embodiment enables Iphis to marry Ianthe, of course, but also to marry into the temporal frameworks of patrilineal history and reproductive futurity that grant security and intelligibility to her/his miraculously preserved life.

Throughout this analysis, I refer to Iphis as trans*, in part because her/his life's continuation is predicated on movements across, in, with and through ontological categories such as male and female, life and death, and subject and verb.[1] However, I also read his/her life as trans* because it depends on transitions across the various temporal landscapes that undergird and sustain these categories. In Eva Hayward and Jami Weinstein's formulation of trans*, the asterisk operates as a metonym for the concept itself, not designating a category, an identity or a collectivity but, rather, operating as a typographical symbol that enables relationships. The asterisk 'foregrounds and intensifies the prehensile, prefixial nature of *trans-* and implies a suffixial space of attachment', so that trans* becomes a movement *out*, *through*, *across* and *toward* instead of a category, an object or a specific point in time or space.[2] This formulation draws on the work of other transgender theorists, including David Valentine, who emphasise transgender's flexibility as category that can expand, contract and change meaning across and within situated contexts and specific texts.[3] Hayward and Weinstein expand on this notion, explaining that trans* 'is not a thing or a being. It is the process through which thingness and beingness are constituted'.[4] In this formulation, trans* resists stabilisation as a generic category, operating, instead, as an incitement to a 'proliferative specification and speciation' that materialises only in particulars and is discernible only as movement and process.[5] Understanding trans* as a 'movement' and a 'force of materialisation that may become matter but only prepositionally so', Hayward and Weinstein locate trans* matter *before* any position, as an 'expressive force' that 'enables the asterisk to stick to particular materialisations'.[6] Trans* can therefore be understood as a process of living, engendering, and embodiment that both invites and resists mapping in time and space. Trans* is not about identification, classification or plotting points but, rather, the multi-sensory experience of ever-shifting intensities and always-incipient transformations that destabilise ontological claims.

I focus on the temporal dimension, the 'beforeness' or the '*event*ualisation of trans life',[7] in the fourteenth-century *Ovide moralisé*'s 'Iphis and Ianthe', which includes a translation of the Ovidian tale followed by a historical and then a religious explication added by the translator. In this version of the story, Iphis's gender-crossing is predicated on a stretching, clipping, reshaping, reforming and reimagining of time – a tampering with temporality that enables sex change. This reshaping of time occurs in the mode of Iphis's lament, which both stalls the forward flow of the story's narrative and dissolves the binary divisions upon which that narrative is built – including distinctions among past, present and future, and between subjects and objects, nouns and verbs, identities and bodies. Iphis's lament is a trans* force in that it undermines the binary narrative logics whereby knowledge and transformation are built out of discrete events. Her lament reimagines subjects and bodies as continuous processes that incorporate past, present and future, dissolve nouns into verbs and transform deferred death into prolonged life. Iphis's lament and its turn toward death evince that the tale's investment in temporality and its shaping of time affects the representation of bodies, throughout the story and in the appended historical and allegorical interpretations. Equally important and equally salient to the concept of time is the concept of 'foolish hope', a repeated phrase that indicates hope for a future that is incompatible with the subject's identity and body. 'Foolish hope' operates as a future-oriented affect and enables trans* survival through the reshaping or trans*-ing of the flow of time. This process, which I term 'trans* time', enacts a deferral of death, of ontological classification and of decisive moral judgment that grants the speaking subject time to challenge and transform the fundamental categories used to identify her/his body and to track its movements across time. These categories include life and death, female and male, as well as the past, present and future. In trans* time, the speaking subject can dissolve and rearrange the divisions among these categories, a process I trace in the grammar, metaphors and repeated structures, names and terms that emerge in the mode of lament, across the three major sections of the text. Relationships among past, present and future are shown to be malleable, as new kinds of bodies, subjects, and desires materialise and endure.

The Grammar of Lament

Iphis's lament over her impending marriage to Ianthe, which delays the flow of narrative time, troubles the divisions between subject and object, noun and verb, and living and dying. The speaker's assumption of the status of subject is slow and never certain. The lament's central metaphor of death works like a suture, holding unlike meanings and temporally slippery concepts together, and reshaping the relationships among past, present and future. The lament begins by naming the marriage day, as Iphis complains:

> The longed-for marriage day draws near, and fair Ianthe will be mine. But what good is this joy to me? Surrounded by water, we will die of thirst. For I will not be able to do with her what a husband should do with a wife. Hymen and Juno, what business would you have at our nuptials? Whoever heard of a marriage without a husband? We will both be married and yet both without husbands![8]

> Or vient li dessirrables tens
> Dou mariage, à quoi je tens,
> Et bele Hyenté sera moie,
> Mes que me vaudra ceste joie?
> En mi l'iaue morrons de soi,
> Quar ne porrai fere de soi

> Ce qu'espous doit d'espouse faire.
> Imen et Juno, quel afaire
> Avez vous d'estre à tel noçailles?
> Qui vit onques mais espousailles
> Sans espous? Nous noçoierons
> Andeus et sans mari serons!
> (*Ovide moralisé* 9: 3007–18)

The speaking subject of this lament is Iphis, as she describes not only her inability to play the husband's role in sex with Ianthe, but also her incapacity to elicit sympathy from the marriage gods, as well as a sense of waning strength and life. At the level of grammar, however, the subject that sets the lament in motion is the 'marriage day', or more literally the marriage 'time' (*tens*). It is the movement of 'time' to the head of the complaint – enabled by Iphis's inabilities both to take the active role and to slow, stop or alter time's forward flow – that inspires the lament. Time is the agent that will bring Ianthe to her, an inevitability that renders Iphis powerless, just as it puts her in possession of the wife she desires.

The rest of the lament elaborates Iphis's incapacity and solidifies her loss, as she fails in various ways to inhabit the subject position of her own sentences and as possibilities for action or even the elicitation of positive affects are foreclosed. When Iphis steps into the subject position, the sentence describing the consummation turns negative. She 'cannot do with [Ianthe] what a husband should do with a wife' ('ne porrai fere de soi / Ce qu'espous doit d'espouse faire', 9: 3012–13). Iphis's voice then slips beyond this impasse by way of apostrophe, in the form of hypothetical questions: 'Hymen and Juno, what business would you have at our nuptials?' ('Imen et Juno, quel afaire / Avez vous d'estre à tel noçailles?' 9: 3014–15). Addressing the god and goddess who personify marriage and female sexuality, her mournful tone presupposes a response of 'none'. She continues: 'Whoever saw a wedding without a husband?' ('Qui vit onques mais espousailles / Sans espous?' 9: 3016–17). The subject here is neither a person nor a personification, but merely a non-specific 'who' or 'whoever' (*qui*) that is negatively inflected – a 'who' that implies 'not Iphis', even as it is Iphis who gives the possibility articulation. Furthermore, while Iphis fails to inhabit the subject position of her own declaration of sadness and loss, she also fails to fully differentiate herself from her sentences' objects. Although Ianthe is the stated object of Iphis's desire, the direct object in the first sentence is the possessive pronoun 'mine' (*moie*) – a placeholder that melds speaking subject and desired object. This possessive and composite object, 'mine', is then poised to fall apart with the next question, 'But what good is this joy to me?' ('Mes que me vaudra ceste joie?' 9: 3010). Even though Iphis still exerts some force of possession at the end of the hesitant question to Hymen and Juno about why they should attend 'our wedding' – or literally 'such a wedding' ('tel noiçailles') – the progressive displacement of Iphis as possessive presence is discernible across the arc of the passage. In the question that follows, 'Whoever saw a wedding without a husband?', the wedding falls into the realm of the indefinite hypothetical; it becomes 'such a wedding' ('tel noçailles'), one that no longer belongs to Iphis and Ianthe and might never occur at all.

Iphis thus speaks her lament from an uncertain location *between* the subject and the object position: we hear her echo in 'whoever saw' but spot her/his outline in the 'wedding without a husband'. She tangoes with a cross-gender self better able to conjugate wives and verbs in a dance that culminates in that self's emphatic negation: 'We will both be married and yet both without husbands!' ('Nous noçoierons / Andeus et sans mari serons!' 9: 3017–18). Unlike Narcissus who falls into the substance of his own desire, Iphis dissolves from a possessive object pronoun in a sentence driven by time, to the incapable subject of a declaration, to the tenuous hypothetical subject – or maybe object – of a hopeless question. Yet even as Iphis disappears from both subject and object position, her voice continues, somewhere in between, as the lament's animating force.

The affect that orients and sustains the lament is described at several points as Iphis's 'foolish hope'. Iphis reprimands herself, saying that she must let go of such 'foolish hope' ('fole esperance', 9: 2979). 'It harms you and holds you back, for you are not, by nature, worthy to be joined to such a creature' ('Ce te nuit, ce te desavance / Que tu n'es digne par nature / D'estre jointe à tel creature', 9: 2980–2). Despite Iphis's slippage across, through and between the grammatical units of her sentences, this flow is punctuated by the 'foolish hope' that 'holds [her] back' ('[se] desavance'). These lines figure hopes and desires that lead Iphis astray from the unspecified timeline that 'counts' as movement, as stasis, delay and 'holding back'.[9] Desire for the wrong kind of marriage registers as a stopping of desire's and life's forward movement in time. In her next breath, 'Your sex destroys your hope' ('Li sexes te nuit solement'), Iphis explicitly attributes the fading of hope to her female sex, which, even before her birth, has already destroyed her prospects (9: 2983).

The connected processes of hope and death are no less present at the centre of Iphis's life as they are at its beginning or end, where death takes the forms of her father's proposed infanticide and her body's demise, respectively. This present death takes the form of a sense of 'dying' from love that Iphis can neither fulfil nor extinguish, an experience that connects her present with her past death and the social and bodily deaths that are to come. Such disruption of the temporal sequence where death constitutes the end of life is also reflected in the structure of the passage's central lament, 'Surrounded by water, we will die of thirst. For I will not be able to do with her what a husband should do with a wife' ('En mi l'iaue morrons de soi, / Quar ne porrai fere de soi / Ce qu'espous doit d'espouse faire', 9: 3011–13). The sentence reaches its dramatic peak, the death by thirst, before the explanation of impotency is added, by the way and after the fact. 'Surrounded by water, we will die of thirst' both precedes and exceeds this future impasse, resulting in a form of sexual failure that requires no crisis or development, because it is poignantly present from the start of the sentence and the story. Because Iphis is already a dispersed and disintegrating subject long before she gets the chance to mortify herself by a failed sexual performance, present and future need not be understood in terms of teleology or opposition. The present emotion of 'dying' from unfulfillable desire conflates the inevitable death of the body – which, according to the terms of Iphis's father's death sentence, should have occurred long before – and the social death that is the exposure of the female body in the failed sex act that is to come. Death thus pulls past, future and present together, in the intimate space of a lament propelled by loss and hope.

An earlier portion of Iphis's lament further explores the temporal implications of same-sex desire by invoking beasts to reflect on the relationships among history, the future and various kinds of bodies. This portion of the lament temporalises desire between women, conflating lust for the wrong 'kind' of body and desire for the wrong kind of future – a future that departs from the repetitive past and the reproductive present. Iphis muses:

> What cow seeks another cow; what mare approaches another mare? Ewes desire rams, and the cow's affection is for the bull. Thus each female seeks a male of her own kind. No female would ever plan or wish to be joined to another female in a lustful manner. But that's exactly what I want, so unwisely! I wish I'd never been born to have such foolish hope.

> Quel vache seult vache requerre,
> Ne quel eque autre eque atoucher?
> Les brebis ont le moton cher,
> Et la vache dou tor s'acointe.
> Ensi veult à male estre jointe
> Chasque femele en son endroit.
> Nulle femele n'entendroit
> Ne de soi joindre n'avroit cure
> À femele en non de luxure.
> Ce quier je come mal senee!
> Je ne vausisse onc estre nee
> Pour avoir si fole esperance.
>   (9: 2934–45)

In the first question, 'What cow seeks another cow' ('Quel vache seult vache requerre'), 'seult' is a modal verb that indicates habitual or repeated action. This opening question and the one that follows, 'what mare approaches another mare' ('quel eque autre eque atoucher'), thus contain the seeds of the continuous flow of past into present that Iphis's 'foolish hope' ('fole esperance') for Ianthe will interrupt. Yet these rules of attraction harden into firm, general statements, 'Ewes desire rams, and the cow's affection is for the bull' ('Les brebis ont le moton cher, / Et la vache dou tor s'acointe'), as Iphis continues to map her situation by means of this habitual mode – where the past runs seamlessly into the present. She generalises further: 'Thus each female seeks a male of her own kind' ('Ensi veult à male estre jointe / Chasque femele en son endroit'). The logics of species likeness and binary gender difference work together by means of cross-sex desire to integrate the orderly past into an orderly present. This is a present where 'No female would ever plan or wish to be joined to another female in a lustful manner' ('Nulle femele n'entendroit / Ne de soi joindre n'avroit cure / A femele en non de luxure'), and yet this present is also a hypothetical one, as indicated by the shift into the conditional mode seen in 'would [n'entendroit] ever plan'. Here, the verb tense describes the way the present world should be – and yet is not. Rather, Iphis's particular configuration of body and desire undermines her efforts to carry the rules of kind, sex and lust from the past into the present – and from the world of the animals into the domain of the human. She explains: 'But that's exactly what I want, so unwisely!' ('Ce quier je come mal senee!'). In this frustrated exclamation, it is the verb to 'want' ('quier') that links Iphis's present embodied state 'unwisely' ('mal senee') to an inappropriate future. This unwise 'want' is the present tense action that diverts the conventional flow from present to future, disrupting the steady rhythm of reproductive temporality. The coupling of two women is thus figured as a threatening future that can only be stopped in a world where Iphis has never been born.

The invocation of Iphis's death in the final lines further complicates the relationships among past, present, future and the body. In voicing the wish 'that I'd never been born to have such foolish hope', the lament turns from an impossible future union with Ianthe toward an impossible past, where life and death are extinguished at once, through the reversal of mortal time. This wish constitutes a second 'foolish hope', located in a longed-for past, born out of and in order to free her from the first one. The impulse to withdraw backwards in time, to undo her whole life rather than die, gestures toward the notion that Iphis's deepest transgression lies in troubling the divisions between a present that repeats the neat, cross-sex couplings of the reproductive past and an unpredictable future. Iphis's desire thus constitutes a site of overlap between the temporal worlds based on reproduction and variation, a point of convergence between their different frequencies. From the point of her/

his birth, Iphis has subsisted though interference between a patriarchal death sentence and a life that runs counter to it. Moreover, this was all enabled by the 'hope' for the child's survival and safety that Isis gave to Telethusa. This incompatibility between the child's body and its future survival is further elaborated when Ligdis names her Iphis, after his grandfather, at which point the narrator digresses:

> The girl's grandfather, did I say? He was called Iphis and she was called Iphis (but Ligdis thought she was a 'he'). The mother rejoiced since the name was suitable for both male and female. She was pleased that her daughter had this name, which could be given to a woman, since it meant that she could truly speak her name without revealing the deception.

> Aiol, di ge, de la pucele?
> Yphis ot non cil, Yphis cele,
> Dont Ligdus cuide que 'cilz' soit.
> La mere se resbaudissoit
> Pour le non qui comuns resamble
> À malle et à femele ensamble
> Bien li plot que tel non eüst
> Qui à fame avenir peüst,
> Si que sans nul apercevoir
> Peüst de son nom dire voir.
> (9: 2875–84)

Iphis, her mother, her nurse and the reader are therefore privy to this transmission of secret attachment. Iphis and her mother repurpose the name, enabling a trans* life through the performance of masculinity while also reflecting Iphis's female gender – as a hidden truth or a spectral trace. Additionally, it hardly needs saying that Iphis sounds like Isis. The two names alliterate and rhyme; they are only distinguishable by one consonant sound, so that the echo of Isis inheres in Iphis, imbuing it with a sense of latency, expectation and promise of rebirth.

For this select audience of mother, nurse and reader, then, 'Iphis' accrues texture and vitality through encompassing incompatible meanings: the name is male and female, false and true; it is a concealed 'reality' and an unrealised eventuality; it contains past, present and future embodiments; and it survives what ought to be its death. As body and word, Iphis catalyses transmutations across, into and through these various categories. She thus exposes the fragility of gender as a means by which the male subject can be distinguished from the female as stronger, more animate or morally superior – and better able to continue a lineage. As trans*, Iphis operates, instead, to erode such divisions, enabling a range of temporal processes to constellate in their wake

– his/her asterisk gathering such diverse bodies-in-time as the patrilineal, the reproductive and, as the allegorisation shall show, even the eternal and the immortal, within its 'fingery' reach.[10]

Although I shall in a moment discuss some strategies that the tale employs to re-solidify gender difference and delineate the processes through which gender is rendered knowable, I want to emphasise first that these efforts are always-already undermined – and perhaps in some ways amplified – by the fact that the narrative does not specify exactly when or where this gender change occurs. It must happen while Telethusa is praying in the temple of Isis or directly after: Isis appears with her retinue, the altar trembles and the signs of Iphis's transformation start to appear immediately after these events. The physical evidence of Iphis's transformation is then given in the voice of the narrator, who does not pin the change to a single point in time, a specific site on the body or even one particular quality of the body's movements:

> Telethusa left the church, happy with the sign she saw. Iphis, her daughter, followed her, with a longer stride than she used to take. Her face became less white than it had been; her strength and boldness grew; her hair became shorter. Her body, which used to be slender, became much more vigorous than before, more vigorous than a woman would be.

> Theletusa ist dou moustier
> Liee dou signe qu'elle voit.
> Hyphis, sa fille, la sivoit
> À plus grant pas qu'el ne seult faire,
> S'a mains de blanchour ou viaire
> Qu'elle n'y avoit ains eüe.
> Force et fierté li est creüe,
> Et si chevoul sont abregié.
> Tout son cors seult estre alegié,
> Si fu plus viguereuse assez
> Qu'el n'iert esté au temps passez
> Et que feme ne peüst estre.
> (9: 3080–91)

The verbs fluctuate from the continuous past tense, or imperfect, of Iphis's gait as she 'followed' (*sivoit*) Telethusa, to the present tense description of Iphis's face, which literally 'has less whiteness' ('s'a mains de blanchour'), and then on to the pluperfect, or the past of the past, in 'than had been there before' ('quelle n'y avoit ains eüe'). The verbs that describe the changes in Iphis's body and its movements thus fluctuate between past and present tense. While Old French narrative verse may move between the past tense and a narrative present tense, here the variation suggests the difficulty of distinguishing between ongoing and completed actions. The temporal relationship between the transformation and its narration remains uncertain, but the way her/his body moves in time has clearly changed. What is more, it is only after the substantial accumulation of these physical characteristics and qualities of movement that the speaker at last concludes, 'Iphis the daughter had become a son' ('Yphis fille est devenus filz', 9: 3095), adding, 'this was certain and sure!' – or more literally, 'of this they could be certain and sure!' ('De ce soient seürs et fis!', 9: 3096).

Bracketing for the moment the question of who, exactly, was 'certain and sure' of Iphis's transformation, I suggest that the manipulation of the relationship between time and sight – and thus the shaping of our perception of time – is a strategy through which the impression of fixed, materially stable gender difference is produced. In addition to the fact that it is the accumulation of 'masculine' characteristics gleaned through a *process* of looking that establishes Iphis as a 'son', it is also the memory of a recent Iphis, who looked just a little different than the present version, that secures this knowledge. The physical traits that the speaker lists as evidence are not inherent features of Iphis's new body; they are, instead, qualities that emerge relationally, through comparison between the old body and the new one. Moreover, a temporal gap constitutes a necessary precondition for the seeing speaker and corroborating 'they' to see the change at all. This delay in perception thus creates the *before* and *after* by means of which the certainty of the transformation can be established and verified. It is through the subtle manipulation of time that gender transformation becomes visible and knowable and is rhetorically produced as 'certain'. It is by means of such tampering with temporality that gender change is secured as something other and more stable than an ambiguous name, a delayed marriage or a 'foolish' hope.

Just as the ontological question of when Iphis's transformation occurs is never answered with precision, the epistemological questions of when, how and to whom that change became (and might still become) known are equally unclear, even when the change is 'certain and sure'. By the end of the walk, an undefined 'they' are certain that Iphis's sex has changed, but this knowing group expands dramatically over the next three lines: 'Telethusa made generous offerings, gifts and sacrifices at the temples. Everyone, high and low, knew that Iphis the daughter had become a son' ('Offrandes et sacrefices amples / Et dons vait presenter aus temples, / Si sorent tuit, grant et menus, / Qu'Yphis fille est filz devenus', 9: 3099–102). By the time Telethusa has given thanks and offerings at the temple for her daughter's transformation into a son, 'everyone' ('tuit') knows what has happened. The question left unanswered, however, is how long this giving of offerings and spreading of knowledge takes. Here again, causality is implied through the narrative sequencing of events. Because Telethusa's offerings at the temple occur just before the assertion that 'everyone ... knew', we are left to assume that the former action precipitates the latter –

that Telethusa's offerings and gifts were the means by which 'everyone' came to know. Temporal sequence thus operates as a proxy for the explanatory framework of gender change that never quite materialises in the tale. What this passage on Iphis's transformation offers in the place of explanation is narrative sequence and the repetition of such terms as the knowing 'they' that expands as Iphis's gender ambiguity hardens into gender change. The subject and object of knowledge alter each time the topic of Iphis's sex and its transformation in invoked: developing from a hidden femininity known only to child, mother, nurse and reader, to an emergent masculinity described in ambiguous terms by an anonymous narrator, to a clear and apparent sex change ascertained by a 'them' that quickly expands to include 'everyone'. This knowing 'they' is sticky, like trans* itself, gathering new subjects into its fold as the object of knowledge travels and transforms. It is a 'they' that verges on 'we' as the story of Iphis's sex change reaches new readers and audiences.

The temporality of gender transition's emergence as a concept is just as uncertain as the temporality of its materialisation and recognition in the context of Iphis's body. It is never clear how or when Telethusa comes to know sex change as a possible solution to her daughter's dilemma. Are readers to imagine that sex change is what Telethusa had in mind when she turned to Isis in prayer, or are we to believe that the concept of sex change as a possibility emerges as narrator and observers recognise the changes in Iphis's body? The narrative does not specify exactly what Telethusa prays to Isis *for*, other than 'help' ('secours') (9: 3061). Telethusa's prayer to Isis continues as follows:

> Now is our hour of need. Help us, I beg you! Following your counsel, my daughter has lived in hope until now. Now I beg you that you proceed straightaway and without delay to save her and care for her. For I cannot keep the secret any longer if you will not intervene.

> Ore est mestiers qu'ele nous vaille.
> Or nous secour, toie merci!
> Par ton conseil a jusque ci
> Vescu ma fille en esperance.
> Or te pri que sans demorance
> D'ore en avant t'en entremetes
> De la saveur et cure i metes,
> Quar je n'i puis plus conseil metre,
> Se tu ne t'en veulz entremetre.
> (9: 3062–70)

Iphis 'has lived in hope until now' ('jusque ci / Vescu [Iphis] en esperance'), but the hope that threaded her past through the present here reaches its breaking point. Isis's 'help', which both constitutes and occludes the solution to the impossible but inevitable marriage, thus becomes the site of hope's concentration. Any other objects that hope might be imagined to take are subsumed under 'help', which places the specifics of the solution in the hands of the mediator. This 'help' could, at this point, be imagined to take a number of different forms, including sex change, but also a temporal transformation such as the wedding's infinite deferral. Indeed, the tale has shown that the shaping of time is entangled with the reshaping of the body. In the instant of Telethusa's prayer, the seamless fabric of narrative time seems to split wide open.

II. History and Allegory

In the *Ovide moralisé*'s 'Iphis and Ianthe', the complex temporality of embodiment and transformation extends beyond the Ovidian tale into the translator's commentary, which takes the dual structure of a historicisation that looks backward in time and an allegorisation that looks forward, beyond the body's death. The historicisation, which is the much shorter of the two, comes first; it explains that there might have been – and indeed there was – an ancient woman who dressed as a man and deceived those around her, until another woman fell in love with her disguise. This deceitful woman solicited the help of a procuress, who introduced her to the idea of a 'false member' ('membre apostis', 9: 3149) and taught her how to use it. The historical woman then used this object and knowledge to consummate the marriage, only to have the deception perceived by her new wife and revealed to everyone. The condemnable nature of the deception thus constitutes the justification for the translator-commentator's quick dismissal of this interpretation and his turn to the tale's allegorical and 'better meaning' ('meillor sentence', 9: 3158). In this allegorisation, Ligdis represents God, who condemns the sinful soul, and Telethusa represents the Holy Church that provides time and space for repentance. Iphis represents the sinful soul's 'female nature' ('femeline nature', 9: 3202), and her transformation occurs in two phases: the acts of repentance she performs in mortal time, and the rebirth of her immortal soul that is deferred beyond her body's death, pushed into an uncertain and faintly hoped-for future.

Where the tale concretises gender difference in the present tense through the dissolution of Iphis's femininity into the past, the historicisation renders gender entirely immutable for the duration of human life. The allegory then extends the delay of transformation, so that it spills over from the voice of lament, beyond the condemnation of the historical woman and beyond the mortal life of the soul. The commentator thus parses and dissects Iphis's ever-shifting relationships to the categories of male and female, life and death, and past, present and future, using his own neat divisions between metaphor and meaning, the material and the eternal, and the saved and the condemned soul. Hope and lament, however, destabilise these divisions in all three sections of the text, creating moments of permeability that invite the imagination to drift beyond the bounds of Christian categories of being, as well as the reproductive, mortal, and eternal temporal landscapes that co-constitute them.

The historical woman's lament is not for something as diffuse and innocuous as 'help', but specifically for the fulfilment of her 'evil desire' ('mal desirrer') to marry another woman and consummate the marriage. This lament is different from the others, however, in that it is recounted in the third person. The temporal effects of the elision of a full imagining of the woman's lament, voiced in the first person, serve the interests of the clerical translator-commentator, who seems to want to dispose of this historical narrative quickly:

> This one, who was attempting such foolish love, lamented and languished until, through the cunning art and advice of a witch (a hideous old crone), she fulfilled her evil desire. She married the woman whom the laws of marriage forbade her from having. In order to fulfil her duty to her wife, she deceived her with a false member.

> Tant se complaint et demena
> Cele, cui fole amours tempta,
> Que par l'art et par la mestrie
> Et par le conseil d'une estrie,
> C'est d'une orde vilz maquerele,
> Traist à chief la fole pucele
> Le mal desirrer qu'ele avoit.
> Cele espousa qu'el ne devoit
> Par loy de mariage avoir,
> Et pour lui rendre son devoir
> Par membre apostis la deçut.
> (9: 3139–49)

The 'evil desire' ('mal desirrer') condenses and materialises, through lament and the aid of the 'hideous crone' ('vilz maquerele'), in the form of the false member. The commentator-translator thus mobilises a logic of metonymy to contain the 'evil desire' in a specific, removable part of the body. This formulation is also predicated on the assumption that the use of the 'member' constitutes an imitation of masculinity – and that the member itself must be classified as 'false' instead of simply variant. For when sex is located specifically in the member, the logic of truth and falsehood can easily take hold, enabling the narrator to quickly discard the historical interpretation from his discussion. The 'too-easy intelligibility' of the false member replaces more complex and less easily identifiable workings of same-sex desire,[11] and the story's provocative energy fades.

The historicisation need not continue long beyond this isolation of the sex change's cause, nature and moral implications. However, the commentator continues:

> When the maiden realised what was happening, the trick could no longer be concealed, but was fully revealed: everyone talked about it, and the woman was thoroughly shamed, as she so richly deserved. May no one desire to undertake such an act, for it is most damnable and vile.

> Quant la meschine l'aperçut,
> Ne fu la chose plus celee,
> Ains fu en apert revelee,
> Si en tenoit chascuns son conte,
> Et la fole en fu mise à honte,
> Qui bien ot honte desservie.
> De tele oeuvre n'ait nulz envie,
> Quar trop est et dampnable et vis.
> (9: 3150–7)

The woman's actions are thus revealed to 'everyone' ('chascuns'), the way Iphis's transformation was also revealed to the world – except instead of eliciting celebration, this woman is 'thoroughly shamed, as she so richly deserved' ('mise à honte, / Qui bien ot honte desservie'). The translator's warning, 'May no one desire to undertake such an act, for it is most damnable and vile' ('De tele oeuvre n'ait nulz envie, / Quar trop est et dampnable et vis'), reinforces the imperative not to give this historical explanation any further discussion. The woman's death is thus transformed from a slow process that accommodates life to a swift extinction of the immortal soul. Readers who desire and act as this woman did, it is implied, will follow the same quick and deadly course.

Where the historicisation neatly curtails the hope for bodily transformation, the subsequent allegorisation operates to prolong such hope for the duration of human life – and beyond. The temporal function of the allegory is to place the transformation firmly in a hoped-for future, while at the same time dematerialising the sex change, rendering Iphis's femininity a metaphor for sin and death. 'The female' is thereby explicitly linked to weakness, sin, death and recidivism.[12] The Mother Church, who does not want to see her daughter suffer, lets the soul be baptised and live. Yet, even when baptism has given hope of redemption, the soul's sinful nature erupts again when she gives in to 'folly' ('folie'), 'vanity' ('vanité') and 'empty pleasures' ('vaine chetivité'), '[gives] herself over to mortal sin' ('à mortel pechié s'amort') and is 'condemned to die' ('jugiee à mort', 9: 3227–30). This relapse into sin maps onto Iphis's 'foolish hope' for Ianthe, and her figurative death from thirst becomes a very real death, the damnation of a Christian soul. Yet even after this spiritual death, the mother keeps 'pious hope' that she will 'gain true penitence' ('bone esperence / Qu'el a de voire penitance', 9: 3233-4) and be saved from damnation through 'Divine Mercy' ('divine misericorde', 9: 3238). The translator then tethers this lingering hope to Isis, who, in representing an allegorised Confession, enables the soul to 'live in good hope, avoiding the harsh sentence' ('fet vivre en bone esperance / D'eschiver la dure sentence') of God (9: 3265–6). The classical Isis is thereby linked to a hope for the soul's rebirth, this time through Confession and Christian mercy. Through Isis-as-Confession's intervention, restoration to the 'real-time' of eternity can, it turns out, still be hoped for after damnation.

It is the lament of the repentant soul, however, that most effectively amplifies the temporal instabilities present in the tale. The complex temporality of Confession requires that the soul look backward on past sins and forward toward a future union with God. The commentator-translator thus explains, in an aside, that the temporality of Confession is shaped like the body of Isis:

> In addition, I believe that Confession must have two glowing horns on her forehead: one illuminates all the sins that the soul used to commit so that she may recognise and acknowledge them; the other lights the correct path that the soul should take so that she can attain and savour heavenly joy.

> Ancor doit avoir, ce m'est vis,
> Deux cornes luisans en son vis
> Confession, dont l'une esclaire
> Aus maulz que l'ame soloit faire
> Recognoistre et manifester;
> L'autre alume et fet aprester
> L'ame à droite voie tenir,
> Pour adrecier et pour venir
> Au deduit de joie celestre ...
> (9: 3289–97)

Confession maintains the two horns that characterise Isis, a bodily feature that links this Christian figure to its classical predecessor. These horns also harken back to the beasts of Iphis's lament, which included such horned male animals as the bull and the ram, along with their hornless female counterparts, figuring the pairs as the embodiment of an idealised past governed by the laws of nature and reproductive futurity. The temporality of Confession, however, resituates the past of the reproductive animals – as well as the classical world of the tale itself – in a history of personal and collective 'ignorance' ('non savoir') that must be remembered and overcome through the work of repentance, in the hope of future salvation (9: 3375). And yet Confession also contains the trace of the 'sinful' past, as well as the prefiguration of the soul's hoped-for transformation, in the very shape of its temporal structure. The allegory that aligns Iphis's transformation, located in the classical past, with the future transformation of the soul achieves this task by invoking the very bodily feature that made Isis androgynous and part animal.[13] In this graceful act of repurposing, the Isis figure from the pre-Christian past becomes the present tense of Confession, where the soul turns both toward and away from her history of sin to 'carry out her penitence' ('Face en repost ses pentinances', 9: 3327), so that she might some day be joined with God. If Iphis's body, which transforms from female to male, prefigures the transformation and purification of the Christian soul, then Isis's body, with one horn in the past and the other in the future, reflects that soul's path in time. The past is bodily, animal and female, the future is spiritual, masculine and pure, but the present tense of life, death, hope, longing and lament stretches through the uncertain time-space in between.

In evoking the horned beasts and the figure of Isis from the Ovidian tale, the temporality of repentance thus re-creates temporal and bodily structures from the tale, but also articulates a shift in the transformation's relationship to the past, present and future. In Confession, the animal past is no longer the prototype for the ideal present and future; it is, rather, a history of sin to be remembered, confessed and thereby overcome. The future thus breaks with the continuous flows of desires, identities and bodies that characterise the sinful soul's past and present. The act of confession does not transform the body in the present tense, but instead converts the soul – turning it in the right direction, inspiring and then redoubling its hope to 'live in an altered state' ('vivre par amendement') beyond death: a lost state of immortal grace that can only be regained in a distant future (9: 3395). The present, however, remains rooted in the body and its history of sin.

This deferral of the transformation into an uncertain future rests on a gentle shift in the nature of time, kind, and body catalysed by Christian hope. For in spite of its deferral of the soul's purification to a future that lies outside mortal time, the lament of the penitent Christian soul both imagines and enacts a reshaping of time and the embodied souls that move through it. The soul's crisis is explained in terms of an incommensurability between the temporalities of atonement and mortal life: 'There is so much folly in her that in all of her life she could never atone for the sins that she has committed' ('Et qu'ele a tant fet de folie / Qu'el ne porroit pas en sa vie / Les maulz qu'ele a fais aquiter', 9: 3369–71). The desire to outlive the mortal body thus transforms the voice of prayer into a lament that death will prevent the soul's work of penitence from ever reaching completion. The soul laments that the time required to attain salvation is impossible to secure, just as Telethusa prayed from the 'hour of need' ('ore est mestiers qu'ele nous vaille', 9: 3062) when she 'cannot keep the secret any longer' ('n'i puis plus conseil metre', 9: 3069). In both instances, the imminent transformation – of body in the first instance and soul in the second – is explained in terms of a desire and failure to stretch and refashion time. Iphis, Telethusa, and the Christian soul *are all short on time*; all three figures are running up against a death sentence that deprives them of the power to gain the thing they want, as well as limiting their abilities to delay death and further loss. Yet the delays that these three figures' complaints lament, they also enact. For, the laments slow the progress of the narrative, building suspense but also reshaping the moving-in-time of the body. Iphis's body can move forward in time as it becomes male, just as the soul's lament expands its temporal frame to include a history of sin and a future of hope, help, and resurrection beyond penitence and the grave. Furthermore, the allegory itself operates as a sort of lament, pushing metamorphosis, joy, and fulfilment out of mortal life into a hoped-for future. These laments constitute an expressive force between the world that is and the worlds that might be – transforming both as the lament unfolds.

In the allegory, lament transmutes its own fundamental categories, identities and bodies by reshaping time – foregrounding the eternal over the mortal, and connecting these timescales through hope. Although this wish for salvation replaces the miraculous sex-change as the 'solution' to the soul's predicament, the turn to hope also undermines the division between damnation and salvation, death and eternal life, and even 'feminine' weakness and its unnamed opposite, rendering all of these categories mutable through their very impermanence. In the long delay before the Final Judgment, nothing is certain, and the soul can still hope to 'live in an altered state' ('vive par amendement', 9: 3395) at some point in a longed-for future – although none of this holds true for the human body, for which such categorical distinctions last as long as life. The moralisation's binary divisions fail most provocatively at its climax, when the narrator describes an especially impassioned and ardent lament of the soul:

> Then she weeps and laments and humbles herself, repenting of her foolishness, seized by fear and trembling. This intensifies and redoubles her love, for joy which seems a little hopeless is desired all the more. And the more the soul is fearful, the more she is ardent and desiring because she hasn't completely abandoned hope. So she suffers, works, undergoes fasts and privations, afflictions and penitence, and prays for divine grace, that she should be given time and space to live in an altered state. When God sees the soul's repentance, her good works and her good intentions, He wishes to give her sweet repose.

> Lors plore et plaint et s'umelie
> Et se repent de sa folie,
> Si est en doute et en cremour.
> Ce fet croistre et doubler l'amour,
> Quar assez plus est desirree
> La joie un poi desesperee,
> Et quant plus l'ame en est douteuse,
> Plus est ardans et desirreuse
> Pour qu'esperance ne li faille,

> Si se paine, si se travaille,
> Si fet jeüne et abstinence,
> Affliction et penitence,
> Et prie la divine grace
> Que lie doinst terme et espace
> De vivre par amendement.
> Quant Diex voit son repentement,
> Sa bone oeuvre et son bon propos,
> Il la veult traire au dous repos.
> (9: 3381–98)

The allegory concludes in a climax without fulfilment, in 'fear and trembling' ('en doute et en cremour') that 'redoubles' the soul's 'love' ('doubler l'amour') for a future that seems 'a little hopeless' ('un poi desesperee'). The translator thus harnesses the transformative power of lament and hope to reorganise the 'natural' sequence of seduction, pleasure, hope and death, and to break down the divisions among physical and emotional states that these sequences uphold. Resolution and fulfilment, though mentioned in the final sentence, are only a wish – albeit the wish of God. The embodied soul that trembles, loves, suffers and works is left hoping for a future redemption it lacks the time and strength to earn.

The incompatibility of present body and desired future that sequestered Iphis from her community and history, that made her exceptional and thus marginal, is here universalised. Christian love for God becomes misdirected in its object, because the subject can never fully deserve the 'repose' ('repos') God's love promises. Yet this future is all the more to be desired, in spite of the union of incommensurate bodies and beings that it will bring. In its efforts to sublimate same-sex desire and sex change into metaphor, the allegorisation thus renders Christian hope a little bit 'foolish', like Iphis's 'foolish' desire for Ianthe and like the historical woman's attempts at 'foolish love'. These subjects are 'foolish' to articulate desires that threaten the coherence of bodies, selves and the steady flow of time. Nevertheless, 'foolish hope' enables these laments and their speaking subjects to endure, as their voices transform narratives, bodies and temporal worlds. The text's final image of the ecstatic lament thus slips beyond the bounds of its context – in a voice that breaks open the body of time.

Although the *Ovide moralisé*'s last word on 'Iphis and Ianthe' occurs in the voice of the repentant soul's lament, this voice resonates with and through the multiplicity of prior laments in the tale and the historicisation. This final re-emergence of 'foolish hope' and lament thereby undermines the text's organising logic, as well as its status as a translated classical tale that is followed by two increasingly illuminating medieval explications. For, if the translator-narrator's decision to situate the allegorisation as both the 'better' ('meillor') and last explication suggests a desire to replace Iphis's 'foolish hope' for Ianthe and her/his gender transformation with Christian hope for redemption and spiritual transformation, this effort fails in some productive ways. The tale's turn and the allegorisation's *return* to lament, instead, capacitate a regeneration and proliferation of 'foolish hopes' – both at the level of the individual narrative and across the text's heterogeneous classical, historical and allegorical layers. The teleology implied in the structure of tale and interpretation thus dissolves – at least in part – into lament's recursion.

'Foolish hope' and lament reorient bodies and subjects, so that they continually move against the forward flow of normatively constructed time, both within and across the three layers of the *Ovide moralisé*'s 'Iphis and Ianthe' and its explications. For the very hope that 'holds' Iphis 'back' – that drives her to wish she had 'never been born' and, later, compels the allegory's repentant soul to look back on her sins – this hope also orients the subjects of lament toward a desired future. In precipitating lament, these 'foolish' hopes and loves catalyse the shift into trans* time, where past, present and future intermix, along with the embodied identities that these temporal divisions uphold, both within and beyond each segment of translation and interpretation. The laments of the *Ovide moralisé*'s 'Iphis and Ianthe', that is, *make* the time to transform the very concepts that bound and differentiate bodies, moments and speaking subjects – a process that enables 'foolish hope', as well as those afflicted by it, to survive narrative, historical and allegorical time's deadly forward flow.

Notes

1. Mills, *Seeing Sodomy*, usefully employs 'transgender' as a provisional category through which to make sodomy and gender variance visible and analyse their interrelationships in this text.
2. Hayward and Weinstein, 'Tranimalities', p. 196.
3. Valentine, *Imagining Transgender*, pp. 14–40.
4. Hayward and Weinstein, 'Tranimalities', p. 196.
5. Ibid., p. 196.
6. Ibid., p. 196.
7. Ibid., p. 196.
8. Translations of *L'Ovide moralisé* are from Griffin et al., trans., in Appendix A.
9. Row, 'Queer Time on the Early Modern Stage', explores the relationship between same-sex desire and temporality in Benserade's seventeenth-century stage play *Iphis et Iante*, arguing that the speed, direction or 'velocity' of time can express queer desires and generate erotic experience that are not rooted in notions of origins or futurity. I argue that the way time moves from the past to the future influences representations of bodies, as well as the concepts used to classify them and their capacities for change.
10. Hayward and Weinstein explain that the 'multipointed asterisk is fingery; it both points and touches', 'Tranimalities', p. 198.
11. Traub, *The Renaissance of Lesbianism*, argues that prior to the rise of the episte-

mology of the closet, the framework for understanding female-female desire was one in which one type of representation supplanted others in the process of achieving intelligibility. The intelligibility of the tribade, for example, was produced through the erasure of difference and complexity within the discourses, rhetorics and representations of female-female sexuality, p. 345.
12. The emphasis on 'female nature's' alignment with sin reflects Christian notions of Eve as the source of original sin and human mortality, as well as baptism and devotion as the means to restore the soul's eternal life. It was also a tendency of medieval commentaries on Genesis to interpret Eve's sin as a failure of discernment, foregrounding what these commentators claim was an inability to see the difference between truth and lies. See McCracken, *In the Skin of a Beast*, p. 99.
13. Isis is a female figure, but horns are typically attributes of male animals.

BIBLIOGRAPHY

Hayward, Eva and Weinstein, Jami, 'Tranimalities in the Age of Trans* Life', *TSQ: Transgender Studies Quarterly* 2: 2, 2015, pp. 195–208.

'"Iphis and Ianthe" from the *Ovide moralisé*', Miranda Griffin, Blake Gutt and Peggy McCracken (trans.), in Valerie Traub, Peggy McCracken and Patricia Badir (eds), *'Iphis and Ianthe' and Its Medieval and Early Modern Transversions* (Edinburgh: University of Edinburgh Press, forthcoming).

L'Ovide moralisé. Poème du commencement du quatorzième siècle, publié d'après tous les manuscrits connus, ed. Cornelius de Boer, Martina G. de Boer and Jeannette Th. M. van't Sant, Vol. 3 (Books 7–9) (Amsterdam: J. Müller, 1931).

McCracken, Peggy, *In the Skin of a Beast: Sovereignty and Animality in Medieval France* (Chicago: University of Chicago Press, 2017).

Mills, Robert, *Seeing Sodomy in the Middle Ages* (Chicago: University of Chicago Press, 2015).

Row, Jennifer E., 'Queer Time on the Early Modern Stage: France and the Drama of Biopower', *Exemplaria* 29: 1, 2017, pp. 58–81.

Traub, Valerie, *The Renaissance of Lesbianism in Early Modern England* (Cambridge: Cambridge University Press, 2002).

Valentine, David, *Imagining Transgender: An Ethnography of a Category* (Durham, NC: Duke University Press, 2007).

3

GOWER'S RIDDLES IN 'IPHIS AND IANTE'

Karma Lochrie

'Let me tell you about when I was a girl, our grandfather says.' So begins Ali Smith's modern reboot of the 'Iphis and Ianthe' story, a story that, as the author tells us in her acknowledgments, is inspired by Ovid's tale of the same two women, one of whom becomes transformed into a man. Of all Ovid's tales of metamorphosis, Smith avers, this tale of Iphis and Ianthe 'is one of the cheeriest. . . one of the most happily resolved of his stories about the desire for and the ramifications of change' (Smith 163).[1] An odd reading, this, considering the way in which Ovid's story first marks the desire of Iphis for Ianthe as 'strange and monstrous' before it repairs the miscreant desire by transforming Iphis from a woman into a man. Strange, too, that Smith's 'cheeriest' of endings is made possible only as a solution to the 'problem' of Iphis's body: that her genital makeup is out of sync with her desire for Ianthe and her masculine identity.

Long before Ali Smith's contemporary novelisation of Ovid's story in *Girl Meets Boy*, the Middle Ages encountered Ovid's *Metamorphoses* cross-dressed, in a sense, 'beyond recognition, encrusted in an integument of allegorisation, whether in marginal notes, commentaries, or vernacular adaptations'.[2] Ovid's story of Iphis and Ianthe summarised below would have appeared to the medieval reader in a disguise, of sorts, analogous to Iphis's gender disguise: an Ovidian tale about a woman's transformation into a man and love fulfilled, decked out in medieval hermeneutic accessories, including allegorical, historical and revisionary transformations, often of the less 'cheery' variety. Ovid in medieval drag was decked out in so many moral and spiritual exempla, framed by glosses and interpretive apparati that overwhelmed the original stories.

John Gower, the late fourteenth-century contemporary of Chaucer, offers a singular and intriguing exception and even riposte to this medieval rendering of Ovid in his collection of tales, the *Confessio Amantis* (*Confession of the Lover*, 1393). Gower's *Confessio Amantis* is organised around the confession and consolation of the lover, Amans, by Genius, who presents hundreds of tales of diverse genres and derivations in octosyllabic couplets under the rubric of the seven deadly sins against love. The tale of Iphis and Ianthe occurs in Book IV as a counterexample of the sin of Sloth in matters of love. As the discussion of this text below demonstrates, Gower retains the skeletal structure of Ovid's tale, but without the moral condemnation of Iphis's love or the problem of her betrothal to Ianthe (or Iante, in Gower's version). Gower's story recasts the love between the cross-dressed Iphis and her beloved as both innocent and exemplary and the transformation of Iphis as less a correction than a logical extension of that love. Instead of Ovid's riddle of same-sex love that can only be solved by the transformation of Iphis into a man and a happy, heterosexual solution, Gower installs riddles in his story of Iphis that pose questions about what constitutes natural love, sex and gender and what we think we know about sex, which challenge the very medieval tradition of moralising Ovid itself. Gower's project in his brief retelling of Ovid, I will be arguing, is less about what Smith calls 'the desire for and ramifications of transformation' than it is about the epistemological certainty that constrains transformation and interpretation in the first place.

Ovid's Gender Trouble

Before Iphis's transformation into a man, she is disguised in male attire by her mother, Telethusa, in order to circumvent her husband's decree that if his pregnant wife's child turns out to be a girl, she should be put to death because 'girls are more trouble, and fortune has denied them strength' ('onerosior altera sors est, et vires fortuna negat').[3] The cruelty of Lidgus's command is tempered by his own tears and prayer that he 'be pardoned for the impiety' (IX.51), but he remains undeterred from his decision even in the face of his wife's entreaty.[4] With the collusion of Isis, goddess of childbirth, Telethusa announces the birth of a boy when her girl child is born. All sorts of odd coincidences seem to conspire with the mother's deceit: for one, the father names the child Iphis, which is her grandfather's name but also, coincidentally, a name that is not gender specific. Even as the mother dresses Iphis as a boy, Iphis's own body seems likewise to align with her masculinity, for 'the features would have been counted lovely whether you assigned it to a girl or boy' ('facies, quam sive puellae, sive dares puero, fuerat formosus uterque', IX.54). Beyond her male disguise and her mother's 'pious fraud' (IX.55), Ovid renders Iphis's gender genuinely non-binary.

The problem begins with the desire Iphis both feels for Ianthe and elicits from her. Ovid curiously frames a naturalised portrait of their desire on the basis of a series of equivalencies: the two were of 'equal age and equal loveliness' (IX.55), and they were educated by the same teachers. Hence ('hinc'), writes Ovid, 'love came to both their hearts all unsuspected and filled them both with equal longing' ('amor ambarum tetigit rude pectus, et aequum vulnus utrique dedit', IX.54–5).[5] And yet, Iphis knows better. Iphis knows that she is possessed of a 'novel and monstrous love' ('quam prodigiosa novaeque cura tenet Veneris', IX.54–5) that can find no parallel in nature. It is worth noting here that the Latin adjective, *prodigious*, could mean both 'unnatural, monstrous' and 'marvellous', even though Loeb and other translators seem to take their cue from Iphis's appeal to nature which follows by translating the word to mean 'monstrous'. Ovid's text allows for either meaning, particularly in view of his introduction to the story as the tale of a wonder ('miracula', IX.50). Although Iphis herself seems to favour the 'monstrous' sense of prodigious, Ovid's text might indeed leave her predicament somewhere between marvellous and unnatural.[6] For Iphis, however, her desire is mocked by nature, making it prodigious in the monstrous sense: 'Cows do not love cows, nor mares, mares . . . there is no female smitten with love for female' ('nec vaccam vaccae, nec equas amor urit equarum . . . femina femineo conrepta cupidine nulla est', IX.54–7). Even Pasiphaë's love for a bull was less mad than Iphis's love for Ianthe because 'she had some hope of her love's fulfillment' ('illa secuta est spem Veneris', IX.56–7).

Riddles begin to emerge in the Ovidian story: is their love prodigious in the sense of wondrous and marvellous, or is it monstrous, as Iphis seems to regard it? Furthermore, what makes Iphis and Ianthe's desire 'mad' ('furioso') by comparison with Pasiphaë's? As scholars of Ovid have pointed out, it is not simply that both are women, nor that nature abhors sex between women, exactly, but that such sex is ultimately impossible. It is a classic example of *amor impossibilis*, in Valerie Traub's coinage, that would characterise love between women until the end of the eighteenth century.[7] *Amor impossibilis*. When pigs fly. For Iphis there is no hope of fulfilment of her passion, not even with all the 'ingenuity of Daedalus himself' (IX.57) at her command. Iphis admonishes herself to 'banish from your heart this hopeless, foolish love' and 'see what is lawful, and love as a woman ought to love' (IX.57)! The irony here is that while their love (being equal) is natural, their impending sexual relations are not.[8] Whose prejudice against the naturalness of women desiring women does Ovid's tale ventriloquise, Iphis's or Ovid's, or both?[9]

The problem of Ovid's Iphis is famously solved by her miraculous transformation into a man at the hands of Isis. As Iphis and her mother leave Isis's temple having pleaded for her assistance in solving this disaster of an impending marriage between two women, Iphis is transformed mid-stride:

And Iphis walked beside her [mother] as she went, but with a longer stride than was her wont. Her faced seemed of a darker hue, her strength seemed greater, her very features sharper, and her locks, all unadorned, were shorter than before. She seemed more vigorous than was her girlish wont. In fact, you who but lately were a girl are now a boy! (IX.59–61)

Sequitur comes Iphis euntem, quam solita est, maiore gradu, nec candor in ore permanet, et vires augentur, et acrior ipse est vultus, et incomptis brevior mensura capillis, plusque vigoris adest, habuit quam femina. Nam quae femina nuper eras, puer es! (IX.58–60)

Iphis's performance of masculinity is here supplemented with a new embodiment of that gender – a longer stride, greater strength, sharper features and new vigour, among other things. Ovid assures us of Iphis's genital transformation in the story's final line: 'and the boy Iphis gained his Ianthe', with a wink at the verb 'gained' ('potiturque', IX.60), since taking possession sexually is understood by Romans to require a penis. Ovid's solution, however, fails to address some of the questions the story has raised. First, for all of the tale's naturalising of the passion of Iphis and Ianthe, it never dispels the unnaturalness of Iphis's complaint about her monstrosity compared to the animal world or of Ovid's own introductory tagline: 'The story of this new monstrosity (of the previous tale of Byblis's incestuous passion for her brother Caunus) would, perhaps, have been the talk of Crete's hundred towns, if Crete had not lately had a wonder of its own in the changed form of Iphis' ('Fama novi centum Cretaeas forsitan urbes implesset monstri, si non miracula nuper Iphide mutata Crete propiora tulisset', IX.50). Ovid's wording seems to suggest that the story of Iphis and Ianthe raises the monstrosity bar on stories of incest at the same time that it resolves sexual monstrosities into wonders. Is the 'problem' of Iphis and Ianthe's love that it is physically 'impossible' and therefore tragic in the vein of failed *amatori*, or that it is improper and monstrous because it is between two women? What is the relationship between the masculinity of the embodied subject, Iphis, and her maleness, between the sexual embodiment and gender performance?[10] And finally, to pose Smith's reading of this tale in the form of a question: what does Ovid's story have to say about the 'desire for and ramifications of change', and how happily resolved, really, is it?

Gower Riddles Ovid

Iphis's lament in Ovid's story riddles us this: how can a female desire another female, and what is to be done with an 'impossible love' such as Iphis and Ianthe's? His riddle depends both on the impossibility and monstrosity of Iphis's love and a sympathy for her predicament, arising as it has from a scheme to save her life. As riddle, it raises an impossible situation that nevertheless exists: Iphis desires Ianthe despite the fact that such love does not exist in nature. What is to be done? Iphis must be made a man, not just a woman performing masculinity. Ovid's riddle relies on all those presumptions voiced by Iphis: that we know what the marriage debt demands, that even women identifying as men lack the means to have sex and that such love is therefore wondrous, but also monstrous if it is not repaired through Iphis's embodiment as a man.

John Gower's story eliminates all of the presumptive knowledge that undergirds Ovid's riddle and substitutes that knowledge with riddles of his own – riddles that, far from merely confirming the presumptions about what we know about sex and gender, instead undermine epistemological certainty where sex and gender and their relationship to nature are concerned and build a radical new possibility out of that uncertainty. Gower's *Confessio Amantis* is organised around the confession and consolation of Amans by Genius – a priest of Venus, but also a personification of the imaginative faculty. Genius's stories, many of which are derived from Ovid, serve as a kind of therapy for Amans, by which he is meant to be guided and consoled regarding the nature of love.[11] The story of Iphis and Iante appears, curiously enough, as Genius's counter-example for the subspecies of Sloth, pusillanimity or cowardice in love.[12] Gower's framing of Ovid's tale in the context of one of the seven deadly sins would seem to suggest a moralistic intention along the lines of the French *Ovide moralisé*, but this is not the case. Genius's response to Amans's request for help with his love distraction becomes a very complex and wide-ranging 'strategy of using entertainment for the winning of mental health and God's pardon'.[13] Many of the tales, such as that of Iphis and Iante, produce surprising interpretations that seem antithetical to a strictly moral agenda, as will become apparent.

The plot of Gower's story differs at the outset from its Ovidian source. Genius begins the story with King Ligdus's threat to kill Thelacuse's child if it is born a girl, a threat that seems unmotivated by his rationale in Ovid's story that women are more trouble and, besides, fortune has given them less strength. Isis appears to the queen when she gives birth to a girl to urge her to keep the child and raise it as her son. The mother names the daughter Iphis and declares her a boy. When Iphis is betrothed at the age of ten to a duke's daughter, Iante, the two children become playmates, and in one of the dearest descriptions of their friendship, Genius notes that 'often abed / These children lay, she and she' ('ofte abedde / These children leien, sche and sche' (IV.478–9).[14] Abed is where Genius introduces a puzzling and tantalising new element to this story:

> Lying abed upon a night,
> Nature, which causes every person
> To reflect upon her law,

> Compels them, so that they use
> Things [a thing] which was completely unknown to them.

> Liggende abedde upon a nyht,
> Nature, which doth every wiht
> Upon hire lawe for to muse,
> Constreigneth hem, so that thei use
> Thing which to hem was al unknowe.
>
> (4.483–7)

While Genius uses the pronoun 'sche' for both Iphis and Iante, his story leaves unaddressed Iphis's own awareness of her gender disguise or her sexual 'lack'. Unlike Ovid's Iphis, who is aware of her own 'lack' when it comes to sexual intercourse with another woman, neither Gower's Iphis (nor Iante) seem to encounter any constraints against their love or sexual play. The Middle English verb 'constreinen' means to compel or induce persons, to govern or control things, but not necessarily to restrict.[15] Their only 'constraint' is that of Nature, which serves both as the source of their inducement to experiment sexually as well as the governor of their desire. Instead of anxiously fearing the wedding night, as Ovid's Iphis does, Gower's Iphis is obliged by Nature to do something with Iante that was unfamiliar to them until that moment. Her masculinity never encounters its own limits as it does in Ovid's story, where gender performance balks before biological sex and sexuality.[16]

What exactly do these two, 'she and she', do? 'They use / Things [a thing] which to them was entirely unknown' ('Thei use / Thing which to hem was al unknowe', 4.486–7). Here is the heart of the first riddle of Gower's text: what is that 'thing that was utterly unknown to them', how did they come to 'use' it and what is Nature up to in compelling them to become so sexually inventive? Robert Mills suggests that the 'thing' in this passage 'designates some appendage, accouterment, or body part for which even the users themselves have no name'.[17] In my translation, though, I allow for the reading of 'thing' as collective 'things' in the sense of 'using things' or 'practising things', a formulation that the Middle English also allows for with a verb such as 'to do' followed by 'thing' without an article or plural ending.[18] Gower has it both ways in the sense that we could read these lines to mean the two girls 'used some thing' or that they 'engaged in an activity' without the involvement of any 'things' per se. Middle English often drops the article before 'thing', as it does here, when it is used in conjunction with a verb to indicate action. To 'use thing' could thus mean to 'do things' or engage in activity ... that was utterly unknown to them. What is not ambiguous is the fact that the girls were utterly ignorant of the thing or activity before that moment, and their unknowing is proof of Nature's marvellous direction.

Gower's riddle does not necessarily ask to be solved. Instead it confronts the reader with his or her own sexual ignorance of what it is the two girls are doing, and in this respect the reader shares in their ignorance, if not their ingenuity. What the girls are doing and with what instruments is as 'utterly unknown' to us as it is to them (and, perhaps, even to Gower for that matter), albeit for different reasons. Traub's insistence on the opacity of sexual knowledge can find no better illustration than this moment in Gower's text and his cryptic allusion to sexual activity. The 'thing' in this passage is this very opacity, and not dildos per se – it is not, in other words, the solution to Gower's riddle.[19] Gower opens up a space of opaqueness courtesy of Nature and the desires of Iphis and Iante – a space that seems deliberately resistant to sexual epistemology, either the knowing of the two girls involved, Gower's knowledge or our own. Without knowing the 'thing' or its use, but also not entirely ignorant or innocent, readers of Gower's text can nevertheless see how it introduces possibility within the realm of what was often regarded as impossible, that is sexual relations between women. This is a riddle, therefore, that requires precisely that we not try to solve it, that we suspend our desire to know in the face of the radical possibility Gower has injected into the story.

What Looks Like a Gloss, But Doesn't Behave Like One?

Gower's riddling on the sexual congress of Iphis and Iante is complicated by the Latin gloss he inserts next to the beginning of the tale.[20] Genius's introduction to the tale is reproduced by Gower's Latin gloss, which appears next to it on the page in some manuscripts, although sometimes the gloss is situated in the textual columns along with the poem (Figure 3.1).

The gloss summarises Genius's narrative regarding the king's threat, Thelacusa's raising of her child as a son on Isis's advice, and Iphis's betrothal to Iante. At this point in the story, however, the gloss parts ways with Genius's version in a curious return to Ovid. According to the Latin gloss, 'when Yphis did not possess the wherewithal to render her debt to her bride, she called upon the gods for help' ('cum Yphis debitum sue coniugi vnde soluere non habuit, deos in sui adiutorium interpellabat').[21] As the discussion above suggests, not only does the Iphis of Genius's story possess plenty of 'wherewithal', but she is entirely unaware of any lack or problem with respect to her desire; moreover, she is already engaged in sexual activity with Iante long before her marriage with its attendant Christian expectations of mutual sexual indebtedness. She never prays to the gods for help (as she does in Ovid), because . . . why would she? Gower's gloss, far from providing any summary perspective or interpretive purchase on his text, instead calls attention to its own lack of wherewithal to gloss the text at hand.

This is not the first time that Gower's Latin gloss plays fast and loose with his Middle English text. The entire *Confessio Amantis* is accompanied by Latin

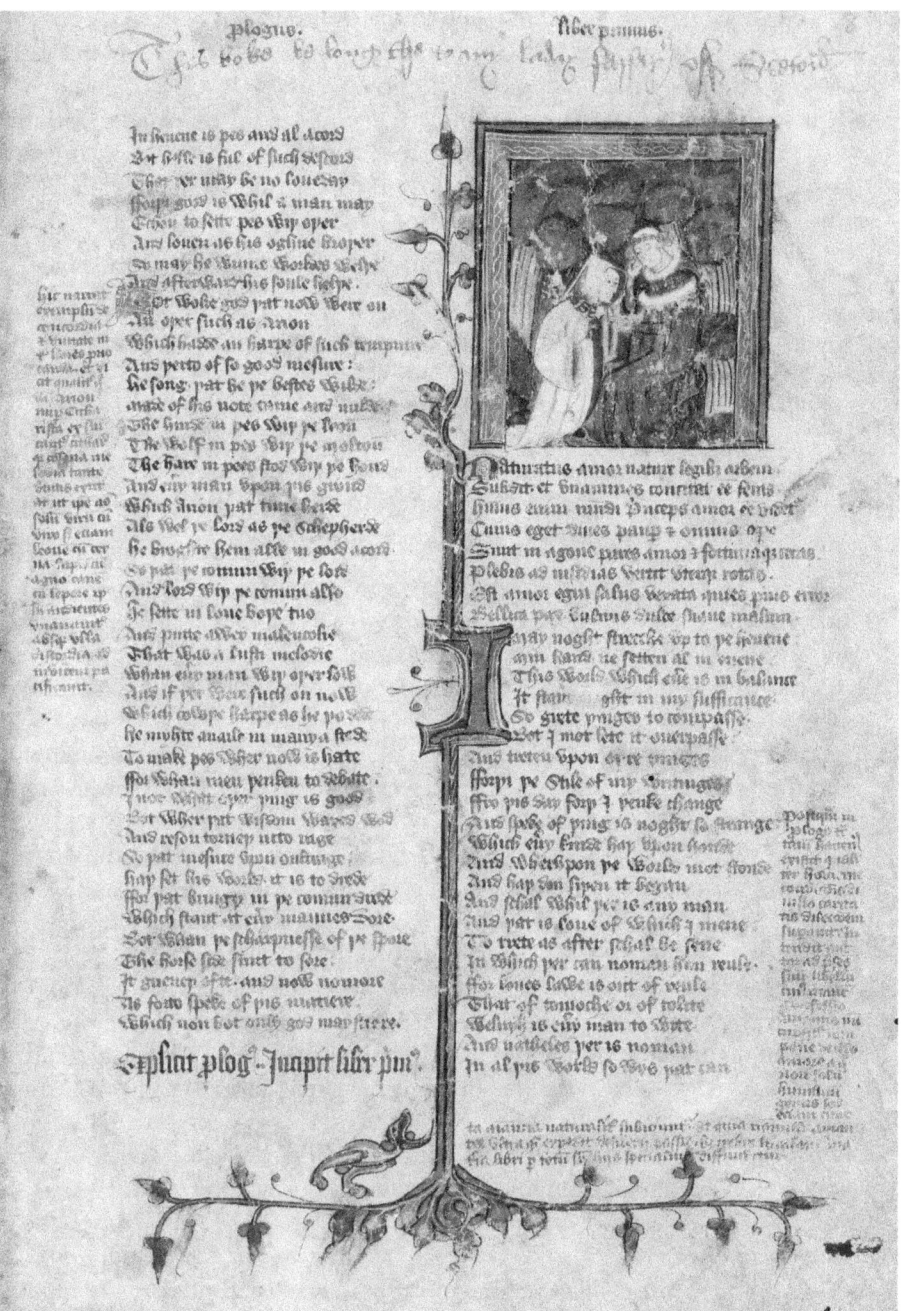

Figure 3.1   Oxford Bodleian Library, MS Fairfax 3, folio 8r.

prose glosses thought to be supplied by Gower himself that behave strangely.[22] Scholars who have studied the Latin commentaries note that Gower's Latin glossing often inverts the function of traditional glosses. Instead of authorising the text with exegesis, Gower's Latin commentary is 'often equally confused (and so confusing) and tangential to what seems to be the "point"'. In short, Gower's glosses do not 'behave as glosses usually do'.[23] Gower's gloss of Genius's 'Iphis and Iante' behaves oddly indeed, summarising a different story than the one the poem tells, calling its own 'wherewithal' as authoritative gloss into question. As Winthrop Wetherbee observes:

> Gower's elaborate framing of the *Confessio* makes explicit and central the confrontation between the traditional authority of Latin and a vernacular with its own claims to meaning ... The uneven perspective of the glosses ... express[es] the difficulty of invoking the authority of the Latin pedagogical tradition as a control on the vernacular text, and so collaborate[s] in Gower's assertion of his status as a vernacular author. The effect is a distancing of traditional *auctoritas*.[24]

In addition to privileging his vernacular text against the Latin pedagogical tradition, Gower's glossing is engaging in two more types of riddles, the first having to do, again, with our own sexual ignorance, and the second concerning the tradition of Ovid in the French moralised tradition that Gower most likely used.

First, Gower's emphasis on epistemological ignorance. By summarising Ovid rather than the Middle English text to which it is attached, Gower's Latin gloss calls attention to the difference between the Ovidian Iphis story (and its moralisations), which is the one most of his readers would have known, and his singular vernacular retelling. The misprision or misreading created by the discrepant story and gloss dismantles the presumption of truth – or, more importantly, of *knowing* – that glossing typically fabricates.

In addition to its deliberate misprision of the Middle English story, Gower's dysfunctional gloss likewise imitates in a less systematic way the very glossed tradition of Ovid that was predominant in the Middle Ages. Medieval Ovid, as I have already suggested, was encountered primarily in glossed form through the early fourteenth-century *Ovide moralisé* and Pierre Bersuire's Latin prose *Ovidius moralizatus* (c.1340).[25] In addition to these versions, there were two French prose versions of the moralised Ovid, one of which texts served as the source for William Caxton's 1483 English translation, *The Booke of Ovyde Named Methamorphose*.[26] Like Ovid's Iphis and that of the *Ovide moralisé*, Caxton's Iphis deplores her 'fowle amorous rage' ('foul amorous rage') and cites the absurdity of 'maryage without a man' ('marriage without a man').[27] Caxton skips the allegorical interpretation of the tale found in the *Ovide moralisé*, the *Ovidius moralizatus* and one of the French prose texts, limiting his gloss to its historical interpretation. The historical gloss links the Iphis story to a purportedly true story from ancient times in which a woman disguised herself as a man à la Iphis and soon desired sex and marriage with another woman. Because she lacked 'the instruments of nature', this proto-Iphis consulted an old and evil bawd who provided her with 'a member apostate' with which she could fulfil her desires. Once the wife discovers the apostate member, she exposes her to her community, bringing shame on herself and causing her 'husband' to flee in exile. The gloss ends with a clear condemnation of such 'villainous' behaviour.[28]

Gower's glossing of the 'Iphis and Ianthe' story, like his glosses of many of the Ovidian and non-Ovidian tales in the *Confessio Amantis*, seems to riff off the habit of glossing that would have been identified with most of the textual traditions of Ovid's *Metamorphoses* in the Middle Ages. Without necessarily imitating the allegorical or historical structure of the *Ovide moralisé* glossing tradition, Gower instead draws attention to the interpretation itself, particularly as that interpretation fails to explain or expand upon the primary text. Whatever Gower might have thought of what strikes the modern reader as far-fetched allegorical interpretations of Ovidian stories, he seems to have brought his own Latin glosses to bear on the unreliability and irrelevance, in some cases, of glossing itself. Gower's gloss is perfectly suitable to Ovid's text or the medieval moralised texts of Ovid, but it is also ignorant of and unresponsive to the text at hand.

A comparison of Gower and Caxton raises a question, too, about the potentially uncanny connection between the two: what is the relationship between the 'thing that was completely unknown' to Iphis and Iante and the 'apostate member' of Caxton's historical interpretation? In accordance with the French tradition of the moralised Ovid, Caxton alludes to the 'member apostate' by which the cross-dressed woman was about to 'achieve her desire' of sex with her wife until she was discovered. This 'apostate member' translates as a 'rebellious instrument' or 'heretical tool' by means of which a perverse desire is enabled.[29] This 'apostate member' that brings shame upon both women and exile upon the wielder of it provides the fulcrum for the glossarial condemnation of the gender impersonation and sexual transgression involved. Gower's riff, if I may call it that, on the 'apostate member' consists of simultaneously evacuating the term of the knowledge it presumes and the moral outrage its sponsors. Use of 'thing(s) that were to them unknown', in fact, installs two ignorances into the story: the innocence of the two young girls engaged in sex and the text's own refusal to know what even the girls do not. Gower's gloss never mentions the 'apostate member' of the moralised texts, but in placing his own story in tandem with the moralised one, he not only mimics the glossed Ovids of his time, but he also installs in his gloss the opacity of sexual knowledge for practitioners, readers, authors and moralists alike at the heart of his revision.

Gower's Two Natures

Nature having constrained the two girls to practise mysterious love-making, Cupid becomes involved in Gower's tale to 'take pity' on their 'great love' (IV.489). Cupid's intervention, which importantly does not occur in Ovid or any of the other moralised versions, consists of placing love above Nature so that the two women may 'be excused for their desire' (4.492). Gower's tale up to this point has already 'excused them for their desire' on the basis of their innocence, their passion and the fact that Nature provides them with the wherewithal that they did not already possess and could not have learned. And yet, Cupid seems to discern a problem where there has been none: 'For love hates nothing more / Than things which stand against the teaching/ Of what nature has naturally established' ('For love hateth nothing more / Than thing which stant agein the lore / Of that nature in kinde hath sett', 4.493–5)). Championing Love over Nature, Cupid waits until just the right time when 'each of them had kissed the other' and 'transforms Iphis into a man'. Not only does Iphis now enjoy 'natural love' with his wife, but the two live a life 'that was no offence to nature' (4.505).

Ovid's riddle of how two girls can engage in physical love is displaced in Gower's text, as it actively – if mysteriously – imagines just such a possibility. It is replaced with another, more shadowy riddle about the position this physical love between women occupies with respect to nature. Iphis's transformation awards him the bliss of sex and 'natural love' with Iante and yet he seemed already to possess both. The riddle that Gower installs in the story works precisely in the opposite direction of most riddles: instead of presenting an enigma that the riddle solves, Gower frames Iphis and Iante's sexual love as both possible and nature-driven – no riddle at all, in other words, even if it does retain a certain mystery surrounding that pesky 'thing'. If 'the thing' is the riddle, Iphis's transformation does not solve it. The solution that the tale applies – the normalising of their love so that 'it was no offence to nature' – is itself another riddle, because it introduces the offence to nature where there was previously none. Is it simply a gratuitous solution where there was no problem? Or does the solution gesture towards a different problem, not so much of Iphis and Iante's love or sex, but of Nature's complicity with it?

Scholars have puzzled over Gower's philosophical understanding of Nature in the *Confessio Amantis* generally. Hugh White maintains that Gower's poem contains 'contradictory attitudes towards Nature': sometimes it 'covers a certain basic instinctual order', while at others, it represents a 'moral authority'.[30] Winthrop Wetherbee points out that Gower in fact invented in the Latin Prologue to the *Confessio* a new idea, *naturatus amor*, or 'natured love'.[31] It is an intriguing idea, but as Wetherbee notes, Gower's meaning is not at all transparent: it could refer to love in the service of nature, love that sustains nature or love 'reduced to the state of nature', binding humans with the animal world.[32] Even the lines in which the term appears can be translated to mean very different things: 'Naturatus amor nature legibus orbem / Subdit, et unanimes concitat esse feras' ('Natured love subjects the world to the laws of nature, and incites harmonized ones to wildness [or, wild ones to harmony]').[33] Gower's invention of a 'natured love' asserts an inextricable relationship between the two forces, whether that means that love serves Nature or love reduces humans to the level of nature, including beasts. The second line is a peculiar sort of paradox in which two opposed meanings are equally possible, although they cannot both be true. As with sex, so too with Nature in Gower's text: instead of embracing the certainty of Nature's alignment with God and procreation, and all things unnatural with immorality, Gower imagines a 'natured love' that straddles the nature of human desires and the Nature of moral authority.

The naturing of love occurs twice in Gower's tale, first with Nature's urging the girls to pursue their desire with 'things unknown to them', and second with Love's establishment of itself over Nature and the transformation of Iphis. It is interesting that Gower uses two different words available in Middle English in order to suggest the two natures of medieval natural philosophy. 'Nature', a word borrowed from French, is used three times in the tale, first as the force governing the creative sexual resources of Iphis and Iante (4.484), second as a body of teaching (4.495), and third as that which Cupid observes in his transforming of Iphis into a man (4.498). 'Kinde', a native English word, is used three times: as a noun designating that domain in which nature establishes her teaching (4.495) and as the moral register that approves their new love (4.505), and as an adjective – 'kinde love' – that Iphis wins when she becomes a man (4.502). Although 'nature' and 'kinde' were used interchangeably to refer to the moral realm governed by reason and the natural world of sexual instincts, in Gower's tale the two do not seem to be synonymous. Gower's 'nature' seems to govern the narrow field of sexual impulses and desires, while 'kinde' represents the moral authority that demands Iphis's transformation.[34] Gower's tale thus has it both ways: Nature teaches them to act on their desire *and* Nature demands Iphis become a man. A paradox . . . and a different riddle entirely than Ovid's. Iphis's metamorphosis is unnecessary, yet it allows for an alliance of the two kinds of sexual love – between women and between a man and a woman – and the two concepts of nature, leaving no meaningful opposition between either set of binaries.

Gower's nature stands apart from other medieval conceptions in another important way insofar as it is 'profoundly secular', according to Galloway. William Langland's nature, for example, is characterised by its pervasive association with the divine, while Gower's nature is essentially Stoic.[35] Gower analogises Cicero's advocacy of a 'mind well-molded by nature' to his ethical principle in the *Confessio* of a 'love well-molded by nature'.[36] This leads in his poem to the rather unusual medieval claim that the incest of Canace and Mahaire is driven by the 'laws of nature' (3.157) and the love-making of Iphis and Iante is both compelled and guided by nature. Even though the tale's signature metamorphosis of Iphis from a woman into a man, therefore, seems to appease a Christian (and classical) view of nature, Gower's own tale provides an alternative ethics – one in which natured love finds a way to integrate the love of Iphis and Iante with the moral law of Nature, which otherwise seems to have little to do with them. The impetus for the metamorphosis is neither moral outrage over their monstrous passion nor Iphis's angst about her marriage night, but the very passion that the two women have already indulged.

The miraculous gender transformation in mid-stride as Iphis leaves the Temple of Isis in Ovid's tale is entirely missing from Gower. Iphis is transformed into a man at the moment that she kisses Iante, but Gower does not detail either her bodily changes or the effects such a metamorphosis would have had on both women in the midst of their sexual contact. On the one hand, this oversight strikes this reader as a disappointing missed opportunity. On the other, it is consistent with Gower's refusal to distinguish in his tale between Iphis's masculinity and her gendered embodiment. Iphis's sudden embodiment of masculinity is irrelevant either to her ability to engage sexually with Iante or to her own sense of herself. She is not afflicted with guilt over her gender 'deception' or the prospect of marrying and having sex with Iante.[37] Gower's oversight is thus consistent with his refusal to identify Iphis's masculinity and sexual congress with Iante as a riddle to be solved in the first place. The climactic mutation of Iphis that finally answers Ovid's riddle – how can a woman desire another woman when she has no hope of sexually acting on that desire? – is written on the body that departs the Temple of Isis. For Gower, Iphis's transformation is epiphenomenal: it is not the story of Iphis and Iante's love but the epiphenomenon of that love, the virtuous transformation made possible by their own passion for one another. Iphis's masculinity exists before she becomes a man, making embodiment less the mark of gender than Iphis's dedicated (because Iphis seems to believe in it) performance of it is.

From the perspective of modern transgender and intersex studies, however, we should pause to consider Iphis's own desire with respect to Cupid's miraculous alteration of her. Unlike Ovid's Iphis, who seeks a solution to her gender dysphoria, Gower's Iphis does not, nor can we be certain that Cupid's intervention is felicitous for the two women. Gower has removed Iphis's voice – and Iante's too – so that their choice in the matter of Iphis's gender and sexual performance is eliminated altogether as an issue. How different, one might ask, is Cupid's intervention from modern medical interventions in gender dysphoria wherein the subject is given no choice?[38] Genius will suggest a key difference in that it is Iphis's desire (if not her voice) that causes the metamorphosis in the first place.

The Thing That Is Due to Love

Following the Iphis and Iante story Genius glosses his tale for Amans as an object lesson in the sin of Sloth in matters of love: 'Love is benevolent / To those who endeavour / With busy hearts to follow / The thing that is due to love' ('Love is welwillende/ To hem that ben continuende / With besy herte to poursuie/ Thing which that is to love due', 4.507–10). The mysterious 'thing' that carries the weight of Iphis and Iante's sexual practice returns uncannily in Genius's gloss, perhaps aligning itself with the inventiveness that Iphis and Iante somewhat more unknowingly wielded. A certain playful unknowing is once again invoked in terms this time around of the 'thing' that is due to love. Genius's 'thing that is due to love' further removes his tale from those Ovidian distinctions between monstrous and natural, possible and impossible, loves, replacing those binaries with the lovers' devoted service to the demands of love.

While 'the thing that is due to love' leaves open many possibilities, Genius cites the amorous 'business' (or 'diligence', 'steadfast pursuit', 4.513) exemplified by the two women as especially worthy of mention. His gloss thus recasts the metamorphosis of Iphis from a reparative act against Nature's offence and the impossibility of female sexual love, to a remunerative one, a reward for their mutual and erstwhile passion. No longer does the transformation of Iphis into a man work to appease Nature – or at least, this is not its only function; instead, it is, in a sense, the very product of their 'natured' love.

Smith's reading of Ovid places the 'desire for and the ramifications of change' at the centre of the 'Iphis and Ianthe' story. I would argue that Gower's story is cheerier (to adopt her word) than Ovid's for a different reason: by installing the riddle of 'the thing that was unknown to them' at the centre of his tale, Gower undoes the epistemological certainty that provokes moral condemnation lodged against the sex between Iphis and Iante and the very need for change in the first place. Gower rebuffs such certainty with respect to gender and to sexuality, creating epistemological opacity where there was none in four ways: first with 'the thing' we don't know but take on faith that satisfied the two girls; second with a Latin gloss that misreads, in effect, his own story in terms of Ovid's story and other moralised Ovids; third by grounding their love in a Nature that already endorses their love and ultimately welcomes the transformation made possible by that love; and finally with Genius's counter-intuitive exegesis of the story as the tale of diligent, persistent and ultimately creative amorous pursuit of 'the thing that is due to love'.

Gower's tale is itself the vehicle of that metamorphosis of which Smith speaks, the desire for and ramifications of change. His 'Iphis and Iante' is a tale about miraculous transformation, yes, but more than that, it is a tale that, in refusing to solve its riddles or provide the interpretive wherewithal of its gloss, creates the possibility for another kind of change – a metamorphosis, if you will, in the very moral and epistemological rubrics with which we read gender, sex and bodies.

NOTES

1. Smith, *Girl Meets Boy*, p. 163. I would like to thank Peggy McCracken, Valerie Traub and Patricia Badir along with the other contributors to the volume for their helpful suggestions for this essay. I would also like to extend my appreciation to Andrew Galloway, who generously shared his extensive knowledge and work on Gower's use of Ovid.
2. Harbert, 'Lessons from the Great Clerk', p. 83. Galloway echoes this idea: 'Gower read Ovid by way of a sizable set of medieval apparatus' [sic], 'Gower's Classicizing Vocations', p. 274; and 'Unlike many other classical authors, Ovid's works did not arrive in medieval culture with scholiae from late antiquity; this meant Ovid's poetry was glossed and assimilated anew by medieval culture', 'Gower's Ovids', p. 442.
3. Ovid, *Metamorphoses Books IX–XV*, p. 51. Quotations from this edition are hereafter designated in the text by book and page number.
4. Pintabone, 'Ovid's Iphis and Ianthe', notes that Ovid's Ligdus is 'somewhat sympathetic' insofar as he grieves his own decision and asks for forgiveness, pp. 261–2.
5. Pintabone, 'Ovid's Iphis and Ianthe', notes Ovid's emphasis on the girls' equality of upbringing and love, p. 263. Ormond points out the dynamics of passivity and activity in the love story, pp. 94–5.
6. Daston and Park, *Wonders and the Order of Nature*, lay out the medieval overlap between 'prodigies' and 'wonders' or 'marvels', although 'prodigies' was reserved for portentous individuals who conveyed 'deliberate messages, fashioned by God to communicate his pleasure or … his displeasure with particular actions or situations', p. 52. The *OED* locates the association of monstrosity with the word 'prodigious' in the sixteenth century. Ormond argues for a more ambiguous sense of the word in his analysis of Ovid's story as treating Iphis's love 'with considerable empathy', pp. 79–80.
7. Traub's term in *The Renaissance of Lesbianism* corrects the grammar of a similar term, *amor impossibilia*, coined by Terry Castle, in *The Apparitional Lesbian*, pp. 30–1.
8. This is how Pintabone, 'Ovid's Iphis and Ianthe', also characterises the 'irony' of Ovid's story (p. 270).
9. In fact, Hallett, 'Female Homoeroticism', argues that 'Ovid's narrative displays immense sympathy with Iphis's plight' (p. 217), while Pintabone, 'Ovid's Iphis and Ianthe', suggests that Ovid's solution proves Iphis wrong in her self-recrimination (p. 269). Ormund, 'Impossible Lesbians', likewise argues that Ovid treats their love not as a 'moral failing' but as a 'thorny and near-tragic problem' (pp. 79–80). Contrast their readings with that of Makowski, 'Bisexual Orpheus', who finds the Iphis story to constitute 'Ovid's most damning denunciation of homosexuality' (pp. 30–1).
10. See Mills's discussion of Ovid's story and its many versions, *Seeing Sodomy*, pp. 98–107. Pintabone, 'Ovid's Iphis and Ianthe', argues for reading Ovid's tale as a kind of 'riddle' in which the love between the two women is deemed natural but sex requires a 'solution' (p. 270). Ormund, 'Impossible Lesbians', makes the case for the impossibility (not undesirability) of the desire, and in addition argues for understanding that impossibility in Roman terms of the active and passive

principles of sexuality, which makes Iphis a failed lover due to her passivity (p. 97).
11. For a full discussion of Gower's poem, its genre, influences and borrowings from other tales, see the Introduction to the TEAMS edition.
12. For discussions of Gower's version of 'Iphis and Ianthe', see Watt, *Amoral Gower*, pp. 73–6, and 'Sins of Omission', pp. 542–6; Mills, *Seeing Sodomy*, pp. 107–11; Dinshaw, *Getting Medieval*, pp. 10–11; Gallacher, *Love, the Word, and Mercury*, pp. 67–8; and Woolf, 'Moral Chaucer and Kindly Gower'.
13. TEAMS edition of *Confessio Amantis*, Introduction.
14. Middle English quotations are taken from the TEAMS edition of *Confessio Amantis*, Book 4, ll. 451–515, http://d.lib.rochester.edu/teams/text/peck-gower-confessio-amantis-book-4#4.451. All citations appear in the text by book and line number. The modern English translation is my own in consultation with Andrew Galloway's translation notes in the TEAMS edition.
15. *Middle English Dictionary*, s.v. *constreinen*, v., http://quod.lib.umich.edu/cgi/m/mec/med-idx?type=id&id=MED9437 (accessed 28 August 2017).
16. Mills, *Seeing Sodomy*, argues for this distinction in Ovid's tale between masculinity as gender performance and as sexual embodiment, p. 101.
17. Mills, *Seeing Sodomy*, p. 108; Mills goes on to explicitly reference 'dildo' as the thing that could not be named, p. 109.
18. The *Middle English Dictionary* lists 5(a) 'thing' as 'an action' or practice in conjunction with 'don', 'to do', to suggest a general practice, as opposed to 'don (a)' to suggest a specific action. Although the dictionary gives no parallels to Gower's use of 'usen thing', I am suggesting this as a possibility. 'Usen' can mean 'to make use of', but also more generally in the sense of 7(g) 'to perform', which is the way I am suggesting it be translated in the second possibility. *Middle English Dictionary*, s.v. *thing*, n. http://quod.lib.umich.edu/cgi/m/mec/med-idx?type=id&id=MED45301 and *usen*, http://quod.lib.umich.edu/cgi/m/mec/med-idx?type=id&id=MED50630 (accessed 14 June 2017).
19. I am indirectly invoking Traub's use of the opacity of sexual knowledges in *Thinking Sex with the Early Moderns* to advocate a sexual historicism in which 'we confront what we *don't* know as well as what we *can't* know about sex in the past', p. 5.
20. Gower's entire Latin précis goes as follows:

> Hic ponit exemplum super eodem, qualiter Rex Ligdus vxori sue Thelacuse pregnanti minabatur, quod si filiam pareret, infans occideretur: que tamen postea cum filiam ediderat, Isis dea partus tunc presens filiam nomine filii Yphim appellari ipsamque more masculi educari admonuit: quam pater filium credens, ipsam in maritagium filie cuiusdam principis etate solita copulauit. Set cum Yphis debitum sue coniugi vnde soluere non habuit, deos in sui adiutorium interpellabat; qui super hoc miserti femininum genus in masculinum ob affectum nature in Yphe per omnia transmutarunt.

> Here he presents an instructive example about the same thing, how King Ligdus threatened his pregnant wife Thelacuse, that if she bore a daughter he would kill the baby. But nonetheless later, when she had issued forth a baby girl, Isis the goddess of birth, then being present, instructed her to call her daughter Yphis by name and to raise her in the manner of a son. The father, believing he had a son, joined her at the usual age in marriage to the daughter of a certain prince. But when Yphis did not possess the wherewithal to render her debt to her bride, she called upon the gods for help; and these, taking pity on this on account of what nature desires, entirely transformed Yphis' gender from feminine to masculine. (IV.451n.)

21. Galloway, trans., *Confessio Amantis*, IV, TEAMS edition online. The Latin adverb, 'unde', meaning 'whence' or 'from which place', here does the work of a noun, direct object of 'habeo', to mean something like 'that with which', or to borrow Galloway's translation, the 'wherewithal'.
22. Emmerson, 'Reading Gower', p. 148.
23. Echard, 'With Carmen's Help', pp. 8 and 13–14. Pearsall, 'Gower's Latin', understands the Latin glosses as 'instructions on how to read it according to the conventions of a specific code of reading', p. 24; Copeland, *Rhetoric, Hermeneutics, and Translation*, comments that 'the exegetical system dominates at all levels and junctures of this text', p. 203.
24. Wetherbee, 'Classical and Boethian Tradition in the *Confessio Amantis*', p. 183.
25. See the translation of the *Ovide moralisé* in the Appendix of this volume. See also McCracken's essay in this volume, 'Moralizing Metamorphosis'. For the relationship between Gower and this glossed tradition, see also Hiscoe, 'Ovidian Comic Strategy', p. 375; Minnis, 'John Gower', p. 158; Wetherbee, 'Classical and Boethian Tradition', pp. 181–2; Galloway, 'Gower's Ovids', p. 438; and McKinley, 'Gower and Chaucer', p. 199. In addition to the glossed tradition, as McKinley points out, 'school texts' provided unmoralised Latin texts of Ovid's verse (p. 199).
26. For the first prose French version (*c*.1466–7) see C. de Boer; the second prose version (*c*.1480) has not been edited. It survives in three manuscripts: London, British Library, Royal MS 17.E.iv; Paris, Bibliothèque nationale de France, MS français 137; and St Petersburg, Rossijskaja Nacional'naja Biblioteka, MS F.v.XIV.1.
27. Caxton, p. 310.996 and p. 311.1022.
28. Caxton, p. 312.1078
29. The *MED* and *OED* list only adjectival definitions that apply to persons rather than things. Caxton is carrying over the phrase 'apostate member' directly from the *Ovide moralisé*, requiring an extension of the Middle English's adjective's meaning to cover things.
30. White, *Nature, Sex, and Goodness*, pp. 199, 193–4. White misreads the Iphis and Ianthe story, in my view, as hinting at the 'naked, unconditioned, undifferentiating sexual impulse that suggests something morally anarchic at the bottom of the totality one calls Nature' (p. 193).
31. I am borrowing Galloway's translation of this Latin phrase in 'Gower's Ovids', p. 446, because I think it captures Gower's innovation in this tale of understanding nature.
32. Wetherbee, 'Classical and Boethian Tradition', p. 181.
33. I am using Galloway's translation of the phrase *naturatus amor* as 'natured love', which as he points out, seems to recall a related phrase in the vulgate gloss on Ovid's account of the creation of the world, 'natura naturata', or 'natured nature', referring to 'a certain inherent force in things procreating similar things from similar things', 'Chaucer's Ovids', p. 446. Wetherbee, 'Classical and Boethian Tradition', translates Gower's Latin as 'love bound to nature', p. 189. I am using Galloway's translation of the second line from the TEAMS edition of the *Confessio Amantis*. The second part of this translation comes from Wetherbee's note to the TEAMS edition of the *Confessio Amantis*, but where he rewords 'natured love' in this translation, I want to retain it.
34. Bychowski claims that 'kinde' can mean 'gender' in Middle English, but the *Middle English Dictionary* limits that meaning to grammatical gender, 'Unconfessing Transgender', p. 13.

35. Galloway, 'Gower's Classicizing Vocations', p. 272; for an analysis of the Christian conception of Nature in William Langland's *Piers Plowman*, see Davis, *Piers Plowman and the Books of Nature*.
36. Quoted from Cicero's *De officiis* 1.4.13, in Galloway, 'Gower's Classicizing Vocations', p. 271.
37. As Watt states, 'Iphis does not undergo any sort of identity crisis', *Amoral Gower*, p. 75.
38. Bychowski raises this issue in conjunction with Gower's tale and the contemporary medicalisation of gender dysphoria, 'Unconfessing Transgender', pp. 1–4.

Bibliography

Boer, C. de (ed.), *Ovide moralisé en prose: Texte du quinzième siècle*, in *Verhandelingen der Koninklijke Akademie van Wetenschapaen te Amsterdam, Afdeeling Letterkunde, nieuwe reeks* 61: 2 (1954).

Bychowski, M. W., 'Unconfessing Transgender: Dysphoric Youth and the Medicalization of Madness in John Gower's "Tale of Iphis and Ianthe"', *Accessus: A Journal of Premodern Literature and New Media* 3: 1 (2016), pp. 1–38.

Castle, Terry, *The Apparitional Lesbian: Female Homosexuality and Modern Culture* (New York: Columbia University Press, 1993).

Caxton, William (trans.), *The Booke of Ovyde Named Methamorphose*, ed. Richard J. Moll, Studies and Texts 182 (Toronto: Pontifical Institute of Mediaeval Studies, 2013).

Copeland, Rita, *Rhetoric, Hermeneutics, and Translation in the Middle Ages: Academic Traditions and Vernacular Texts* (Cambridge: Cambridge University Press, 1991).

Daston, Lorraine and Park, Katharine, *Wonders and the Order of Nature, 1150–1750* (New York: Zone Books, 1998).

Davis, Rebecca, *Piers Plowman and the Books of Nature* (Oxford: Oxford University Press, 2016).

Dinshaw, Carolyn, *Getting Medieval: Sexualities and Communities, Pre- and Postmodern* (Durham, NC: Duke University Press, 1999).

Echard, Siân, 'With Carmen's Help: Latin Authorities in the "Confessio Amantis"', *Studies in Philology* 95: 1, 1998, pp. 1–40.

Emmerson, Richard K., 'Reading Gower in Manuscript Culture: Latin and English in Illustrated Manuscripts of the *Confessio Amantis*', *Studies in the Age of Chaucer* 21, 1999, pp. 143–86.

Gallacher, Patrick J., *Love, the Word, and Mercury: A Reading of John Gower's Confessio Amantis* (Albuquerque, NM: University of New Mexico Press, 1975).

Galloway, Andrew, 'Gower's Classicizing Vocations', in Ana Sáez-Hidalgo, Brian Gastle and R. F. Yeager (eds), *The Routledge Companion to John Gower* (New York: Routledge, 2016), pp. 266–80.

Galloway, Andrew, 'Gower's Ovids', in Rita Copeland (ed.), *The Oxford History of Classical Reception in English Literature: Volume 1: 800–1558* (London: Oxford University Press, 2016), pp. 435–64.

Gower, John, *Confessio Amantis, Vol. 2*, ed. Russell A. Peck, trans. Andrew Galloway (Kalamazoo, MI: Medieval Institute Publications, 2013), http://d.lib.rochester.edu/teams/publication/peck-gower-confessio-amantis-volume-2.

Hallett, Judith, 'Female Homoeroticism and the Denial of Roman Reality in Latin Literature', *Yale Journal of Criticism* 3: 1, 1989, pp. 209–27.

Harbert, Bruce, 'Lessons from the Great Clerk: Ovid and John Gower', in Charles Martindale (ed.), *Ovid Renewed: Ovidian Influences on Literature and Art from the Middle Ages* (Cambridge: Cambridge University Press, 1988), pp. 83–97.

Hiscoe, David W., 'The Ovidian Comic Strategy of Gower's *Confessio Amantis*', *Philological Quarterly* 64.3, 1985, pp. 367–82.
McKinley, Kathryn L., 'Gower and Chaucer: Reading of Ovid in Late Medieval England', in James G. Clark, Frank T. Coulson and Kathryn L. McKinley (eds), *Ovid in the Middle Ages* (Cambridge: Cambridge University Press, 2011), pp. 197–230.
Makowski, John F., 'Bisexual Orpheus: Pederasty and Parody in Ovid', *Classical Journal* 92: 1, 1996, pp. 25–38.
Mills, Robert, *Seeing Sodomy in the Middle Ages* (Chicago: University of Chicago Press, 2015).
Minnis, A. J., 'John Gower, Sapiens in Ethics and Politics', *Medium Ævum* 49, 1980, pp. 207–29.
Ormund, Kirk, 'Impossible Lesbians in Ovid's *Metamorphoses*', in Ronnie Ancona and Ellen Greene (eds), *Gendered Dynamics in Latin Love Poetry* (Baltimore: Johns Hopkins University Press, 2005), pp. 79–110.
Ovid, *Metamorphoses Books IX–XV*, ed. and trans Frank Justus Miller, 3rd edn, rev. G. P. Goold, Vol. 2, Loeb Classical Library 43 (Cambridge, MA: Harvard University Press, 1984).
Pearsall, Derek, 'Gower's Latin in the *Confessio Amantis*', in A. J. Minnis (ed.), *Latin and Vernacular: Studies in Late-Medieval Texts and Manuscripts. York Manuscripts Conferences: Proceedings Series*, Vol. 1 (Cambridge: D. S. Brewer, 1989), pp. 13–25.
Pintabone, Diane T., 'Ovid's Iphis and Ianthe: When Girls Won't Be Girls', in Nancy Sorkin Rabinowitz and Lisa Aunger (eds), *Among Women: From the Homosocial to the Homoerotic in the Ancient World* (Austin: University of Texas Press, 2002), pp. 256–85.
Smith, Ali, *Girl Meets Boy: The Myth of Iphis* (New York: Canongate, 2007).
Traub, Valerie, *The Renaissance of Lesbianism in Early Modern England* (Cambridge: Cambridge University Press, 2002).
Traub, Valerie, *Thinking Sex with the Early Moderns* (Philadelphia: University of Pennsylvania Press, 2016).
Watt, Diane, 'Sins of Omission: Transgressive Genders, Subversive Sexualities, and Confessional Silences in John Gower's *Confessio Amantis*', *Exemplaria* 13: 2, 2001, pp. 529–51.
Watt, Diane, *Amoral Gower: Language, Sex, and Politics* (Minneapolis: University of Minnesota Press, 2003).
Wetherbee, Winthrop, 'Classical and Boethian Tradition in the *Confessio Amantis*', in Siân Echard (ed.), *A Companion to John Gower* (Cambridge: Brewer, 2004), pp. 181–96.
White, Hugh, *Nature, Sex, and Goodness in a Medieval Literary Tradition* (London: Oxford University Press, 2001).
Woolf, Rosemary, 'Moral Chaucer and Kindly Gower', in Mary Salu and Robert T. Farrell (eds), *J. R. R. Tolkien, Scholar and Storyteller: Essays in Memoriam* (Ithaca, NY: Cornell University Press, 1979), pp. 221–45.

4

FORTUNE'S TOUCH: READING TRANSFORMATION IN CHRISTINE DE PIZAN'S *MUTACION DE FORTUNE*

Miranda Griffin

INTRODUCTION: CHRISTINE'S TRANSFORMATION

The tale of Iphis is one of several stories told in Christine de Pizan's 1403 narrative allegorical poem, *La Mutacion de Fortune*, in order to give credence to the change in gender that the narrator describes having undergone.[1] Most of this work (just over 15,000 lines of the 23,000) recounts the history of the world (based on the chronicle, *L'Histoire ancienne jusqu'à César*) in the form of an ekphrastic description of the murals painted in the citadel of Lady Fortune as Fortune herself expounds them to the narrator. However, the first thousand or so lines recount an allegorical autobiography, in which Christine discusses her parentage and relates her early life, from childhood through adolescence to her happy marriage to Etienne du Castel and his death in 1389, leaving her a widow at the age of twenty-five with three children. In the terms of the allegory, we are informed that Christine is raised by her mother, Lady Nature, then sent into the protection of Lady Fortune, who, in turn, sends her by sea, to the court of Hymenaeus – in other words, she arranges for Christine to be married. The description, still within this allegorical setting, of Christine's husband is warm and loving, and they enjoy a happy marriage for ten years. But then disaster strikes: Fortune sends Christine and Etienne (the 'captain of the ship' in the allegory) on another journey, and although Etienne is a very accomplished pilot, he dies in a storm at sea. Shipwrecked and alone, Christine has nevertheless not been abandoned by Lady Fortune:

99

> Then my mistress [Fortune], who diminishes many people's joy, came to me, and touched me everywhere on my body. I well recall that she handled and held in her hands each limb. Then she left and I remained; and, as our boat sailed over the waves, it struck a rock with force; I woke up, and it happened that I felt that I had swiftly and certainly been transformed. My limbs felt stronger than before and the sadness and weeping which had previously afflicted me, were gone.

> Adont vers moy vint ma maistresse,
> Qui a plusieurs la joye estrece,
> Si me toucha par tout le corps;
> Chacun membre, bien m'en recors,
> Manÿa et tint a ses mains,
> Puis s'en ala et je remains,
> Et, comme nostre nef alast
> Aux vagues de la mer, frapast
> Contre une roche moult grant cas;
> Je m'esveillay et fu le cas
> Tel qu'incontinent et sanz doubte
> Transmuee me senti toute.
> Mes membres senti trop plus fors
> Qu'ainçois et cil grant desconfors
> Et le plour, ou adés estoie,
> Auques remis.
> (1325–40)

The result of this consoling, transforming touch is, announces Christine, that 'I had become a true man' ('vray homme fus devenu', 1361).

In his sensitive reading of the *Mutacion*, Robert Mills uses the pronouns 'he' and 'him' to refer to the poem's narrator.[2] I shall follow this example, taking Christine the narrator at his word: after all, he insists that he is still a man to this day:

> As you hear, I am still a man, and I have been for more than thirteen whole years.

> Comme vous ouës, encore suis homme
> Et ay esté ja bien la somme
> De plus de XIII. ans tous entiers.
> (1395–7)

Christine de Pizan the extra-textual author, however, did not, in the years between Etienne's death and the composition of the *Mutacion*, claim a masculine identity: she (and I will use she/her to talk about Christine de Pizan the author) is depicted as a woman in her later texts, most notably *La Cité des dames* (1405), and in the illustrations of her in the manuscripts of her work, manuscripts whose creation the author herself often supervised.[3] By adhering to this gender difference in my terminology for author and character, I want to make a distinction between these roles, a distinction which can often be less clear when it comes to women authors.[4] I want also to preserve a sense of the strangeness with which Christine de Pizan is experimenting here, by making the first-person persona insistently masculine. Scholars tend to refer to Christine de Pizan as 'Christine', since her patronym – a French version of her father's name, da Pizzano – is a prepositional phrase indicating the family's geographical origins, rather than functioning in the same way as a modern surname (her father, Tomasso da Pizzano, also known as Thomas de Pizan, was astrologer to King Charles V of France). In this essay, however, for the sake of clarity, I shall refer to Pizan the author and Christine the (masculine) narrator of the *Mutacion de Fortune*.[5]

To support the credibility of Christine's transformation, the narrator relates three stories taken from Ovid's *Metamorphoses*: those of Circe, Tiresias and Iphis; he also briefly refers to the tale of Ceyx and Alcyone. While Pizan read Latin,[6] the text in which she would have had her earliest and most frequent encounters with Ovid's tales would have been the fourteenth-century *Ovide moralisé*. The first full-length translation of the *Metamorphoses* into French, appending historical and Christian interpretations to each tale, the *Ovide moralisé* was popular and widespread in the royal and aristocratic libraries from the time of its production.[7] Pizan, the daughter of the court astrologer, would have had access to the library compiled by the learned king: the inventories of his collection indicate that he owned three manuscripts of the *Ovide moralisé* and one of the *Metamorphoses*, glossed in Latin.[8]

The reworked Ovidian tales in the *Mutacion* are therefore retellings of translations, participating in the rich network of medieval *translatio*, whereby classical tales are adapted, translated and repurposed for a secular, courtly, Christian audience. The essays by Peggy McCracken and Laurel Billings in this volume address the *Ovide moralisé*'s presentation of the tale of Iphis and Ianthe: in my essay, I explore Pizan's retelling of the tale, focusing also on the tale's interaction with the other tales of metamorphosis as they are related in the *Ovide moralisé* and recounted by the *Mutacion*'s narrator to make sense of his own transformation. In this personal project of *translatio*, Christine resembles Ovid's Iphis, who casts about for figures who might reflect the impossible love she feels for Ianthe. Iphis summarises the story of Pasiphaë, who contrived to have sex with a bull with the help of a cow-disguise fashioned by Daedalus, but rejects her as a role model,[9] understanding her own desire as even more unnatural than Pasiphaë's.[10] Where Iphis tries and fails to find an equivalent to her love in narrative, Christine tries out several tales to summarise or support his bereavement and transformation, recalling the tales of Circe and Tiresias before he touches on Iphis, making himself the next term in a series of Ovidian retellings.

While Christine's autobiography in the *Mutacion* relies on the retelling of myth and the actions of allegorical personifications, it is also insistently presented as truth.[11] As the narrator puts it:

> And it is neither lie nor fable to speak according to metaphor which posits nothing but truth.
>
> Et si n'est mençonge, ne fable,
> A parler selon methafore,
> Qui pas ne met verité fore.
> (1032–4)

The word 'fable' is a clear signal of Pizan's engagement with the *Ovide moralisé*, since this text describes the tales it translates from the *Metamorphoses* as 'fables',[12] as opposed to the moralisations (the word the *Ovide moralisé* uses for these is 'sentences', which I will discuss in more detail later in the essay). The four lines from the *Mutacion* quoted above intertwine lie, truth, fiction and metaphor to indicate a practice of interpretation and rewriting which has much in common with the imbrication of classical myth, historical origins and Christian truth to be found in the *Ovide moralisé*. The gender transition portrayed in the *Mutacion* cannot be dismissed as 'just' a metaphor, then, although it is generally understood as a means for Pizan to explore the radical rethinking of her corporeal and intellectual selfhood as a result of her widowhood.[13] Metaphor, allegory and *translatio* can all be understood as self-consciously literary figures of substitution, where an experience, person, emotion or story is reworked with recourse to learned tradition, and reread and transformed into fiction, in a process which chimes with the notion of transversion central to this volume.

In this essay, I make two interrelated arguments about the use of Ovidian material in the *Mutacion*'s representation of its narrator's transformation. Firstly, that an interwoven reading of the tales of Iphis, Circe, Tiresias and Alcyone in the *Mutacion* and their sources in the *Ovide moralisé* enables the articulation of a narrative of gender change with that of the precarity of a reciprocated love between two partners. In Ovid's tale of 'Iphis and Ianthe', gender change is seen as necessary for married love to take place; in Christine's own story, gender change takes place after married love is no longer possible. Secondly, I argue that the representation of this gender change is mediated strongly through the sense of touch. In the *Mutacion*, reading emerges as a haptic process, sensuous in that it involves more than just the sense of sight, but also the sense of touch, which is implicated in sensuality and seduction as well as epistemological certainty.[14] The tender embrace of Fortune on the newly-widowed Christine's skin both mimics the embrace between husband and wife and offers consolation in its absence; it also recalls the touch of hand on parchment which characterised the experience of manuscript reading in the Middle Ages. For Pizan reading in the royal library or in the private study in which she is so often depicted,[15] encounters with books would have involved this intimate contact, the touch of skin on skin. Bringing these arguments together, I conclude that this emphasis on the sensuality of the reading encounter is useful in reflecting on Pizan's use of Ovidian tales of desire and transformation to think through her widowhood. Widowhood, like virginity or chastity, is a position which is taken up in relation to the erotic, even if it does not involve sex:[16] for Pizan, it is not a renunciation of sexuality, but a reimagination of it via sense memory – remembered on the body, memorialised in skin and recreated via the sensuous processes of reading and writing.

RETELLING IPHIS IN THE *MUTACION* AND THE *OVIDE MORALISÉ*

While Christine de Pizan did not always cite Ovid or the *Ovide moralisé* approvingly, nor quote them verbatim,[17] her *oeuvre* shows meticulous engagement with the *Metamorphoses* and its French translation and moralisation.[18] In the *Mutacion*, Christine recounts a series of three Ovidian tales in order to emphasise that Fortune can often intervene in order to change people's appearances, although transformations in the *Metamorphoses* are generally effected by the gods rather than the personification of Fortune.

> For Fortune certainly has the power to perform great miracles for those over whom she holds sway, often transforming animals into lords, when she wishes.

> Car Fortune a bien la puissance
> Sur ceulz de son obeisance
> Faire miracles trop greigneurs,
> Et souvent bestes en seigneurs
> Fait transmuer, quant il lui gree.
> (1035–9)

It is noteworthy that Christine emphasises Fortune's transformative power as effecting transition between animal and human rather than from one gender to another. Indeed, the first Ovidian tale cited by Christine is that of Circe, who gave a potion to Ulysses' men, which turned them into pigs. The next two tales Christine relates do involve transgender experiences: first is that of Tiresias, who makes two transitions during the course of the story, from man to woman and back to man again. Finally, and perhaps bearing most similarity to the experience that Christine relates, he tells the story of Iphis.

In relating this transformation, however, Christine makes some changes of his own, abridging the tale considerably, demonstrating a practice of *translatio* that weaves between fidelity to the *Metamorphoses* and the *Ovide moralisé*, and redistributing details from each of these source texts throughout the narrative of this first part of the *Mutacion*. Most importantly, the *Mutacion* makes no mention at all of Ianthe. Erasing Iphis's partner presents the crucial gender change less in the context of a desire which may or may not be reciprocated, and more as an embodied, sensory experience, enacted by a merciful deity, chiming with Christine's own transfiguration. Iphis's mother, Telethusa, although she is not named, plays an important role in Christine's retelling, and rather than the humble Ligdus of the *Metamorphoses*, Christine makes Iphis's father a 'king of Lydia' ('roy de Lide', 1094). The *Ovide moralisé* might be seen as a staging post in this promotion up the social ranks, since it relates that Iphis' father was called Ligdus, who was 'a baron who was both rich and noble' ('Un baron riche et noble ensamble', 9: 2773). Christine's account endows this man with a 'hatred' ('haÿne', 1095) of women: he orders his pregnant queen to burn or otherwise kill the child she is carrying if it turns out to be a girl. This is in sharp, and surprising, contrast to the account in the *Metamorphoses*: Ovid's Ligdus does not hate women but argues that they have a more difficult lot in life than men, especially, perhaps, those who are born to relatively impoverished families like his own. In the case of such disadvantaged women, he points out, 'fortune denies them strength' ('fortuna vires negat', 9: 677). This reference to fortune is not quite the fully-fledged, complex personification of Fortune that we encounter in the *Mutacion*, but a place of agency nonetheless, in a point of view which might be read as sympathetic to the female condition rather than the misogynist attitude displayed by Iphis's father in the *Mutacion*.[19] The *Ovide moralisé*, like Christine, does not mention fortune (or Fortune) at this point, but gives Ligdus a much more dismissive (and detailed) view of women:

> For there is too much trouble in a woman; I know of no heavier burden. Woman lacks strength and valour. Many men are caused pain by women.
>
> Quar trop a en feme d'anui.
> Ains fais si chargant ne conui.
> Fame est sans force et sans valour.
> Par fame est maint home à dolour.
> (9: 2789–92)

The *Ovide moralisé*'s Ligdus, like Ovid's, voices his sorrow at having to issue the command that any daughter of his be killed (*Met.* 9: 679; *OM* 9: 2798). The *Mutacion* does not relate Telethusa's dream of Isis, and her decision to bring up her daughter as a boy is portrayed as stemming from the queen's 'maternal nature' ('nature de mere', 1108), which prompts her to protect the baby girl from death. When the time comes for Iphis to be married, Christine portrays only Iphis's mother's fear: Iphis's anguished monologue, in which she speaks passionately yet hopelessly about what she sees as her impossible love for Ianthe, is not relayed in the *Mutacion* at all.

Ianthe's absence from this retelling of Iphis's tale removes any mention of Iphis's anxiety about same-sex love.[20] In Christine's story, Telethusa, while unnamed, eclipses Ianthe, and also takes on some of the characteristics of Ovid's Iphis. In the *Mutacion*, Vesta, not Isis, is the goddess to whom Iphis's mother prays and who effects the climactic transformation: Mills reads this substitution as a domestication of Iphis's transgendering, moving it into the purview of the goddess of hearth and chastity and away from Isis, whose legend includes the detail that she fashioned for her husband a replacement penis.[21] While mother and daughter visit Isis's temple together in the *Metamorphoses* and the *Ovide moralisé*, in the *Mutacion* Iphis's mother prays alone to Vesta. The gender transformation is marked in Ovid's description as Iphis adopts 'a longer stride' ('maior gradu', 9: 787) on leaving the temple, and in the *Ovide moralisé* she walks 'with a longer step than was her wont' ('A plus grant pas qu'el ne seult faire', 9: 3083). In the *Mutacion*, this adaptation is seen not in Iphis's gait, but it is her mother who 'jumps from the temple door' ('du temple sault de la porte', 1148).

Christine reworks the tale of Iphis, transferring elements of it into his own allegorical autobiography. While Ovid's meticulous description of the changes wrought on Iphis's body is missing from the account of this tale in the *Mutacion*, Christine does incorporate it into the portrayal of his own gender transition. As he leaves the temple, Ovid's Iphis is stronger and more vigorous and his features sharper. Similarly, Christine's 'flesh was changed and stronger, my voice much lower and my body harder and swifter' ('ma chiere / Estoit muee et enforce / Et ma voix forment engrossie / Et corps plus dur et plus isnel', 1348–51). It is notable that, where the *Ovide moralisé* adds the detail that Iphis's 'body [. . .] used to be slender' ('Tout son corps seult ester alegié', 9: 3089), the *Mutacion* uses the notion of being light as a masculine quality, possessed by Christine after his transformation, perhaps as a reference to the burden of grief which he feels has been lifted from him with this transition. Christine echoes the *Ovide moralisé*'s use of the verb 'souloir' (to have the custom or habit of doing something), but with the inverse effect: 'I felt lighter than before' ('Si me senti trop plus legiere / Que ne souloye', 1347–8). Fortune's touch on Christine's body has an inverse gendered effect to that which is described by Ligdus in the *Metamorphoses*, although the transformation it effects supports his judgement: rather than denying her strength, Fortune has endowed Christine with it – and thereby made him a man.

The closing lines of Book 9 of the *Metamorphoses* evoke the union between Ianthe and the newly-male Iphis on their wedding night: the sun rises, 'and the boy Iphis gained his Ianthe' ('potiturque sua puer Iphis Ianthe', 9: 797). The *Ovide moralisé* concludes its translation of this section of the *Metamorphoses* with an emphasis on the joy experienced by Iphis at this union: 'Iphis was happy and full of joy. He took Ianthe as his own' ('Yphis fu liez et plains de joie. / Hyenté prist come la soie', 9: 3111–12). But in the *Mutacion*, this joy is shared with Iphis's mother:

> The goddess performed a great miracle, for that night she brought great happiness to the queen and Iphis her daughter, who became a son, thanks to the ingenious goddess Vesta, who undid her woman's body and made him a son.
>
> Miracle y fist grant la deesse,
> Car la nuit rempli de leece
> La roÿne et Yplis sa fille,
> Qui filz devint, par la soubtille
> Deesse Vestis, qui deffit
> Son corps de femme et filz le fit.
>   (1153–8)

If Isis in the *Metamorphoses* and the *Ovide moralisé* performs Iphis's gender change in order to reinvent Iphis as a husband for Ianthe, then, in the *Mutacion*, Vesta 'undoes' Iphis's body to make her a son rather than a daughter: this resonates with Christine's own allegorical autobiography in the early stages of the *Mutaction*.

Inherited Knowledge and Sensual Memory

The early stages of the *Mutacion* portray Christine's learned, poetic persona as a result of the talents and qualities he has inherited from his parents. The very skills which form the basis of the *Mutacion* – the ability to read, understand, remember and retell both life experience and literary encounters – are portrayed as jewels inherited from his parents. While the father Christine describes is recognisable as Tomasso da Pizzano, Christine de Pizan's historical father, Pizan's historical mother is written out and replaced with the allegorical figure of Nature.

Christine tells us that he is the 'son of a noble and famous man' ('Filz de noble homme et renommé', 171). All the manuscripts of the *Mutacion* have the reading 'filz' (son) for this line, as if the transformation at the end of the Iphis story Christine will later relate has already been effected at his birth. But Christine tells us later that 'I was born a girl/daughter, this is no fairytale' ('Si fus nee fille, sanz fable!' 392). Yet, it appears he cannot sustain the narrative of his birth as a son without a 'fable'. While Christine's father is not portrayed as being brutal as Ligdus is in his dismissal of a daughter, he is depicted as possessing a 'great desire to have a male offspring' ('tres grant voulenté d'avoir / un filz masle', 381–2). The emphasis placed by the *Mutacion* on Iphis's shift as being one from daughter to son can be read as an answer to this desire, and is reflected in the narrator's own gender transition.

Christine relates that, when he was born, he resembled his father almost entirely, 'apart from sex alone' ('Fors du sexe tant seulement', 396): in everything else, they were indistinguishable. Because of this difference in sex, Christine relates that he was unable to inherit any of the jewels of wisdom his father had accumulated – including some taken from the Ovidian location of art and wisdom, the fountain of Helicon, where the nine Muses bathe.[22] This denial of the learning he so craved made him resemble a thwarted lover:

> I am like ardent, desiring lovers, who cannot see nor hear that of which they wish to take pleasure.

> Si suis comme les amoureux
> Bien ardans et bien desireux,
> Qui ne peuvent veoir, n'ouyr
> Ce dont desirent a jouir.
> (439–42)

The figure of the lover whose desire is only increased by the unattainability of the object of desire is a well-worn medieval topos of courtly love. But the setting of this topos in the *Mutacion* evokes Iphis, another woman destined to become a man, whose gender at birth cuts her off from the object of her desire and who laments her inability to be united with her beloved. In the *Ovide moralisé*, the coincidence of her proximity to Ianthe and her anxiety about consummating her love only strengthens Iphis' love: 'This intensified and redoubled the love which inflamed the maiden Iphis for fair Ianthe' ('Ce fet l'ardour croistre et double, / Qui plus embrace la pucele / Hyphis pour Hienté la bele', 9: 2916–18). The *Ovide moralisé*'s allegorical reading reiterates this formula: Iphis is understood as the soul which repents of its foolish actions, and desires the forgiveness of God which it believes it has forfeited through its sinful ways: 'this intensifies and redoubles her love, for joy which seems a little hopeless is desired all the more' ('Ce fet croistre et doubler l'amour, / Quar assez plus est desiree / La joie un poi desesperee' (9: 3384–6)). Christine's reading of the tale of Iphis in the *Ovide moralisé* and its recasting in the *Mutacion* thus reconfigures knowledge, cross-sex union and divine forgiveness as states which might all be fervently desired, withheld and finally attained.

In the *Metamorphoses* and in the *Ovide moralisé*'s translation, Iphis blames nature for preventing her from consummating her love for Ianthe: 'the only one who disapproves is Nature, who opposes us all. She vetoes everything that we desire and is much more powerful than all of us put together' ('Mes seule desveult, ce me samble, / Nature contre tous enasamble, / Qui desdist ce que tuit loons / Et plus puet que tuit ne poons', 9: 3003–6). Nature is also a powerful force in the *Mutacion*, since it is her intervention, as Christine's allegorical mother, which has caused Christine to be born a woman: 'For my mother, whose power was greater than his [Christine's father's], wanted to have a female who resembled her' ('Car ma mere, qui ot pouoir / Trop plus que lui, si voult avoir / Femelle a elle ressemblable', 398–91). Rather than inheriting the wealth of her father's learning, Christine, as a girl, inherits allegorical jewels from mother Nature. Christine describes how this inheritance consisted of a crown beset with four gems: Discretion, Consideration, Retention and Memory. Discretion and Consideration enable Christine to behave in a seemly way at court. The influence of the last two gems can be traced throughout the rest of the *Mutacion*, specifically in the way in which Christine weaves together the Ovidian tales he relates to reflect on his bereavement and gender change.

Retention, set at the front of the crown, enables its wearer to recollect experience acquired using bodily senses: 'that which one hears and feels and sees, / and all that the heart conceives' ('Ce que l'en oit et sent et voit, / Et tout ce que le cuer conçoit', 615–16). Set at the back, Memory has a complementary power:

> Whatever one has heard or seen or heard speak of or read in the past, whether it was to do with knowledge or history, this stone gives one the ability to remember it all, and thus it is called Memory.
>
> Ceste de tout le temps passé,
> Quoyqu'on eust ouÿ ou veü
> Ou ouÿ dire ou leü
> Fust en science ou en histoire,
> Faisoit de tout avoir memoire,
> Aussi est Memoire appellee.
> (624–9)

These two jewels and the descriptions of them, then, create a distinction between the way in which sensory information and learning are remembered. Retention enables one to attend to the way in which embodiment conditions learning and memory; Memory stands for a more abstract, cognitive engagement with scholarship and collective knowledge.

In the *Mutacion*, Christine relates reading as a memory that is recalled via touch, using the power of the allegorical gem Retention along with the less embodied Memory. Retention and Memory complement one another, set together as they are in Christine's crown, enabling him to look forward and backwards, and to recall the 'science' and 'histoire' he has encountered, and put them into practice in narrating his own embodied life. Both 'science' and 'histoire' are hard to translate in this context, 'science' being a term for learning (Charles V's library contained, Pizan writes in her 1404 encomium to the late king, 'all forms of learning' ['toutes sciences']),[23] and 'histoire' straddling, as it does in modern French, both factual history and fictional story. The transforming touch of Fortune that Christine recalls in his allegorical autobiography and the Ovidian tales he tells are recollected with the help of these gems, and these retellings are also characterised by a focus on the blending of intellectual and sensory memory. In other words, Memory and Retention enable the articulation and the proliferation of the stories that support Christine's gender transition.

Transformation Remembered

The tale of Circe features in both the *Metamorphoses* and Boethius's *Consolation of Philosophy*. Neither of these texts mentions Fortune in connection with Circe's transformation of Odysseus' men into pigs but, as Christine relates the story in the *Mutacion*, he adds the detail that it was Fortune herself who brewed the magic potion that effected the metamorphosis.[24] While the inclusion of Circe is surprising in a list of tales supposed to reflect and guarantee the veracity (if not the verisimilitude) of a narrative of gender change, the appearance of this tale in the *Mutacion* may be explained by the way in which it is articulated in both the *Metamorphoses* and the *Ovide moralisé* as a sense memory. In Book 14, Macareus, who sailed with Odysseus, might be said to be using his powers of Retention when he recalls the effect his transformation had on the surface of his body. The *Ovide moralisé* follows the *Metamorphoses* faithfully at this point: Macareus recollects his transformation by Circe, who touched the men on their hair with her wand. This magic touch had an unsettling effect on his skin: 'My hairs started to bristle, to stiffen and stand up' ('Le poilz me prist à hericier, / A redir et à redrecier', 14: 2463–4; compare *Metamorphoses* 14: 279). Macareus becomes a pig from the outside in, giving a graphic account of how it feels to transform, his face lengthening and his neck thickening (*Met.* 14: 282–4; *OM* 14: 2470–4). When Ulysses secures his men's disenchantment, this metamorphosis is reversed, once more starting with the skin: 'we lost our bristles' ('nous desheriçons', 14: 2546), recalls the *Ovide moralisé*'s Macareus. Both Macareus and Christine change shape (Macareus becoming a pig, Christine taking on masculine physical features) and are able to narrate their transformations in retrospect. The *Ovide moralisé*'s moralisation of this tale reinforces the connections between Circe and the senses: Circe is read as the Whore of Babylon mentioned in the Apocalypse, who intoxicates earthly rulers with her potion of lust: the pigs represent those sinners who are overcome with gluttony and lust, whose sensuous appetites are running amok.

The second Ovidian story Christine recounts in order to apprehend his new sense of embodiment is a story of transgender, but one which flickers between masculine and feminine, leading to a secret body of knowledge that not even the gods can fathom. Like the story of Macareus, it is a tale in which the memory of transformation, as much as the transformation itself, plays an important role. The *Mutacion*'s version relates that the man Tiresias encountered two snakes mating, struck them and was transformed. 'He immediately perceived that his entire body had been transformed and had instantly changed into a woman' ('incontinent s'apperceut / Que tout son corps fu transmué, / En femme fu tantost mué', 1072–4). The terms in which Tiresias's transformation is described closely echo those of Christine's: it happens 'incontinent' and the newly feminine Tiresias is 'transmué' (cf. ll. 1335 and 1336, quoted above). Both characters are depicted noticing their transformation using verbs which evoke the senses as a means of revelation. While Christine 'felt' ('senti') his transformation, Tiresias 'perceived' ('s'apperceut') his: this visual perception prefigures the blindness Juno will later inflict on Tiresias.

For seven years, Tiresias lives as a woman; at the end of this period, Tiresias meets the snakes again, strikes them once more and is returned to masculine form. The *Metamorphoses* introduces Tiresias at a moment in his life after these two transformations, as he is called upon by Jupiter and Juno to arbitrate their drunken debate about whether men or women enjoy greater pleasure in sex. Having experienced both masculine and feminine embodiment, Tiresias can make this pronouncement with confidence (although presumably only from an individual point of view).[25] When he declares that women experience the most pleasure, Juno, in anger, blinds him, but Jupiter gives him the gift of prophecy. Once again, Christine relates the tale of a character whose embodied memory can enable him to recount an extraordinary experience from a first-hand perspective. Just as Macareus can recall in detail the feeling of his skin being transformed by a supernatural figure, so Tiresias can, from the perspective of a male body, remember feminine sexual pleasure so clearly that he can definitively declare its superiority before the gods themselves. So, too, Fortune's touch is recalled by Christine so vividly that after thirteen years he still feels her transformative effects. As Tiresias retains the memory of being a woman even when he has been transformed back into a man, so Christine recalls the experience of hardening himself against the devastation of bereavement.

Iphis's Sentences: The Meanings of Transversion

Pizan's source text, the *Ovide moralisé*, gives more than one interpretation to the story of Iphis and Ianthe. As is usual in this text, a pseudo-historical, euhemerist reading is offered first, and then another interpretation is given:

It seems to me that I could give this tale a better meaning, through allegory, and gloss the text differently: this is the preferred meaning.

Meillour sentence, ce m'est vis,
Par allegorie y puis metre
Et gloser autrement la letre,
Si doit ceste estre miex amee.
(9: 3158–61)

This second reading understands the story as an allegory of the inherent corruption of the soul (which is gendered feminine and linked to 'feminine nature' ('femeline nature'), 9: 3202) and its consequent need to be purified through confession. The 'historical reading' ('historial sentence', 9: 3115) claims that the story of Iphis and Ianthe has its origins in a less supernatural and rather more sordid account of a woman who dressed as a man in order to deceive another woman into sexual relations. This she achieved, the moraliser alleges, with the help of a 'false member' ('membre apostis', 9: 3149), akin to the false penis that legend claims Isis fashioned for her husband. The disapproval provoked by this artificially created false member is in stark contrast to the loving refashioning of Christine's own limbs ('membre[s]', 1328 and 1337) by the goddess Fortune. Rather than one false member being imposed on this transgendered body, Fortune 'handled and held in her hands each limb' ('Chacun membre, [. . .] / Manÿa et tint a ses mains', 1328–9), dispersing her transformative touch all over the surface of Christine's transformed, consoled body.

For the *Ovide moralisé*, Iphis's body becomes a tale to be read, to be interpreted according to various 'sentences'. Furthermore, in the allegory of the Iphis story, the *Ovide moralisé* exploits the polyvalence of the word 'sentence' itself: it also has a meaning closer to the modern English usage of 'sentence' to mean a legal judgement. In the *Ovide moralisé*, Telethusa is advised by Isis to disregard her husband's command ('Si deçoi la sentence au pere', 9: 2849). In the moralisation, God the father (the allegoresis of Ligdus) is portrayed as pronouncing a 'bitter and harsh verdict' ('sentence amere et dure', 9: 3201) on the feminine nature of the soul. If the soul renounces her wicked ways, then, declares the moraliser, God 'will certainly commute the sentence' ('relaschera sans doute / La sentence', 9: 3335–6). Just as the *Ovide moralisé* offers more than one meaning to the tale of Iphis, and to the word 'sentence' itself, Christine explores various readings and judgments of his own body via the Ovidian tales he recounts.

Conclusion: Grief and Gender on the Surface

In the *Ovide moralisé*'s translation of Tiresias's story, the meaning of 'sentence' as 'judgement' is used once more, as Tiresias's pronouncement on the relative pleasure of men and women is called a 'sentence' (3: 1051). The interpretation given to the tale of Tiresias by the moraliser summarises the medieval view of the elements' role in gender. It is thanks to the mutability of earthly material figured by Tiresias, explains the moraliser, that we can understand the created world:

> For according to their changes, we understand the quality of elements and natures which sustain and nourish all things.
>
> Quar selon les muabletez
> Cognoissons nous les qualitez
> Des elimens et les natures
> Par lesqueulz toutes creatures
> Sont soustenues et norries.
> (3: 1151–5)

As a reader of the *Ovide moralisé*, Christine de Pizan would certainly seem to support the view that 'muabletez' are valuable ways of understanding the world: the stories of mutability related by Ovid enable her to establish contact between her life and the books she has encountered. In deploying Ovidian narratives, these stories of changeable bodies are used as judgments and interpretations of Christine's own widowhood and the resulting experience of a refigured gender identity.

Christine refers to one other Ovidian tale to structure the allegorical autobiography in the *Mutacion*: the tale of Ceyx and Alcyone, told in Book 11 of the *Metamorphoses*. In this tale, King Ceyx drowns at sea; Morpheus, the son of the God of Sleep, appears in Ceyx's form to his widow, Alcyone, in a dream. Upon awaking, Alcyone finds her husband's corpse at the sea's edge and the couple are reunited in the form of birds. In the *Mutacion*, Christine touches briefly on this tale, declaring that he would have rushed to join his husband in his watery grave had he not been restrained (11: 1257–62). The parallels between the tales of Alcyone and Christine are clear: they both involve the devastation of widowhood and a subsequent bodily transformation.[26] Whereas Alcyone is transfigured into a bird, however, Christine's makeover resonates more with Morpheus's ability to take on the shape of Ceyx. And while Ceyx and Alcyone transform together, one from a corpse, one from a live human body, to be reunited in non-human form, Christine undergoes metamorphosis alone: his transformation is more redolent of those visited on Iphis and Tiresias.

While Morpheus takes on Ceyx's shape, Christine does not become Etienne, but his embodiment is reconfigured, his outline redrawn, as masculine. Naomi Segal, writing on the psychoanalyst Didier Anzieu's work on skin as an organ through which we experience intimacy, and a metaphor via which we articulate the connections between intimacy, erotic desire and gender, observes that 'the skin keeps alive and safe the memory of what is lost'.[27] As Christine recalls stories which imagine transformative embodiments and recollections of those stories, he keeps safe in his skin the memory of his husband. From this perspective, the touch of Fortune on Christine's skin effects an exchange between Christine and Etienne: the woman vanishes and the man appears. Crucially, this disappearing act is only possible through the processes of reading – in both senses of allegorical interpretation and the physical interaction with the book.[28] The consoling, transformative touch of the allegorical personification of Fortune on the surface of the suffering Christine can, therefore, be compared to the consoling practice of reading, which brings comfort to Pizan as she finds echoes of her own grief and recovery in Ovidian tales. In contrast to Christine's use of the story of Alcyone, the *Ovide moralisé* places much more emphasis on the ship in which Ceyx drowns than on the heart-rending story of his bereaved wife.[29] Its oarsmen are interpreted as the five senses, which guide us through 'the troubled sea of the world' ('La troubleuse mer dou monde', 11: 3884). In a later work, *L'advision Christine*, Christine uses a metaphor of shutting down her senses to convey the solitude and study she sought after the death of her husband: 'Then I closed my doors, which is to say, my senses' ('Adonc cloy mes portes, c'est assavoir mes sens').[30] In the *Mutacion*, the body is conceived less as an architectural structure to be sealed off to the world, and more as a mobile locus of gender transition, with vulnerability lent strength by the sense of touch and sensory memory.

To think of the skin as the locus on the body where gender is expressed is to envisage an understanding of gender and its transversion which does not focus exclusively on genitalia and the need for a 'false member'.[31] Whereas the *Ovide moralisé*'s historical reading, its 'historial sentence', of the tale of Iphis and Ianthe concentrates on the resolution of a perceived lack in terms of genitalia, Christine's transformation, like that of Iphis in the *Metamorphoses*, involves a reconfiguration, a re-membering of the entire surface of the body and the way it moves through space: Christine is transformed by touch while Iphis's transition is interpreted via a reading of his gait. Gender, in other words, is dispersed all over the surface of the body, rather than specifically localised at various points on that body. The emphasis is more on the sensory embodied experience of a subject, and less on the visual perception of a body by others. In *La Mutacion de Fortune* Christine de Pizan presents an image of sexuality and gender which is written through touch, on the surface of the body and on the surface of the page.

Acknowledgment

I would like to thank Blake Gutt for his extremely helpful comments on an earlier draft of this essay.

NOTES

1. References are to *Le Livre de la Mutacion de Fortune*, ed. Solente; line numbers are given parenthetically in the text. Translations are my own, taken from the version in Appendix C.
2. 'Christine's narrator aims, in part 1, to trace his [sic] own development as author of the present book, following the death of his husband' (Mills, *Seeing Sodomy*, p. 122). Thompson, 'Medea', also uses masculine pronouns to refer to the narrator-character in the *Mutacion*.
3. See Ouy, Reno and Villela-Petit, *Album Christine de Pizan*, p. 17.
4. As Nora Ephron opined, 'I've noticed, over the years, that the words "thinly disguised" are applied mostly to books written by women' (*Heartburn*, Kindle edition).
5. A similar convention is often adopted by scholars writing on the distinction between author and narrator in the texts of Guillaume de Machaut (c. 300–1377), whose work also engages with Ovidian material, and who was an influence on Pizan's *oeuvre*.
6. Fenster, '"Perdre son latin"'.
7. References are to *Ovide moralisé*, ed. C. de Boer (*OM*); and Ovid, *Metamorphoses*, trans. Miller, rev. Goold (*Met.*), hereafter given in parentheses in the body of the essay. Translations from the Iphis and Ianthe section of the *Ovide moralisé* are taken from the translation in Appendix A; translations of other sections of the *Ovide moralisé* are my own; translations from the *Metamorphoses* are taken from Miller (with occasional silent emendations for context).
8. Delisle, *Recherches*, vol. 2, p. 174. On the *Ovide moralisé* in Charles' library, see Griffin, 'Imagining Ovid and Chrétien'.
9. Pintabone, 'Ovid's Iphis and Ianthe', pp. 268–9.
10. In the *Metamorphoses*, Iphis's is the most detailed telling of this story; in the *Ovide moralisé*, a glancing reference to it by Scylla in Book 8 of the *Metamorphoses* (8: 136–7) is amplified into a graphic account of the various ways in which Pasiphaë wooed the bull. This culminates in the narrator exclaiming over the wonder Pasiphaë felt when beholding the bull's 'vit' ('penis', 8: 765), and then issuing a fulsome apology for having uttered such an offensive word (see Armstrong and Kay, *Knowing Poetry*, pp. 84–5). It is worth noting that the *Ovide moralisé* narrator shows no such compunction in the next book, where the historical interpretation of the Iphis story relates that Iphis' mother betrothed her daughter to a woman, 'Tout n'eüst elle point de vit' ('even though she had no penis', 9: 3130).
11. On truth and fiction in the *Mutacion*, see Griffin, 'Transforming Fortune'; and Blumenfeld-Kosinski, *Reading Myth*, pp. 178–9.
12. See Blumenfeld-Kosinski, *Reading Myth*, pp. 178–9.
13. See Lechat, *'Dire par fiction'*, pp. 371–83; Kellogg, 'Transforming Ovid'; Kelly, *Christine de Pizan's Changing Opinion*, p. 96; Kay, 'Allegory and Melancholy'; Margolis, 'Christine de Pizan'; Huot, 'Seduction and Sublimation'; Desmond, *Reading Dido*, pp. 195–6.
14. See Harvey, 'Introduction', p. 2.
15. See Cerquiglini-Toulet, 'Fondements et fondations'; and Desmond, 'Introduction'.
16. My position is therefore distinct from Brownlee's in 'Widowhood' and Weisl's in 'The Widow as Virgin'. For a sensible account of sublimation and gender, see Huot, 'Seduction and Sublimation'.
17. See Kellogg, 'Transforming Ovid'.
18. See Brownlee, 'Ovide et le moi'.
19. See Pintabone, 'Ovid's Iphis and Ianthe', pp. 261–2.

20. Mills, *Seeing Sodomy*, pp. 126–8.
21. Mills, *Seeing Sodomy*, pp. 123–5. On this aspect of the story, see also McCracken's essay in this volume.
22. See Tarnowski, 'Maternity and Paternity', p. 119.
23. *Le Livre des fais et bonnes meurs*, 42
24. On Pizan's use of the myth of Circe, see Blumenfeld-Kosinski, *Reading Myth*, pp. 176–7.
25. See Griffin, *Transforming Tales*, pp. 142–5.
26. Mühlethaler, 'Entre amour et politique', p. 11.
27. Segal, *Consensuality*, p. 229.
28. Kay also offers insights into the connections between loss, allegory and Christine's *oeuvre* in 'Allegory and Melancholy'.
29. See Kellogg, 'Transforming Ovid'.
30. Christine de Pizan, *Le Livre de l'advision Cristine*, p. 110. Christine also depicts the senses as doors in the *Epistre Othéa*, p. 268. See Cerquiglini-Toulet, 'Le Schéma', p. 66.
31. As Segal comments, 'if the skin is the "leading organ" this makes it possible to think about bodily difference and individuation in a way that avoids the grosser gender presumptions of the penis-phallus, castration, and the rest', *Consensuality*, p. 56.

Bibliography

Armstrong, Adrian and Kay, Sarah, *Knowing Poetry in France: From the Rose to the Rhétoriqueurs* (Ithaca, NY and London: Cornell University Press, 2011).

Blumenfeld-Kosinski, Renate, *Reading Myth: Classical Mythology and Its Interpretation in Medieval French Literature* (Stanford: Stanford University Press, 1997).

Brownlee, Kevin, 'Ovide et le moi poétique "moderne" à la fin du moyen âge: Jean Froissart et Christine de Pizan', in Brigitte Cazelles and Charles Méla (eds), *Modernité au moyen âge: Le Défi du passé* (Geneva: Droz, 1990), pp. 153–73.

Brownlee, Kevin, 'Widowhood, Sexuality, and Gender in Christine de Pizan', *Romanic Review* 86, 1995, pp. 201–9.

Cerquiglini-Toulet, Jacqueline, 'Fondements et fondations de l'écriture chez Christine de Pizan: Scènes de lecture et scènes d'incarnation', in Margarete Zimmermann and Dina De Rentiis (eds), *The City of Scholars: New Approaches to Christine de Pizan* (Berlin: Walter de Gruyter, 1994), pp. 79–96.

Cerquiglini-Toulet, Jacqueline, 'Le Schéma des cinq sens, d'une théorie de la connaissance à la creation de formes littéraires', *I cinque sensi; The Five Senses, Micrologus*, 10, 2002, pp. 55–69.

Christine de Pizan, *Le Livre de la Mutacion de Fortune*, ed. Suzanne Solente, 4 vols (Paris: Picard, 1959).

Christine de Pizan, *Le Livre des fais et bonnes meurs du sage roy Charles V*, ed. Suzanne Solente, 2 vols (Paris: Champion, 1936).

Christine de Pizan, *Le livre de l'advision Cristine*, eds Christine Reno and Liliane Dulac (Paris: Champion, 2001).

Christine de Pizan, *Epistre Othéa*, ed. Gabriella Parusa (Geneva: Droz, 1997).

Delisle, Léopold, *Recherches sur la librairie de Charles V*, 2 vols (Paris: Champion, 1907).

Desmond, Marilynn, 'Introduction: From Book-Lined Cell to Cyborg Hermeneutics', in Marilynn Desmond (ed.), *Christine de Pizan and the Categories of Difference* (Minneapolis: University of Minnesota Press, 1998), pp. ix–xix.

Desmond, Marilynn, *Reading Dido: Gender, Textuality, and the Medieval Aeneid* (Minneapolis: University of Minnesota Press, 1994).
Ephron, Nora, *Heartburn* (London: Virago, 2008).
Fenster, Thelma, '"Perdre son latin": Christine de Pizan and Vernacular Humanism', in Marilynn Desmond (ed.), *Christine de Pizan and the Categories of Difference* (Minneapolis: University of Minnesota Press, 1998), pp. 91–107.
Griffin, Miranda, 'Imagining Ovid and Chrétien in Fourteenth-Century French Libraries', *French Studies*, 70, 2016 (Special Issue: The Medieval Library), pp. 201–15.
Griffin, Miranda, 'Transforming Fortune: Reading and Chance in Christine de Pizan's *Mutacion de Fortune* and *Chemin de long estude*', *Modern Language Review* 104, 2009, pp. 55–70.
Griffin, Miranda, *Transforming Tales: Rewriting Metamorphosis in Medieval French Literature* (Oxford: Oxford University Press, 2015).
Harvey, Elizabeth D., 'Introduction: The "Sense of All Senses"', in Elizabeth D. Harvey (ed.), *Sensible Flesh: On Touch in Early Modern Culture* (Philadelphia: University of Pennsylvania Press, 2003), pp. 1–21.
Huot, Sylvia, 'Seduction and Sublimation: Christine de Pizan, Jean de Meun and Dante', *Romance Notes* 25, 1985, pp. 361–73.
Kay, Sarah, 'Allegory and Melancholy in Luce Irigaray, Julia Kristeva and Christine de Pizan', in Gesche Ipsen, Timothy Mathews and Dragana Obradovic (eds), *Provocation and Negotiation: Essays in Contemporary Criticism* (Amsterdam; New York: Rodopi, 2013), pp. 125–40.
Kellogg, Judith L., 'Transforming Ovid: The Metamorphosis of Female Authority', in Marilynn Desmond (ed.), *Christine de Pizan and the Categories of Difference* (Minneapolis: University of Minnesota Press, 1998), pp. 181–94.
Kelly, Douglas, *Christine de Pizan's Changing Opinion: A Quest for Certainty in the Midst of Chaos* (Woodbridge: Boydell & Brewer, 2007).
Lechat, Didier, *'Dire par fiction': Métamorphoses du je chez Guillaume de Machaut, Jean Froissart et Christine de Pizan* (Paris: Champion, 2005).
Margolis, Nadia, 'Christine De Pizan: The Poetess as Historian', *Journal of the History of Ideas* 47, 1986, pp. 361–75.
Mills, Robert, *Seeing Sodomy in the Middle Ages* (Chicago: University of Chicago Press, 2015).
Mühlethaler, Jean-Claude, 'Entre amour et politique: métamorphoses ovidiennes à la fin du Moyen Âge', *Cahiers de recherches médiévales* 9, 2002, DOI: 10.4000/crm.76 (last accessed 21 March 2017).
Ouy, Gilbert, Reno, Christine and Villela-Petit, Inés, *Album Christine de Pizan* (Turnhout: Brepols, 2012).
Ovid, *Metamorphoses*, trans. Frank Justus Miller, rev. G. P. Goold (Cambridge, MA and London: Loeb Classical Library, Harvard University Press).
Ovide moralisé: Poème du commencement du quatorzième siècle, ed. C. de Boer and others, *Verhandelingen der Koninklijke Akademie van Wetenschapaen te Amsterdam, Afdeeling Letterkunde* 15 (1915) (Books 1–3), 21 (1920) (Books 4–6), 30 (1931) (Books 7–9), 37 (1936) (Books 10–13), 43 (1938) (Books 14–15 and appendices).
Pintabone, Diane T., 'Ovid's Iphis and Ianthe: When Girls Won't Be Girls', in Nancy Sorkin Rabinowitz and Lisa Auanger (eds), *Among Women: From the Homosocial to the Homoerotic in the Ancient World* (Austin: University of Texas Press, 2002), pp. 256–85.
Segal, Naomi, *Consensuality: Didier Anzieu, Gender and the Sense of Touch* (Amsterdam and New York: Rodopi, 2009).

Tarnowski, Andrea, 'Maternity and Paternity in *La Mutacion de Fortune*', in Margarete Zimmermann and Dina De Rentiis (ed.), *The City of Scholars: New Approaches to Christine de Pizan* (Berlin: Walter de Gruyter, 1994), pp. 116–26.

Thompson, John Jay, 'Medea in Christine De Pizan's *Mutacion de Fortune*, Or How To Be a Better Mother', *Forum for Modern Language Studies* 35, 1999, pp. 158–74.

Weisl, Angela Jane, 'The Widow as Virgin: Desexualized Narrative in Christine de Pizan's *Livre de la cité des dames*', in Cindy L. Carlson and Angela Jane Weisl (eds), *Constructions of Widowhood and Virginity in the Middle Ages* (London: Macmillan, 1999), pp. 49–62.

5

BECOMING SCATTERED: THE CASE OF IPHIS'S TRANS*VERSION AND THE ARCHIPELOGIC OF JOHN FLORIO'S *WORLDE OF WORDES*

Marjorie Rubright

Trans*

The year 2014 marked the publication of the inaugural issue of *Transgender Studies Quarterly* (or *TSQ*). Its editors, Susan Stryker and Paisley Currah, set out on a lexicographic venture providing readers with a two-volume dictionary of keywords for the recently institutionalised field of transgender studies. Between its covers, the lexical entries, each uniquely authored, range from critically current keywords in gender and sexuality studies (cross-dresser, identity, intersex, performativity) to an as yet less critically varnished vocabulary (capacity, error, handmade, monster, somatechnics). But it was an entry for something other than a word that most captured my attention: the entry for 'asterisk'.

There has always been something queer about the asterisk. Both word and thing, it operates 'as a wildcard character', according to the entry's author, Avery Tompkins.[1] Its use among queer communities, Tompkins argues, emerged from the use of asterisks in computing language to designate an open-ended search. If we enter 'trans' plus asterisk (trans*) into a search engine, our results yield any word beginning with trans. Figured as *TSQ**, the journal mobilises the asterisk in its logo as a symbol of this open-ended search in the field of transgender studies and, as the journal's editors explain, a 'gesture toward the inherently unfinishable combinatorial work of the *trans-* prefix'.[2]

What does it mean to put the asterisk to bodies? Lingering at the edge of *TSQ* the asterisk reminds us that thinking 'trans' entails holding open, even moving between, at least three perspectives onto sexed and gendered embodiment. The first is binary and oppositional; male and female are held apart as the work of the prefix *trans* performs a conveyance across a difference that it also insistently punctuates. This, we might say, is the conventional etymological work of trans: a prefix derived from the Latin preposition meaning 'across, through, over, to or on the other side of, beyond, outside of, from one place, person, thing, or state to another'.[3] In other words, trans conveys. The second meaning of trans (let's imagine this as trans- hyphen) operates as a live circuitry animating the possibilities between; in this instance, MTF and FTM are not only identities that challenge the male-female binary, but processes that emphasise becoming, transformation, metamorphosis, conversion. Trans- lives in a shifting current, flowing both ways between the shores of M and F, eroding the sharp edges of categorical distinction between male and female. Trans- disrupts divisions. Thirdly, trans* (with an asterisk) scatters our attention beyond the M/F binary. Trans* both confounds the directionality of trans (from one to another) and exceeds the circuitry of trans-. 'That trans is agitation, operation, locomotion, localisation and action underscores how trans* troubles ontological states', Eva Hayward and Jami Weinstein argue; trans* 'is moving mattering'.[4] Trans* jams the teleology of ontological conversion across kind (trans: one then another) to make possible an epistemological engagement with the 'inherently unfinishable combinatorial work of the trans prefix'.[5] Trans* multiplies.[6]

Now move the asterisk around. Place it in the middle of a word and suddenly it becomes a hypothesis. For instance, consider S*X. Multiple possibilities surface in the mind: sex, six, sox, sax; and we may hear others: sux (sucks). For the queer philologist, Jeffrey Masten, the asterisk signals not only the multiplicity of potential semantic meanings resident in S*X but raises to the surface the matter of the interpreter's hermeneutics. S*X asks me: to experience my own interpretive biases in meaning-making (why do I see 'sex' first? does what I see first establish itself as primary in my list of other possibilities?); to confront my own skills for solving the question (is sax really a word? have I missed anything?); to experience *jouissance* or discomfort when I do not arrive at any one solution with certainty (should I even be trying to solve this?). S*X is less a puzzle to solve than an invitation for play, one that generates and turns on the interpreter's self-scrutiny.[7] In this way, asterisks make us aware of our own interpretive promiscuity and its parameters.

What does it mean to put the asterisk to language? Asterisks themselves are a promiscuous form of punctuation finding their way into all kinds of company. In early modern dictionaries, to which I will turn momentarily, the asterisk served as a mark of barbarousness, unmasking foreign words in drag as natives. The Letter to the Reader in John Rider's *Dictionarie* of 1612 concludes: 'For the Dictionary Etymologicall. First note, (besides that which is already noted in the Epistle to the Reader) that in the first part, those words

> For the Dictionary Etymologicall. First note,(besides that which is already noted in the Epistle to the Reader) that in the first part, those wordes which haue this marke * are barbarous, and crept in thither by chance.

Figure 5.1 John Rider, *Riders dictionarie corrected* (1612). RB 302497, The Huntington Library, San Marino, California.

which have this marke * are barbarous, and crept in thither by chance' (Figure 5.1).[8]

There are many layers of irony in Rider's purist impulse to police the very linguistic borrowings that give rise to his lexicographic enterprise, not the least of which is that 'barbarous' itself is a term 'crept in [to English] by chance'. If * marks the spot of illicit linguistic border-crossing in Rider's *Dictionarie*, then in John Bullokar's *English Expositor* (1616), which offers interpretations of the 'hardest words in our language', the asterisk marks literary archaisms, or words 'onely used of some ancient writers, and nowe growne out of use'.[9] Here, the asterisk casts a long shadow over the life of language, serving as a gravestone to the dead or dying. Though Bullokar's intention is to mark a word's decay in current discourse ('growne out of use'), the asterisk's energy – the difference it introduces on the page – may, conversely, encourage a word's resurrection and revival. Reading against the grain, the dictionary reader who scans the page for asterisks wittingly conveys herself back in time in an effort to rediscover (even relish) the strangeness of the past materialised in the present. Against its stated purpose, Bullokar's asterisk aids readers in plucking words from the fallow ground of literary archaism to plant them anew on the tip of their tongues, as many Renaissance poets and antiquarians were keen to do. Like 'barbarians', asterisks are as likely to go astray of boundaries as they are to demarcate them.

As a symbol that footnotes*, or as marker of difference within a list (violets, chrysanthemums, peonies, *paperclips), the asterisk points beyond the word it accompanies, directing attention to some supplement elsewhere: the footnote, the caveat, the alternative gloss. Curious and curiosity-inducing, asterisks are queer cousins among their punctuating kin. They are indefinitive. They don't stop meaning (.), or give it pause (,), raise questions (?), convey emotion (!), bridge ideas (;), join words (-) or send a thought trailing off (. . .).[10] Instead, inviting substitutions, suggesting expansions, signalling alternative possibilities, marking the strangeness of the foreign or the past resident within, and insistently encouraging interpretive reorientations, the asterisk *scatters* our orientation onto bodies, language and texts.

If *TSQ* introduces a lexicon for transgender studies both by way of introducing new vocabulary and repurposing old signs (*) it is not because dictionaries strike today's readers as inherently sexed territory. In 1598, however, with the publication of John Florio's *A Worlde of Wordes*, dictionaries were understood as sexed objects.[11] They might be male, female or/and trans; so too their genealogies and legacies were decidedly queer, as we'll discover in the stories of Bacchus and Iphis that feature centrally in the prefatory framework of Florio's dictionary. Before heading to market, Florio's text – the first Italian–English bilingual dictionary published in England and, at the time, the most monumental lexicographic accomplishment to date in the English language – would undergo a sex change: from female to male. This essay explores the ontological and epistemological conversions that transpire as Florio turns, first, to the Ovidian myth of Bacchus and then to the story of Iphis and Ianthe for embodied analogues by which he imagines his dictionary's sex transition. Ultimately the story of Iphis directs Florio's attention beyond linguistic and somatic matters of transformation and toward the terrestrial landscape of his Italian ancestry, the Aegean archipelago known as the Sporades. In his effort to imagine an answer to an implicit question – if dictionaries were embodied, what forms would they take? – the lexicographer asks his readers not only to imagine the possibility that a dictionary might change its sex, but that, in so doing, it might also find its most apt analogue in the terrestrial sphere: the dictionary as archipelago.

In what follows, I trace the linguistic, somatic and terrestrial figures through which Florio imagines his *Worlde of Wordes* in an effort to illuminate the various ways of thinking about metamorphosis and conversion that they effect. Moving between thinking trans, trans- and trans*, our early modern dictionary-maker imagines his way toward solving a problem central to his lexicographic enterprise: its culturally effeminised copiousness. Florio puts the asterisk to his *Worlde of Wordes* in an effort to conceptualise and lend new cultural value to what it meant to traffic in language. The story of Iphis and Ianthe proves the fulcrum around which Florio's thinking – particularly his movement from thinking trans- to trans* – turns. The story generates a productive mode of scattered thinking onto/about/across both human and terrestrial bodies. Implicit in Florio's progression through thinking trans, trans- and trans* is a proposition: that becoming scattered makes possible the fullest representational expression of and interpretive engagement with the ontological paradoxes and epistemological puzzles to which Iphis's story gives rise.

A WORLDE OF WORDES

A self-described 'English Man in Italian', living and working in London, John Florio was a French and Italian language tutor turned lexicographer who, shortly after the publication of his dictionary, secured his place in English literary history with his translation of Michel de Montaigne's *Essais* (1603).[12] *A Worlde of Wordes* is of significant historical importance as it was the

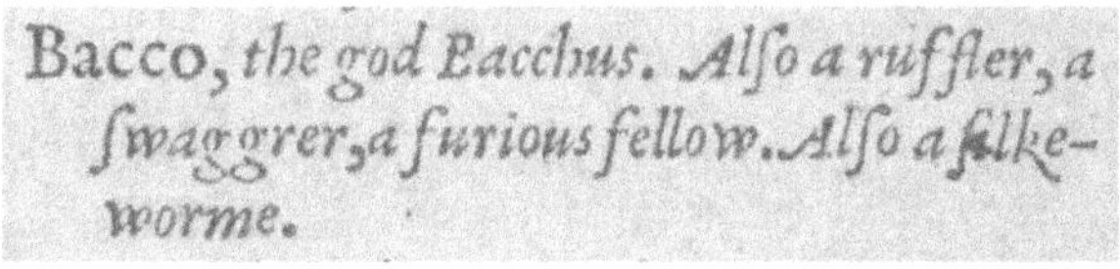

> Bacco, *the god Bacchus. Also a ruffler, a swaggrer, a furious fellow. Also a silkeworme.*

Figure 5.2   John Florio, *A Worlde of Wordes* (1598). RB 59838, The Huntington Library, San Marino, California.

first attempt at a comprehensive bilingual Italian–English dictionary in the Renaissance and, at the time of its publication, offered the single largest compilation of the English language in any dictionary on the European market.[13] Throughout his dedicatory epistle, Florio dwells on a problem arising from the gendered body of his dictionary. It risks, he fears, running ashore of the period's disparaging associations of linguistic copiousness with femininity. As Patricia Parker has demonstrated, in the sixteenth and seventeenth centuries in England, 'manliness of style is described as inseparable from manliness of body and manner'.[14] Plain, restrained style – what Parker characterises as 'virile style' – free from the imported flourishes of foreign tongues was regularly juxtaposed to the loquacity of eloquence and its attendant association with the female sex. The problem is pressing for Florio since copiousness is precisely what is on display, for sale and enabled by his dictionary. With 46,000 Italian headwords matched with thousands more words in the English glosses, the work is indeed all words.[15] Even proper nouns are copiously defined, as we witness in the entry for Bacchus: 'Bacco, *the god Bacchus. Also a ruffler, a swaggrer* [sic], *a furious fellow. Also a silkeworme*' (Fig. 5.2).[16]

The dictionary runs counter not only to Renaissance valorisations of masculine, restrained, 'virile style', but also to classical celebrations of (masculine) deeds above (feminine) words.[17] For these reasons, Florio worries that the body of his book is potentially scandalous.

Three implicit questions about embodiment shape the arc of Florio's epistle: how to imagine the body of a bilingual speaker (the problem of two in one); how to conceive of the bodies of language that a single speaker sets into relation (translation from one into another); and, most urgently, how to fashion the enterprise of compiling a world of words into the body of a single book (the multiple as one). Each of these questions animate different tensions between singularity and multiplicity in the sphere of language and compel Florio to explore different possibilities for thinking trans, trans- and trans* across linguistic embodiment(s). Throughout his epistle, Florio turns to Ovid to ponder these queer configurations of embodiment (two in one, one into another, multiple as one). In Florio's imagination, Ovid dramatises dilemmas of embodiment-in-metamorphosis whose varied processes of conversion (horticultural grafting, transgendering and terrestrial scattering) offer useful corollaries to a lexicographer bent on lending positive value to his philological enterprise.

TRANSPLANTATION: GRAFTING BACCHUS

Prior to *A Worlde of Wordes*, Florio published two bilingual Italian–English dialogue books entitled *Firste Fruites* and *Second Frutes* [sic].[18] Comparing these earlier ventures to his dictionary, Florio writes:

> Now where my rawer youth brought foorth these female fruites, my riper yeers affording me I cannot say a braine-babe, *Minerva*, armed at al [sic] assaies at first houre; but rather from my Italian *Semele*, and English thigh, a bouncing boie, *Bacchus*-like, almost all names.[19]

Even by Ovidian standards, as myths of generation go the births of Minerva and Bacchus are remarkable. Minerva, cleaved from Jove's head, springs fully formed and armed for battle, while Bacchus is violently uprooted from Semele's womb and grafted to Jove's thigh. Bacchus is later 'twice-born' when Jove unseams his son into the world. In an effort to re-gender his life's work, Florio replaces the feminised fruits of his past linguistic productions with a vision of masculine futurity. As the story of Bacchus conveys, this future depends upon a fantasy of divine, male sexual reproductivity that itself depends on the art of husbandry.

Lionised as England's talented grafter, Florio's linguistic productions had long been celebrated in horticultural terms. He is lauded as 'The Graffer FLORIO' in the prefatory encomia of his *Firste Fruites*.[20] T. C. '*in commendation of Florio his first Fruites*' imagines Florio as a botanist who 'settes the slips in English lande, / Of *Tuscane* tongue, to spring and stande'.[21] Good grammar instruction and good husbandry were often analogised in humanist education,[22] even as the conceit of grafting languages onto human stock produced unsettling figurations of embodiment.[23] Bilingualism is 'straunge' because of its two-in-oneness. R. H. Gent explores bilingualism as a paradox of embodiment in his poem, '*in commendation of* the Authours wel imployed tyme', which appears at the opening of Florio's *Firste Fruites*:

> If it were straunge, one selfe same necke should beare
> two sundry heades, and faces more then one:
> It was as straunge, one selfe same head should weare
> two sundry hornes, where Nature grafted none.
> And is more straunge, to see one selfe same face,
> Two sundry tongues, and speaches to imbrace.[24]

In the first two lines of this stanza, bilingualism is imagined as the bifurcation of features of human embodiment that are usually considered distinctly singular: one neck, two heads; one face, two tongues. The final two lines reinforce the notion that bilingualism doubles the self-same by splitting it. Sandwiched between these estranging images, an altogether more perplexing portrait of the bilingual speaker emerges: one who exhibits doubleness where 'nature grafted none'. Taken together, one plus one does not yield two; cross-sex pollination is nowhere in evidence. Instead, the queer arithmetic of bilingualism either yields two from one (division), or two 'where Nature grafted none' (a compounding of nothing that somehow yields double).

In Florio's account, Bacchus's story stands in both for Florio's own professional transition from grammar instruction to lexicographic production and for Italian–English bilingualism in the figure of the 'grafted' child.[25] This is neither a happy image of Italian–English doubleness nor a celebratory veneration of autochthonous bilingualism. Alternatively, as a drama of bilingual reproduction, Bacchus's birth implicitly conveys a violent effacing of the feminine foreign origins of the lexicographer's Italian roots. We recall that Bacchus is 'twice-born' from Jove's thigh because his mother, in whose womb he began his gestation, has died; Semele is destroyed in the act of sexual consummation with Jove.[26] In an Ovidian context, 'my italian Semele' is not a counterpart to Florio-as-Jove's 'English thigh'. Rather, Semele is all but faintly re-membered there. Indeed, it is more apt to say that she is dis-membered, as the son she never bears is grafted to a divine, male body that stands, in this instance, for 'Englishness' in the form of the English language.

Through a set of associations, the story of Bacchus renders once feminine fruits (mothers / wombs / Italians / foreigners / mortals / grammar instruction) destroyed as the act of generation is *trans*ferred to the father / thigh / English / native / divine / lexicography. Bacchus-as-graft stages a transfantasy of unidirectional, irreversible ontological conversion. Florio's Bacchus embodies a fantasy of linguistic translation that valorises not the shifting back and forth of a reader's engagement with Italian and English (precisely the movement that Florio's own dictionary makes possible), but an uprooting and transplantation that enriches masculine English lexicography and hollows out feminine Italian ground.

Trans-gendering: The Case of Iphis

This veneration of masculine English lexicography (Jove) over feminine Italian grammar instruction (Semele) does not resolve Florio's larger problem: that the very copiousness of his lexicographic practice was negatively associated with effeminacy. The problem is not simply that Florio traffics in the wrong words (foreign / feminine / Italian). The trouble is he trafficks only in words. In his epistle, Florio therefore worries that his work will be mistaken for the 'female' sex:

> Some perhaps will except against the sexe, and not allowe it for a male-broode, sithens [*sic*] as our Italians saie, *Le Parole sono femine, e i fatti*

sono maschij. Wordes they are women, and deeds they are men. But let such know that *Detti* and *fatti*, words and deeds with me are all of one gender. And though they were commonly Feminine, why might not I by strong imagination . . . alter their sexe?[27]

With this question, Florio's text opens onto the Ovidian tale of Iphis: 'Or at least by such heaven-pearcing devotion as transformed *Iphis*, according to that description of the Poet.'[28] If Iphis can grow more virile in her style then why might not Florio's dictionary do so too? On its face, Iphis seems the perfect Ovidian analogue for Florio's project of altering the sex of his wordbook from female to male. If words are feminine, then – like Iphis, the once girl made boy – so too might they 'alter their sex', thereby transforming *A Worlde of Wordes* into a masculine project and pursuit.[29] But the story of Iphis, as the essays throughout this collection demonstrate, was never simply a story of transformation so much as a story of trans*version.

In bringing Iphis's story to bear on his lexicographical project, Florio turns to Giovanni Andrea dell'Anguillara's *Le metamorfosi di Ovidio*,[30] an Italian (Tuscan) translation of Ovid's *Metamorphoses* first published in 1561. As he translates Anguillara's text into English, he presents his readers with a single stanza that captures the moment of Iphis's metamorphosis:

> Feeling more vigor in each part and strength
> Then earst, and that indeede she was a boy.
> Towards hir mother eies and wordes at length
> She turns, and at the temple with meeke joy
> He and his nurse and mother utter how
> The case fell out, and so he paid his vow.[31]

Florio's pronouns amplify paradoxes of embodiment animated by Iphis's story. First, as a girl-dressed-as-a-boy, Iphis begins to 'feel' an increased 'vigor' in her body's parts. What's new at this moment, in Florio's account, is not the outward expression of Iphis's gender identity (after all, from her birth onward she has convincingly played the seeming boy); rather, Iphis's affective responses to her gender expression change at the temple. She begins to *feel* like a boy. That is, she feels as if she 'was a boy' because she feels as boys do: vigorous. Had Florio concluded his Ovidian story thus, Iphis might indeed have served as an emblem of ontological conversion (from female to male embodiment): 'she was a boy' might be taken to mean that she now *is* a boy, as her outward expression of gender (all along boyish) aligns with a new sense of internally felt and outwardly expressed vigour. And yet, this somatic and affective correspondence is fleeting. At the very moment when the text seems most poised to crystalise an ontological conversion in the form of a narrative of transformation across binary difference ('indeede she was a boy'), Iphis is shuttled apace back and forth across male and female pronouns, effectively unweaving the conviction of Florio's declarative, 'indeede'. As the vigorous 'boy', 'she' turns toward 'hir' mother. 'She turns' again as 'he' when, together with mother and nurse, 'he . . . utter[s] how the case fell out, and so he paide his vow'. If the story of Iphis is precedent – an analogue for Florio's dictionary's sex change – then it is all the more striking that, at the very moment when Iphis's ontological metamorphosis is dramatised, the reader discovers herself engaged not with questions of the ontological (has the sex transition occurred?), but the epistemological instead. What do we think we see?

For the reader alive to the movement of FTM, MTF and back again, the story of Iphis is a *trans*-narrative. Florio's account is decidedly not unidirectional (from F *toward* M: trans), but instead animates the circuitry of the hyphen, conveying both Iphis and the reader back and forth across the quick-shifting currents of somatic and grammatical conversion. Perhaps we imagine that Iphis's sexed embodiment shifts with every pronoun change. Or, perhaps, the back and forth of pronouns suggests conversion is processural, not instantaneous. There is yet another interpretative possibility. For the readers who begin to see both at once – male and female – in Florio's grammar and syntax, this scene presents us with a *trans** story: a story of trans*version that captures this concept's neither here-nor-there and both-at-once kineticism.

As Valerie Traub remarks in the Introduction to this collection, transversion is a term that comes into English during the Renaissance. In his *Glossographia* of 1656, Thomas Blount introduces the word for the first time in the history of English lexicography: 'Transversion [*transversio*] a turning away or crosse, a traversing, or going athwart'.[32] It is this final gloss – 'going athwart'– that best captures the epistemological effects of attempting to arrive at any ontological certainty about the sexed embodiment of Florio's Iphis. As a figure of trans*version, Iphis both thwarts attempts to pin down his/her ontological embodiment and unsettles epistemological conviction regarding what and how we see this body. About Florio's Iphis, we might simply say that 'indeed she *is* a boy'.

In important ways, the back-and-forth movement between gender pronouns in Florio's version of this story is an effect of conveying Iphis's story into the English language. Florio puts the asterisk to Iphis's body by way of exploiting restrictions inherent to English. In Ovid's Latin, Heather James reminds us, 'the very last words of *Metamorphoses* Book 9 home in on the still open question of gender translation: *potiturque sua peur Iphis Ianthe* (line 797)'.[33] In Latin

> the feminine possessive adjective, *sua,* attaches to the direct object (Ianthe) regardless of the gender of the subject (Iphis) of the sentence. Only in English are readers required to make a choice between trans-

lating the possessive as 'his' or 'her': in Latin, there is active and fully appropriate ambiguity.[34]

In Anguillara's Italian translation, from which Florio drew his account of Iphis's story, a somewhat different ambiguity arises in the final lines of Book 9: 'E col favor de l'arme elette, e sante, / Ifi godè fatt'huom la bella Iante' ['with the blessing of the elect and holy souls, Iphi[s] took pleasure of the fair Iante made man'].[35] Strictly speaking, the Italian grammar of this line leaves open the question of whether the subject or object of the sentence has been 'made man'.[36] The metamorphic event – 'fatt'huom' ('made man') – is suspended mid-line between the verb ('godè' [took pleasure]) and its object, thus emphasising the drama of the conclusion without definitively resolving the ontological question of whether Iphis is indeed now a man. Florio's Englished Iphis differs from these Latin and Italian textual antecedents in an important way. By shifting between Iphis's gendered grammatical coordinates, Florio Englishes the grammatical ambiguities resident in Ovid's Latin and Anguillara's Italian by way of encouraging the reader to experience contradictory fixations (she *then* he *then* she; or s/he) in making sense of Iphis's case. By way of Englishing Iphis's story, Florio turns ontological questions about sexed embodiment into epistemological ones.

Crucially, Iphis emerges as something other than a figure of ambiguity in Florio's 'strong imagination'. If ambiguity is a wavering doubt and uncertainty in the mind of the interpreter then, in this instance, uncertainty pertains to an open ontological question: what is Iphis's sex? No doubt, Florio's story of Iphis raises this question. But this uncertainty is not the limit of the epistemological effect of Florio's Englished Iphis. Florio in fact offers a direct, albeit paradoxical, answer to the ontological quandary of Iphis's sex: 'indeed she was a boy'. Translated out of Latin and Italian into English, Iphis emerges grammatically as a figure of paradox. The epistemological puzzle is no longer limited to the question of which sex we think we see (as it is for any translator attempting to convey Latin 'sua' into English). More, the interpreter must now face a new challenge of holding all possibilities in mind simultaneously: she then he; she and he (both and); neither fully she nor he (not quite one or the other).

Another English version of the Iphis story with which Florio was surely familiar was Arthur Golding's English translation of 1567. Golding's complete *Ovid's Metamorphoses* was republished regularly throughout Florio's writing life in London (1575, 1584, 1587, 1593, 1603 and 1612). In his epistle, Florio telescopes what in Golding's translation is narrated step by step and part by part. In Golding, each somatic part of Iphis is transformed as s/he leaves the temple and runs after her beloved, Ianthe:

> And Iphis followed after her with larger pace than aye
> She was accustomed, and her face continued not so white.

> Her strength increased, and her look more shaper was to sight.
> Her hair grew shorter, and she had a much more lively sprite
> Than when she was a wench.[37]

Here, Iphis's strides grow longer, hair shorter, face darker, even her style sharpens as s/he grows more virile. Strikingly, there is a missing part in this story, a part that seems not to partake of all this trans-formation. Does Iphis undergo a sex transition here? What of her genitals? Her breasts? Are we to imagine, as Florio explicitly does, that Iphis's 'case' falls out? Or, before our eyes, is she now passing – being passed by Golding and by the reader – in new ways? Golding's account ignites a key interpretive question: as readers, are we witness to an ontological transformation or experiencing an epistemological trans*ition that situates us as in-the-know, learning, step by step, how to see both at once, male and female?

In Florio's account, Iphis's final metamorphosis is conveyed by way of a single word: case. The word 'case' provides a masterful pun at this moment in the story. It comes into English via French (*caas*), from the past participle of 'to fall' in Latin (*cāsus*).[38] In its colloquial sense 'how the case fell out' simply means 'how something happened'. A case refers broadly to a situation, or a position, as it still does today. Case was also a bawdy pun for female genitalia.[39] Florio's pun suggests that a metamorphosis of Iphis's sexed embodiment has transpired, at least as it might have been imagined within the Galenic humoral system. Understood to be imperfect men, women's sexed bodies may experience conversions that transform them *into* men: the woman's case, her sexual organs, may 'fall out', transforming her into a man (or, alternatively, into a woman with the 'part' of a man).[40] Understood in this framework, Iphis's story might be understood as one of sex *trans*formation: female to male.

And yet the dictionary (for which Iphis serves as analogue) is not constrained by the processes and practices of translation – the conversion of one language *into* another. Florio's primary concern is not with human embodiment per se but with bodies of language. As such, the book encourages readers to hold side by side Italian and English, both at once, as we also move back and forth between headword and gloss. By way of a grammatical pun on 'case', Florio converts the Iphis story from one of transformation to one of trans-formation. The pun works in this way: unlike Latin – the language of the original source text – as well as Italian, English does not retain a strong sense of marked grammatical case. The case, in grammar, is the form of a noun (or pronoun) telling us about its grammatical function in a sentence. The case tells the story of a sentence's relational dynamics. As Iphis's story is translated out of Latin into Italian, and then out of Italian into English, its grammatical cases indeed fall out. In the English language, Iphis is evacuated of grammatical case. Through this triple entendre on 'case' (its situational, embodied and grammatical registers) the lexicographer holds the linguistic at the centre of the portrait of Iphis's trans-formation. Florio translates Iphis's transgendering by way of a pun on case that amplifies interpretive pressure on the question of how the reader thinks 'trans'.

Thus far, I have been arguing that the Iphis story dramatises an epistemological shift in Florio's epistle, from thinking in terms of oppositions that require translation and transition (Italian vs English, Semele vs Jove, words vs things, feminine vs masculine, grammar instruction vs lexicography, copiousness vs plain, virile style), to thinking with and through trans-itions as movements that might run both ways (feminine then masculine, and back again; cases falling out), to thinking trans* (both-and as well as neither-nor: 'indeed she was a boy'). In short, Iphis has exceeded – s/he has gone 'athwart' of – Florio's explicit agenda for her.

In so doing, Iphis emerges more as an avatar for Florio's readers than for his book. The point of Florio's dictionary, after all, was not simply to offer Italian speakers in London an opportunity to translate Italian into English. Rather, the bilingual dictionary was primarily marketed to and popular with English-speaking readers who, in an effort to learn better Italian, would have moved back and forth between Italian and English as they read. Linguistically speaking, to see both at once (Italian and English) side by side in Florio's *Worlde of Wordes* is to experience doubleness: two tongues present together on the page. So too, readers experienced multiplicity within singularity (that is, English to English equivalents). Practically speaking, in Florio's *Worlde*, single Italian headwords often do not yield single equivalent glosses (or synonyms) in English. Instead, the reader is invited to peruse a multiplicity of correspondents in English (as with the entry for *Bacco* in Figure 5.2, above). In Florio's *Worlde*, one yields many.

As the largest compilation of the English language on the dictionary market, Florio's work was no doubt engaged by some readers 'athwart': reading only in English, thereby transforming the bilingual dictionary into a study of English-to-English equivalents. Florio asks his readers to think the many-in-one both at the level of word entries and at the level of his larger lexicographic project. The reader's attention is not directed or directional so much as it is scattered about, promiscuously 'going athwart' of the more conventional task of unidirectional translation. In other words, *A Worlde of Wordes* primes its readers – both by way of inviting engagements with multiplicity and by way of connecting the body of the dictionary to the epistemological dilemmas animated by the story of Iphis – to think trans*. In the third and final movement of his epistle, Florio imagines this epistemological challenge in terms of a process of 'scattering'.

Trans*version: Becoming Scattered

Having turned to Iphis to underwrite the sex-conversion of his dictionary (however imperfect the results), Florio takes up the challenge, lingering in the story's background, to explore ways of thinking with, through and about multiplicity itself. And fittingly so, since multiplicity is at the core of a lexicographer's dilemma and craft: how to gather up, organise and make sense of the world of words and the ever-evolving polysemy of their meanings. The figure of Isis – the goddess who first spared Iphis's life and to whom her mother later prays on the evening before the wedding to Ianthe – informs how Florio takes up this challenge. There is no overt mention of Isis in Florio's epistle. She is, however, a spectral presence, heralded through address at the temple. She is the audience of the prayer and the divine agent of intervention in Iphis's trans*version. As such, she is the corollary to Florio's 'strong imagination'.

In addition to learning the story of Isis by way of Golding's *Ovid's Metamorphoses*, Florio may have read Plutarch's account of the myth, which Susanne Wofford characterises as an 'extraordinary syncretic and imaginative rethinking of the myth of Isis and Osiris in his essay of that name'; Plutarch's essay was 'widely available in Latin and in French by the second half of the sixteenth century even before it was translated in 1603 into English by Philemon Holland.'[41] In it, Isis is a figure of both doubleness and multiplicity. Hers is not a story limited to self-metamorphosis; rather, she is catalytic of generation itself:

> They say also that *Isis* (which is no other thing but generation) lieth with him; and so they name the Moone, Mother of the world; saying that she is a double nature, male and female: female, in that she doth conceive and is replenished by the Sunne: and male, in this regard, that she sendeth forth and sprinkleth in the aire, the seeds and principles of generation.
>
> For *Isis* is the feminine part of nature, apt to receive all generation [. . .] yea and the common sort name her *Myrionymus*, which is as much to say, as having an infinite number of names, for that she receiveth all forms and shapes, according as it pleaseth that first reason to convert and turn her.[42]

Isis is a paragon of shape shifting, even among the Gods. A figure of 'double nature' whose 'infinite number of names' (μυριώνυμος in Greek) signals her capacity for generating and taking on 'all forms and shapes', Isis is 'Mother of the World'. As both male and female, s/he is 'generation' itself: a 'moving mattering' that also moves other matter ('sprinkleth' even the air with 'seeds and principles of generation'). Isis is catalytic, trans*forming both the self and the world dialectically. The story of Isis is all trans*.

Golding's version of the Iphis-Isis connection plies Florio with a rich vocabulary for thinking trans*. With her wedding to Ianthe set for the following day, the cross-dressed Iphis enters the temple with her mother to pray to the goddess Isis for help. Golding's account describes Telethusa 'taking from her head the kerchief quite away / And from her daughter's head likewise, with scattered hair she laid / Her hands upon the altar and with humble voice thus prayed'.[43] Golding's verb choice is evocative of a longer mythological history informing Iphis's story. Lingering in the background of this scene of prayer is another scattering – that of Osiris, Isis's once brother, now husband, 'whom the folk of Egypt ever seek / And never can have sought enough'.[44] Following Osiris's dismemberment by his brother, Isis gathers up the scattered pieces of Osiris's body, all but for a single part (the phallus), which remains forever lost.[45] Isis's story animates the tension between holding (gathering together) and scattering that will emerge as the central epistemological challenge arising from Florio's final figuration of his *Worlde of Wordes* as the Sporades.

In this moment, as we witness Telethusa's prayer at the altar to Isis, we too are never far from this archetypally scattered body-in-parts. The story of Iphis is, in many ways, about parts: (1) Iphis's transformation occurs *in parts* (or stages, step by step in Golding); (2) her transformation is *of parts* (features of her body: hair, stride, complexion, etc.); (3) her desire might be understood as desire *for a part* (the phallus) she lacks; and (4) she desires to play a part (the role of husband) in her wish to fulfil Ianthe's 'hopes to see her husband' on her wedding night.[46] As the *Oxford English Dictionary* makes evident, this entire semantic range was alive and flourishing in early modern English usage of the word 'part'.[47]

Attuned to this multivalence, Golding cannily conveys Iphis's frustrated desires by way of a pun on the word part: 'Iphis loves whereof she thinks she may not be Partaker'.[48] The first appearance of the word 'part' in an English wordlist occurs in the form of precisely this conjunction in the *Catholicon Anglicum* (1483): 'a Part-takynge' glossed '*participacio*'.[49] Nearly three-quarters of a century later, in *Principle Rules of Italian Grammar* (1550), William Thomas glosses the Italian headword *participare* as 'to take part, to make partetaker'.[50] Florio characteristically expands the English equivalents when, in *A Worlde of Wordes*, he glosses *partecipare* as 'to participate, to partake, to communicate, to take part with, or be partaker'.[51] Throughout the sixteenth century, when Golding was translating Ovid, a 'partaker' was a participant, one who desired to 'take part with' another. The word is fundamentally relational.

The word 'part' cut both ways in the period; it could be marshalled to convey ideas of jointure or division. 'Part' was so multivalent and ubiquitous in English that, in 1582, Richard Mulcaster included it among his list of eight thousand 'hard words' he hoped an English dictionary would soon define.[52] A search for the word 'part' in *Lexicons of Early Modern English*, a database of dictionaries, vocabularies and lexicons from the period, produces over twelve thousand results, eight thousand of which occur as glosses of other words.[53] In its verbal form, 'to part' meant 'to divide', as readers of Antonio del Corro's *The Spanish Grammar* (1590) would learn.[54] It also conveyed the sense of 'to sunder'.[55] As a noun, 'part' had long been loaded with sexual connotation in English, reaching at least back to Chaucer's *Parson's Tale*.[56] Florio trafficks in this sexual euphemism when, in his dictionary, he calls upon the word to define both male and female sex organs ('*Cucitusa*, a part of a mans privities; *Cunno*, a womans privy part').[57]

In the context of Iphis's metamorphosis, the word 'partaker' emerges as a crystallising triple entendre for the drama of her trans*version:

- it names Iphis's desire. She desires *to partake* in sexual union *with* Ianthe, but 'thinks' she cannot without the male genital 'part';[58] she desires the role of *partaker*;
- it animates this crisis of (potentially) thwarted desire by way of an aural pun that provides Iphis with an epithet. She is the *part-acher*, the girl who aches for a part (phallus) whose lack – in this heteronormative fantasy – denies her the ability to consummate her nuptials (or so she 'thinks');[59] and finally
- it instantiates the sexed metamorphosis that the tale implicitly suggests occurs. If we believe Iphis has transitioned from girl to boy, then she becomes the *part-taker*, claiming, by way of a sexual transformation, the very part Osiris lost as his body was scattered in parts.

The polyvalent pun works kaleidoscopically on the reader's imagination, scattering our attention across all dimensions of Iphis's desire, her dilemma(s) and his/her embodiment(s).

I propose that it is precisely Golding's constellation of images of scattering – the women's 'scattered hair' at the temple, the story of Osiris's scattered embodiment lingering in the background of the prayer to Isis and the pun on Iphis as 'Partaker' – that catalyses the final movement of Florio's epistle. The process of scattering emerges as an epistemological proposition – a way of putting the asterisk to thought – in an effort to encourage interpretative reorientations onto how we see the *Worlde* and the bodies in it.

Having attempted the requisite sex transition of his dictionary, Florio invites his patrons to baptise the book as their 'god-child' even as he worries that his patrons may take offence at his having already named it:

> It may be demanded how is it, your Honors gave not him his name? Heerein (right Honorable) beare with the fondnes of his mother, my Mistress *Muse*, who seeing hir female *Arescusa* turn'd to a pleasing

male *Arescon* (as *Plinie* tels of one) beg'd . . . that to the fathers name she might prefixe a name befitting the childes nature. So cald she him, A worlde of words: since . . . as words are types of things, and everie man by himselfe a little world in some resemblances; so thought she, she did see as great capacitie . . . and therefore as good cause to entitle it. If looking into it, it looke like the Sporades, or scattered Ilands [*sic*], rather then one well-joynted or close-joyned bodie, or one coherent orbe: your Honors knowe, an armie ranged in files is fitter for muster, then in a ring; and jewels are sooner found in severall boxes, then all in one bagge.[60]

With this, *A Worlde of Wordes* begins to perform a new kind of epistemological work: a way of imaging bodies – human and terrestrial, as well as bodies of language compiled in this bilingual dictionary – as intrinsically multiple and scattered rather than 'coherent' and 'close-joyned'. The Sporades, an archipelago in the Aegean, takes its name from the Greek word σποραδικός: scattering. They are, literally speaking, the ones that have been scattered. The etymological connection resounds fully in early modern English. Indeed, every English dictionary throughout the seventeenth century that glossed the word 'Sporades' did so by describing the archipelago as 'scattered'.[61] Crucially, Florio's Sporades provides a terrestrial corollary not only to his *Worlde of Wordes* but to the paradoxes of human embodiment that animate and are animated by the story of Iphis. Both Iphis and the Sporades encourage perceivers to embrace the epistemological utility of making sense of 'moving mattering' by becoming 'scattered'.

Archipelogic

In Ovid's *Metamorphoses* archipelagoes catalyse ontological and epistemological transformations in those who encounter them. In Book 8, a God's eye view of the Sporades and Cyclades heralds the fall of Icarus. Soaring above the Mediterranean, Icarus scans the sea beneath, suddenly comprehending what no human before has: the entirety of an archipelago (the many as one, all at once). At this very moment, 'the boy a frolic courage caught to fly at random'.[62] The narrative sequence intimates that this new comprehensive perspective on and capacity for comprehending the archipelago disorients Icarus in flight, igniting a desire to fly off course ('at random'). Having gone athwart of the middle path, Icarus rises toward the sun, whose wax-melting rays moult the wings from his back. Plummeting to his watery death, Icarus would forever have been lost but that his feathers 'swim upon the waves' and scatter across the aquatic landscape like an archipelago of death.[63] Spotting the feathers adrift on the sea, Daedalus hauls up his son's body from the deep and names the isle where he buries him *Ikaria*. As his body becomes island, the terrestrialised and memorialised Icarus takes his place as one among the many scattered islands. Later in Book 8, an archipelago seen from a distance gives rise to Theseus's knowledge that his eyes deceive him when what appears, at first glance, to be one island turns out to be many. The river God, Achelous, clarifies that 'the distance of the place / doth hinder to discern between each isle the perfect space'.[64] The archipelago, Theseus learns, is made up of 'sometime waternymphs' whom Achelous transformed into islands in revenge for being forgotten by the nymphs during their celebrations. Ovid's archipelagoes force matters of perspective, discernment and understanding to the fore. So too they enmesh the somatic, linguistic and terrestrial realms.[65]

Renaissance readers would not need to have attempted Icarus's flight to explore the Sporades and Cyclades and the epistemological questions to which they gave rise. Over the course of the fifteenth and sixteenth centuries in Italy, a genre of encyclopedic books known as *isolarii* (island books) offered readers stunning visual engagements with the earth's archipelagoes. Neither fully cartographic nor chorographic, *isolarii* are 'a genre that belongs somewhere within the shadowy bounds of geographical, historical, and travel literature and nautical manuals', George Tolias contends; they are characterised by historians of cartography as 'cosmographic encyclopedia[s] of islands, with maps'.[66] The first *isolario*, the manuscript *Liber insularum archipelagi* by the Florentine priest and traveller Cristoforo Buondelmonti, appeared in the early fifteenth century (c.1420) and 'may be described as a randomly arranged encyclopedic and antiquarian atlas of the Greek islands'; unlike itineraries or medieval portolan charts used by merchant sailors in the Aegean, 'the choice of islands and the order in which they appear are not governed by any strict geographical criteria, nor do they represent a likely itinerary through Greek waters' (Figure 5.3).[67] Rather, Buondelmonti describes his work as 'an illustrated book of the Cyclades and the various other islands surrounding them, with a description of the events that took place there in antiquity and up to our times'.[68]

Buondelmonti's dedication of his manuscript to Cardinal Giordano Orsini makes clear that the *isolario* was 'to be read for pleasure':[69] 'I am sending this to you ... so that you can have the pleasure of letting your thoughts wander when you are tired.'[70] In *Archipelagoes: Insular Fictions from Chivalric Romance to the Novel*, Simone Pinet argues that Buondelmonti's *Liber insularum archipelagi* seeks not to aid the sailor but 'to entertain and please the armchair traveller ... to whom the work is dedicated'; 'as the more than sixty extant manuscripts in three different redactions emphasize', the work was quite popular and fast 'constituted itself as the model for future *isolarii*, which until the seventeenth century derived from it not only the content but the structure itself, and, quite often, the maps'.[71]

The first printed *isolario* is that of Bartolomeo dalli Sonetti of 1484 (Figure 5.4).[72] Sonetti was a Venetian ship captain who 'adopted the pen name ...

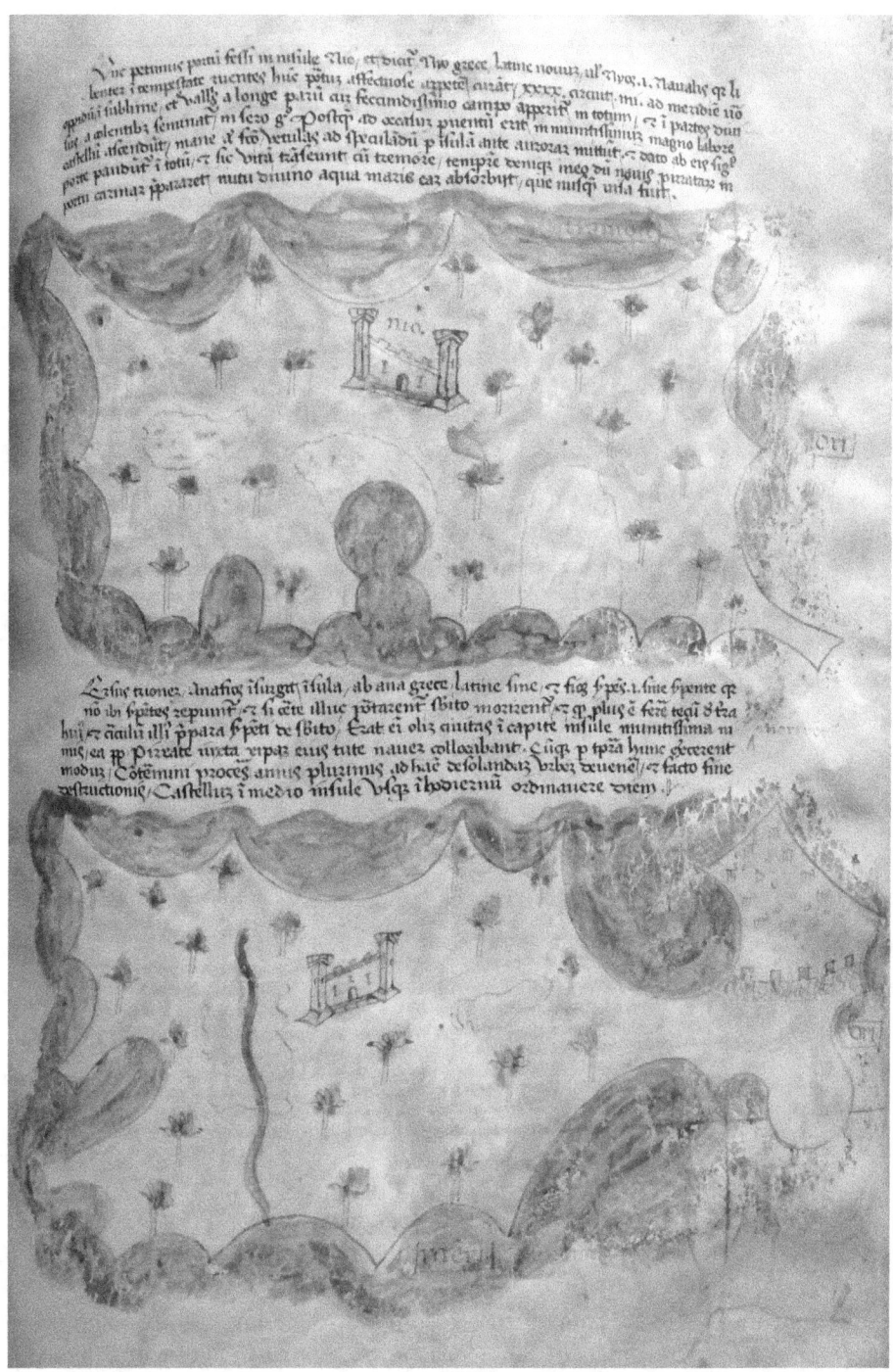

Figure 5.3 Cristoforo Buondelmonti, *Liber insularum archipelagi* (c. 1420). Mich. MS. 162, Special Collections Research Center, University of Michigan, Ann Arbor, Michigan.

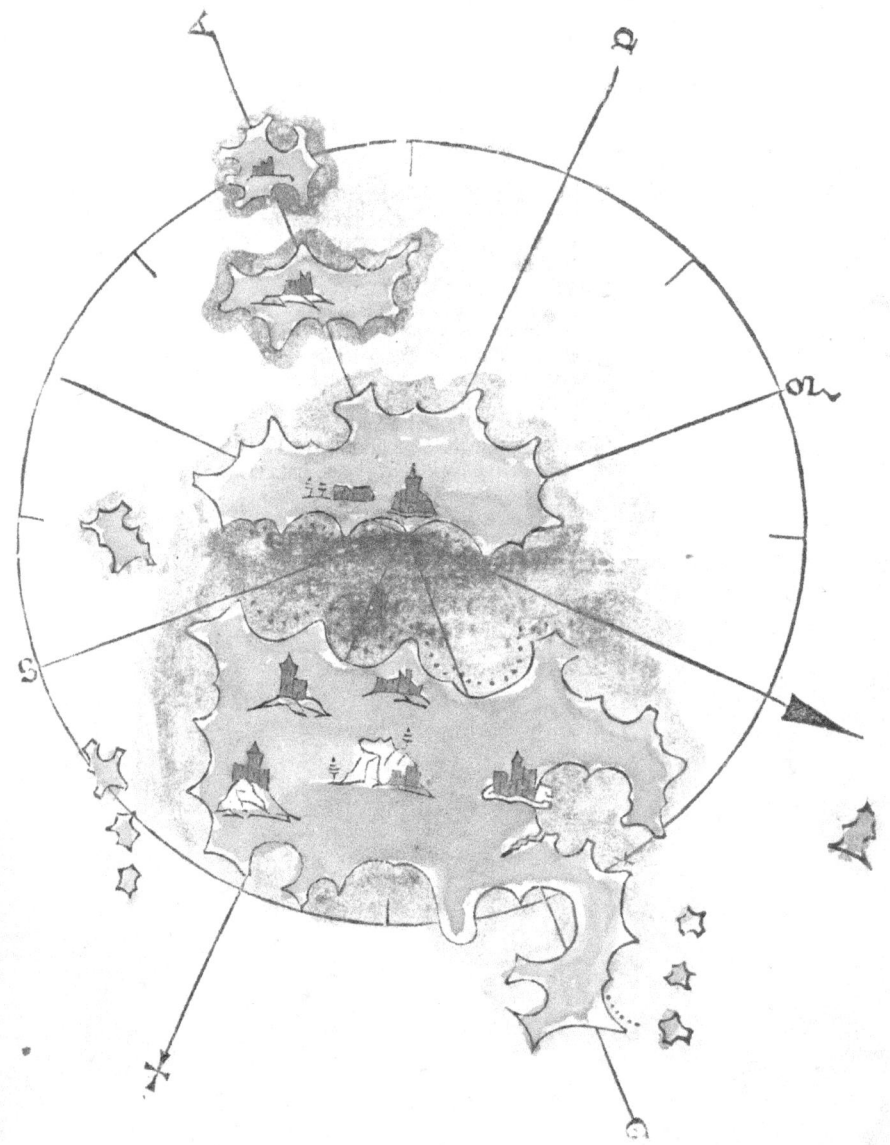

Figure 5.4   Bartolomeo dalli Sonetti, *Isolario* (1484). RB 84726, The Huntington Library, San Marino, California.

Sonetti in allusion to the sonnets that accompany the book's 48 woodcut maps' depicting the major islands of the Aegean sea.[73] Across each opening, a sonnet (an island of text) describes the island, or small cluster of islands, pictured on the facing page. As the reader holds the codex in hand, the archipelago itself risks slipping our grasp. As reader-viewers, we are struck less by the maritime connectivity and archipelagic assemblage whose weight registers in the palms of our hands than by the singularity of individual isolated landforms and their poetic correspondents. Tom Conley argues: 'In both the Petrarchan tradition and the *Isolario* the writing of the sonnet becomes a practice that spatializes knowledge in terms of a drive to contain the world within an infinity of variation on the same form.'[74] In Sonetti's *Isolario*, the singular sonnets and their terrestrial corollaries on facing pages create a world unto themselves, their own 'insular fiction'.[75] The armchair traveller *cum* sonnet reader who finds herself enchanted by a particular opening may indeed let her 'thoughts wander' within the scope of a single sonnet/island as the archipelago drifts out of mind.

Combining maps and poetic or narrative-historical chorography, *isolarii* were 'didactic' rather than 'technical', 'intended first and foremost as objects of contemplation . . . and only secondarily for their geographical accuracy', Theodore Cachey has demonstrated.[76] Conley likewise emphasises the 'virtuality' rather than representational nature of Sonetti's work:

> [A]lthough it seems to be based on the experience of travel in the Aegean (and the accompanying text underscores the eye-witness account on the part of the writer), the reality it projects is not something that is represented, but that is entirely simulated. It is a book of real islands that are the product of the labors of a poet and a woodcutter. The reader of the book experiences the history and the space of the archipelago as he or she never would be able to do within the limiting and unreliable process of travel and notation of a world seen.[77]

As is true for all atlases, an important aspect of the reader's experience pertains to how she thinks about the relation of parts (in this case, islands) to a whole that is itself a series of parts (here, the archipelago). In world atlases produced in northern Europe in the sixteenth and seventeenth centuries, 'a world map typically introduces the volume, and then a continent map is followed by plates of different countries and regions, sometimes islands, and cities and towns. Rather than attain a mental picture of the world in an instant', Valerie Traub has argued, 'the reader of an atlas either reads selectively or undergoes a sequential process of scrutiny, accretion, and collation, during which segments are imaginatively pieced together into a composite whole.'[78] If Sonetti's *Isolario* likewise sparked a desire to piece together a 'composite whole', it did so without orienting its readers to a 'mental picture' of the archipelago as a whole, or to the terrestrial and aquatic boundaries that surround and situate it in space. Pinet argues that the archipelago 'emphasizes unity in diversity'.[79] A terrestrial landform of scattered singularities, the archipelago encourages onlookers to think similitude across difference (and distance), unity in multiplicity, coherence in diversity. And yet, the *mis-en-page* of Sonetti's *Isolario* also encourages an alternative perspective. Viewing islands in juxtaposition, one after the next, page by page, 'involves the simultaneous perception of infinite "singularities"', Conley observes,[80] and, as Frank Lestringant argues, the recognition that 'the island engenders the archipelago'.[81]

The archipelago is a terrestrial paradox. Epistemologically speaking, archipelagic encounters entail both thinking 'similitude across difference' and perceiving (and holding in mind) 'infinite singularities'. To be sure, this is not straightforward synechdoche, where one part stands in for the whole, even as it is also true that the island 'engenders the archipelago'. The parts (islands) are themselves whole (worlds unto themselves) even as they are also part(s) of a larger form itself constituted of scattered parts (the archipelago). The archipelagic paradox exceeds the limits of synechdochic logic; here distinction between parts and wholes is pulled apart. For the reader who 'ever seek[s]' for the archipelago in Sonetti's *Isolario*, it would seem that, like Isis, we 'never can have sought enough'.

If the earliest *isolarii* were intended as objects of contemplation (catalysts for 'the pleasure of letting your thoughts wander'), what, then, might their readers have contemplated? With the exception of occasional marginal marks indicating latitude or longitude and consistent marginal inscriptions indicating east and west, Buondelmonti's maps are devoid of orientation guides altogether. The large asterisk-like compass rose that dominates Sonetti's page, in contrast, puts orientation itself to the question.[82] The compass points and rhumb lines convey a seductive, yet false, sense that a viewer might locate this archipelago in space. For, visually speaking, the majority of islands are untethered to anchoring references to the European, African and Near Eastern shorelines that buttress the Mediterranean and Aegean seas.[83] The page offers its viewer no single orientation point.[84] Apparently, to ask where precisely on earth we are is to miss the epistemological point. Sonetti's *Isolario* is indeed an object of contemplation, but one that foremost enlivens the reader-viewer to her own processes of contemplative engagement.

Across the pages of Sonetti's *Isolario* a variety of island forms are displayed. While some pages are filled with clusters of islands (as in Figure 5.4), others offer vertical views of single islands. In the figure of Hiere Island (Figure 5.5), the compass rose dominates the page. The island's legendary monastic inhabitants were 'widely reputed' to give 'refuge to bellicose pirates' who were pulled up from the sea by means of 'a huge balance and pulley set on a fulcrum placed on a cliff'.[85] Less situated than jettisoned, Hiere Island is thrust to the page's edge by the compass-as-asterisk that puts the viewer's orientation to the question. As a close examination of these two images from Sonetti's book makes evident, even the compass rose itself spins about as the reader turns from page to page. East, marked with the figure of a cross, revolves from the bottom left quadrant in the first image to the top right in the image of Hiere Island.[86] The

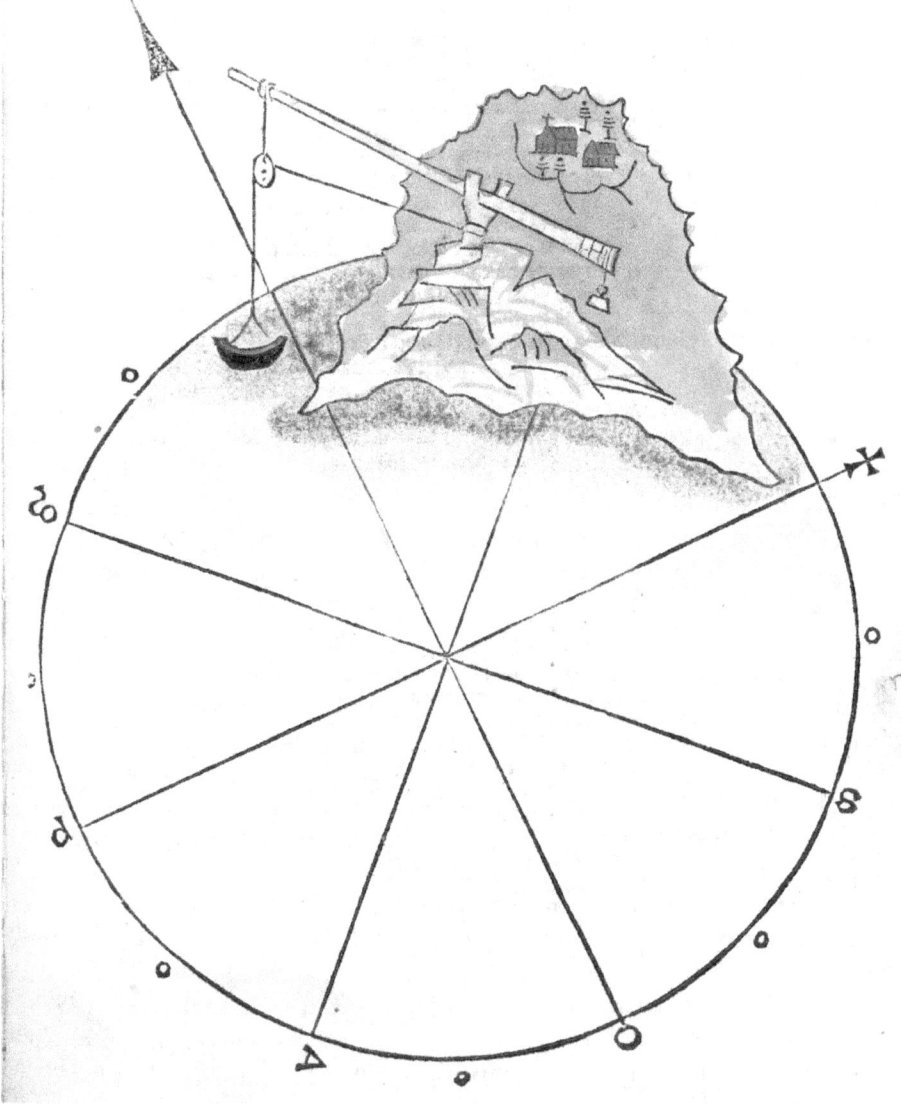

Figure 5.5   Bartolomeo dalli Sonetti, *Isolario* (1484). RB 84726, The Huntington Library, San Marino, California.

compass-as-asterisk serves as a reminder that – like the islands themselves – we too have been scattered.

Like an asterisk that sends a reader's attention off in multiple directions (into a footnote, caveat or gloss, or back through time to consider the presence of archaisms in current speech, or off to the border's edge to encounter 'barbarians'), here the compass-as-asterisk colludes with the islands within, and just beyond, its circumference to generate an epistemological puzzle whose only apparent solution lies in the increased capacity of the reader-viewer to become and remain 'scattered'. To glimpse an archipelago here requires what Florio characterises as a 'great capacitie'. As my own eye scans from the page's centre to its edge and back again, I labour to hold the multiplicity of (insular) parts together (as archipelago) in mind. Turning from one page to the next, I endeavour to hold the larger archipelago in mind as I travel, in no apparent order or consistent direction, from island to island (page to page) across the bodies that constitute the (book as) archipelago. The more I strive to be a partaker of this archipelago, the more challenging is the cognitive work of holding the multiplicity of its terrestrial form(s) in mind. Sonetti's *Isolario* does not offer the viewer a bird's-eye view of the archipelago; the reader is not conveyed along Icarus's flight. Instead, we are tasked with Isis's ever-ongoing search.

As Sonetti's audience confronts the archipelago in and as parts, so too Florio's readers confront the world of words in Florio's dictionary. There is, after all, no such thing as a bird's-eye view onto a language. Not even a dictionary gives us that. The whole of any language must be gathered and distributed in parts, word by word. To page through Florio's *Worlde* is to encounter a Sporades of words and, in so doing, adopt what I characterise as an 'archipelogic': a scattered way of thinking that entails imagining bodies, both human/mythological and terrestrial as well as bodies of language compiled in bilingual dictionaries, as intrinsically multiple. Readerly engagement with these bodies, in turn, engenders a 'great capacitie' for sustaining the tension between our desires to hold wholeness in mind while also attending to the scatteredness of form(s) by sustaining multiple perspectives onto the 'moving mattering' of languages, human bodies and terrestrial landscapes.

Thinking of Florio's dictionary as the Sporades opens up not only an alternative system of valuation – that is, lexicography's inherent copiousness might be positively revalued if recast as a strategic strength (as Florio puts it, armies ranged in files, jewels sooner to be found). More, like archipelagoes, *A Worlde of Wordes* displays what is correspondent across difference (Italian/English), as it also showcases multiplicity alive in singularity (many English words for every Italian one). Archipelagoes, such as the Sporades of the Aegean or the lexico-landscape of a bilingual dictionary, are at once one and many 'things'; as such, they paradoxically hold our attention by scattering it.

Trans, Trans-, Trans*: Iphis in Retrospect

As Florio's archipelago performs the work of the asterisk, Iphis emerges (retrospectively) more and more like an archipelago: a body we never see fully all at once, a body never fully finished (the case fell out) and a body whose relations with other bodies shapes it (Iphis's desire to 'partake' in love-making with

Ianthe; Ianthe's desire for Iphis to play the role of husband). I thus propose that we add Iphis – in all his/her ontological, epistemological and poetic expressions explored throughout this collection – to our expanding catalogue of 'keywords' for trans*studies. In so doing, we press the questions animating our conversation about Ovidian transversions to the fore of transgender studies. To borrow Kathleen Perry Long's formulation, we 'make Ovid our theorist' of embodiment of all sorts.[87] In this essay, I have argued that the archipelago, the dictionary and Iphis emerge not as figures of fluidity but of multiplicity, not as figures of endless flux but as variable, temporarily situated embodiments that function differentially in space yet simultaneously in time. They require their perceivers both to experience and sustain contradictory fixations (island/archipelago, part/whole, English/Italian, male/female) and to explore the range of possibilities for movement across and relations between these fixations. As we explore the tensions and overlaps in thinking trans/trans-/trans* and embrace an archipelogic way of thinking about language, as well as somatic and terrestrial bodies, we discover ourselves engaged ever more fully by the central epistemological questions of the Iphis story: what do we think we know and how do we think when we attempt to know it?

Acknowledgments

I wish to thank the members of the following audiences for their rich engagements with earlier incarnations of this work: University of Michigan's *Metamorphosis, Transformation, and Conversion: A Symposium on Ovid, Lyly, and Benserade* (2015); *Early Modern Conversions* Team Meeting (2016); Cornell University's *Transforming Bodies* Conference (2017); the 5-Colleges Renaissance Seminar (2018); and Stanford University's Renaissance Focal Group (2018).

Notes

1. Tompkins, 'Asterisk', pp. 26–7.
2. Stryker and Currah, 'Introduction', p. 1.
3. 'trans-, prefix.' *OED Online*. Oxford University Press, June 2017. Web: 27 June 2017.
4. Hayward and Weinstein, 'Introduction', p. 197.
5. Stryker and Currah, 'Introduction', p. 1.
6. In March 2018, 'trans*' was added as a unique headword entry in the Oxford English Dictionary Online: 'trans*, adj.' *OED Online*. Oxford University Press, March 2018. Web: 4 June 2018. Characteristically slow to capture neologisms, particularly English-speaking cultures' 'lavender lexicons', the *OED Online* does not suggest the controversy already underway regarding 'trans*'. While trans* continues to be mobilised urgently and productively in the academy (e.g. Halberstam, *Trans* A Quick and Quirky Account of Gender Variability*, 2018), for some in queer activist and gender non-binary online communities, trans* has become a controversial, even outmoded, term. In 'Why We Used Trans* and Why We Don't Anymore', the online collaboration, 'transstudent.org', argues that the asterisk

lingering on the edge of trans is 'unnecessary and should not be used' because 'it's often applied in inaccessible, binarist, and transmisogynist ways', Trans Student Educational Resources, 2014 (http://www.transstudent.org/asterisk), Web: 4 June 2018. In her blog 'Whipping Girl', Julia Serano weighs in on what she characterises as the 'activist-language-merry-go-round' surrounding trans*. For Serano, trans* has suffered, together with other terms, a form of 'word-sabotage': 'Because many people viewed the asterisk as imparting broad inclusion, suddenly the use of the terms transgender and trans sans asterisk – which I have used in a broad inclusive manner for well over a decade – would sometimes be questioned, or might be interpreted as promoting exclusion.' Serano concludes, 'The word trans* is not inherently inclusive or trans-misogynistic. Rather, like all words, it gets its meaning from the way in which people use it. And it may be utilized towards positive or negative ends. Just because some people may use it in an exclusionary way doesn't mean that the word itself is disparaging or exclusionary' (http://juliaserano.blogspot.com/2015/08/regarding-trans-and-transgenderism.html), Web: 4 June 2018. Throughout this essay, I mobilise trans* not as an identity category but as a signifier of the mode of thinking catalysed by the various forms of human embodiment, terrestrial matter and linguistic difference that I trace throughout. It is my conviction that, as an invitation for epistemological engagement with multiplicity and polyvalence, trans* is a salient and powerful neologism in the English language and may continue to prove useful to gender non-binary/gender expansive and queer communities.
7. For the queer philologist, this unresolvability is both the pleasure and rich potential of S*X. Jeffrey Masten proposes that, in the context of editing so-called textual 'cruxes' in early modern literature, we ought not strive toward clarifying emendations that 'not only narrow ... but also potentially *prophylactic[ally]*' protect readers from engaging with a semiotic or semantic crux. Instead, Masten encourages practices 'of glossing that recognize that dwelling on ... unstable boundaries may *also* produce "sense"' (*Queer Philologies*, p. 228). The asterisk is helpful to the practice of queer philology since, pedagogically, 'the oddity of an asterisk in the middle of a word – and its suggestion of euphemized or bleeped-out language – might send students ... into the glosses [of early modern texts] more forcefully than ... a bracketed [crux]' might (ibid., 229).
8. Rider, *Riders dictionarie corrected*, n.p.
9. Bullokar, 'Instruction to the Reader', n.p.
10. Laurie Maguire argues that *etcetera* (or the typographically abbreviated '&c'), works to direct 'the eye to a vacancy', playing a 'conceptually sophisticated tease of hide and seek with boundaries and cusps, with abruption and continuation, with suspension and extension of meaning'; in their shared capacities to generate both heuristic and epistemological puzzles, the asterisk and the etcetera are kindred typographic embodiments. See Maguire, 'Typographical Embodiment', p. 528.
11. All references are to *John Florio: A Worlde of Wordes*, ed. Haller. Hereafter, Florio, *Worlde*.
12. For Florio's biography, see ibid., 'Introduction', pp. ix–xl; and Yates, *John Florio*. The self-description, 'An English Man in Italian', appears printed in Italian ('*Italis ore, Anglus* pectore') below Florio's engraved portrait in *Queen Anna's New World of Words* (1611), a subsequent and revised edition of *A Worlde of Wordes*.
13. William Thomas' *Principle Rules of the Italian Grammar* (1550) offered approximately 8,000 Italian words translated into English. A predecessor to Florio's *Worlde*, this word list did not aspire to comprehensiveness but instead focused primarily on the Italian of Boccaccio, Petrarch and Dante.
14. Parker, 'Virile Style', p. 207. See also Parker, 'On the Tongue'.

15. On the significance of the *Worlde*'s influence on the history of English lexicography, particularly as the source of the earliest appearance of 1,149 English words that would later appear in the second edition of the *OED*, see Wyatt, *The Italian Encounter*, p. 230–1.
16. Florio, *Worlde*, p. 82.
17. Parker, 'Virile Style', pp. 201–2.
18. Florio, *Florio his firste fruites*, 1578; *Florios second frutes* [sic], 1591.
19. Florio, *Worlde*, p. 4.
20. 'John Cowland in commendation of the Authour', n.p.
21. 'T.C. in commendation of Florio', n.p.
22. See Bushnell, *A Culture of Teaching*, esp. pp. 117–43.
23. On early modern metaphors of grafting as expressive of deviations in human generation and embodiment, see Feerick, 'Botanical Shakespeares' and 'The Imperial Graft'; Nardizzi, 'Grafted to Falstaff'; Wilson, 'Bastard Grafts'; and Ellerbeck, 'A Bett'ring of Nature'. On the entwining of horticultural practice and metaphoricity of grafting in early modern literature, see Bushnell, *Green Desire*.
24. 'R. H. Gent. *in commendation of* the Authours wel imployed tyme', n.p.
25. Florio's mother was Italian and father English, making this 'bacchus-like' boy an apt (if matricidal) avatar of Florio himself.
26. Unless otherwise noted, all Ovidian citations are from Golding's *Ovid's Metamorphoses*, and are given in book and line number, here 3: 398.
27. Florio, *Worlde*, p. 6.
28. Ibid.
29. For an alternative reading of this passage, see Wyatt, *The Italian Encounter*, 251. Wyatt argues that Florio emphasises the 'neutered' aspects of the English language and 'appears to be rewriting . . . the terms of his cultural mediation, translating its Italian coordinates into those of an English culture whose neutered language tends by default to favor masculine discourse, given that there is nothing in its grammatical structure to privilege the feminine' (ibid.).
30. Anguillara, *Le metamorfosi di Ovidio*. Florio includes the corresponding lines from Anguillara's translation: '*Et ogni membro suo più forte e sciolto / Sente e volge alla madre il motto, e 'l lume. / Come vero fanciullo esser si vede / Iphi va con parole alme, e devote / Al tempio con la madre, e la nutrice, / e paga il voto. E 'l suo miracol dice*' (*Worlde*, p. 6). Although Florio presents this passage as if it were a single unified stanza, he silently drops fourteen lines from Anguillara's text, thus drawing more closely together the action in the first sentence ('Feeling more vigor') and the conclusion of the second ('The case fell out'). In Anguillara's text, these actions transpire over the course of three stanzas (Book 9, stanzas 378–80). *Le metamorfosi di Ovidio* was first published in 1561; I have consulted the online digital reproduction of the 1584 edition in the Bibliothèque nationale de France.
31. Florio, *Worlde*, p. 6. The text appears in italics in *Worlde*.
32. Blount, *Glossographia*, n.p.
33. James, 'Ovidian Girlhood', p. 117 n. 29.
34. Ibid., p. 117.
35. Anguillara, *Le metamorfosi di Ovidio*, 9: 385, ll. 7–8.
36. I am grateful to Peggy McCracken and Karla Mallette for their generous assistance in translating and explicating the grammatical ambiguities of the final lines of Anguillara's text.
37. Golding, *Ovid's Metamorphoses*, 9: 924–8.
38. See 'case, n.1.' *OED Online*. Oxford University Press, June 2017. Web: 27 June 2017.

39. See 'vagina, n.2.' *OED Online*. Oxford University Press, June 2017. Web: 27 June 2017. On the semantic fungibility of the term 'case' as a signifier for female and male genital anatomy in the period, see Traub, *Thinking Sex with the Early Moderns*, pp. 181 and 207.
40. On contemporary popular accounts of female-to-male sex transition, particularly stories Florio would have known well by way of his own project of translating Montaigne's *Essais*, see Parker, 'Gender Ideology, Gender Change'. On period-specific distinctions between female-to-male sex transition, female masculinity, the Galenic/Hippocratic belief in hermaphrodites as an 'intermediate sex' versus Aristotelian notions of 'doubled or redundant genitalia', together considered in light of medical discourses regarding sexual difference, see Traub, *The Renaissance of Lesbianism*, esp. pp. 45–51; and Daston and Park, 'The Hermaphrodite and the Orders of Nature'.
41. Wofford, 'Against Our Own Ignorance', p. 165. Wofford makes a strong argument for Plutarch's account of Isis influencing Florio's contemporary, William Shakespeare, whose descriptions of Cleopatra include the phrase, a woman of 'infinite variety', p. 166.
42. Quoted in ibid., p. 166.
43. Golding, *Ovid's Metamorphoses*, 9: 905–7.
44. Ibid., 9: 818–19.
45. On the ways in which the Isis story underpins the Iphis tale with images of 'phallic transfer' in medieval accounts, see Mills, *Seeing Sodomy in the Middle Ages*, esp. 113–14.
46. Golding, *Ovid's Metamorphoses*, 9: 850–1.
47. See 'part, n.1.' *OED Online*. Oxford University Press, June 2017. Web: 30 June 2017. Of the eighteen definitions listed in the *OED Online*, all but one have their origins in late medieval or early modern English.
48. Golding, *Ovid's Metamorphoses*, 9: 850.
49. The anonymous Latin–English wordbook, *Catholicon Anglicum*, was one of the first 'dictionaries' to include the English language. Although the word dictionary is attested as far back as the thirteenth century, it is not until the publication of *The dictionary of syr Thomas Eliot knyght* in 1538 that it is applied increasingly to wordbooks. I therefore use the term 'dictionary' anachronistically.
50. Thomas, *Principle Rules of Italian Grammar*, n.p.
51. Florio, *Worlde*, p. 457.
52. Mulcaster, *The First Part of the Elementarie*, p. 205.
53. Keyword search, 'part'. *Lexicons of Early Modern English*. Online. University of Toronto Press. Web: 30 June 2017.
54. Cited in *Lexicons of Early Modern English*. Online. University of Toronto Press. Web: 30 June 2017.
55. Anon., *Catholicon Anglicum*, 'to sunder: to parte'.
56. The *OED Online* (part, n.1) cites the first use of part as a euphemism for genitals as attested in Chaucer's *Parson's Tale*, but it is likely that this pun reaches further back historically.
57. Florio, *Worlde*, pp. 178–9.
58. On the tradition of Ovidian *amor impossibilis*, which 'thematizes the unnaturalness of female-female love' and the problem ('less desire itself than the intractability of the physical body'), see Traub, *The Renaissance of Lesbianism*, esp. pp. 276–88; here pp. 284 and 288.
59. On the ways in which the dilemma of Iphis's desire for a 'part' amplifies and is amplified by broader ideas about the social dictates of Nature in this period, see ibid., pp. 276–88.

60. Florio, *Worlde*, p. 7. On the surface, the logic linking the military formation of 'rings' to precious 'jewels' implies that scattering (bodies and commodities) is a way of preserving them from loss. Just beneath the surface of the analogy, Florio ventures into the territory of the sexual pun: in the early modern period, rings, jewels, boxes and bags were commonplace innuendos for male and female reproductive anatomy. While Florio doesn't develop the implications of his military/economic/sexual analogy, the reader is urged, by way of this imagery, to ponder, once again, the utility of becoming scattered.
61. 'Sporades' appears as a headword in the Latin–English bilingual dictionary, *The dictionary of syr Thomas Eliot knyght* (1538), wherein the archipelago is defined as the 'yles nygh to Crete or Candy'. By the late sixteenth century, readers of John Thorius's dictionary, *The Theatre of the Earth* (1599), would learn that the Sporades were 'certain scattered islands in the Carpathian sea neere Creet'. Thereafter, every English dictionary that glosses the word 'archipelago' does so by using the word 'scattered'.
62. Golding, *Ovid's Metamorphoses*, 8: 299–300.
63. Ibid., 8: 310–11.
64. Ibid., 8: 741–2.
65. For one early modern lexicographer, the word Ikaria drew to mind both the aquatic and terrestrial realms, blurring more than defining their boundaries. In Thorius's *Theatre of the Earth* (London, 1599), the word fills nearly half a page with entries: '*Icaria*. An isle in the Sea Icarium . . . ; *Icarium*. An isle in the Persian Gulf; *Icarium Mare*. A part of the Aegean sea called *Mar di Nicaria*; *Icarus*. One of the isles Cyclades. Also an isle neer the red sea'. Herein, Icaria emerges as not one but many islands, not merely island(s) but also a sea. The entry stretches the dictionary reader's geographical attention across the Aegean geography of the Cyclades and into the Persian Gulf. Here and elsewhere in early modern dictionaries, the entry for Icarus/Icaria enmeshes the somatic, terrestrial, aquatic and linguistic realms in ways reminiscent of the Ovidian story.
66. Tolias, '*Isolarii*', pp. 263, 264. On the dialectic of text and image in *isolarii*, see Conley, *Self-Made Map*, pp. 167–201. On the expansive network of knowledge communities involved in producing printed *isolarii*, see Stouraiti, 'Talk, Script, and Print'.
67. Tolias, '*Isolarii*', p. 265. In 'Talk, Script, and Print', a study primarily of late sixteenth- and seventeenth-century *isolarii*, Stouraiti explores the ways in which the genre (for instance, Marco Borschini's *L'Arcipelago* (Venice 1658) and Vincenzo Maria Coronelli's *Isolario* (Venice 1696)) came to function as reference works, 'for consultation *ad locum* rather than linear reading', p. 226.
68. Buondelmonti, quoted in Tolias, '*Isolarii*', p. 266. Buondelmonti's *Liber* is not, strictly speaking, limited to representations of terrestrial islands; crucially, it includes Constantinople as the 'anchoring' city-island, visually featuring the city in the form of an island (Pinet, *Archipelagoes*, p. 71).
69. Tolias, '*Isolarii*', p. 266.
70. Buondelmonti, quoted in Tolias, '*Isolarii*', p. 266.
71. Pinet, *Archipelagoes*, pp. 46–7. To view colour images of these manuscripts, visit the online digital library of Bibliothèque nationale de France: http://data.bnf.fr/12378926/cristoforo_buondelmonte/. Web: 1 October 2017. Black and white reproductions are also published in Cachey, 'From the Mediterranean to the World', and Pinet, *Archipelagoes*, pp. 54–9.
72. It is considered 'one of the incunabula from Venice', Tolias, '*Isolarii*', p. 268.
73. Cachey, 'From the Mediterranean to the World', p. 2
74. Conley, 'Virtual Reality and the *Isolario*', p. 129.

75. I borrow the phrase from the subtitle of Pinet's *Archipelagoes*.
76. Cachey, 'From the Mediterranean to the World', p. 9. In drawing this distinction between technical and didactic maps in the history of cartography, Cachey wittingly rehearses the argument of Schultz, 'Jacopo de' Barbari's View of Venice'.
77. Conley, 'Virtual Reality and the *Isolario*', p. 121.
78. Traub, 'Cartography', p. 268.
79. Pinet, *Archipelagoes*, p. 69.
80. Conley, 'Virtual Reality and the *Isolario*', p. 130.
81. Cited in ibid., p. 126 n. 4.
82. Although I have not had the opportunity to examine manuscripts of Buondelmonti's *Liber insularum archipelagi*, the high-resolution, digital reproductions of the Tuscany (1465–1475) mss, available through the Bibliothèque nationale de France (http://gallica.bnf.fr/ark:/12148/btv1b55010482q), and that of the *c.*1420 mss, available through the Royal Museums Greenwich (http://prints.rmg.co.uk/artist/27752/cristoforo-buondelmonti), reveal the absence of compass lines (Web: 1 October 2017). The University of Michigan mss. (Mich. MS. 162) is similarly devoid of compass lines and, in contrast to the manuscript at the Bibliothèque nationale de France, features no marginal notation regarding longitude or latitude. While Sonetti's indebtedness to Buondelmonti is evident in the visual depictions of some of his islands, the dominance of the compass and rhumb lines structuring Sonetti's *mise-en-page* is a striking departure from Buondelmonti's *Liber*. I am grateful to librarian and curator Dr Pablo Alvarez for providing photographs of the Michigan manuscript.
83. In a few instances, the mainland appears in the margins of the *mis-en-page*; see the islands of Chios, Lesbos, Rhodes, Simi, Samos and Agathonissi in Sonetti.
84. Like other *isolarii* in the period, the 'geographic indeterminacy' of individual islands in Sonetti's *Isolario* functions to increase 'their imaginative resonance' (Cosgrove, *Apollo's Eye*, p. 94). If 'on portolanos the alignment of words and symbols assumes an immobile eye and a revolving image whose orientation is continuously adjusted to the fixed viewing position', the *Isolario*, conversely, assumes a radically unfixed, mobile and yet partial viewing position that never brings the full archipelago into view (ibid., p. 86).
85. Conley, *Self-Made Map*, p. 174.
86. A complete survey of extant copies of Sonetti's *Isolario* would be required to determine whether or when changes were introduced to clarify matters of directional orientation, island to island and page to page. It is interesting to note that in the *c.*1485 copy at the National Maritime Museum, Greenwich, London, east appears on every page at the right outer edge of the compass (45 degrees), giving a consistent north, east, south, west orientation to all of the islands pictured throughout the *Isolario*. Conversely, the Huntington Library copy, also dated *c.*1485, reveals a tolerance for dis/orientation – what I've characterised as 'a going athwart'. What these two copies would seem provisionally to suggest is that questions of orientation may have arisen for readers not only within the scope of engagement with a single volume, but across various imprints too.
87. I am grateful to Kathleen Perry Long for this formulation, which she shared as part of her opening remarks at the Cornell 'Transforming Bodies' conference (21 April 2017).

BIBLIOGRAPHY

Anguillara, Giovanni Andrea dell', *Le metamorfosi di Ovidio ... in ottava rima*. Venice: 1584. Bibliothèque nationale de France, http://gallica.bnf.fr/ark:/12148/bpt6k58750d/f370.item. Web: 1 October 2017.

Anon., *Catholicon Anglicum*, 1483.
Blount, Thomas, *Glossographia: or A dictionary, interpreting all such hard words*. London: 1656.
Bullokar, John, 'Instruction to the Reader', *An English expositor teaching the interpretation of the hardest words used in our language*. London: 1616.
Buondelmonti, Christoforo, [De Insulis Archipelagi], 1440. University of Michigan Special Collections, Mich. MS. 162, n.p.
Buondelmonti, Christoforo, *Liber Insularum Archipelagi*, Italie (Toscane): 1465–1475. Bibliothèque nationale de France, http://gallica.bnf.fr/ark:/12148/btv1b55010482q. Web: 1 October 2017.
Bushnell, Rebecca, *A Culture of Teaching: Early Modern Humanism in Theory and Practice* (Ithaca, NY: Cornell University Press, 1996).
Bushnell, Rebecca, *Green Desire: Imagining Early Modern English Gardens* (Ithaca, NY: Cornell University Press, 2003).
Cachey, Theodore J., 'From the Mediterranean to the World: A Note on the Italian "Book of Islands" (*isolario*)', *California Italian Studies* 1: 1, 2010, pp. 1–13.
Conley, Tom, 'Virtual Reality and the *Isolario*', *Annali d'Italianistica* 14, 1996, pp. 121–30.
Conley, Tom, *The Self-Made Map: Cartographic Writing in Early Modern France* (Minneapolis: University of Minnesota Press, 1996).
Cosgrove, Denis, *Apollo's Eye: A Cartographic Genealogy of the Earth in the Western Imagination* (Baltimore: Johns Hopkins University Press, 2001).
Cowland, John, 'John Cowland in commendation of the Authour', in *Florio his firste fruites*, n.p.
Daston, Lorraine and Park, K., 'The Hermaphrodite and the Orders of Nature: Sexual Ambiguity in Early Modern France', *GLQ: A Journal of Lesbian and Gay Studies* 1, 1995, pp. 419–38.
Ellerbeck, Erin, 'A Bett'ring of Nature: Grafting and Embryonic Development in *The Dutchess of Malfi*', in Jean Feerick and Vin Nardizzi (eds), *The Indistinct Human in Renaissance Literature* (Basingstoke: Palgrave Macmillan, 2012), pp. 85–99.
Elyot, Thomas, *The dictionary of syr Thomas Eliot knight*. London: 1538.
Feerick, Jean, 'Botanical Shakespeares: The Racial Logic of Plant Life in *Titus Andronicus*', *South Central Review* 26: 1–2, 2009, pp. 82–102.
Feerick, Jean, 'The Imperial Graft: Horticulture, Hybridity, and the Art of Mingling Races in *Henry V* and *Cymbeline*', in Valerie Traub (ed.), *The Oxford Handbook of Shakespeare and Embodiment: Gender, Sexuality, and Race* (Oxford: Oxford University Press, 2016), pp. 211–27.
Florio, John, *A Worlde of Wordes*, ed. Hermann W. Haller (Toronto: University of Toronto Press, 2013).
Florio, John, *Florio his firste fruites*. London: 1578.
Florio, John, *Florios second frutes* [sic]. London: 1591.
Florio, John, *Queen Anna's New World of Words*. London: 1611.
Golding, Arthur (trans.), *Ovid's Metamorphoses*, ed. Madeleine Forey (Baltimore: Johns Hopkins University Press, 2001).
Halberstam, Jack, *Trans* A Quick and Quirky Account of Gender Variability* (Oakland, CA: University of California Press, 2018).
Hayward, Eva and Weinstein, J., 'Introduction: Tranimalities in the Age of Trans* Life', *TSQ: Transgender Studies Quarterly* 2: 2, 2015, pp. 195–208.
James, Heather, 'The Ovidian Girlhood of Shakespeare's Boy Actors: Q2 Juliet', *Shakespeare Survey: An Annual Survey of Shakespeare Studies and Production* 69, 2016, pp. 106–22.

Maguire, Laurie, 'Typographical Embodiment: the case of etcetera', in Valerie Traub (ed.), *The Oxford Handbook of Shakespeare and Embodiment: Gender, Sexuality, and Race* (Oxford: Oxford University Press, 2016), pp. 527–48.
Masten, Jeffrey, *Queer Philologies: Sex, Language, and Affect in Shakespeare's Time* (Philadelphia: University of Pennsylvania Press, 2016).
Mills, Robert, *Seeing Sodomy in the Middle Ages* (Chicago: Chicago University Press, 2015).
Mulcaster, Richard, *The First Part of the Elementarie*, London: 1582.
Nardizzi, Vin, 'Grafted to Falstaff and Compounded with Catherine: Mingling Hal in the Second Tetralogy', in Vin Nardizzi, Stephen Guy-Bray and Will Stockton (eds), *Queer Renaissance Historiography: Backward Gaze* (Burlington, VT: Ashgate, 2009), pp. 149–60.
Parker, Patricia, 'Gender Ideology, Gender Change: The Case of Marie Germain', *Critical Inquiry* 19: 2, 1993, pp. 337–64.
Parker, Patricia, 'On the Tongue: Cross Gendering, Effeminacy, and the Art of Words', *Style* 23: 3, 1989, pp. 445–65.
Parker, Patricia, 'Virile Style', in Louise Fradenburg and Carla Freccero (eds), *Premodern Sexualities* (London and New York: Routledge, 1996), pp. 201–22.
Pinet, Simone, *Archipelagoes: Insular Fictions from Chivalric Romance to the Novel* (Minneapolis: University of Minnesota Press, 2011).
'R. H. Gent. *in commendation of* the Authours wel imployed tyme', in *Florio his firste fruites*, n.p.
Rider, John, *Riders dictionarie corrected*, Oxford: 1612.
Schulz, Juergen, 'Jacopo de' Barbari's View of Venice: Map Making, City Views, and Moralized Geography Before the Year 1500', *Art Bulletin* 60: 3, 1978, pp. 425–74.
Serano, Julia, 'Regarding Trans* and Transgenderism' [blog post], 27 August 2015. Retrieved from http://juliaserano.blogspot.com/search?q=trans*+and+transgenderism.
Sonetti, Bartolomeo dalli, *Isolario*, Venice: c.1484. The Huntington Library, RB 84726.
Stouraiti, Anastasia, 'Talk, Script and Print: Making of Island Books in Early Modern Venice', *Historical Research* 86: 232, 2013, pp. 207–29.
Stryker, Susan and Currah, P., 'Introduction: Keywords', *TSQ: Transgender Studies Quarterly* 1: 1–2, 2014, pp. 1–18.
'T. C. in commendation of Florio and his first fruites', in *Florio his firste fruites*, n.p.
Thomas, William, *Principal Rules of the Italian Grammar*, London: 1550 (Menston: Scolar Press, 1968).
Thorius, John, *The Theatre of the Earth*. London: 1599.
Tolias, George, '*Isolarii*, Fifteenth to Seventeenth Century', in David Woodward (ed.), *The History of Cartography*, Vol. 3 (Chicago: Chicago University Press, 2007), pp. 263–84.
Tompkins, Avery, 'Asterisk', *TSQ: Transgender Studies Quarterly* 1: 1–2, 2014, pp. 26–7.
Trans Student Educational Resource (2014) 'Why We Used Trans* and Why We Don't Anymore', http://www.transstudent.org/asterisk/ (accessed 4 June 2018).
Traub, Valerie, 'Cartography', in Bruce Smith (ed.), *The Cambridge Guide to the Worlds of Shakespeare: Shakespeare's World 1500–1660*, Vol. 1 (Cambridge: Cambridge University Press, 2016), pp. 265–76.
Traub, Valerie, *The Renaissance of Lesbianism in Early Modern England* (Cambridge: Cambridge University Press, 2002).
Traub, Valerie, *Thinking Sex with the Early Moderns* (Philadelphia: University of Pennsylvania Press, 2016).

Wilson, Miranda, 'Bastard Grafts, Crafted Fruits: Shakespeare's Planted Families', in Jean Feerick and Vin Nardizzi (eds), *The Indistinct Human in Renaissance Literature* (Basingstoke: Palgrave Macmillan, 2012), pp. 103–17.

Wofford, Susan L., 'Against Our Own Ignorance', in Dympna Callaghan and Suzanne Gossett (ed.), *Shakespeare in Our Time* (London and New York: Bloomsbury Arden Shakespeare, 2016), pp. 158–66.

Wyatt, Michael, *The Italian Encounter with Tudor England: A Cultural Politics of Translation* (Cambridge: Cambridge University Press, 2009).

Yates, Frances A., *John Florio: The Life of an Italian in Shakespeare's England* (Cambridge: Cambridge University Press, 1934).

6

ALCHEMY, HUMANISM AND THE USES OF DISKNOWLEDGE IN JOHN LYLY'S *GALATEA*

Katherine Eggert

The prologue of John Lyly's 1580s play *Galatea*, an address to Elizabeth I, includes an analogy that, though appropriately obsequious to the queen and modest on the part of the players, grows odder and odder the closer one examines it.

> So have we endeavoured with all care that what we present Your Highness should neither offend in scene nor syllable, knowing that as in the ground where gold groweth nothing will prosper but gold, so in Your Majesty's mind, where nothing doth harbour but virtue, nothing can enter but virtue.[1]

Despite being penned by Lyly, whose facility with balanced prose style knows no equal, this analogy's parallelism trips us up. We can see its flaws immediately if we parse it backward, the second half first. The second half of the analogy asserts that her majesty's virtuous mind, which 'harbours' virtue, can admit nothing that is not virtuous. The first half establishes that the analogy to Elizabeth's mind is a particular kind of ground, one where gold 'groweth'. What sort of ground is this? The sort of ground where gold grows – ground that is as extraordinary as her majesty's mind is extraordinary. So far, so good. But this sentence's very last phrase introduces a problem. It is not just the case that her majesty's mind *harbours* virtue, it is also the case that virtue *enters* her mind. Virtue is not necessarily inherent in Elizabeth's mind but also something that may be admitted there. This statement makes sense in terms of supplicating the queen's gracious reception of Lyly's virtuous play, but it makes no sense in terms of the metallurgy of the first part of the analogy. How does gold get in the ground? Is gold introduced to the ground from the outside, just as the virtue that enters the queen's mind is introduced from the outside? If so, then we start to get sceptical. The prevailing science in the late sixteenth century of how metals form in the earth followed Aristotle's *Meteorologica*. According to Aristotle, the sun's heat produces 'exhalations' of two sorts in the earth, moist and dry, and when the dry exhalations contained in rocks encounter the moist exhalations contained in looser dirt, they congeal into metal such as gold.[2] Aristotle includes nothing about external agency or influence in this process. Gold is not like plants; it doesn't grow from a seed of itself that is introduced into a growth medium.

That is, not unless you are growing gold alchemically. Alchemists were as indebted to Aristotle as every other early modern proto-scientist was.[3] But in order to validate growing gold or other valuable metals in the workshop instead of in the earth – that is, in order to justify their own agency in the process – alchemists had to replace Aristotle's earth science theory with his theories of sexual generation. The alchemical process is like a pregnancy, instigated by the introduction of seed into a receptive medium. The advantage of theorising alchemical production as sexual reproduction is that the alchemist may envision multiplying the product far beyond the initial ingredients. With alchemy, as with the generation of life from seeds, you can get more – infinitely more – at the end of the process than was put in at the beginning. Although many sceptics protested alchemy's fast and loose treatment of classical scientific theory in this regard, most alchemists made no bones about subscribing to a metallurgical science that according to prevailing standards was patently incorrect.[4]

My sense is that there is very good reason for the gold of *Galatea*'s prologue to be grown alchemically rather than in proper Aristotelian metallurgical fashion. As it turns out, the entirety of *Galatea* is in some sense about the blatant and unrepentant practice of and adherence to false knowledge. This false knowledge comes to include not only the enterprise of alchemy, one of the occupations tried on by Rafe, the aspiring and criminally minded young man who is the centre of the play's comic subplot; it also includes the very underpinnings of Lyly's play both in Ovidian transformation and in the humanistic education that has made Ovid's text accessible and meaningful to Lyly's audience. The same humanistic education, it must be said, on which Lyly's own livelihood and aspirations depended.

It is not surprising, of course, that alchemy shows up in a late sixteenth-century play about Ovidian transformation, since alchemy, whose popularity in England was on an upswing that would continue through the mid-seventeenth century, offers a treasure trove of tropes for metamorphosis.[5]

But alchemy is more than a convenient set of associations in this play. *Galatea* is among a group of literary texts of the sixteenth and seventeenth centuries that use alchemy to signal the way that individuals and cultures can hold in their minds two states of knowledge at the same time, one known to be credible and one known to be incredible. In a recent book, I argue that alchemy can serve this purpose because of its own unusual status as a discipline of study and practice in the sixteenth and seventeenth centuries.[6] Unlike other branches of natural philosophy whose status gradually shifted from orthodox to doubtful in the sixteenth and seventeenth centuries – for example, Galenic medicine or Ptolemaic astronomy – alchemy had drawn enthusiasm and scorn in equal measure ever since its introduction into Europe in the twelfth century. As a result, alchemy held different truth values in different settings and for different practitioners and audiences. Depending on one's purpose or intellectual inclination, alchemy could be a practical occupation crafting useful and saleable products; an esoteric pursuit of spiritual, transformative wisdom; a madman's delusion; or a con man's game. At every historical moment of its European heyday, alchemy taken as a whole was thus both true and false.

My interest lies not in sorting early modern responses to alchemy into fans and foes, but rather in those literary writers of the period who understand alchemy's multiple truth values as granting a special and important epistemological status: alchemy can be characterised as knowledge that is also non-knowledge. More precisely, these authors deploy alchemy to signal a mode of choosing not to know what one knows to be true. Or, to put it the other way around, they deploy alchemy to signal a state of knowing something isn't true but choosing to believe it anyway. My own word to describe this peculiar epistemological manoeuvre is 'disknowledge'. In a state of disknowledge, one prefers the alternative fact to the proven fact, the admittedly wacky theory to the established theory, the unworkable idea to the well-established practice. And one does so knowing full well that the choice is to be wrong rather than right, thereby defining truth as an operative rather than a verifiable function.

After the prologue, it takes some time for *Galatea* to associate alchemy with the state of disknowledge, and, as we shall see, the play arrives at this association only by way of Ovidianism. In the comic secondary plot of Lyly's play, in which the masterless young man Rafe seeks an apprenticeship that is lucrative no matter its ethical standing, alchemy is at first labelled as knowledge that is simply false, even if usefully false. For example, alchemy is useful as a generator of sophisticated jargon that will bamboozle anyone who encounters it. Moreover, alchemy is not the only profession with a difficult technical vocabulary. The first occupation that Rafe lights on is that of a sailor, but he wilts in the face of mastering the very first thing a mariner must know, the points on the compass. Encountering the vocabulary of 'North. North and by east. North northeast. Northeast and by north' and so on, Rafe first bumbles the exercise and then exclaims, 'I will never learn this language. It will get but small living, when it will scarce be learned till one be old' (I, iv, 59–60, 73–4). Alchemy, similarly, is also identified as a craft with special 'terms' and particular 'points' one must learn, as the alchemist's apprentice Peter puts it (II, iii, 53–4). When Rafe meets up with him, Peter is complaining to himself that alchemy 'is a very secret science, for none almost can understand the language of it: sublimation, almigation, calcination, rubification, incorporation, circination, cementation, albification, and [frementation], with as many terms unpossible to be uttered as the art to be compassed' (II, iii, 11–16).[7]

The difference between alchemy and seamanship, as the play soon reveals, is that alchemy is good for nothing, as Rafe complains after the alchemist fails in his promise to make of Rafe's 'silver thimble . . . a whole cupboard of plate' and 'of a Spanish needle . . . a silver steeple' (III, iii, 11–13). Alchemy is no more than licensed thievery, as Peter makes clear when he turns the alchemical goal of 'multiplication' into the art of subtraction, taking things away: 'such a beggarly science it is, and so strong on multiplication, that the end is to have neither gold, wit, nor honesty' (II, iii, 31–3). Or it is no more than a slick art for manipulating people, whether for sex or for money. Later on, Rafe jokes that the only kind of 'multiplying' he saw his alchemist master perform was on 'a pretty wench come to his shop, where with puffing, blowing, and sweating he so plied her that he multiplied her.' How? 'By the philosophers' stone', which he keeps in 'a privy cupboard' (V, i, 20–8). When Rafe first meets Peter and is promised that the alchemist is able 'to pave ten acres of ground' with a mere 'one pound of gold', he eagerly asks, 'How might a man serve him, and learn his cunning?' (II, iii, 50–2). While Rafe's phrasing pairs 'cunning' with its venerable sense of 'learning', his aim is not alchemical wisdom but rather the recently coined sense of 'cunning' as 'skillful deceit'.[8] Alchemy, Rafe recognises, is utter flimflam, and despite his disappointment at not having a wealth of silver made out of his thimble, Rafe has known alchemy to be flimflam all along. Indeed, whatever discipline Rafe adopts, he is in the 'cunning' business only for profit that is ill-gotten. He was interested in the sailor's art only because he mistook the mariner's mastery of the compass, the shipman's 'one card', for the 'cunning at the cards' employed by the successful card sharp (I, iv, 35, 42–3). Similarly, in the end, he leaves the alchemist's service as much because the alchemist isn't a successful rogue as because the alchemist isn't a successful transmogrifier of metals.

Yes, alchemy is a sham. And yet, by way of Ovidian metamorphosis, alchemy is also something else. It has a special status as the one discipline, among all those that Rafe tries to master, that takes physical transformation as its métier and its aim. The alchemist himself is introduced by his apprentice Peter in Ovidian terms, as a hybrid between the human and the divine: 'A little more than a man, and a hair's-breadth less than a god' (II, iii, 42–3). Before this explanation, Rafe mistakes the alchemical terminology Peter is reciting for a very different kind of change: he thinks it is demonic. 'Let me cross myself! I never heard so many great devils in a little monkey's mouth!' (II, iii, 17–18). But his horror at what he presumes to be the black magic of Peter's string of words dissipates at almost the exact moment of Peter's corrective explanation that the alchemist is in fact quasi-divine. With alchemy we are in the world of Ovid, not the world of Satan. And it is this Ovidian reference to a demigod that introduces Rafe's potential state of disknowledge. Rafe understands alchemy to be both true and false, both efficacious and mendacious. Hearing of the alchemist's capacity to create untold wealth, Rafe willingly accepts Peter's claim that the alchemist is godlike – 'if he can do this, he shall be a god altogether' (II, iii, 47–8) – despite having just praised alchemy for Peter's revelation that it has no honesty about it and having declared himself a similar kind of thief: 'Then am I just of your occupation' (II, iii, 34).

Even when he is about to abandon his alchemical apprenticeship later in the play, Rafe maintains this dual expression of alchemy as both transcendent and preposterous. When Rafe complains that he hasn't seen his master create much of anything, the alchemist excuses his failure with the explanation that it isn't often that 'the just proportion of the fire and all things concur' well enough to ensure success. 'Concur? Condog!' Rafe exclaims (III, iii, 26–8). Repeating the alchemist's Latinate term for the exceptionally precise and hence chancy conditions of alchemical success, when all of the operation's elements 'concur', Rafe's expostulation expresses frustration at the alchemist's substitution of fancy language for solid results: a 'cur' is a 'dog', hence to 'concur' may be mocked as to 'condog'. But even in his frustration, Rafe does not deny that such a concurrence might be possible, even if it is highly unlikely ('Nay, if you must weigh your fire by ounces, and take measure of a man's blast, you may then make of a dram of wind a wedge of gold' (III, iii, 21–3)). Alchemy's efficacy, its 'concurrence', is so proximate to its status as claptrap, its 'condoggery', as to make no difference.

The same conflation of bad knowledge and good knowledge, true and false, appears in the play's repetitions of the word 'mystery', which carries the connotation both of something terribly occult and of something easily explicable. A mystery, on the one hand, is a truth of religious faith that is accessible only in a transcendent moment of divinely inspired understanding. We get a whiff of this meaning of 'mystery' when the apprentice alchemist Peter undiplomatically refers to alchemy as a 'craft'. 'Craft, sir boy?' objects the alchemist. 'You must call it mystery' (II, iii, 113). But 'craft' or 'skill' is another early modern definition of 'mystery', which may be used to denote a trade, something acquired through teachable motions and dogged repetition. Rafe immediately deconstructs the distinction, saying, 'All is one: a crafty mystery and a mystical craft' (II, iii, 114). Equating divinely inspired knowledge with ordinary knowledge, Rafe also turns both senses of 'mystery' toward the purpose of 'craftiness' as underhanded subterfuge.[9] But all is one: knowing that alchemy is a sham does not cause Rafe to discount alchemy as not a 'mystery' in the revelatory sense. Both possibilities are allowed to stand. Similarly, we learn two reasons why the alchemist is beggarly in appearance, not decked out as you would expect a man who can make gold to be. First, as Peter puts it, the alchemist 'is so ravished with his art that we many times go supperless to bed, for he will make gold of his bread; and such is the drought of his desire that we all wish our very guts were gold' (II, iii, 128–31). In this case, the alchemist is in genuine pursuit of alchemy; the implication is either that he buys alchemical supplies rather than food for his apprentices, or that he is in fact successful at making gold of bread, leaving his apprentices nothing to eat. Second, however, the alchemist is in rags because dressing well would draw the attention of a patron; the alchemist would 'be compelled to work for princes, and so be constrained to bewray [his] secrets' (II, iii, 81–2). While ostensibly Peter is claiming that the alchemist is good enough at his craft to 'work for princes', the subtle suggestion is that he doesn't want to look too prosperous because then he would attract patrons who would expect him to accomplish alchemy, which he can't. Here the alchemist's 'secrets' also hint at the double sense of 'mystery': what he keeps secret are both his occult means of alchemical transcendence and his (lack of) command of his craft. The alchemist seems both to be intent on making miracles happen in his furnace, and also to be just blowing smoke.

The dual nature of 'mystery' in this play returns us to how the disknowledge that characterises the pursuit of alchemy also characterises Ovidian transformation. Rafe, disappointed with the meagre outcome of alchemy, shifts his allegiance to an astronomer, who promises that his own 'cunning' – that word again – can go so far as to 'measure how many yards of clouds are beneath the sky' (III, iii, 47–8). Once again, Rafe's eagerness for profitable service couples his faith in the astronomer's divine wisdom with his equating that very knowledge with the skills of a rogue and a petty criminal. He says, 'Happy am I, for now I shall read thoughts, and tell how many drops of water goes to the greatest shower of rain. You shall see me catch the moon in the clips [eclipse], like a cony in a purse-net' (III, iii, 67–70). Cony-catching, as an early modern synonym for scamming, once again weds the astronomer's 'cunning' erudition with 'cunning' flimflammery – but Rafe does not mind the equation, not at all.

In fact, this equation is what leads Rafe to his most transcendent Ovidian experience. Once Rafe gains this 'astrological wisdom', the astronomer promises, his 'cunning shall sit cheek by jowl with the sun's chariot' (III, iii, 80–1). Rafe, too, envisions this future in the empyrean: 'Then I shall be translated from this mortality!' (III, iii, 78). Extraordinary, this deliverance from the shackles of earth and the limitations of the human. Extraordinary: but also impossible, and it is because we know our Ovid that we know this to be so. For a human to sit cheek by jowl with the sun's chariot is for him to imitate the folly of Phaeton, destined for a fall.[10] Thus when the astronomer promises Rafe that 'thy thoughts shall be metamorphosed, and made hail-fellows with the gods' (III, iii, 85–6), we hear not only the promise of Ovidian change but also its attendant failures. In the context of the Phaeton story, Lyly's subtle pun on 'hail' reminds us that Phoebus's unruly steeds are the agents of earth's first climatological disaster, as, in the unskilled charioteer's hands, the sun veers first too close to heaven and then too close to earth.[11] Metamorphosis is, in this case, a calamity resulting from stupidity and hubris. This is where Rafe's 'cunning' will lead him if he pursues this astronomer's blatantly overblown claims.

But pursuing untruth as if it were true is exactly what the play commits itself to. The word 'mystery' next recurs in the play's main plot, derived from Ovid's story of Iphis and Ianthe. In Act IV, Galatea and Phillida, both dressed as boys but by now well aware that they are both girls – Phillida admits as much when she tells herself, 'thou . . . lovest one that, I fear me, is as thyself is' (IV, iv, 40–1) – toy with linguistic tricks for changing the sex of one of them so that they may fulfil their desire for each other. Phillida offers to call Galatea 'mistress' as a way of making a show of love palatable. Galatea says, 'I accept that name, for divers before have called me mistress.' Phillida wants to know why, but Galatea demurs, saying, 'Nay, there lie the mysteries.' Her status as 'mistress' is the 'mysteries', she hints as she puns (IV, iv, 20–3).[12] Calling her female identity a mystery is a blatant lie, as both of the girls know; the true sex of each of them by this point falls into the category of an 'open secret', a secret that one continues to guard even though one is fairly certain everyone knows the truth.[13] But it is a lie that both of them continue to accept. And it is a lie that works out well enough when it comes to the 'mystery' that enwraps the end of the play, as Venus offers to change one of the couple into a boy, but refuses to reveal which one will be so changed until they are on the brink of their wedding: 'Neither of them shall know whose lot it shall be till they come to the church door' (V, iii, 184–5). Given the girls' earlier voiced suspicions that each has fallen for someone of her own sex, their protestations of surprise when their respective fathers identify them in this scene as 'my daughter' seem rather disingenuous (V, iii, 118). But divinity ultimately gilds the unsubtle but enabling falsehood that has allowed the girls' love to develop. Similarly, Venus's promise to turn one of the girls into a man operates both through mysterious divine agency and by means of that homeliest of agential forces, choosing by 'lot' (V, iii, 185). At that literally liminal place, the church's threshold, that place that is neither sacred nor secular, neither holy nor workaday, the mystery joins the mistress: occult knowledge ratifies as true that obvious, wholly quotidian subterfuge that we suspected to be false all along.

The out-and-out lie that works out well as truth gives us a way to read not only this play's ambiguous, offstage conclusion, but also its intellectual allegiances and its position on the social standing of learning. To make these connections I begin by noting one peculiarity about alchemy in the play. Whether we are to take alchemy seriously or whether we are to take it mockingly, alchemy in *Galatea* is unusual in that it is strikingly unambitious. On the whole, it is devoted not to creating something entirely new, but to creating like from like. Recall how in the prologue, the virtue of Queen Elizabeth's mind entertains more virtue, just as the ground that already has gold in it produces more gold. Similarly, alchemy in this play generally takes something small to create something that is more or less identical, just more of it. Rafe gives the alchemist a stolen silver thimble and expects him to transform it into a cupboard full of silver dinnerware, for example, just as Peter claims the alchemist can cover 'near . . . ten acres of ground' with gold by use of a pound of exactly that, gold (II, iii, 50–1).[14] In the same fashion, the alchemist himself boasts of being able to make eight thousand pounds of silver out of a single ounce of silver, not of something else (II, iii, 84–8). True, we hear claims that the alchemist made a golden shower 'of a spoonful of tartar alum', astringent mineral salts – in other words, not like from like (II, iii, 103–4). On the other hand, however, we also hear that his power to transform disparate ingredients into something else entirely is strictly limited: 'with the fire of blood and the corrosive of the air he is able to make nothing infinite' (II, iii, 104–6). Either this combination of elements produces very little – 'nothing infinite' – or, as the phrase jokingly suggests, it produces 'infinite nothing'. Better stick to starting with silver to get more silver.

With alchemy, so with transformation in the play as a whole: it is likeness – likeness of metals, likeness of sex – that creates the conditions for metamorphosis and perhaps is even the aim of metamorphosis. There is a telling similarity, in the end, between the two girls' resolution to go 'into the grove, and make much of one another' (III, ii, 64–5) and Venus's promise to make their marriage realisable: both forms of 'making much' rhetorically suspend transformation between instituting and not instituting true difference. Having previously recognised that Galatea is a girl, Phillida first backtracks on this insight and then resolves to pursue Galatea regardless: 'I will after him, or her' (IV, iv, 47). Male or female, either sex seems acceptable to Phillida. Similarly, despite Venus's assurances that 'one [of the girls] shall be' a man once the couple arrive at the church, both characters remain girls at play's end (V, iii, 185–6). Metamorphosis in this play implies perhaps not a remarkable transformation of species but rather, quite possibly, a fairly mundane reproducibility of the same.

Such a reproducibility comports with Laurie Shannon's observations on the way the early moderns valued friendship as an ideal likeness, a figure of the self in the other. Shannon refers this portrait of friends as an identical pair to Lorna Hutson's description of how 'a new pattern of subjectivity resulted from humanist strategies of teaching through *copia*'.[15] *Copia*, the rhetorical technique taught by Erasmus and others for increasing the matter of one's discourse, seems to promise limitless abundance, an increase of eloquence beyond our wildest dreams, just as Renaissance humanism itself promises access to an endless and endlessly proliferating world of newly accessed texts. But in practice, humanist pedagogy offered a rather narrow corpus of acceptable texts, many of those edited to remove unacceptable parts or to excerpt passages from their context so as to make their content less controversial.[16] What looks like abundance is actually conformity; what looks like invention is actually reproduction of the same. Hutson remarks on how *copia* must be 'husbanded', marshalled into the decorum proper to the rhetorical occasion.[17] Similarly, alchemy is identified in this play as operating, when it operates, under conditions of absolute controllability. Remember that the alchemist claims that the reason he and Rafe haven't made unlimited riches is that for alchemy to work, 'the just proportion of the fire and all things [must] concur' (III, iii, 26–7). Were such conditions ever to pertain, the predicted outcome of alchemy would eventuate, and the alchemist would fulfil his promises. But the fact that the alchemist has predicted fairly precise and delimited outcomes – enough silver to fill a 'cupboard of plate' or 'a silver steeple' – implies that in a successful alchemical operation the truly unexpected would never happen, and change would never be as surprising as the term 'metamorphosis' would suggest. In the same way, the humanist curriculum tends not to produce earth-shaking innovation; it tends instead to reproduce itself.

We know this to be true, just as the sixteenth century knew it to be true. And yet we choose, just as the sixteenth century chose, to believe otherwise. And so does Lyly's play choose otherwise, wrapping its occult transmutations in the pages of humanist schoolbooks. In the last act of *Galatea*, Rafe tells his brother Robin, with whom he has just been reunited, about the shortcomings of all of the masters he has served. The alchemist could multiply nothing but the child in his pretty wench's womb, and the astronomer imparted to Rafe no revelations except the fact that Rafe 'was a Jovialist, born of a Thursday' and thus will 'be a brave Venerian and get all [his] good luck on a Friday' (V, i, 46–8). These are mundane, unsurprising and non-transformative instances of knowledge. But immediately, the text turns that non-transformation into something rich and strange. Robin remarks on the astrologer's forecast that Rafe will have 'good luck' – by which he means 'get lucky' as we moderns would use the slang phrase – on Fridays, since ''tis strange that a fish day should be a flesh day' (V, i, 49). At which point Rafe enters upon an almost operatic set of transformations, taken both from Ovid and from the quotations of Ovid's *Heroides* that Lyly's grandfather William Lily included in his *Institutio compendiaria totius grammaticae*, the standard elementary Latin grammar in English schoolrooms for more than two hundred years: 'O Robin, *Venus orta mari*; Venus was born of the sea. The sea will have fish, fish must have wine, wine will have flesh, for *caro carnis est muliebre*' – flesh is feminine in gender (V, i, 50–2).[18] In quick succession in this speech, sea foam begets a goddess, the fish of the sea transform into flesh and flesh transforms back into the feminine by means of the gender of the Latin for 'flesh' and 'of flesh': *caro, carnis*. Lyly the humanist, by means of his grandfather the grammarian, has bested Pygmalion. He has conjured up a goddess and turned her into flesh.

This is an Ovidian metamorphosis in truth and indeed. Moreover, it is only because of the humanist's mastery of text that this metamorphosis can come about. Other kinds of mortal skill will not suffice. The play's last scene opens with Neptune, angry that his plans to sacrifice virgins have been disrupted, fuming, 'do men begin to be equal with gods, seeking by craft to overreach them that by power oversee them?' (V, iii, 10–11). Through the word 'craft', Neptune demotes what has been the play's dual sense of 'mystery' to a single, secular sense: human effort is not mystery as divine revelation, it is just a skilled artisan's 'craft' or a sneaky mortal's 'craftiness'. But Venus, who promises that one of the girls will be metamorphosed in the end, has a different take than merely labelling change as either artisanal *techne* or expedient falsehood. In order to make the transformation that she promises believable, Venus has to refer to herself as an intertextual being, one who can exist and have power only because, like good Renaissance schoolboys, we already know the story of a metamorphic change in sex from reading our Ovid: 'What is to love, or the mistress of love, unpossible? Was it not Venus that did the like to Iphis and Ianthes?' (V, iii, 145–6). Galatea's earlier pun on 'mysteries' as uniting the sacred and the mundane, the inexplicable and the ordinary, resurfaces here. In the person of the goddess, the *mistress* of love enacts the *mysteries* of love. But love may prove mysteriously transformative and truly metamorphic only because a humanist reading list has made the allusion legible. Venus must cite the Ovidian story of Iphis and Ianthe in order to cement her divine capacity. Only then do Galatea, Phillida and their fathers, along with Diana, Cupid and Neptune himself, all consent to the proposed change (V, iii, 147–72).

The play's fantasies of humanist power, however, are undercut in the same way that all transformation is undercut in the play. Venus's self-referential textuality blatantly calls attention to the fact that her citation of Ovid is in error. The answer to her ostensibly rhetorical question, 'Was it not Venus that did the like to Iphis and Ianthes?', is 'no'. In the *Metamorphoses*, Venus is not the goddess who accomplishes the transformation of female to male and thus makes the couple's marriage possible; it is Isis.[19] Perhaps Lyly is slyly indicating that humanistically educated sixteenth-century English students did not typically get as far in the *Metamorphoses* as the Iphis and Ianthe story, located in the ninth of fifteen books, and thus is making a joke appreciable only by those few who would notice this Venus-for-Isis error.[20] Or perhaps the joke is that he is reproducing the kinds of mistakes that a weary pedagogue might hear from students liable to recall the name of the familiar Roman goddess, Venus, in place of that of an unfamiliar Egyptian one, Isis. The two names sound similar and either one scans perfectly well, so why not substitute Venus for Isis, no matter how incorrect? In either case, the mistake highlights the fact that the Ovidian text was seldom transformative in the way that we scholars wishfully assume it must have been. Andrew Wallace has argued that the teaching of Ovid and Virgil inspired in humanist educators a sense of parallelism between these authors' typical tales of frustrated love and the teacher's experience of frustrated pedagogy – the schoolboy, after all, seldom becomes what William Lily's Latin grammar optimistically calls '*Amator Studiorum*, A lover of studies'.[21] Combined with its deferral of sex change until some unknowable future moment, *Galatea*'s misidentification of one goddess for another arguably marks the failure of both kinds of metamorphosis, amatory and intellectual.

The play's winking acknowledgment of Ovid as a pedagogical failure lends itself to another dimension of disknowledge that, as we shall see, implicates not only the text of *Galatea* but also both Lyly himself and his boy performers. What, exactly, is the status of the classical text in a humanist education and among England's educated classes? The first aspect of this question involves the status of the *Metamorphoses* as a pillar of the sixteenth-century grammar school curriculum.[22] I discussed above the way that alchemy in *Galatea* and humanism in early modern English schools share a goal of predictable reproducibility rather than radical transformation. When it came to maintaining textual control in this fashion, however, the destabilising ethos of the *Metamorphoses* and its erotic paganism posed particular difficulties in the early modern schoolroom. On the one hand, the long medieval tradition of moralising Ovid continued to have considerable presence and influence in sixteenth-century England in a way that assisted the pedagogical project of channelling Ovid for moral purposes. The first full English version of the *Metamorphoses* was not directly from Latin but rather a translation of the French *Ovide moralisé* (William Caxton's translation, completed in 1480). When Arthur Golding does translate the *Metamorphoses* directly from Latin in 1567, he adds a preface that recommends reading Ovid's pagan gods according to allegorical principles, so that 'Jove and Juno', for example, signify simply 'all states of princely port'.[23] This tradition easily comports with the humanist practice, widely employed in the schoolroom as well as outside it, of 'framing' exempla from classical texts so that the reader absorbs only fragments rather than confronting the textual whole.[24]

On the other hand, however, Golding and other sixteenth-century translators and interpreters of Ovid evince a conflict between knowing they ought to bring Ovid into line with Christian morals, and advocating for reading the *Metamorphoses* as a whole text, not as a series of detachable snippets.[25] The schoolroom, too, was at least theoretically open to a more complete reading of the Ovidian text, at least for those students whose Latin was advanced enough to undertake one. Ian Green notes that while early modern English schoolmasters 'were aware of the need to defend the use in class of Ovid's accounts of the dubious behavior of the Greek gods', these teachers 'as far as we can see used unexpurgated versions of Ovid, unlike their French counterparts'.[26] Shakespeare, to name one alumnus of sixteenth-century English grammar schools, notably mines the entirety of the *Metamorphoses* for material.[27] Susan Wiseman describes the *Metamorphoses* as so 'lodged in the vernacular and . . . built into the environment' of post-Reformation England that it amounted to a form of vernacular knowledge, even structuring descriptions of natural phenomena.[28] Given both this text's ubiquity and the potential dangers to one's morals and perhaps even one's salvation of having the *Metamorphoses* fully present in unmediated fashion, one might see the necessity of hedging Ovid's poem about with means for not taking it as gospel truth.

The tradition of moralising the *Metamorphoses* is one way of channelling Ovidian effect in acceptable directions, but a Christianised Ovid does not strike what I am arguing is the optimum heuristic and epistemological balance aimed for in *Galatea*: a state of belief in what one knows to be utterly untrue. We might find such a handling of Ovid, however, in the larger circumstances surrounding the writing and production of *Galatea*. Lyly's own career shows an approach to the classical text that takes advantage of its cultural capital while nonetheless undermining its truth value and disarming its capacity to change hearts and minds. Lyly himself received exactly the kind of humanist education that, in its advertised form, would have made him either a cleric or a courtier. Lyly's education, like his family lineage, had prepared him to be the kind of public man envisioned by the ideal of civic humanism: that is, a man equipped by his training in classical rhetoric and classical texts to improve himself and better his world. These principles had led an earlier generation of Tudor polemicists and schoolmasters, including Lyly's grandfather William Lily, to establish the *studia humanitatis*, including grammar, rhetoric, poetry and moral philosophy, as the core – indeed practically the entirety – of the grammar school curriculum. The idea was to train young men whose grounding in ancient wisdom, such as that found in Ovid, would suit them for a civil society on a par with that of ancient Rome. By the last decades of the sixteenth century, however, humanism had been evacuated of its efficacy, as I have discussed extensively elsewhere.[29] While the shift from knowledge as a kingdom of letters to knowledge as a field of empiricism was decades in the future, the end of the sixteenth century nonetheless saw the considerable erosion of the principle that general learning, and hence civic accomplishment and moral virtue, would ultimately be founded on the command of humane letters. And yet as an educational system, there was nothing to replace humanism. As is so often the case in pedagogical routine, the programme was followed even though it was suspected to be no longer adequate.[30]

Lyly's career, I would suggest, represents a solution of sorts to the hollowing out of the ideals of humanist education: as an author, he fully exploited humanism while nonetheless both satirising and frittering away its ideals. Lyly's grandfather and uncle, William Lily and George Lily, had put humanism into practice in their roles as co-founder of St Paul's School and as secretary to Cardinal (later Archbishop) Reginald Pole, respectively.[31] The vaunted education that his grandfather established and upon which his uncle based a public career launched John Lyly, in contrast, into a life of composing fripperies. Though patronised by the likes of Lord Burghley and the Earl of Oxford, Lyly made his fame not as a dedicated public servant but as the author of the phenomenally popular two volumes of *Euphues*, in which humanist curricula and humanist didacticism are both consistently undermined by prodigals who quote the classics but never successfully use them to turn society to good ends.[32]

After his splashy start with the *Euphues* volumes, Lyly turned his ambitions to writing plays for the newly formed boys' theatre companies. Lyly's plays, traditionally described as static and 'talky', have recently been re-evaluated as deeply committed to theatrical form and spectacle, a fact that we must take into account as we analyse their relationship to the humanist enterprise.[33] For many decades, modern critics assumed that the boys' companies' performance style *ipso facto* was parodic no matter how serious or didactic the dramatic content of the play being performed, a fact that, if true, in and of itself might have undercut the humanistic underpinning of a play like *Galatea*; however, this assumption has been debunked in more recent work on theatrical history.[34] But *Galatea*'s status as a narrative designed for the stage erodes the humanistic educational enterprise in other ways. Not only does Galatea's and Phillida's same-sex equality – an equality emphasised by the characters both being played by boys – erode the traditional master–pupil hierarchy on which a humanist education depends, as Elizabeth Mathie argues in her essay in this volume, but the play's commitment to a theatrical experience also tends to downgrade the very basis of humanist pedagogy, the written text. Kent Cartwright argues that in *Galatea*, Lyly explicitly stresses how humanistic conceptualisation and rhetoric fail in the face of 'the physical, kinetic, and emotional dimensions of experience'.[35] Lynn Enterline suggests, in turn, that such a failure was unwittingly built into humanistic education when it incorporated techniques of embodiment and theatricality into teaching students to imitate the classics. In this fashion, the humanist schoolroom unintentionally encouraged students to rely on emotions (even if not their own) rather than precepts, undermining humanism's purported faith in letters.[36] Lyly's turn to the stage thus might be understood as a genre-specific means by which to both exploit and diminish the humanist education in which he was brought up. Lyly seems to have devoted himself to that very literary form that would most demolish his eruditional background's validity while still showing it off.

This vocational form of disknowledge, in which one's occupation depends on an education to whose ideals that career does not ascribe, also applies to the boys' playing companies for whom Lyly wrote, the Children of Paul's and the Children of the Chapel Royal. Technically attached to schools, these companies were headed by masters who, as Andrew Gurr drily puts it, 'maintained with varying degrees of truth the claim that their play-acting was part of the educational curriculum'.[37] A boy actor's career sometimes began with impressment and indenture, not with the grammar-school curriculum. To be fair, it would be a mistake to describe the boy players solely as exploited, the equivalent of 'student athletes' in the US college sports system whose service is institutionally justified by the often dubious promise of an education. In many respects, a boy actor's career resembled a regular apprenticeship in the guild system. Records from the early seventeenth century show that a number of the actors and choristers from the boy companies progressed to careers as adult actors, and some, like Nathan Field, even became prominent playwrights.[38] Nonetheless, Lyly's own involvement with the boy companies demonstrates that, just as his work expressed a kind of gleeful cynicism regarding humanism as a means of inculcating morality and good judgment, so too did the theatrical enterprise into which Lyly threw himself evince cynicism regarding the enterprise of humanism as a means of social advancement. The boy players' careers gave the lie to the assumption that a humanist education might lead to a permanent place at court and lifelong status as a civic leader, and Lyly's own career gave the lie to the dream of educators like Richard Mulcaster that the theatre would be both training ground for and promulgator of humanism on a broader scale.

Lyly's theatrical career eventually devolved into his involvement in a somewhat shady and certainly shoddy shell structure of leases and subleases to play in Blackfriars that ultimately collapsed when the property owner, who complained that he understood his house would be used only for teaching and not as a 'continuall howse for plays', sued to recover the use of the property.[39] David Bevington argues that Lyly's complaint in the epilogue of *Endymion* about 'the malicious that seek to overthrow us with threats' refers to the fact that *Galatea*, which was first entered in the Stationers' Register in 1585 but perhaps not performed until 1588, was held up precisely because of Lyly's embroilment in the uncertain legal status of the Blackfriars playing space.[40]

Just as Rafe's stint as an alchemist's apprentice garners him, in the end, plenty of learning but no advancement – he emerges with 'a full head and an empty belly' (V, ii, 65) – so too does Lyly's theatrical career ultimately reveal that humanist learning and professional success have little to do with each other.

It is tempting, then, to refer the disknowledge that links alchemy, humanism and Ovidian metamorphosis to how Lyly seems to have himself viewed the course of his career. In the same way that Rafe's full awareness of the inefficacy of alchemy coexists with his ongoing sense that alchemy might actually work, and in the same way that Venus's mangling of Ovid at the end of *Galatea* coexists with her assurance of the truth of Ovidian metamorphosis, Lyly's career in the last decade of the sixteenth century seems to have blended his cognisance that an ambitious man in the late Elizabethan age must be prepared to shift vocational direction on a moment's notice with his insistence that the well-worn strategy of taking one's humanist credentials to court ought to be a sure path to success. The very author who built his career on being ahead of the curve in shifting literary fashion began, quite contrariwise, to expect loyalty and constancy from the milieu he was trying to please.[41] For many years, scholars acquiesced to G. K. Hunter's view of Lyly's professional hopes being dashed by the end of the time that *Galatea* was written and then revised, in the late 1580s and early 1590s. Hunter's analysis was based on Lyly's own word: by the 1590s, Lyly was complaining to Queen Elizabeth that his talents and selfless efforts had unfairly gone unrewarded.

> Thirteen yeares, y[ou]r: Highnes servant; Butt; yett nothinge, Twenty ffrindes, that though they say, they wilbee sure, I ffinde them, sure to[o] slowe, A thowsand hopes, butt all noethinge; A hundred promises, but yett noethinge, Thus Casting vpp: An Inventorye of my ffrinds, hopes, promises, and Tymes, the; Sum[m]a Total[is]: amounteth to Just nothinge.[42]

Lyly sounds for all the world like Rafe, a disbeliever in alchemy who is nonetheless exasperated that his silver thimble has not become a cupboard full of plate.

The scholarship of Leah Scragg and others has recently revised the portrait of Lyly that we might get from this whinging that all his work has come to nothing. While Lyly may not have gotten the offices he desired, he became a Member of Parliament and seems to have kept powerful friends; he also seems to have continued to compose entertainments for the queen. If he died in debt, it was not for lack of connections or lack of work.[43] However self-generated, though, Lyly's frustration reminds us that *Galatea*'s pun on 'mystery' as both sacred and mundane is a matter of etymological accident: the root of 'mystery' as a mere craft is not *misterium* or secrets, as it was often taken to be, but rather *ministerium* or servitude. Preferring to believe that your keen mind and superior education will necessarily get you the position you deserve may be quite attractive, even if, like Lyly, you were one of a late-humanist generation who were attempting to blaze alternative paths to success. From the vantage point of those who realised that true influence was to be gained from weightier occupations than writing fictions, the reason that Lyly was not part of Queen Elizabeth's inner circle was no mystery. But, on the evidence of his petitions to the queen, that was not what Lyly seems to have chosen to believe. He would prefer to attribute his failure to metamorphose into a man of influence to a monarch who will not, alas, rise to the level of Venus, the beneficent goddess of *Galatea*: the goddess for whom nothing, she says, is 'unpossible'. So she says. If we take what she says for true, it is not out of ignorance that it is false. We take it for true not because it is true, but because we wish it to be so.

The fact that Lyly's monarch is not just his ruler but also a queen makes the relation between our obviously unfounded but still unshakeable hopes in Venus's powers and Lyly's obviously unfounded but still unshakeable hopes in Elizabeth more than just a fortuitous analogy. Analysing both the Sudeley entertainments for Queen Elizabeth (1592), which were possibly authored by Lyly, and Lyly's late 1580s play *Love's Metamorphosis*, Cora Fox has described Lyly as matching his own plays' Ovidianism to the queen's changeable gender identity and to her power to modulate the register of men's various modes of desire for her. Lyly, Fox argues, founds his theatrical career on the literal prospect of queenly metamorphosis.[44] This circumstance might not only help us understand why Lyly might have been peeved that Elizabeth, as subject and instigator of change, had not, in all those years, changed her mind about rewarding him. It might also help us evaluate *Galatea*'s exploration of the centrality of knowledge practice to civic life.

Let me make explicit what I have been implying during the course of this essay. Part of the brilliance of *Galatea*'s structure is that its comic subplot helps reveal how the main plot raises disknowledge from being a cornerstone of vocational enterprise, as it is in Rafe's career, to the level of epistemological principle. At the end of the play, unlike in Ovid's Iphis and Ianthe tale, we don't know which girl will change to a boy (or even *whether* a girl changes to a boy), just as we don't know what happens to the virgin who, at the beginning of the play, had been left 'as a peace offering to Neptune', bound and immobile before the predations of Neptune's sea monster: 'Whether she be devoured of him, or conveyed to Neptune, or drowned between both, it is not permitted to know and incurreth danger to conjecture' (I, i, 60–2). The effect of this inconclusive conclusion on the play's treatment of same-sex desire has been much debated.[45] I would like to maintain focus, however, on the fact that we don't know if Venus does or even can do anything at all. In light of her fellow goddess Diana's scepticism about Venus's powers ('Is it possible?'), Venus's defence – 'What is to ... the mistress of love unpossible?' – starts to sound like an effort at either special pleading or skilful con-artistry (V, iii, 153–4). The omission of the results of divine action may evacuate divinity; what looks like Venus's mystery may be her audience's sheer ignorance. Or perhaps not: perhaps some extraordinary metamorphosis may yet occur. Venus's word 'unpossible' (a variant often used by Lyly) somehow focuses the matter. A word attached to alchemy earlier in the play, as Peter complains that alchemical terminology is 'unpossible to be uttered' (II, iii, 15), the 'unpossible' also appears in Galatea's illogical epilogue, which declares Cupid 'a conqueror' of the ladies in the audience 'sith it is unpossible to resist', even while this presumably inevitable outcome is enabled by Venus's ability to do what can't be done: 'make constancy fickleness, courage cowardice, modesty lightness, working things impossible in [the female] sex' (Epi., 11, 2–4).

The result of this uncertainty? What the gods do is mysterious and workaday, mighty and ineffective, horrific and unremarkable, transformational and static. At the end of *Galatea* all characters remain in a state of disknowledge, not knowing metamorphosis to be true, but believing nonetheless. Why? Because it satisfies. Galatea and Phillida declare themselves content because, whether the transformation happens or not, they may still 'embrace' and 'enjoy' each other (V, iii, 158–9). Their fathers are content because their dispute over which of their daughters must be made male has been adjudicated by Venus. Whether the transformation happens or not, they accept her ruling 'because she is a goddess' (V, iii, 177). And Rafe and his brothers are 'never better content' because Venus engages them to 'sing Hymen *before* the marriage' (V, iii, 208–10, my emphasis). Having discharged their duties before the moment at which the transformation either does or doesn't take place, they 'shall be sure to fill [their] bellies' regardless (V, iii, 210–11). In this constellation of contentment, sexuality and sustenance are sanctioned by authority and governed by law. What else could we ask for in a blueprint for a well-functioning civil society? Even if it is one based on the 'alternative facts' promulgated by disknowledge.

Notes

1. Lyly, *Galatea*, ed. Scragg, Pro., 13–17. All subsequent references to *Galatea* are to this edition and are cited parenthetically in the text. Composed between 1583 and 1585, *Gallathea* appeared in print in a 1592 quarto that refers to the play's having been 'played before the Queen's Majesty at Greenwich, on New Year's day', probably in 1588. The prologue may have been written for that specific performance. See Lyly, *Gallathea and Midas*, ed. Lancashire, pp. xiv–xv; and Lyly, *Galatea; Midas*, ed. Hunter and Bevington, p. 5.
2. Aristotle, *Meteorologica*, 3.6.378a.13–378b.6.
3. See Crane, *Losing Touch with Nature*.
4. Eggert, *Disknowledge*, p. 160. On the intersections between alchemy and theories of sexual identity and sexual reproduction, see, for example, Long, 'Odd Bodies'; Cislo, *Paracelsus's Theories of Embodiment*; and Eggert, *Disknowledge*, pp. 160–8.

5. There is even a widespread tradition in medieval and early modern alchemical writing that some of the tales of the *Metamorphoses* are allegories of alchemical processes. See Willard, 'The Metamorphoses of Metals'.
6. This paragraph and the next sum up the argumentative framework of Eggert, *Disknowledge*; this book, however, does not treat Lyly or *Galatea*.
7. I have restored the spelling 'frementation' from the first quarto of *Galatea* in place of the typical modern editorial correction 'fermentation' because the error seems to me deliberate on Lyly's part (Lyly, *Gallathea* [1592], C3r). Peter's list of terms indicates that learning alchemical lingo is part of the difficulty of learning alchemy itself, whose practices, like its disciplinary language, ranged from intentionally obfuscatory to necessarily inventive. Many alchemical words were so useful that they quickly became part of the jargon of what we would now call 'materials science', and many then crossed by way of metaphor into ordinary language. We owe terms like 'sublimation', for example, to alchemy. Other alchemical terms, however, were mocked by contemporary writers for their over-complication of processes that could have been described more simply. The joke of Peter's complaint is that these words are 'difficult' both in the sense of being simply hard to say and in the sense of being brand new. He gets wrong a relatively familiar alchemical word ('fermentation') that had been in broader circulation since Chaucer's alchemical *Canon's Yeoman's Prologue and Tale*, but he also posits a brand-new word, 'circination', that Lyly seems to have invented himself (*OED*, 'circination' n.1.a); R. Warwick Bond's surmise that this is an error for Chaucer's 'citrinatioun', meaning 'turning yellow', is implausible (Lyly, *The Complete Works*, vol. 2, p. 433). 'Almigation' may also be a Lylian neologism. Usually glossed by editors as an error for 'amalgamation', a word Lyly could have found in Reginald Scot's *Discoverie of Witchcraft* (1584), 'almigation' is as likely to be a Lylian coinage based on Latin *almus*, 'nourishing'.
8. The *OED* cites Richard Stanyhurst's translation of the *Aeneid* (1582) as the first use of 'cunning' as 'skillful deceit' (*OED*, 'cunning' n^1.5.a).
9. 'Crafty' had been used in the sense of trickery since at least the early thirteenth century (*OED*, 'crafty' adj.3.a and adj.3.b). Like much of his alchemical terminology, Lyly seems to have gotten the bifurcated meaning of 'craft' as both profession and sneakiness from Chaucer's *Canon's Yeoman's Prologue and Tale*. Chaucer does not, however, associate alchemy with 'mystery' and thus avoids its association with religious sublimity.
10. Ovid, *Metamorphoses*, 2: 31–328.
11. Ovid, *Metamorphoses*, 2: 167–272.
12. Lancashire asserts that 'mistress' is an 'obsolete plural form of *mysteries*' (Lyly, *Gallathea and Midas*, p. 56 n. 20), but I have not been able to verify this claim. It is, of course, unnecessary for this 'obsolete plural form' to have existed for Lyly's pun on mistress/mysteries to work.
13. Miller, *The Novel and the Police*, p. 207.
14. While exaggeratedly impressive, gilding ten acres of land with a pound of gold is not Midas-like in its extravagance. In 2013, the dome of the Colorado state capitol building in Denver was re-gilded with only 65 ounces of gold, using a process for extra-thin gold leaf that has been employed by the contractor, Giusto Manetti Battiloro of Florence, since the seventeenth century. The 65 ounces furnished 140,000 gold leaves, each of them $3^1/_8$ inch square, enough surface area to cover about 0.22 acres in total. Proportionally, it would take just under 185 pounds of gold to gild ten acres. See the *Denver Post*, 'Gold Leaves'; Giusto Manetti Battiloro S.p.A., 'The Manetti History'; and the State of Colorado, 'Dome Restoration'.
15. Shannon, *Sovereign Amity*, p. 25; Hutson, *The Usurer's Daughter*.

16. See Nauert, *Humanism and the Culture of Renaissance Europe*, pp. 214–15.
17. Hutson, *The Usurer's Daughter*, pp. 48–9.
18. For the longevity of William Lily's Latin grammar, see Jewell, *Education in Early Modern England*, p. 3.
19. Ovid, *Metamorphoses*, 9: 666–797.
20. Ian Green remarks that from the historical and bibliographic evidence, it is 'not clear if students were expected to get through all 15 books of *Metamorphoses* ... [Schoolmaster] John Clarke of Hull focused on the first six or seven books, which he recommended going through twice with students' (Green, *Humanism and Protestantism*, p. 225).
21. Wallace, *Virgil's Schoolboys*, p. 76.
22. Green describes Ovid as standard in the curriculum of grammar schools' upper forms, and notes that the *Metamorphoses* was in so much demand in schools that 'a new edition was published every three or four years from the 1580s to the 1740s' (Green, *Humanism and Protestantism*, p. 223).
23. Golding, *Ovid's Metamorphoses*, p. 59. For the afterlife of Caxton's translation of the *Metamorphoses* in sixteenth-century England, see Oakley-Brown, *Ovid and the Cultural Politics of Translation*, pp. 165–91.
24. See Crane, *Framing Authority*.
25. See Lyne, *Ovid's Changing Worlds*, pp. 34–53.
26. Green, *Humanism and Protestantism*, p. 224.
27. Bate, *Shakespeare and Ovid*, p. 23.
28. Wiseman, *Writing Metamorphosis in the English Renaissance*, p. 56.
29. See Eggert, *Disknowledge*, pp. 14–26 and *passim*.
30. Ibid., p. 17; Dolven, *Scenes of Instruction*, pp. 8–11.
31. Hunter, 'Lyly, John'.
32. See Helgerson, *The Elizabethan Prodigals*, pp. 58–78. There is a long critical history of exploring how *Euphues* undermines humanistic values. See Lunney, 'Introduction'. Recently, Arthur Kinney has argued that the entire structure of *Euphues* – its plot, setting and prose style – works to dismantle verity in general and classical verities in particular (Kinney, 'John Lyly's Poetic Economy'). Katharine Wilson persuasively describes the Euphues volumes as handbooks for how to fake morality, as Lyly 'sweep[s] his readers into agreeing that enjoying a story of adulterous gods is a moral duty' (Wilson, *Fictions of Authorship*, p. 56).
33. See, for example, Scragg, 'Speaking Pictures'.
34. The assumption that the boys' companies' playing style was always parodic derived from the satire-based repertory of the second phase of boys' companies in London, a decade or more after Lyly's plays. The earlier boys' companies seem to have cultivated performance expertise in a wider range of styles. See Lamb, 'Boys' Plays', p. 83.
35. Cartwright, *Theatre and Humanism*, p. 171.
36. Enterline, *Shakespeare's Schoolroom*.
37. Gurr, *The Shakespearean Playing Companies*, p. 218; see also Lamb, *Performing Childhood*, pp. 102–3.
38. Lamb, 'Boy's Plays', pp. 91–2; Williams, 'Field, Nathan'. For the bifurcated behaviour of the boys' companies as both exploiting and nurturing their young talent, see Lamb, *Performing Childhood*, pp. 55–65.
39. Chambers, *The Elizabethan Stage*, vol. 2, p. 496.
40. Lyly, *Endymion*, pp. 196, 49.
41. Not only did Lyly invent euphuism, which became the height of literary fashion for about a decade, he also led off what Daniel Moss calls the 'Ovidian vogue' of the 1580s and early 1590s (Moss, *The Ovidian Vogue*). Andy Kesson argues that

Lyly ought to be regarded as ahead of the curve, as well, in creating a role for the playwright as literary author. He was the first playwright to see a series of his plays into print, anticipating the likes of Ben Jonson by a decade or more (Kesson, *John Lyly and Early Modern Authorship*). Derek Alwes reads Lyly's plays as advertising his capacity to undertake any number of vastly disparate positions and roles, at court and beyond (Alwes, 'I would faine serve').

42. 'Another; L're: to, Queene, Elizabeth: ffrom John: Lillye', British Library Harleian MS. 1323, fol. 250, qtd. in Lyly, *The Complete Works*, vol. 1, pp. 70–1. Lyly had written a similar letter to the queen some three years earlier; see *The Complete Works*, vol. 1, pp. 64–5.
43. Scragg, 'The Victim of Fashion?'; Scragg, 'Angling for Answers'. For Lyly's late-in-life state of indebtedness, see Hunter, 'Lyly, John'.
44. Fox, *Ovid and the Politics of Emotion*, pp. 46–58. Jacqueline Vanhoutte, similarly, describes Lyly as tailoring his plays' rejection of normative, heterosexual marriage to the anomalous marital career of his queen (Vanhoutte, 'A Strange Hatred of Marriage').
45. Valerie Traub, for example, argues that the deferral of the sex change beyond the frame of the play leaves the two girls suspended in a state of mutual desire based on their mimetic similarity to each other (Traub, *The Renaissance of Lesbianism*, pp. 327–8). Mark Dooley, in contrast, argues that the play's conclusion lends itself to imagining that same-sex love persists past and outside the end of the performance (Dooley, 'Inversion, Metamorphosis, and Sexual Difference').

BIBLIOGRAPHY

Alwes, Derek, '"I would faine serve": John Lyly's Career at Court', *Comparative Drama* 34 (2000–1), pp. 399–421.
Aristotle, *Meteorologica*, trans. H. D. P. Lee (Cambridge, MA: Harvard University Press, 1952).
Bate, Jonathan, *Shakespeare and Ovid* (Oxford: Clarendon Press, 1993).
Cartwright, Kent, *Theatre and Humanism: English Drama in the Sixteenth Century* (Cambridge: Cambridge University Press, 1999).
Chambers, E. K., *The Elizabethan Stage*, 4 vols (Oxford: Clarendon Press, 1967).
Cislo, Amy Eisen, *Paracelsus's Theory of Embodiment: Conception and Gestation in Early Modern Europe* (London: Pickering & Chatto, 2010).
Crane, Mary Thomas, *Framing Authority: Sayings, Self, and Society in Sixteenth-Century England* (Princeton: Princeton University Press, 1993).
Crane, Mary Thomas, *Losing Touch with Nature: Literature and the New Science in Sixteenth-Century England* (Baltimore: Johns Hopkins University Press, 2014).
Denver Post, 'Gold Leaves for Colorado Capitol Building Return from Italy', 18 June 2013, http://www.denverpost.com/2013/06/18/gold-leaves-for-colorado-capitol-building-dome-return-from-italy/ (last accessed 26 June 2017).
Dolven, Jeff, *Scenes of Instruction in Renaissance Romance* (Chicago: University of Chicago Press, 2007).
Dooley, Mark, 'Inversion, Metamorphosis, and Sexual Difference: Female Same-Sex Desire in Ovid and Lyly', in Goran V. Stanivukovic (ed.), *Ovid and the Renaissance Body* (Toronto: University of Toronto Press, 2001), pp. 59–76.
Eggert, Katherine, *Disknowledge: Literature, Alchemy, and the End of Humanism in Renaissance England* (Philadelphia: University of Pennsylvania Press, 2015).
Enterline, Lynn, *Shakespeare's Schoolroom: Rhetoric, Discipline, Emotion* (Philadelphia: University of Pennsylvania Press, 2012).

Fox, Cora, *Ovid and the Politics of Emotion in Elizabethan England* (New York: Palgrave Macmillan, 2009).
Giusto Manetti Battiloro S.p.A., 'The Manetti History', http://www.manetti.com/en/company/ (last accessed 26 June 2017).
Golding, Arthur (trans.), *Ovid's Metamorphoses*, ed. Madeleine Forey (Baltimore: Johns Hopkins University Press, 2001).
Green, Ian, *Humanism and Protestantism in Early Modern English Education* (Farnham: Ashgate, 2009).
Gurr, Andrew, *The Shakespearean Playing Companies* (Oxford: Clarendon Press, 1996).
Helgerson, Richard, *The Elizabethan Prodigals* (Berkeley: University of California Press, 1976).
Hunter, G. K., 'Lyly, John (1554–1606)', *Oxford Dictionary of National Biography* (Oxford University Press, 2004; online edn, May 2008), http://www.oxforddnb.com.colorado.idm.oclc.org/view/article/17251 (last accessed 26 June 2017).
Hutson, Lorna, *The Usurer's Daughter: Male Friendship and Fictions of Women in Sixteenth-Century England* (London: Routledge, 1994).
Jewell, Helen M., *Education in Early Modern England* (Basingstoke: Macmillan, 1998).
Kesson, Andy, *John Lyly and Early Modern Authorship* (Manchester: Manchester University Press, 2014).
Kinney, Arthur F., 'John Lyly's Poetic Economy', *Connotations* 22 (2012/13), pp. 1–12.
Lamb, Edel, 'Boys' Plays', in Michael Hattaway (ed.), *A New Companion to English Renaissance Literature and Culture*, 2 vols (Chichester: Blackwell, 2010), Vol. 2, pp. 80–93.
Lamn, Edel, *Performing Childhood in the Early Modern Theatre: The Children's Playing Companies (1599–1613)* (Basingstoke: Palgrave Macmillan, 2009).
Long, Kathleen P., 'Odd Bodies: Reviewing Corporeal Difference in Early Modern Alchemy', in Kathleen P. Long (ed.), *Gender and Scientific Discourse in Early Modern Europe* (Farnham: Ashgate, 2010), pp. 63–85.
Lunney, Ruth, 'Introduction', in Ruth Lunney (ed.), *John Lyly* (Abingdon: Routledge, 2016), pp. xi–xxxix.
Lyly, John, *The Complete Works of John Lyly*, ed. R. Warwick Bond, 2 vols (Oxford: Clarendon Press, 1902).
Lyly, John, *Endymion*, ed. David Bevington (Manchester: Manchester University Press, 1996).
Lyly, John, *Galatea*, ed. Leah Scragg (Manchester: Manchester University Press, 2012).
Lyly, John, *Galatea; Midas*, eds George K. Hunter and David Bevington (Manchester: Manchester University Press, 2000).
Lyly, John, *Gallathea* (London, 1592).
Lyly, John, *Gallathea and Midas*, ed. Anne Lancashire (London: Edward Arnold, 1969).
Lyne, Raphael, *Ovid's Changing Worlds: English Metamorphoses, 1567–1632* (Oxford: Oxford University Press, 2001).
Miller, D. A., *The Novel and the Police* (Berkeley: University of California Press, 1988).
Moss, Daniel, *The Ovidian Vogue: Literary Fashion and Imitative Practice in Late Elizabethan England* (Toronto: University of Toronto Press, 2014).
Nauert, Charles G., Jr, *Humanism and the Culture of Renaissance Europe* (Cambridge: Cambridge University Press, 1995).
Oakley-Brown, Liz, *Ovid and the Cultural Politics of Translation in Early Modern England* (Aldershot: Ashgate, 2006).

Ovid, *Metamorphoses*, trans. Frank Justus Miller, rev. edn trans. G. P. Goold, 2 vols (Cambridge, MA: Harvard University Press, 1984).

Scragg, Leah, 'Angling for Answers: Looking for Lyly in the 1590s', *Review of English Studies* n.s. 67 (2016), pp. 237–49.

Scragg, Leah, 'Speaking Pictures: Style and Spectacle in Lylian Comedy', *English Studies* 86 (2005), pp. 298–311.

Scragg, Leah, 'The Victim of Fashion? Rereading the Biography of John Lyly', *Medieval and Renaissance Drama in England* 19 (2006), pp. 210–26.

Shannon, Laurie, *Sovereign Amity: Figures of Friendship in Shakespearean Contexts* (Chicago: University of Chicago Press, 2002).

State of Colorado, 'Dome Restoration', https://www.colorado.gov/capitol/dome-restoration (last accessed 26 June 2017).

Traub, Valerie, *The Renaissance of Lesbianism in Early Modern England* (Cambridge: Cambridge University Press, 2002).

Vanhoutte, Jacqueline, 'A Strange Hatred of Marriage: John Lyly, Elizabeth I, and the Ends of Comedy', in Laurel Amtower and Dorothea Kehler (eds), *The Single Woman in Medieval and Early Modern England: Her Life and Representation* (Tempe, AZ: Arizona Center for Medieval and Renaissance Studies, 2003), pp. 97–115.

Wallace, Andrew, *Virgil's Schoolboys: The Poetics of Pedagogy in Renaissance England* (Oxford: Oxford University Press, 2010).

Willard, Thomas, 'The Metamorphoses of Metals: Ovid and the Alchemists', in Alison Keith and Stephen Rupp (eds), *Metamorphosis: The Changing Face of Ovid in Medieval and Early Modern Europe* (Toronto: Centre for Reformation and Renaissance Studies, 2007), pp. 151–64.

Williams, M. E., 'Field, Nathan (bap. 1587, d. 1619/20)', *Oxford Dictionary of National Biography* (Oxford University Press, 2004), http://www.oxforddnb.com.colorado.idm.oclc.org/view/article/9391 (last accessed 26 June 2017).

Wilson, Katharine, *Fictions of Authorship in Late Elizabethan Narratives: Euphues in Arcadia* (Oxford: Clarendon Press, 2006).

Wiseman, Susan, *Writing Metamorphosis in the English Renaissance, 1550–1700* (Cambridge: Cambridge University Press, 2014).

7

THE PROBLEM WITH LOVE: UNTOWARD ENGAGEMENT AND HUMANIST PEDAGOGY IN *GALATEA*

Elizabeth Mathie

To be untoward in early modern England is to be 'difficult to manage, restrain, or control; intractable, unruly, [or] perverse' – to be untrainable.[1] The definition is simple enough. However, the task of determining what constitutes 'untoward' behaviour, especially in the humanist classroom where students were expected to be both obedient and inventively independent, is not so straightforward. Pedagogues in the period subscribed to an educational regime that embraced the contradictory goals of producing creative and eloquent performers and fashioning adult men who would dutifully fit into (and perpetuate) pre-existing hierarchical systems in an intensely stratified English society. While the transformation of schoolboys into independent adults was built into the concept of education, student obedience was fundamental to maintaining harmonious order among students and instructors of disparate social status. This essay examines John Lyly's *Galatea* for how it plays with the problems such contradictions present, especially in the context of a particular pedagogical claim that students could be made self-motivated, obedient and successful through the power of a single affective force: love.

Written to be performed by a schoolboy troupe for Queen Elizabeth I, *Galatea* is ostensibly a love story about two shepherdesses – Galatea and Phillida – who fall in love while they are both disguised as boys. The play has been fruitfully read by scholars for what it reveals about the radical potential and the conservative limits of early modern English sexuality.[2] By turning attention to the pedagogical and hierarchical setting in which it would have been performed, I shift attention to an important element of the play which, though intertwined with issues of sexuality, has been less explored. While scholars of sexuality have persuasively shown that Lyly's play is unique in representing homoerotic love as both possible and even, according to a few scholars, preferable to patriarchal heterosocial institutions like marriage,[3] viewing the play with education in mind reveals that the similitude that characterises homoerotic love in the drama also encourages humanist scholarly goals. At the same time, the play suggests that homoerotic love does not necessarily bolster the hierarchical structures central to English education. The represented coequality of homoerotic love that threatens patriarchal claims for the necessity of difference in marriage and sexual consummation also threatens to undo the categories of master and subordinate – categories that schoolmasters seek to maintain.

Humanist Pedagogy in *Galatea*

The language of love used in *Galatea*, especially as it appears between the central romantic pair, is not exclusively sexual or romantic. In contemporaneous humanist treatises, love is often described as a central component of how masters seek to cultivate a necessary affective engagement in their students. In an effort to foster love of learning – resisting long-standing stereotypes of schoolmasterly cruelty – humanists work actively to impress upon their audiences that gentleness is central to effective teaching.[4] In his authoritative treatise on education, *The Scholemaster* (1570), Roger Ascham writes that 'from seauen yeare olde, to seauentene, loue is the best allurement to learninge', stressing that love does not just ease master–student relations but also leads pupils to desire training from their instructor.[5] Love relatedly, and importantly for Ascham, encourages students to want the approval of their tutor – a useful motivation for the obedience educators require.[6] For Ascham, love helps to promote a desirable 'towardness' in students – that is, a willingness and aptness to learn paired with a useful docility and tractability – a trainability.[7]

Ascham was not alone among pedagogical authorities in his emphasis on love and care in schooling, nor was he alone in supporting gentler instructional methods on pragmatic rather than purely ideological grounds.[8] The Puritan schoolmaster John Brinsley writes in his *Ludus literarius: or, the grammar schoole* (1612) that a good school requires 'constancy in good orders ... with continual demonstration of loue in the Masters towards the Schollars, & a desire to do them the vttermost good' because that caring 'shall ouercome the most froward in time; and vsed with the rest, shal vndoubtedly bring forth the fruit of their [the schoolmasters'] desires'.[9] Similarly, humanist pedagogue Richard Mulcaster cautions against sending children to school too early because frustration may cause their schoolmasters to beat them and ruin students for years to come, 'whom if we beat we do the children wrong in those tender yeares to plant any hatred, when loue should take roote, & learning grow by liking'.[10] Masterly commitment to nurturing pupils' loving inclinations was in turn expected to inspire students to put in their own form of affective work.[11] The instructor's careful approach could only make it possible for love of learning to develop and continue to grow in properly 'toward' students. To make full use of the opportunity love presented, schoolboys also had to embrace it as a motivator for themselves. In other words, they had to labour to passionately engage with and enjoy the material given them by their master.[12] Subordinate agency is therefore at the heart of the loving labour that these pedagogues hope to cultivate in their collaborative but clearly structured classrooms.

Even aside from its emphasis on love, *Galatea* exemplifies the labour schoolboys did in the classroom. Performance was central to early modern English schoolboys' academic success. Humanist pedagogues were particularly well positioned to take an interest in the inner motivation of their pupils, and therefore to acknowledge the value of love in the learning process, in part because of their use of performative instruction. An emphasis on 'imitatio' and rhetorical presentation, in particular, meant that pupils were taught rhetorical prowess not only by learning the texts and languages they were assigned, but also by imitating their master's delivery of those texts.[13] Schoolboys were asked to mentally and physically embody the passions and modes of expression exemplified in their texts and by their teacher with the aim that they would eventually incorporate those models into their own identities. By these means, they were expected to become the masculine models they could at first only pretend to be.

Not a simplistic mimicry, the imitation instructors demanded was more like the process by means of which an actor embodied his part.[14] In fact, acting itself was an important element of many early modern English schoolboys' educational experience. Boys' grammar schools and choirs in the mid and late sixteenth century provided students first 'with a thorough grounding in Latin grammar', but then quickly shifted to 'supplementing instruction with exemplary literary illustrations of eloquent and wise uses of language' to 'reinforce a developing mastery of language, including an emphasis on voice, expression, and eloquence'.[15] During these later educational stages, students often read aloud and even performed scenes in the classroom.[16] Paired with drama-centred modes of instruction, several choirs and grammar schools also trained schoolboy troupes – St Paul's choir and grammar school, for example, both included boy actors – which performed at court and elsewhere.[17] Though they would eventually fall out of style, these troupes were immensely popular and successful in the 1580s when *Galatea* was first staged, and they seem even to have surpassed adult companies in certain respects.[18] Text-focused schoolboy performers played a central role in bringing the interior, empathetic and subtly affective acting styles that a literary approach affords to English drama.[19] Passionate, inventive and full-minded engagement with their subjects is part of what made these schoolboys successful, both in the classroom and on the stage.

Encouraging passionate agency among students could have its drawbacks, though. Lynn Enterline has explored some of the complications that arise from schoolmasters' use of affectively engaged performance as 'a method for obtaining compliance with the school's linguistic and social regime',[20] contending that humanism's embrace of 'imitatio' could authorise students to embody both male and female classical models. Thus it allowed male students to identify with modes of expression coded feminine as well as those coded masculine, those resistant as well as those conforming to masculine standards.[21] Scholars have recently disagreed about whether this possibility was inadvertent or actively embraced by pedagogues.[22] Whether or not instructors intended for their trainees to have identificatory access to both ideal civic male models and more divergent forms, however, it is well-established that the participation required of schoolboys encouraged them to go beyond mere mimicry and to engage deeply with their models – whether those models offered a performed civic masculinity or whether they represented passions resistant to that ideal.[23] And indeed, resistance to civic and masculine ideals was available in some literary works introduced into the classroom. Subversion was perhaps especially possible, for example, through the works of Ovid. Though part of the curriculum, Ovid's corpus often strays from the masculine expressions of 'epic duty' found in other humanist standards, potentially allowing boys to identify with erotic and feminine figures 'at some distance from their masters' declared purpose', both on and off the schoolroom stage.[24]

Despite the risk of valuing potentially disorderly student interests when divergent inspiration was abundant, it was practical for educators to acknowledge that students' desire and pleasure were integral to their success in a programme that was dependent on pupils' inventive embrace of their embodied labour.[25] The independent work of the will that performative skill requires meant that, for figures like Ascham, students who were self-motivated by their love of their teacher and their subject (and their according desire to become what their instructor intended them to become) were more likely to succeed. Love, then, was viewed as a good motivator for the work schoolboys were asked to do. In *Galatea*, that agential student love, as well as the labour it inspires, both does and does not work the way humanist educators hope it will.

Lyly's drama represents key humanist educational methods – imitation and performance – as particularly effective in encouraging the kind of independent affective engagement pedagogues required of their pupils. In the process of so representing them, however, *Galatea* demonstrates the predicament that a reliance on subordinate love can pose for hierarchy. It shows how affective labour can work against rather than for social stratification by leading subordinates to exercise too much power in their own subordination, selecting and creating masters of their own choosing. Simultaneously, it shows how love can usher in realisations of similarity, blurring rather than reasserting difference, and thus undermining the authority of instructors who sought obedience as much as affection.

I look at the promises and problems of humanist training posed in *Galatea* partly by considering how transformation pervades the play. While Venus's offer of a sex change is arguably the most literal metamorphosis of the drama, and has accordingly received the most critical attention, the drama's subplots similarly contain figures who seek changes to their forms – the apprentice, Rafe, who is in search of a master, and the maiden Hebe, who is expected to serve as a sacrifice for her nation. The transformations Hebe and Rafe desire are not transgressive or form-defying, but normalising – conducive to the preservation of social order. Especially in the case of education, but in other instances of training in early modern England as well, such as in apprenticeships and household service positions, young subordinates who were being trained to be obedient and loyal to their masters could aspire to serve as masters themselves, even if not surpassing the status of their initial superior. This mobility offers a 'transformation' of sorts, though not a very Ovidian one. These kinds of societally sanctioned transformations are central to the subplots and central story of *Galatea*, and in turn should colour our reading of the plot's final sex change.

Scholars have debated whether we are meant to believe that the transformation Venus offers at the end of *Galatea* will take place.[26] In fact, Katherine Eggert argues in her essay in this collection that the characters believe Venus's transformation is possible, despite evidence to the contrary, only through a conscious embrace of 'disknowledge' – they believe it because it allows their society to function to their satisfaction rather than because they think it is true.[27] I too read Venus's offer as inconclusively possible, focusing instead on how it operates as an after-the-fact authorisation of an educational process which has already occurred. Viewed through pedagogical prescriptions, the play's central transformation is both more quotidian and more problematic for English social structures than Venus's grand gesture seems to suggest. From a modern perspective it might seem necessary to separate Venus's promise from the more common social mobility associated with education, but the distinction would not necessarily be as stark for Lyly's audiences.[28] Schoolboy plays like *Galatea* sometimes joke about their actors' transitional status between childhood and adulthood as the spectacle of boys playing the roles of men and gods lent itself to quips about physical stature and facial hair.[29] Lyly's audience, then, would not have been unfamiliar with thinking about how these actors were on their way to being, but not yet fully made into, men. While transformation might make Lyly's setting in some respects 'a never-never land where Greek gods can appear on the banks of the Humber',[30] it simultaneously insists on that fantasy world's palpable connection to Lyly's lived social world.

GOOD AND BAD SUBORDINATES

Galatea opens with separate scenes that prepare us to read the main lovers in terms of pedagogical training. Each girl is told by her father why she must be disguised as a boy – both girls are beautiful enough that their fathers worry they will be selected as the country's virgin sacrifice to Agar, Neptune's sea monster, who must be appeased, every five years, with the most beautiful maid in order to prevent devastating floods. In both cases, the shepherdesses are submissive to their fathers' wishes despite hesitation about the honourability of the proposed plan.[31] Phillida casts her obedience as a feature of her girlishness. Once disguised, she laments her clothing and how she must perform boyishness with her body: 'I neither like my gait nor my garments, the one untoward, the other unfit, both unseemly' (II, i, 14–15). By calling the gait of a boy 'untoward', Phillida opposes her womanly body to her body disguised as a man. In part, Phillida calls her new gait awkward.[32] Having highlighted her own obedience from the play's beginning, though, Phillida also refers to what her newly disguised body communicates about her tractability. Phillida's characterisation is comical not only because she insults the body of the actor who plays her part, but additionally because she is played (presumably successfully) by a boy – belying the distinction she assumes between her inherent towardness and a boy's natural untowardness. Contrary to the image the shepherdess calls up, the student who plays Phillida presumably succeeds in doing so precisely because he is a 'toward' schoolboy who has learned (and is learning) his lessons.

Phillida mistakes herself as inherently different in her subordination from the many boys who possess, according to humanist pedagogical authors, a 'natural towardness'.[33] The scene of the girls' first encounter jokes about the parallels between character and actor. Each girl expresses surprise at the lack of confidence they see in the 'boy' before them, allowing the audience to laugh about the shepherdesses' failures to comfortably act out the roles newly assigned them by their fathers. In addition, their reactions to each other wink metatheatrically at the actual male schoolboy actors' indistinguishability from the characters they play – that is, their indistinguishability from girls failing to effectively perform masculinity. Galatea says in an aside upon seeing Phillida's embarrassment, 'I perceive that boys are in as great disliking of themselves as maids' (II, i, 18–19). Phillida echoes the joke, remarking of Galatea, 'It is a pretty boy and a fair. He might well have been a woman' (II, i, 21–2). Then, further cementing their link to the schoolboys who play them even as they insist upon their difference from men, Galatea says upon seeing the disguised Phillida: 'I will learn of him how to behave myself' (II, i, 12–13). She thus, along with her counterpart, determines that imitation of a masculine model, paired with her active embodiment of that role in performance, is the best way to successfully become a man.

Within this interplay between their failure to be convincing boys and their failure to find adequate masculinity in one another, the girls fluctuate between identifying their differences and displaying their similarities. The girls are drawn together in part based on what they identify as feminine features in the 'boy' before them, and their speeches mirror each other throughout the play.[34] While their verbal echoing emphasises the similitude integral to their desire, it also, as Valerie Traub suggests, renders their speech similar to that of schoolboys learning their lessons.[35] Each girl exhibits both similarity and imitation as she inadvertently trains her fellow while she seeks training for herself. They learn as schoolboys through both 'imitatio' and performance, mirroring the masculinity they think they find in their fellow and theatrically enacting the masculinity they hope to achieve. Initially hesitant to interact because they fear they might accidentally curtsey or blush, each girl is using the other's performance as evidence of masculinity (and thus apparently providing an adequate performance herself) by Act 3.[36] Assuring herself that Galatea cannot be a girl like her, Phillida reasons, 'Tush, it cannot be; his voice shows the contrary' (III, ii, 36–7). Echoing Phillida, Galatea assures herself of the same: 'Yet I do not think it; for he would then have blushed' (III, ii, 38–9). This shared imitative and performative labour, and the love it inspires in both, sets the shepherdesses apart, as we will see, from the other, less successful subordinate figures in the play.

To understand how exactly their evident success at the end of the play works, even as they imitate a model that, in the world of the play, seemingly would not serve their intended purpose, we can look first to the other subordinate characters' failed attempts at transformation through subordination. The village's choice of a virgin to sacrifice to the monster Agar provides one example. Because the two most beautiful virgins in the land are disguised and hidden in the woods, the citizens select a different maiden, Hebe, to serve as the sacrifice. Hebe expresses amazement along with despair that she should be considered the most beautiful. She begins her speech mourning that she is not in fact lovely enough for her role and yet, by the end of her speech, she seems to have accepted her place as sacrifice, goading Agar to 'Glut thyself till thou surfeit, and let my life end thine! . . . I am fair! I am a virgin! I am ready!' (V, ii, 7–9, 50–3, 56). From initially appearing sceptical that she constitutes a fit offering, Hebe comes to boldly declare that she is fair, possibly even fair enough to serve as a sufficient sacrifice of virgin beauty for the rest of time by adequately 'surfeiting' even the monster's 'insatiable' desire for the foreseeable future. When the monster does not appear, Hebe is, in another twist of mood, disappointed. She cries, 'Nay, unhappy girl, thou art not the fairest ... But alas, destiny would not have it so, destiny could not, because it asketh the beautifullest. I would, Hebe, thou hadst been beautifullest' (V, ii, 65–6, 70–2).

Critics have read the monster Agar as an ominous metaphor for what is undesirable about marriage, from a maiden's perspective.[37] But Hebe's disappointment at not being subjected to Agar draws attention to what she appears to think she has to gain from submitting to the will of her fellow citizens, Neptune and Agar – even if that submission will decidedly be an awful (and likely fatal) experience. Hebe's sudden sense of loss at rejection shows that she had come to anticipate a *post facto* transformation from her forced submission to the sea-monster. The sacrifice would confirm in her a beauty and a use-value she, and her community, did not know she possessed. This hoped-for transformation might not sound terribly appealing, resulting as it does in probable death, but her sacrifice would confirm a clear and culturally valued position for Hebe in her society – maybe even one, she imagines, that could alter her country's future.[38] When the monster fails to accept her, those hopes and expectations are dashed.

The play might not ask us to blame Hebe for her lack of beauty, but it does represent an important case in which a subordinate's embrace of obedience fails to afford her a societally sanctioned transformation like the one promised through education. Hebe cannot make herself into something she is not (a beautiful virgin) by simply being placed in a corresponding subordinate position. In practice, her affective commitment has no effect on whether she can serve the role she is assigned by her superiors. Moreover, even though she comes to identify with the terms of the sacrifice, presumably because she is pleased to be considered more beautiful than she thought she was, her capacity to participate in her subordination is limited by the fact that, in practical terms, the choice was never hers to make.

Hebe's necessarily limited affective engagement in this respect speaks to a distinction that one humanist theorist makes between the commitment of citizens to their king and the superior commitment schoolmasters seek from their students. In a 1581 educational treatise, Mulcaster compares and then differentiates the obedience of citizens from that of students, favouring a student's submission to his schoolmaster over a citizen's submission to his prince. Describing the student, he writes:

> Is not obedience the best sacrifice, that he can offer vp to his prince and gouernour, being directed and ruled by his countrie lawes? And in the principles of gouernment, is not his maister his *monarche*? & the scholelawes his countrey lawes? wherunto if he submit himselfe both orderly in *perfourmance*, & patiently in *penaunce*, doth he not shew a mynde already armed, not to start from his dutie? and so much the more,

bycause his obedience to his maister is more voluntarie, then that to his prince, which is meere necessarie.[39]

Mulcaster here sees the schoolroom as a microcosm of the country: a realm with laws, government and a monarch. He reads the student, in keeping with the humanist educational goal of willing participation, as 'more voluntarie' in his submission than the citizen, and therefore superior in his preparation to act as a political subject. Hebe's ultimate obedience to her country means less from this pedagogical perspective because her willingness can only ever be partial. She evidently embraces her role as sacrifice by the time it becomes clear that Agar will not arrive, but she does so only in the context of a forced submission – she is literally dragged to it by men who similarly act out of necessity to prevent the flooding of their lands.

If we read the maiden's limits alongside the similar stasis of yet another metamorphosis-hopeful subordinate – Rafe, the apprentice – it becomes clear that, despite its many Ovidian references, the world of *Galatea* is not necessarily one of free changeability. Rafe's failure to become something new through a subordinate role is slightly more complicated than Hebe's since, on the surface, Rafe seems more eager than Hebe. After failing to advance as a mariner, he attempts apprenticeships with two separate men who work in mystical arts: the Alchemist promises to transform Rafe into an Alchemist while the Astronomer promises to transform Rafe's capacity for knowledge. Were these training experiences successful, Rafe would gain skills that would afford him upward mobility, or at least a place in society. Rafe himself expresses great enthusiasm for the potential of each position. When the Alchemist offers to take Rafe on as his charge (mostly because his last apprentice has run away), saying 'Come in, and thou shalt see all', Rafe responds excitedly to the thought of his transformation: 'I follow, I run, I fly! They say my father hath a golden thumb; you shall see me have a golden body!' (II, iii, 140–2). Rafe appears to be affectively engaged almost in the same way educators argued humanist students should be. His willingness is evident in how he begins, and after joking about his father's reputation for cheating, he looks forward to his expected reward for subordination to (and training from) the alchemist.

But he puts it oddly. He says he anticipates he will 'have a golden body' rather than simply expressing a desire to become wealthy and to obtain gold (which is what the Alchemist has promised). In expressing his excitement in terms of bodily transformation, he fails to indicate any interest in the art of alchemy itself or the work he would presumably have to do to become skilled in it. Rafe does not look forward to practising alchemy. He does not even look forward to turning things into gold or, in what Eggert describes as the alchemist's mode of work,[40] conning customers for a profit, despite the fact that either form of labour would earn him the wealth for which his eager anticipation of a 'golden body' seems to express desire. Rafe's rather bizarre phrasing even makes his hoped-for future into a passive, unthinking one (that of a golden body), inadvertently exposing the extent to which he expects a reward for no work. Despite his apparent passion for entering into service, Rafe's wording reveals that he is as interested in cutting corners as his 'gold-thumbed' father. Unprepared to actively engage with his training, it is hardly a surprise, in humanist terms, that Rafe fails to benefit from this first apprenticeship.

After quickly abandoning the Alchemist, Rafe expresses a similar hope for transformation when he takes up an apprenticeship with an Astronomer. The Astronomer calls on him to 'come in with me' and learn all of his 'astrological wisdom'. Rafe responds by declaring 'Then I shall be translated from this mortality!' As he leaves with his new would-be trainer, he claims 'I feel my very brains moralized, and as it were a certain contempt of earthly actions is crept into my mind by an ethereal contemplation. Come, let us in!' (III, iii, 78–90). Again, Rafe's expression – 'I shall be translated from this mortality!' – anticipates a transformation whose source is external. The word 'translated' might encourage the audience to consider Rafe's apprenticeship and its work alongside the labour of students who would have earned their own social transformation in part through exhaustive translating (of Ovid and others). The comparison comes out poorly for Rafe, only further emphasising the passivity of his expectations, since he assumes he will be translated rather than realising that he himself will be doing the translating. His lack of diligence, like Hebe's lack of choice, renders transformation through subordination unlikely.

Rafe's failure might well be partially one of selection. In picking first an alchemist and then an astronomer as his master, he selects men practising arts that are in some respects suspect in the period.[41] As Eggert points out, even if we understand the Alchemist to be a con man, he is not a very good one.[42] As we will see with Galatea and Phillida, however, his selection of an unapproved masterly figure might not have been a problem had he nonetheless affectively engaged with his master and committed himself to modelling that which he desired to become. While Hebe and Rafe's desired transformations fail, Galatea and Phillida apparently succeed, through Venus's promise, by committing themselves to their chosen model despite that model's shortcomings from a patriarchal perspective. To understand why Galatea and Phillida might be offered a different fate than Hebe and Rafe, we must turn once again to their schoolboy engagement with one another.

Subordinate Authorisation of Masterly Models

Initially, Galatea and Phillida think they have found in each other something like a tutor of masculinity. But as they continue to identify with their chosen model, they each begin to suspect their guide might be less authoritative than anticipated. Unable to definitively resolve their confusion about whether their instructor is actually a man, Phillida finally proposes to Galatea 'Come, let us into the grove, and make much of one another that cannot tell what to think of one another' (III, ii, 64–6). When they return from the grove four scenes later, the girls are steadfastly in love, but seem not to have determined each other's gender. Their evident continuing lack of certainty has inspired much scholarly discussion about what it is exactly that the girls might have done in the grove. Phillida's proposal can be read as an amorous one,[43] but a close look at the meaning of the phrase 'to make much of' reveals that the girls might enter the grove to continue to treat their partner as their model and master, despite their uncertainty. That is, they might enter the grove as good humanist students, still seeking to affectively engage in their own learning.

In its entry on 'make', the *Oxford English Dictionary* defines 'to make much of' in two ways:

> 12c. *to make much* (also *little, something, nothing,* etc.) *of* (or *on*): to derive advantage from or turn to account, to the degree specified

and

> 29a. *to make much* (also *little, nothing, too much,* etc.) *of* (or *on*): to have an opinion or rate at (the degree specified); to treat with much (little, no, etc.) consideration. *to make much of*: (often) to treat with marked courtesy and show of affection.[44]

The second definition listed (29a) is the one that has most influenced recent scholarship on *Galatea*. This version of the phrase refers to shows of approval and affection, and is often used in the period to describe the affectionate expressions of lovers – a lover might 'make much of' his lady in a letter or in person. The last part of definition 29a bears out that common, romantic sense of the phrase with its emphasis on 'make much of' as a phrase used particularly to express 'marked courtesy' or 'affection'. Scholars have usefully read Phillida's remark according to this definition, since it can be read to suggest that the girls exchange physical and/or verbal affection while leaving open to interpretation how that affection might be sexual.[45]

That same version of 'making much of' as 'displaying affection for', however, can also be used to describe a master rewarding a subject affectionately for successfully obeying instructions. For example, a schoolmaster might 'make much of' a student who learns his lesson quickly, or the author of a horsemanship treatise might encourage readers to 'make much of' a young colt who successfully obeys his rider's command.[46] Under this definition, the fact that Galatea and Phillida 'make much of' their fellow might suggest education as much as erotic exchange. After all, Phillida suggests the girls go to the grove in the first place because they 'cannot tell what to think of one another', not merely because they want to express their mutual love.

In addition to these two slightly different common uses of 'making much' is the first definition listed above (12c): 'to derive advantage from or turn to account'. This definition refers less to what the object or person being made much of gains by the action and more to what the *actor* gets out of that action. While definition 29a emphasises that an actor 'makes much of' someone or something to treat it with affection, the first focuses on the fact that a person only 'makes much' of something as they are 'deriving advantage from' it. In this way, the definition highlights the fact that the actor who 'makes much' gains some value from the object or person acted upon. In its focus on the perspective of the praiser rather than the receiver of praise, it makes clear that, in order for anything or anyone to be 'made much of', some actor has to decide that person or thing is worth it.

A helpful example of how this definition could be used in early modern England appears in another of Mulcaster's treatises on early education. In *The first part of the elementarie* (1582), he uses 'make much' to mean 'turn[ing] to account' and 'deriv[ing] advantage from' several times. One example appears when he describes how tutors and students should approach the reading of unfamiliar words:

> if anie reader find falt with anie word, which is not sutable to his ear, bycause it is not he, for whom that word serues, let him mark his own, which he knoweth, and make much of the other, which is worthie his knowing.[47]

Mulcaster says that the reader should take note of the words he does know, but that he should 'make much of' those that he does not know because they are 'worthie his knowing'. The reader, according to Mulcaster, should 'turn to account' the words he does not know because he expects to 'derive advantage' – become more knowledgeable – from coming to know them. 'To make much of' something here operates as a synonym for making something (or someone) the subject of further study, of giving it (or her) emphasis. To make much of something in this way fits clearly into an educational context, especially from the perspective of the instructor who determines to what his students would be best advised to pay attention.

In response to their unsureness about 'what to think' of their respective tutors of masculinity, I argue that Phillida and Galatea decide to enter the grove to 'make much' in all of the above senses. In doing so, they affectively engage with their peer in part as students engage with their models and masters, cultivating their love for someone they see as their superior (a boy who can serve as a model of the masculinity they each seek to learn – their schoolmaster in the rhetorical performance of masculinity). Simultaneously, they are made into masters by their fellow, who addresses them as such, and who receives their praises as a reward for 'toward' subordinate engagement.

Their effortful interactions with their respective 'superiors' set them apart from Hebe, who has little agency over her decision to take on a subordinate role, and Rafe, who desires transformation but performs no affective labour to achieve it. Galatea and Phillida's loving attitude toward their inadvertent student, similarly, sets them apart from Rafe's unskilled and neglectful masters. They make one another and themselves into 'toward' students and attentive instructors.

In keeping with the claims of pedagogues in the era, Galatea and Phillida's affective engagement affords them success in their training in that it gives them, through Venus, access to a better place in society as husband and wife rather than as children forced to be obedient to fathers whose commands sometimes require them to act unvirtuously. By the time they enter the grove, their respective subordinations are grounded in their own pleasure and motivated by their own desires. This, paired with the labour those motivations lead them to undergo, is represented as integral to their success. The love they have cultivated through that effort is what ultimately earns them Venus's approval. And even the validity of their model in the eyes of society ends up being less important than their motives and methods. Venus makes this clear when, as a condition of offering to transform one of them, she asserts that 'love and faith' cannot be overthrown by 'fortune and nature' and asks the girls 'Is your loves unspotted, begun with truth, continued with constancy, and not to be altered till death?' (V, iii, 146–7). Her preference for love and faith over fortune and nature poses her own interests as the goddess of love explicitly against those of Diana who champions nature. Similarly, it places emphasis on the affective engagement that characterises Galatea and Phillida's loving relationship rather than on the pair's initial social legibility. The girls' defiant commitment to a female model might be considered 'untoward' in that it defies social expectations for masculine authority, but it is 'toward' in that it beautifully executes the combination of individual motivation and dutiful imitation pedagogues valued in their pupils.

The play famously ends without determining which girl will be transformed. Venus does not specify, the girls do not inquire and the epilogue starts before the change occurs. For scholars of early modern sexuality, this ambiguity allows for an affirmation of homoerotic desire despite its simultaneous concession that gender difference is required for the consummation of the girls' marriage.[48] It also ostensibly accepts that neither girl has yet proven herself to be the better teacher or even the better student while determining at the same time that the shepherdesses' mutual education in the grove has been effective enough to earn one (or either) of them the status of man. In the drama's final scene, when the goddess asks the girls if their loves are true and constant, they respond 'Die, Galatea, if thy love be not so!' and 'Accursed be thou, Phillida, if thy love be not so!' (V, iii, 148–9). Then, again, when

Venus asks if they agree 'one to be a boy presently', the lovers echo each other, Phillida saying 'I am content, so I may embrace Galatea' and Galatea replying, 'I wish it, so I may enjoy Phillida' (V, iii, 158–9). These repetitive responses, like the girls' mirrored lines throughout, insistently remind us that the difference Venus promises to provide does not yet exist, that the girls have learned from and with one another without having clearly designated one as teacher and one as student, one as master and one as subordinate. It reminds us, in other words, that the girls' affective engagements throughout have been both toward and untoward – they have imitated each other in one sense as dutiful students seeking to emulate a superior but in another as subordinates who have increasingly committed themselves to an instructor who is not an approved model. Galatea and Phillida have obediently followed the prescription for students to be active and affectively engaged, but that imitative work seems to have directed them away from the masculine authority their methods initially aimed to emulate.

In promising that love can do the 'unpossible' – making the love and pleasure that Galatea and Phillida practise produce a hierarchical relationship of which the other characters can approve – Venus assures the audience that she can make love amenable to early modern societal order, much as did pedagogues who argued for love and pleasure as tools of conformity in the classroom.[49] The actual events of the drama, though, demonstrate unavoidably that love can approve its own masters – Venus and both of the shepherdesses have done so. Moreover, Venus's coyness about which girl will become a boy asserts her – that is love's – ultimate power to decide who makes a sufficient authority. By prioritising the fact that she will choose who becomes a man – asserting herself as authority over and above the male characters around her – rather than clarifying which girl ought to be a man according to those other figures' standards, the goddess of love demonstrates how fundamentally incompatible her own order is with that of the society she promises here to satisfy.

Venus's victory over Neptune and the shepherdesses' fathers finally denies the audience an affirmation of masculine authority that the drama has consistently withheld. Among the characters of the drama, there are not really any successful male masters. Galatea and Phillida's fathers both command their daughters to act against their senses of virtue; Rafe's male teachers prove to be comically inept at their trades; and, in this last scene, even Neptune acquiesces to the will of Venus.[50] Scholars have noted how Venus's promise renders gender difference arbitrary. In the context of humanist training we can see how love also threatens to raise up new models of authority, levelling out hierarchical distinctions or usurping them for its own purposes. And that, for masters seeking to cultivate obedience as much as inventive skill in students, is the problem (or at the very least one of the problems) with love.

NOTES

1. *Oxford English Dictionary Online*, s.v. 'untoward', *adj.* 2a.
2. See Walen, 'Utopian Lesbian Erotics'; Jankowski, 'Queer(y)ing Virginity'; Traub, *Renaissance of Lesbianism*.
3. Traub, *Renaissance of Lesbianism*, p. 327; Walen, 'Utopian Lesbian Erotics'. Shannon, in 'Nature's Bias', argues that Galatea and Phillida's love is presented as more natural, contrary to Diana's suggestion, than love between a man and a woman.
4. For a discussion of the decreasing emphasis on violent discipline in humanist pedagogy in the late sixteenth and early seventeenth centuries see Bushnell, *A Culture of Teaching*, for example p. 29 where she writes: 'Early humanist arguments against pedagogical flogging . . . argue that, rather than encouraging children to learn through pleasure and love, flogging turns them away from books, creating . . . hatred'. See also p. 31, where Bushnell explains how excessive cruelty was seen to lead to 'slavish' servility, which was unreliable and demeaning compared to 'an absolute mastery of love'. See also, Stewart, *Close Readers*, p. 92 and 108, on 'the beating schoolmaster' as a 'stock character' before humanism and on Ascham's gentle tone in *The Scholemaster*, respectively.
5. Ascham, *The Scholemaster*, p. 22.
6. Ibid., p. 9.
7. *Oxford English Dictionary Online*, s.v. 'towardness', *n.* 2.
8. Bushnell, *A Culture of Teaching*, pp. 29–30, describes how theorists 'moved explicit attention from the mastery of mind and body to the "allurement" to learning . . . structuring the relationship of student and teacher as one of love'.
9. Brinsley, *Ludus literarius*, pp. 51–2.
10. Mulcaster, *Positions*, p. 24.
11. Mulcaster, *Positions*, esp. pp. 154, 165–6.
12. Ibid., p. 27.
13. 'Imitatio' means imitation. As Enterline writes in *Shakespeare's Schoolroom*, p. 4, 'imitatio' is a platform of humanist education, according to which students are asked to 'imitate the schoolmaster's facial movement, vocal modulation, and bodily gestures as much as his Latin works and texts'. Such imitation was in turn expected to make students successful orators by enabling them to accurately perform emotions while eloquently expressing their ideas, thus persuading their audiences.
14. See McCarthy, *The Children's Troupes*, pp. 106–9. McCarthy in part credits Quintilian's influence with pedagogues' commitment to producing creative and passionate, not mindlessly mimicking, students.
15. McCarthy, *The Children's Troupes*, pp. 108, 22.
16. Ibid., p. 25.
17. See McCarthy, *The Children's Troupes*, and for the history of St Paul's association with acting, see Gair, *The Children of Paul's*. Play-acting as a feature of education, though it was occasionally a source of scandal, was accepted by experts in the era. For example, Richard Mulcaster himself was a product of education under the 'schoolmaster playwright' Nicholas Udall, and an author of dramas for schoolboys at the Merchant Taylor's school before receiving an appointment as schoolmaster at St Paul's (see McCarthy, *The Children's Troupes*, p. 109).
18. McCarthy, *The Children's Troupes*, see esp. p. 65, argues that schoolboy troupes were at the forefront of the establishment of the text-centred literary playing that would come to characterise early modern drama at large. For resistance to schoolboys acting even during their popularity, however, see Gair, *The Children of Paul's*, pp. 1–13. See also for the troupes' popularity under Elizabeth, for several examples

of their performances, and for how they fit into the theatrical market (partially via commercialisation and partially as part of a gift-giving exchange culture), Michael Shapiro, 'Patronage and the companies of boy actors', pp. 278–84.
19. McCarthy, *The Children's Troupes*.
20. Enterline, *Shakespeare's Schoolroom*, p. 120.
21. Ibid., pp. 131–2, 152. Hutcheon, *Imitating Women*, and Correll, 'Malleable Material, Models of Power' also assert that imitation allowed students to subvert the masculine performance they were expected to learn.
22. Most markedly, since she departs from more common readings of humanist pedagogy (and the troupes it produced) as stiff, stuffy and repressed compared to the art of acting practised in adult troupes, McCarthy, *The Children's Troupes*, esp. pp. 106–8.
23. Ibid., p. xviii.
24. Enterline, *Shakespeare's Schoolroom*, p. 87.
25. Enterline, *Shakespeare's Schoolroom*, p. 4. Disagreeing with Enterline's sense that humanist instruction via imitation partially reflected but was ultimately contrary to dramaturgy, McCarthy, *The Children's Troupes*, discusses at length how mere 'slavish' imitation was considered inadequate for schooling. See esp. pp. 108–15.
26. See Altman, *The Tudor Play of Mind*, and Kemper, 'Dramaturgical Design in Lyly's *Galatea*', for two older works that argue that the transformation does occur. Shannon, 'Nature's Bias', p. 206, argues that the authorisation of Galatea and Phillida's desire for one another on the basis of likeness has a firmer grasp in the play than the transformation which is deferred.
27. Eggert, 'Alchemy, Humanism and the Uses of Disknowledge' (this volume). 'Disknowledge' is Eggert's term for a mode of thinking especially prevalent in Renaissance England according to which one can willingly ascribe to two conflicting sets of knowledge at once – one which is true, and one which is false. See also Eggert, *Disknowledge*, for a fuller discussion of the concept.
28. See Stewart, *Close Readers*, and Orgel, *Impersonations*, esp. pp. 15 and 25. Young girls and boys in England were understood to have much in common and, in fact, were dressed in similar clothing until boys underwent 'breeching' around the age of seven. Though the schoolroom was not the only place where boys were taught to perform a distinct masculinity, it was certainly a central site of their transition into manhood. Stewart, *Close Readers*, p. 102 explains how the passage into masculinity was tied up in the passage into education for boys: 'The "breeching" of a boy at around the age of seven was a major event: Thomas Elyot links the age to the ideal age for the starting of an education. The "breeching" of a boy was not only the entry into his education, but also his institution as a man, now visually distinct from his female companions.'
29. McCarthy, *The Children's Troupes*, pp. 101–5, for a discussion of how schoolboy troupes playfully 'draw notice to the gaps that emerged whenever youths played against type'.
30. Rackin, 'Androgyny', p. 31. Rackin suggests that androgyny can become acceptable in such a world because the fantasy of it 'transcends the social'.
31. Lyly, *Galatea*, ed. Scragg, I, i, 14, 93–4. All subsequent citations refer to this edition and to act, scene and line.
32. Scragg, *Galatea*, p. 56, fn. 15.
33. Mulcaster, *Positions*, p. 27.
34. Traub, *Renaissance of Lesbianism*, p. 328, characterises the play as having an 'investment in presenting these lovers as coequal in everything'.
35. Ibid. While describing the effect of Galatea and Phillida's mirroring speeches, especially at the end of the play, Traub notes that the girls' 'linguistic symmetry' 'makes

for rather stilted dramatic action (suited more for the schoolboys' grammatical exercise than lively stage dialogue)'. Part of the humour of this scene might be the boy actors' reference to the more rote aspects of their early grammatical education, which stands in some contrast to the skilful show they perform now.

36. Galatea fears she will curtsey at II, i, 25–6. Galatea and Phillida both fear they will blush, one after the other (though presumably they do not, since neither observes the other blushing), at II, i, 27 and at II, i, 31–3.
37. Shannon, 'Nature's Bias', p. 200; Jankowski, 'Queer(y)ing Virginity', pp. 15–17; Caldwell, 'John Lyly's *Gallathea*', p. 32.
38. At V, ii, 50–3, Hebe says 'Glut thyself till thou surfeit, and let my life end thine!' hoping that Agar will find her to be more than enough sacrifice (despite being an 'unsatiable monster') and pass away, presumably precluding the possibility that future virgins would share in Hebe's fate.
39. Mulcaster, *Positions*, 151.
40. Eggert, 'Alchemy, Humanism, and the Uses of Disknowledge' (this volume).
41. See Eggert, *Disknowledge*, on early modern attitudes toward alchemy as an art which was both true and false, a practised (and practical) profession and an impossible or ridiculous pursuit. Rackin, 'Androgyny', p. 30, also notes that Rafe and his fellows pursue careers in 'dubious trades'.
42. Eggert, 'Alchemy, Humanism, and the Uses of Disknowledge' (this volume).
43. For example, Traub, *Renaissance of Lesbianism*, reads *Galatea* along with other texts to demonstrate how lesbian desire is depicted here as possible despite the fact that it concedes that gender difference is required for consummation; Dooley, 'Inversion, Metamorphosis, and Sexual Difference', p. 61, reads the tryst in the grove as a sexual encounter, as does Jankowski, 'Queer(y)ing Virginity', p. 22.
44. *Oxford English Dictionary Online*, s.v. 'make'.
45. For example, this definition is useful for Jankowski in 'Queer(y)ing Virginity', where she argues that the girls have a sexual encounter, but because they are virgins and not yet inculcated into a patriarchally restricted notion of sex as reproductive penetration, that sexuality occurs in a realm other than that of the patriarchy. The same definition also works well for Dooley's reading of the scene in 'Inversion, Metamorphosis, and Sexual Difference', since he sees their encounter in the grove as an acknowledgement of the viability of female–female desire, despite the anxiety expressed about it at the end of the play.
46. For example, Blundeville, *The fower chiefest offices belonging to horsemanshippe*, pp. 5 and 15.
47. Mulcaster, *The first part of the elementarie*, p. 268, italics removed from original. See also Mulcaster, *Positions*, p. 241: 'Wherein they haue some reason to mocke at mathematicall heades, as they do tearme them, though they should haue greater reason, why *to cherish*, and *make much of* the matheticall [*sic*] sciences', italics added ('cherish' and 'make much of' are cognates here, and both are used to refer to turning to account or putting academic focus on a subject).
48. Jankowski, 'Queer(y)ing Virginity', p. 26; Walen, 'Utopian Lesbian Erotics', p. 137; Traub, *Renaissance of Lesbianism*, p. 287 and 327–8.
49. At V, iii, 154, Venus says 'What is to love, or the mistress of love, unpossible?'
50. V, iii, 174–81.

BIBLIOGRAPHY

Altman, Joel B., *The Tudor Play of Mind: Rhetorical Inquiry and the Development of Elizabethan Drama* (Berkeley: University of California Press, 1978).

Ascham, Roger, *The Scholemaster* (London: 1570) *Early English Books Online*, 3

April 2017, http://gateway.proquest.com.proxy.lib.umich.edu/openurl?ctx_ver=Z39.88-2003&res_id=xri:eebo&rft_id=xri:eebo:citation:99840125.
Blundeville, Thomas, *The fower chiefest offices belonging to horsemanshippe* (London: 1561) *Early English Books Online*, 28 June 2017, http://gateway.proquest.com.proxy.lib.umich.edu/openurl?ctx_ver=Z39.88-2003&res_id=xri:eebo&rft_id=xri:eebo:citation:99840344.
Brinsley, John, *Ludus literarius* (London: 1612), *Early English Books Online*, 26 June 2016, http://gateway.proquest.com.proxy.lib.umich.edu/openurl?ctx_ver=Z39.88-2003&res_id=xri:eebo&rft_id=xri:eebo:citation:9984230951-52.
Bushnell, Rebecca W., *A Culture of Teaching: Early Modern Humanism in Theory and Practice* (Ithaca, NY and London: Cornell University Press, 1996).
Caldwell, Ellen M., 'John Lyly's *Gallathea*: A New Rhetoric of Love for the Virgin Queen', *English Literary Renaissance* 17: 1, 1987, pp. 22–40.
Correll, Barbara, 'Malleable Material, Models of Power: Woman in Erasmus's "Marriage Group" and *Civility in Boys*', *ELH* 57: 2, 1990, pp. 241–62.
Dooley, Mark, 'Inversion, Metamorphosis, and Sexual Difference: Female Same-Sex Desire in Ovid and Lyly', in Goran V. Stanivukovic (ed.), *Ovid and the Renaissance Body* (Toronto: University of Toronto Press, 2001), pp. 59–76.
Eggert, Katherine, *Disknowledge: Literature, Alchemy, and the End of Humanism in Renaissance England* (Philadelphia: University of Pennsylvania Press, 2015).
Enterline, Lynn, *Shakespeare's Schoolroom: Rhetoric, Discipline, Emotion* (Philadelphia: University of Pennsylvania Press, 2012).
Gair, Reavley, *The Children of Paul's: The Story of a Theatre Company, 1553–1608* (Cambridge: Cambridge University Press, 1982).
Hutcheon, Elizabeth. *Imitating Women: Rhetoric, Gender, and Humanist Pedagogy in English Renaissance Drama*. Dissertation, University of Chicago, 2011.
Jankowski, Theodora, 'Queer(y)ing Virginity: Virgins, Lesbians, and Queers of all Types', in *Pure Resistance: Queer Virginity in Early Modern English Drama* (Philadelphia: University of Pennsylvania Press, 2000), pp. 1–28.
Kemper, Susan C. 'Dramaturgical Design in Lyly's *Galathea*', *THOTH*, Fall 1976, pp. 19–31.
Lyly, John, *Galatea*, ed. Leah Scragg, Revels Student Editions (Manchester and New York: Manchester University Press, 2012).
McCarthy, Jeanne H., *The Children's Troupes and the Transformation of English Theater 1509–1608: Pedagogue Playwrights, Playbooks, and Play-boys*, Studies in Performance and Early Modern Drama Series (London and New York: Routledge, 2017).
Mulcaster, Richard, *Positions wherein those primitive circumstances be examined, which are necessarie to the training vp of children* (London: 1581) *Early English Books Online*, 24 June 2016, http://gateway.proquest.com.proxy.lib.umich.edu/openurl?ctx_ver=Z39.88-2003&res_id=xri:eebo&rft_id=xri:eebo:citation:99848169.
Mulcaster, Richard, *The first part of the elementary* . . . (London: 1582), *Early English Books Online*, 26 June 2016, http://gateway.proquest.com.proxy.lib.umich.edu/openurl?ctx_ver=Z39.88-2003&res_id=xri:eebo&rft_id=xri:eebo:citation:99848167.
Orgel, Stephen, *Impersonations: The Performances of Gender in Shakespeare's England* (Cambridge: Cambridge University Press, 1996).
Rackin, Phyllis. 'Androgyny, Mimesis, and the Marriage of the Boy Heroine on the English Renaissance Stage', *PMLA* 102: 1, 1987, pp. 29–41.
Shannon, Laurie, 'Nature's Bias: Renaissance Homonormativity and Elizabethan Comic Likeness', *Modern Philology* 98: 2, 2000, pp. 183–210.

Shapiro, Michael, 'Patronage and the Companies of Boy Actors', in Paul Whitfield White and Suzanne R. Westfall (eds), *Shakespeare and Theatrical Patronage in Early Modern England* (Cambridge: Cambridge University Press, 2002), pp. 272–94.

Stewart, Alan, *Close Readers: Humanism and Sodomy in Early Modern England* (Princeton: Princeton University Press, 1997).

Traub, Valerie, '"Friendship so curst": *amor impossibilis*, the homoerotic lament, and the nature of *lesbian* desire', in *The Renaissance of Lesbianism in Early Modern England*, Cambridge Studies in Renaissance Literature and Culture (New York and Cambridge: Cambridge University Press, 2002), pp. 276–325.

Walen, Denise A., 'Utopian Lesbian Erotics', in *Constructions of Female Homoeroticism in Early Modern Drama* (New York: Palgrave Macmillan, 2005), pp. 121–48.

8

COASTAL SQUEEZE: ENVIRONMENTAL METAMORPHOSIS AND LYLY'S LINCOLNSHIRE

Patricia Badir

At the end of John Lyly's *Galatea* (1583–5), the play's two heroines are steadfast in love. To move the plot toward marriage and comic resolution, the goddess Venus promises to turn one of them into a boy. However, the play ends as the company proceeds to church, and to the nuptial ceremony, leaving the question of sex change unresolved and the metamorphosis itself withheld. The source text of the sex-change plot is Ovid's 'Iphis and Ianthe' and my interest in Lyly's reworking of this story lies in his oft-remarked upon suspension of the original final resolution.[1] Unlike Iphis whose transformation from girl to boy is carefully detailed in *The Metamorphoses*, Lyly's protagonist leaves the stage female, albeit still disguised as a boy.[2] This essay proposes that Lyly's deferral of the trans-narrative offered by 'Iphis and Ianthe' rests upon his investment in the play's setting – the banks of the Humber Estuary in Lincolnshire – as it is adapted from another Ovidian myth, the story of the sea nymph, Galatea, and her shepherd love, Acis. Lyly's heroines' unending affection for each other, as well as his reworking of the Ovidian ending, can be read, I argue, as a reflection upon the precarious environs of English coastal communities. In order to make sense of what Lyly does and doesn't do with 'Iphis and Ianthe', we need to come to terms with the environmental concerns of 'Acis and Galatea'; the play's curious management of desire, it will become apparent, has everything to do with Lyly's metamorphosis of Ovidian riparian ecologies.

At the beginning of Lyly's play we find Galatea with her father, Tityrus, beneath a 'fair oak' whose leaves defend them from the sun. They are enjoying 'the fresh air, which softly breathes from Humber floods' (I, i, 2–5).[3] The tree is on the verge of a 'pleasant green' upon which flock roam (6–7). In the next scene, the three brothers who wash ashore after the wreck of their ship will tell us that we 'are now in Lincolnshire' and that 'there be woods hard by, and at every mile's end, houses' (I, iv, 15–16). This is one of the most regionally specific rural settings in the early modern dramatic repertoire and Lincolnshire was an area Lyly could have known well.[4]

The Humber is the second-largest coastal plain estuary in the UK after the Severn, and the largest on the east coast of Britain (Figure 8.1). Water collected from this catchment flows to the estuary through many rivers and tributaries, including the Ouse, Trent and Wharfe, along which, as Christopher Saxton's 1576 map of Lincolnshire (Figures 8.2 and 8.3) shows, there can be found a great many historic towns and villages.

Today, as in Saxton's time, this fertile area is of great economic importance to the wider region and the rest of the UK. As a transitional zone between river and sea, it contains a variety of natural environments and habitats that are now protected and preserved by national, European and international designations.[5] The Humber Wetlands, however, are under continuous threat from sea level rise.[6] Over the next 50 years, it is expected that the waters around the estuary will rise by about a third of a metre. This will increase the risk of flooding, particularly when high tides combine with storm surges from the North Sea. Wildlife habitats will change and homes, farms and businesses will become increasingly vulnerable.[7] However, these particular and precarious environmental conditions are not new. Though the landscape as it is known today was significantly altered from the seventeenth century onwards by large-scale drainage projects, recent archeological and archival work confirms that water levels rose steadily after 1250 and the fourteenth, fifteenth and sixteenth centuries are known to have been periods of increasing storminess and regular flooding.[8]

Galatea is a distinctly postdiluvian play: all the elements of plot and character turn around the knowledge that the forest and pasture lands that provide the play's setting have flooded before and could flood again. As they stand beneath an oak tree at the top of the play, Tityrus gives his daughter, Galatea, a lesson in environmental history in which the Anglo-Saxon past converges with Roman mythology and natural history: when their country was invaded by Danes, a temple to Neptune was destroyed, an action that so enraged the sea god 'that he caused [the river] to break [its] bounds'.

> Then might you see ships sail where sheep fed, anchors cast where ploughs go, fishermen throw their nets where husbandmen sow their corn, and fishes throw their scales where fowls do breed their quills. Then might you gather froth where now is dew, rotten weeds for sweet roses, and take view of monstrous mermaids instead of passing fair maids. (I, ii, 22–38)

Figure 8.1 Lincolnshire banks from the Humber Bridge (between Barton-upon-Humber and Hull). Author's photograph.

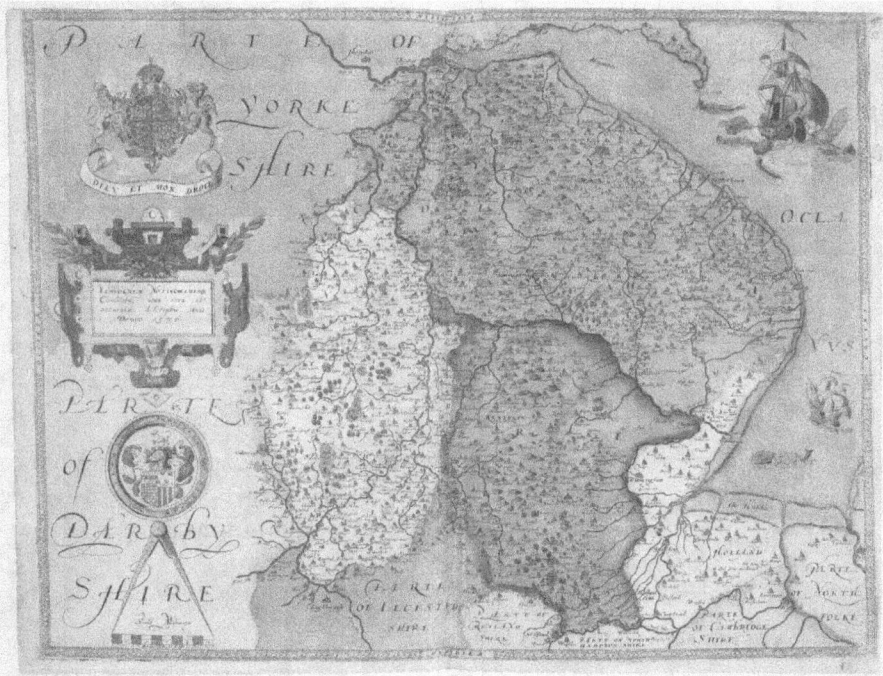

Figure 8.2 Christopher Saxton's Map of Lincolnshire. Royal MS 18.D.III. no. 5. © The British Library.

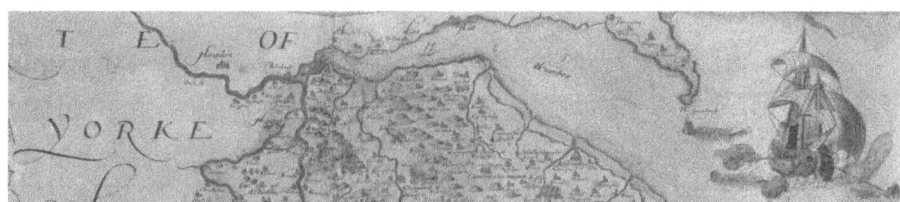

Figure 8.3 Christopher Saxton's Map of Lincolnshire (detail). Royal MS 18.D.III. no. 5. © The British Library.

Tityrus tells Galatea that, unable to survive under such conditions, the townspeople proposed a peace offering wherein every five years their fairest virgin would be bound to the very oak tree beneath which father and daughter now stand and that a sea-monster, the Agar, would take the virgin to Neptune and to a watery fate. When the play begins, the five years are up and Galatea is the fairest of them all. It's her life or the Humber, at Neptune's command, will once again break its bounds and flood the community's pasturelands. Tityrus, unwilling to sacrifice his daughter in fulfilment of the obligation, disguises Galatea as a boy and sends her into the woods. There she meets Phillida, another fair virgin cross-dressed by yet another concerned father.

There is plenty of evidence to suggest that Lyly's contemporaries would have understood the threat of flood posed by Neptune's Humber as real. There are records of regular flooding from the thirteenth century, including the Chronicle of Melsa (1396), which references land and villages lost to Humber floods, and reports one instance in which the destruction of the town of Ravenserodd is attributed to the anger of God, provoked by the rebelliousness of the town's inhabitants.[9] Centuries later, the devastating flood of 1571 was recorded by Holinshed who attributes the loss of land, houses, churches and livestock to the 'terrible tempest of wind and rayn' that ravaged the Lincolnshire coast.[10] Holinshed's account is derived from a pamphlet written in the year of the flood, by Thomas Knell, a preacher, who moralises the catastrophe by declaring that God

> to stirreth vp the Godly to prayse and extoll his majiestie, and mooueth the wicked and stubborn, to feare and dreade of his horrible vengeance [...] turneth the Flouds into a wildernesse, and the springes of water into drie grounde, & a frutefull lande into barrennesse, for the wickednesse of them that dwel therein.[11]

Literary evidence pertaining to the power of the Humber is also plentiful. Spenser gives us 'storming Humber' in *The Fairie Queene* (1590) and 'Humber rough and stout' in his elegy for Sidney, *Astrophel* (1595).[12] John Taylor, the 'water poet', commends the hospitality of the people of Hull by

Figure 8.4   The Humber river from the Lincolnshire banks (at Barton-Upon-Humber). Author's photograph.

stating that 'their Loues (like Humber) ouer-flow'd the bankes' (1622).[13] And John Abbot, writing in 1623, compares pagan iconoclasm to the Humber 'passing his set bounds with waters drowne the over-flowed grounds. / Bridges, and houses which oppse his waie / He carries with him, nothing can him staie'.[14] The massive power of the river is also accentuated by imaginative accounts and news stories of 'mighty monstrous whales' appearing off its shores.[15]

By contrast, there are also accounts of more bucolic Humberside amblings which resonate closely with the soft, fresh air that Tityrus enjoys in his daughter's company (Figure 8.4). Marvell's speaker, for instance, famously exclaims to his coy mistress that had he 'but world enough and time' he would 'by the tide of Humber' sit and complain,[16] and Francis Sabie, in *The fissher-mans tale* (1595), describes the estuarial banks in the dulcet tones of pastoral:

> If on the banks or Poplar-bearing brims,
> Of Cristall *Humber* we do please to walke,
> Great Dolphins shall aboue the water rise,
> And for our solace seeme to make great sport,
> The Marmaids shal looke out from siluer lakes,
> And greet vs with an hundred merrie songs,
> The Naydes, Nymphs, Nereides and Faunes,
> The Satyrs, Fayries, and each rurall power,

> Abandoning their fragrant fields and springs,
> About our lodging shal resort and sing.[17]

In its contribution to this complex figurative tradition of pastoral pleasures and recurrent dangers, *Galatea* is, as Julie Sanders observes, a 'fascinating blend of the fantastic and the rooted, the literal and the figural'.[18]

Lyly's mapping of ecological history is also greatly indebted to his classical sources which resonate against familiar English coastlines. For example, the opening scene of the play, in which we find Tityrus and his daughter beneath the oak, is straight from Virgil's first Eclogue: '*Tityre tu recubans sub legmine fagi*' ('Tityrus, lying in the shadows of a beech tree').[19] Ovid's *Metamorphoses* also functions as what Susan Wiseman calls 'a literary resource' for Lyly's 'history of the natural world'.[20] More precisely, it is Golding's English translation, *Metamorphosis* (1567), which unhinges the classical source from its medieval moralisations, giving it, as Raphael Lynn proposes, 'a new home in England and in English'. Through Golding, Ovid becomes 'more local, regional and even rural', facilitating Lyly's manifold transversions of the verdant world of the *Metamorphosis* into the forests, fields and pastures of Lincolnshire.[21] For instance, the description of Neptune's flood from Golding's translation of Book One, particularly in its use of antithesis and opposition, was clearly one of Lyly's principal sources for Tityrus' description of the Humber flood:[22]

> The floods at random where they list through all the fields did stray;
> Men, beasts, trees, corn, and with their gods were churches washed away.
> If any house were built so strong, against their force to stand,
> Yet did the water hide the top; and turrets in that pond
> Were overwhelmed. No difference was between the sea and ground,
> For all was sea. There was no shore nor landing to be found.
> Some climbèd up to tops of hills, and some rowed to and fro
> In boats, where they not long before, to plough and cart did go.
> One over corn and tops of towns whom waves did overwhelm
> Doth sail in ship; another sits a-fishing in an elm.
> In meadows green were anchors cast (so fortune did provide),
> And crooked ships did shadow vines, the which the flood did hide.
> And where but t'other day before did feed the hungry goat,
> The ugly seals and porpoises now to and fro did float.
> The seanymphs wondered under waves the towns and groves to see,
> And dolphins played among the tops and boughs of every tree.
> (*Metamorphosis*, 1: 339–54)[23]

In this passage, the natural elements – flora and fauna – are, for the most part, Ovid's; however, notably, the translation omits Neptune's distinctively

Mediterranean 'sea-blue' skin colour (327); removes vineyards; translates 'temples and shrines' as 'churches' (340); and adds porpoises (352) to the inventory of marine creatures, creating points of identification for English Christian readers more familiar with the shores of the Atlantic. 'I have him [Ovid] made so well acquainted with our tongue', writes Golding to his readers, 'as that he may in English verse, as in his own, be sung' (*Metamorphosis*, 'Preface to the Reader', 177–8). Elizabeth Jane Bellamy suggests that 'when early modern English writers took their verse to the local water's edge, they did so in the fraught context of a longstanding cultural inheritance from antiquity' that identified the English coastline as bleak, remote, dangerous and inhospitable to poetry.[24] Golding arguably resists such attributes by creating a productive sympathy between classical waterscapes and English wetlands.

In Golding's 'Acis and Galatea', we find the sea nymph Galatea between Scylla and Charybdis, recounting the story of how she was beloved by the Cyclops, Polyphemus – a love she could not return, favouring instead the attentions of the young shepherd, Acis. The setting of the story, as in the original, is amphibious: both pastoral and marine. Polyphemus lives in a cave in the woods near the pastures upon which he tends his sheep. When he spies Galatea frolicking in the sea with Acis, he positions himself on a 'wedgèd point' where 'shoots a hill into the sea whereof the sea doth beat / On either side' (*Metamorphosis*, 13: 918–20). So perched, he sings a song to his aquatic beloved. Terrified by the ferocity of his devotion, Galatea dives into the water, leaving Acis to confront the cyclops alone. Polyphemus throws a boulder at the boy who is crushed, his blood streaming from beneath the rock. The despairing nymph summons her lover's ancestral powers ('Forthwith I brought to pass / That Acis should receive the force his father had before') and the blood turns to water 'at the first a brook with rain distroubled new / Which waxeth clear by length of time'. Then high reeds 'spin up' from the stone out of which the 'bubbling water' begins to flow and Acis emerges as both river and man ('a wondrous matter'), stronger than he was ('Much bigger than he erst had been') and, uniquely in Golding's translation, 'altogether grey'. His skin color is significant because whereas Golding directly translates Ovidian landscape features (fields, forests, rocks, reeds, the sea), the face of Ovid's metamorphosed shepherd is 'wave-blue'; the amendment swaps the River Acis which, in *The Metamorphosis*, flows into the Mediterranean Sea, for the brackish waters of English estuaries (13: 1039–52).

In terms of plot, 'Acis and Galatea' maps unevenly onto Lyly's play; this is a case of capricious and inconsistent borrowing that is tricky to unravel. We can hear in Tityrus's account of Neptune's catastrophic flood an echo of the environmental transformations set in motion by Polyphemus' love for Galatea: 'Of his murderous heart', we read in Golding's translation, 'the wildness waxeth tame', assuring that 'ships may pass / And repass safely' (13: 906-8).

The cyclops could also be a prefiguring of Lyly's sea-monster the Agar, whose name is a remarkably specific local dialect variation of the word 'eagre' which is 'a tidal wave of unusual height, caused by the rushing of the tide up a narrowing estuary [...] chiefly with reference to the Humber (and Trent) and the Severn'.[25] Even the account of Acis's transformation from human to river resonates against the lesson Galatea is supposed to learn: sheep will turn into ships, birds into fish, and girls into monsters.

Ovid's Galatea is the daughter of Nereus, son of Pontus (the Sea) and Gaia (the Earth). Nereus is known as the 'old man of the sea' and he fathers the Nereids (the sea nymphs of which Galatea is the fairest) with ocean nymph, Doris. Galatea's aquatic character is also emphasised by Polyphemus' song that, in Golding's translation, repeatedly draws attention to the fact that his beloved is, in her strength, estuarial:

> More fleeting than the waves, more hard than warried oak to twine;
> More tough than willow twigs, more lithe than is the wild white vine;
> More than this rock unmovable, more violent than a stream.
> (13: 941–3)

Lyly seems to be picking up on this imagery when he has Galatea remark, 'There is a tree in Tylos, whose nuts have shells like fire, and, being cracked, the kernel is but water' (III, ii, 4–5). Her point is that she is not what she seems to be, but she is also indicating, *pace* Ovid and Golding, that her inner nature is aquatic.

In her antipathy for the forest world Phillida, Lyly's milder girl, begs comparison to Ovid's androgynous Acis whose metamorphosis – from shepherd to river – makes Phillida's association with him all the more evocative. Acis, the amphibious son of Faunus and the river-nymph Symaethis, is framed in *The Metamorposis* as the feminine antithesis of the ever-so-virile hairy cyclops:

> For, being but a sixteen years of age, this fair sweet boy
> Did take me to his love what time about his childish chin
> The tender hair like mossy down to sprout did first begin.
> (13: 888–90)

Acis is a very tender boy, in other words – one whose 'sweetness' recalls Jeffrey Masten's account of the term's expression of an inherently queer 'mobile quality of desire, erotics and affect'.[26] The lovers' aquatic affinities are also emphasised in Ovid by the fact that it is Galatea who sees to it 'That Acis should receive the force his father had before', permitting him to transform into a stream (13: 1040). If Phillida is a reworking of Acis, then both of Lyly's heroines are, at least partially, of the water. Moreover, if the union of Acis and Galatea is the union of river and sea, then the union of Galatea and Phillida can be tied to estuarial properties of the Humber. When Lyly's Tityrus speaks of 'monstrous mermaids' taking the place of 'passing fair maids' in the post-diluvian world of days gone by, he is thinking of his daughter in terms of the latter category but, in the light of Lyly's debt to 'Acis and Galatea', we are asked to consider her in terms of the former.

At the beginning of the play, Galatea asks Tityrus to tell her what happens when the sea monster steals away the sacrificial virgin. He responds: 'Whether she be devoured of him, or conveyed to Neptune, or drowned between both, it is not permitted to know, and incurreth danger to conjecture' (I, i, 59–61). The virgin martyr's fate is undetermined and the knowledge itself is deemed enticingly off limits. And yet, for Galatea and Phillida, this 'natural' solution – an uncertain fate in the hands of a sea monster – is more appealing than their fathers' forest caper. 'Nature hath given me beauty; Virtue courage', says Galatea, 'Nature must yield me death; Virtue, honor' (I, i, 85–6).[27] Two possible definitions of nature hover over this passage: the girl's constitutional nature is the meaning likely intended, but Galatea's 'nature' is rooted in the natural world and its natural history which are as central to the play as they are to its Englished Ovidian source.

The second environment important to both *Galatea* and 'Acis and Galatea' is the forest. For Golding, Ovid's forest lands are in fact wetlands, the oddity of which needs some emphasis: we need to imagine river-valley meadows, marshlands of poplar and, closer to the water, grasses, bog and reeds. And it is Venus and Diana who are the masters of these woods and who make them terrifying. For Lyly's Rafe, shipwrecked and washed ashore like an unfortunate crab, these woods are 'nothing but the screaking of owls, croaking of frogs, hissing of adders, barking of foxes and the walking of hags' (II, iii, 3–5). As Alexandra Walsham has shown, 'forests, woods, and groves functioned as the arena in which communication with numinous forces was believed to be possible and individual trees of impressive stature frequently became the focus of cultic behavior.'[28] This is all the more true when that forest is located along an estuary – a liminal space, part land, part sea, part river – possessing all of the captivating qualities of both earth and water. 'Heavy with anthropomorphic symbolism and redolent of divine power', woodlands could be, as Walsham suggests, responsive to human presence; 'care had to be taken to avoid angering the deities that invisibly occupied the physical spaces men and animals traversed.'[29] For Galatea and Phillida, the woods are a murky dangerous place where sensible girls should never go. This is a soggy space of mythological enchantment inhabited by gods and nymphs, a damp sacred grove where sensible humans dare not tread. It is both a wet and earthy place containing at its edge one tree of great significance: the 'fair' oak, beneath which Tityrus and Galatea stand and to which the sacrificial virgin is to be tied. As Leah Scragg has shown, Lyly's euphuistic style renders this all important tree as both shelter and site of sacrifice, 'promoting a view of the world as unstable and capable of metamorphosis to an opposite state'.³⁰ This form of transversion is all the more powerful if located in the Lincolnshire wetlands, themselves a place of transformation subject to the surges and swells of the river Humber.³¹ Lyly's tree has an Ovidian past, but an Englished one whose histories speak of local ecologies.

Tityrus and Phillida's father, Melibeus, are both described as shepherds linked to a third Ovidian environment, also present in 'Acis and Galatea', the pasture. Tityrus's gesture to 'our flock that doth roam up and down this pleasant green' (I, i, 6–7) draws attention to the agricultural lands of Lincolnshire, rescued from the sea by generations of engineering and intervention. At the time of the dissolution of the monasteries, over 40 ecclesiastical foundations could be counted within the boundaries of the Humber Wetlands and the reclamation of wastes, moors and wetlands by these foundations, often seen as a 'conversion of the land' for godly purposes, contributed to the development of the region's important agricultural industry (Figure 8.5).³² From the middle of the sixteenth century, the gentry, profiting in many cases from the dissolution of the monasteries, bought up this land for pasture, resulting in the wide-

Figure 8.5 Humberside fields and pastures. Barton-Upon-Humber. Author's photograph.

spread practice of land enclosure and sheep breeding. Ovid's Polyphemous is a denizen of this world, a country shepherd bound to the pastoral characters in Lyly's play. Golding's gloss of the cyclops in his dedicatory 'Epistle' to the Earl of Leicester enhances this association by domesticating Ovid's monster in the English pastoral tradition: 'in the person of the selfsame giant is set out / The rude and homely wooing of a country clown and lout' ('Epistle': 264–5). This description is developed in the subsequent tale which gives us a besotted Polyphemous tending to his beard rather than his sheep (13: 901–6). In his love song to the sea nymph, moreover, the giant promises her the fruits of his agricultural labours, including cattle with 'udders full', lambs and kids to make her 'good cheese' and 'milk as white as snow' (13: 971–5).

And yet, in *Galatea*, Tityrus and Melibeus seem prepared to sacrifice pastoral prosperity, as secured by allegiance to the gods, for the sake of lineage – a fact that is not missed by Neptune.

> And do men begin to be equal with gods, seeking by craft to overreach them that by power oversee them? Do they dote so much on their daughters that they stick not to dally with our deities? (V, iii, 11–14)

The instability introduced by the patriarchs' disobedience and deception may be a function of the fact that the English landscape that Lyly inherits from Golding is itself undergoing further metamorphoses engineered by human hands. As Vin Nardizzi has shown, timber shortage was already a preoccupation for Elizabethans – something Rafe acknowledges when he beckons his compatriots to 'Come, let us to the woods and see what fortunes we may have before they be made ships' (I, iv, 77–9).[33] By the time Lyly was writing *Galatea*, in other words, many of the wetland villages were in decline, primarily because the agricultural modifications effected upon the land eroded the natural woodland barriers between the towns and the river, making Humberside communities much more vulnerable to flood.[34] By the sixteenth century, we find prohibitions against, and fines for, the pasturing of livestock on marsh banks because it led to soil compression and the destruction of vegetation, and the records of the courts of sewers attest to the laborious and expensive business of building up defence banks in order to preserve towns and fields – a process that A. E. B. Owen describes as 'a losing battle'.[35]

'Coastal squeeze' is the environmental phenomenon in which intertidal habitat is engulfed by the rising sea as it is kept from encroaching on the land by immovable stone defence embankments. As the sea rises up against the man-made walls, the banks beneath the water vanish and along with them their flora and fauna. The water management systems designed to protect humans and their lands from flood essentially destroy coastal ecosystems by preventing them from re-establishing themselves on higher ground as water levels rise over them (Figure 8.6).[36]

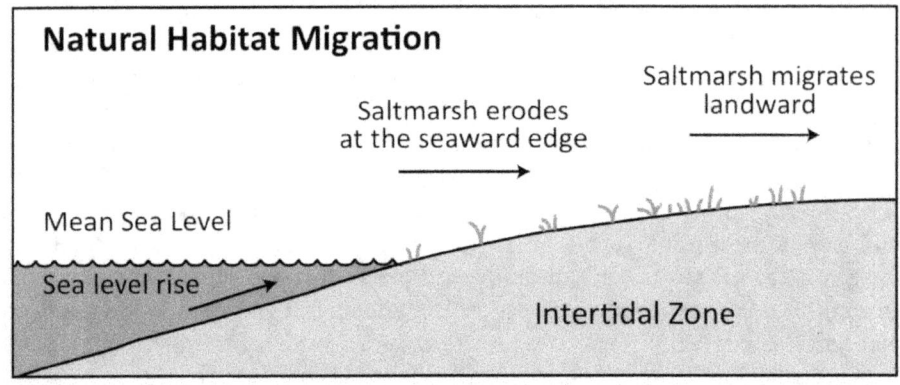

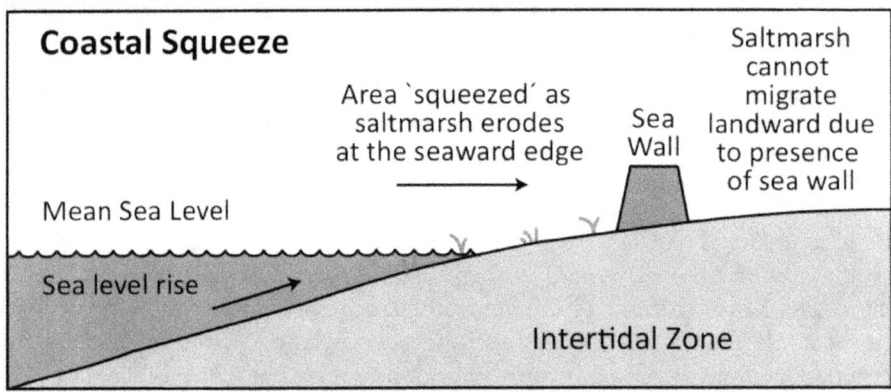

Figure 8.6 'Tide Facts: The Humber Estuary'. TIDE Project.http://www.tide-project.eu/index.php5?node_id=Reports-and-Publications;83&lang_id=1.

Coastal squeeze is a phenomenon that concerns English economists and conservationists today, exacerbated as it is by climate change, but the problem is not new. We see the beginnings of this tension between nature and human engineering in *Galatea*. The coastal woodlands – so crucial to this plot because they are Diana's habitat, and also because they provide the grove in which the girls 'make much of one another' (III, iii, 64–5) – had, by the mid-sixteenth century, all but disappeared over centuries of deforestation in combination with rising sea levels.[37] By the time Lyly transplants 'Acis and Galatea' to Lincolnshire, the forest into which Tityrus and Milebeus send their daughters had already been squeezed, not between Scylla and Charybdis, but between the ocean and the sheep enclosures that protect the 'pleasant greens' and 'plain fields' of early modern Lincolnshire.

Galatea comes to a close when Neptune calls off the virgin sacrifice in order to broker peace between Diana and Venus who are fighting because Cupid, at

Venus's command, had enslaved Diana's nymphs and Diana, in retaliation, was holding Cupid prisoner. Galatea and Phillida, their femaleness confirmed, are to leave the woods and go home where things will return to normal. 'Nature will have it so; necessity must', says Diana (V, iii, 134). This is the point where the same-sex love plot of 'Iphis and Ianthe' overtakes the environmental metamorphoses of 'Acis and Galatea', assuring that, as in Ovid, girl still loves girl. 'I will never love any but Phillida', says Galatea, 'her love is engraven in my heart with her eyes', to which Phillida responds, 'Nor I any but Galatea; whose faith is imprinted in my thoughts by her words' (V, iii, 135–8). Venus (here a transversion of Ovid's Isis) solves the ensuing conundrum by cunningly proposing that one of the girls be changed into a boy. The fathers, who have reappeared in the forest, instantly protest, in one case because a younger male sibling would lose his inheritance. And yet it is agreed that Venus's plan is the best way forward. 'Then let us depart', the goddess says; 'Neither of them shall know whose lot it shall be till they come to the church door' (V, iii, 184–5).

The church had, by Lyly's time, torn itself apart over the question of transubstantiation, making it certain that that any kind of metamorphosis staged in an English church would be charged with meaning and thus best left to the imagination. Furthermore, as Wiseman has pointed out, 'metamorphosis' is not a property readily claimed by any Christian church.[38] Even Golding was at pains to wrestle his translation into a Christian framework, palatable to his Protestant patron and readership. The ancient poets, he suggests, 'took the ground of all their chiefest fables out / Of scripture; which they shadowing with their glosses, went about / To turn the truth to toys and lies' ('Epistle', 529–31). Lyly, in step with his source, reveals mistrust of metamorphosis generally, and of Ovid specifically, in Galatea's response to her father's argument on the merits of his cross-dressing scheme. In defence of disguise, Tityrus argues that 'to gain love the gods have taken the shapes of beasts, and to save life art thou coy to take the attire of men?' to which Galatea retorts, 'they were beastly gods, that lust could make them seem as beasts' (I, ii, 95–8). Golding would agree:

> To eagles, tigers, bulls and bears and other figures strange,
> Both to their people and themselves most hurtful do they change.
> And when the people give themselves to filthy life and sin,
> What other kind of shape thereby than filthy can they win?
> ('Preface', 91–4)

However, while Galatea shudders at the thought of disguise as a means to preserve her life, her community's endorsement of sex-change as the means to resolve the love plot is conceivable, even desirable, as long as it restores the social and economic order (V, iii, 151–88). Likewise, in defence of Ovid's tales of metamorphoses, Golding argues that the fables 'are not put in writing to th' intent / To further or allure vice', but rather encourages his readers to 'seek a further meaning than the letter gives to see' ('Epistle', 541–2, 561–2). Lyly's plot resolution thus seems to follow Golding's humanist insistence that metamorphosis is appropriate, provided it is deserved and aimed toward a greater purpose:

> Now when thou read'st of god or man, in stone, in beast, or tree
> It is a mirror for thyself thine own estate to see.
> For under feignèd names of gods it was the poet's guise,
> The vice and faults of all estates to taunt in covert wise,
> And likewise to extol with praise such things as do deserve,
> Observing always comeliness from which they do not swerve.
> ('Preface', 81–6)

For Lyly's shepherds, bodily conversion is a good thing, if it is decent, appropriate and becoming. The cross-dressing scheme, designed by fathers to protect their lineage, is not, from Galatea's perspective, comely. But paradoxically, love that is itself constant and unchanging, 'unspotted, begun with truth, continued with constancy, and not to be altered til death' (V, iii, 146–67), provides the motive for a metamorphosis that can even be sanctioned, presumably, by the church.

The character of Lyly's church is not at all clear. At the beginning of the play, Tityrus gestures, possibly off stage, toward a 'heap of small pebbles' as he gives his history lesson to his daughter. These are the ruins of the Temple of Neptune, the destruction of which precipitated the first calamitous flood. By the end of the play, however, these stones are forgotten, as is Neptune's wrath and his demand of compulsory sacrifice. Instead, our attention is drawn to an offstage church and a joyful sacramental union. Lyly's anachronistic use of the word 'church' as a substitute for Ovid's 'templum' is modelled on Golding's desire to give classical temples 'a more English shape'.[39] One such translation appears in the account of the flood cited above and another can be found at the climactic moment in 'Iphis and Ianthe', immediately after the mother's prayer is answered and Iphis is declared 'now a boy':

> With offerings, both of you,
> To church retire and there rejoice with faith unfearful!
> They with offerings went to church again, and there their vows did pay.
> (9: 930–1)

Not all of Golding's Christian conversions are particularly charged, but here, in the paratactic paring of the homonyms 'there' and 'their', the translator appears to propose a link between place and subjectivity. As Lyne has shown, Golding is 'promoting Christian values', and while he declines to moralise or provide systematic interpretations of stories, he is invoking a Christian context, aiming these myths 'towards a new home in English culture'.[40] It is telling, then, that in many early modern translations of *The Metamorphoses*,

Telethusa's and Iphis's prayer to Isis is the scene of choice for illustration (see Appendix F) of the story. In the foreground of these images we see mother and daughter kneeling in prayer. 'Have mercy now on twain / And help us', begs Telethusa of Isis. At which point the goddess moves and 'the temple doors did tremble like a reed, / And hornes in likeness to the moon about the church did shine'. Then, to the side we see two figures walking away – Telethusa with Iphis whose transformation has just begun: 'not wholly careless, yet right glad', following 'with larger pace than aye / She was accustomed' (9: 917–25). This scene of prayer and 'conversion' is, for Golding as for Lyly, the most properly Christian moment in the story.

The literary metamorphosis of 'templum' into 'church' has its English architectural analogue in the dismantling of Roman temples which was accompanied by the resanctification of these same sites in the name of Christianity.[41] This process of appropriation and refurbishment was repeated again in the post-Reformation period when acts of anti-Catholic iconoclasm were often accompanied by 'efforts to protect and rehabilitate prehistoric monuments and medieval churches, chapels, and crosses and to incorporate them into newly designed spaces'.[42] Lincolnshire examples possibly known to Lyly include the Church of St Peter's in Barton-upon-Humber. This church, now an English Heritage property, sits on the east coast of the Humber estuary, resting on land that was open to Viking invaders, traders and settlers, some of whom would have converted to Christianity. The first Christian church, built by or in the early eleventh century, is still visible today in the distinctive Anglo-Saxon tower. Here as well, some of the stone has been re-used from earlier Roman buildings (Figure 8.7).[43]

The ending of *Galatea* is a coming together of the old (the classical, the Roman, the pagan) with the new (the modern, the English, the Christian) and also of Ovid with Golding. And the invention that results of these convergences – ecological, historical and literary – is the church that appears near to, or on top of, the sacred ruins of ancient stones.[44] Valerie Traub, in the introduction to this volume, proposes that the virtue of 'transversion' as a heuristic 'is that it asks us to scrutinize such dynamics of location and temporality, to watch movements as they transit forward and back, and to attend to the play of difference as well as similarity.'[45] Lyly's church is an English church built on the foundations of a Roman temple by English shepherds who raise sheep on the verge of an ancient grove that might someday be swallowed by the sea. The layers of this landscape run deep; it is neither natural nor man-made, mythic or real, pagan or Christian, English or Roman, but transversions of all of these.

* * *

Perhaps in some way, by virtue of the marriage promised by Venus, Galatea and Phillida are made to belong, as Ovid was, by being Englished. And yet, I

Figure 8.7 St Peter's Church, Barton-Upon-Humber. Author's photograph.

also hear in Lyly's play the echo of the sea nymph's choice of her gentle river-lover over the virile cyclops, a decision that emphasises water over land and similitude over difference.[46] The sex change and marriage proposed by Venus at the end of Lyly's play is a convenient, magical work-around, squeezed out in the intertidal forest between the raging tides of the ocean and the man-made sheep enclosures that separate the humans from the gods. But there *is* an unruliness in the play's suspension of this ultimate metamorphosis and in the girls' affection for each other which, through its association with the 'Humber floods', is delightfully resistant to the fields on the other side of the enclosures – fields whose defense embankments threaten to destroy the inter-tidal habitat and all of its earthly and divine inhabitants.

'The hungry ocean', Steve Mentz reminds us, 'destabilizes our fantasies of sustainable growth and a harmonious relationship between human culture and the natural world'.⁴⁷ If, as I have been proposing, the unresolved conclusion of *Galatea* asks us to turn from 'Iphis and Ianthe' toward 'Acis and Galatea', it is possible to see in Lyly's ending something of a warning that would have been recognisable to the natives of Lincolnshire: fear the sea. While the Mariner that brings Rafe and Robin to safety on the Lincolnshire shoreline dismisses the ocean as 'but a liquid element' (I, iv, 40), Galatea's initial embrace of her estuarial fate suggests otherwise, as does the inconclusive ending of the play. Everyone setting off to church hopes that Venus's trans-ending will stave off the ocean, ushering in dry days, pastoral prosperity and general concord among the gods, the humans and the natural world. But the Humber, in its tidal storms and destructive floods, is of the sea and, as Lyly's audience would have understood, its presence unsettles the conclusion's flirtation with environmental sustainability. Lyly and his contemporaries lived with the same certainty that haunts England today: the Humber will flood again. No temple, no church, no stone embankment will stop it. These stopgap measures will inevitably fall to ruins.

It is possible, however, to think about Lyly's treatment of imminent environmental catastrophe in broader historical terms. The early moderns, despite their various 'reformed' theologies, continued to imagine their present as historically placed between environmental catastrophes: between flood past and apocalypse to come.⁴⁸ Texts like Golding's *Metamorphoses* or Lyly's *Galatea* gather ancient and contemporary iterations of this cosmic situatedness and anchor them to something local and familiar – something like 'home'. In so doing, they activate affective associations between art and the environment, illustrating that humans cannot live apart from the oceans, rivers, trees and stones that surround them. This idea is salutary for us, as located moderns – no longer poised on the verge of environmental catastrophe but living within it. Might there be a wild, and even somewhat hopeful, incivility to *Galatea* lying in the suggestion that the pastoral Lincolnshire landscape is a man-made work-around that only temporarily forestalls the tides of the mighty Humber, to which these like-minded mermaids might, someday, return?

Acknowledgments

I would like to acknowledge the graduate students in my 2017 seminar, 'Renaissance Conversions: Religion, Theatre and Transformation in Early Modern England', whose careful thinking about this play helped to strengthen my own. I am also grateful for the support of Oecologies Research Cluster and Early Modern Conversions project.

Notes

1. Traub suggests that while the play positions female–female relationships 'as an *amor impossibilis*', Lyly's play 'at the same time, by gesturing toward the

enactment of erotic passion for one's own sex, by mining a tension between what can and cannot *be practiced* [...] helps to make the impossible intelligible and the unintelligible possible (*The Renaissance of Lesbianism*, p. 6). Carter also proposes that the 'conclusion leaves the audience with the same mode of desire demonstrated throughout, the two girls in love with one another', but concludes that 'the homoeroticism of female same sex desire' is ultimately curtailed by the 'prerogatives of the dominant discourse' (*Ovidian Myth and Sexual Deviance*, pp. 109–10). Dooley goes further to argue that 'the end of the play positively encourages the continuation of the relationship between Gallathea [*sic*] and Phillida *as girls*' ('Inversion, Metamorphosis and Sexual Difference', p. 61).

2. This statement does seem to beg some consideration of the boy actors whose performance of the parts of Galatea and Phillida would have been part of the appreciation of the resolutions to this, and other, cross-dressing comedies. However, for my purposes here, the characters that leave the stage are female.
3. All references to Lyly's *Galatea* are to Scragg's edition and appear within the body of the essay.
4. Sanders, in *The Cultural Geography of Early Modern Drama*, proposes that Lyly's knowledge would have been 'first hand' due to his wife's family estate (51). Lancashire, in her edition of *Gallathea*, also makes the argument for Lyly's regional specificity (p. xviii), while Scragg writes that the Humberside setting is described in 'non-naturalistic' terms (*The Metamorphosis of* Gallathea', p. 16).
5. 'The Humber Estuary', Wildlife Trusts, http://www.wildlifetrusts.org/node/5576. See also the 'Habitats and Wildlife' section of *The Humber Environment in Focus*, pp. 24–36, and *The Humber Flood Risk Management Strategy: Planning for Rising Tides*.
6. For discussion of a recent flood, see news coverage from December 2013 (i.e. 'Hull and North Lincolnshire Floods Clean-up Begins', BBC News, 6 December 2013, http://www.bbc.com/news/uk-england-humber-25253833).
7. For footage of the 2013 Humber flood see 'Police Helicopter Films Humber Estuary Flooding', http://www.bbc.com/news/av/uk-england-humber-25260349/police-helicopter-films-humber-estuary-flooding.
8. See Van de Noort, *The Humber Wetlands* 1, 2004, pp. 147–8, 153. For an account of towns damaged and lost in the Middle Ages and the early modern period, see Owen, 'Coastal Erosion in East Lincolnshire', pp. 330–41.
9. *Chronica Monasterii de Melsa*, vol. 3, pp. 120–1. For other instances of Humber flooding see vol. 2, pp. 91, 300; vol. 3 pp. 102, 183, 243, 247. For discussion of the relationship between the wrath of gods and oceanic disturbance see Steve Mentz's chapter, 'Angry Gods: Theologies of the Ocean', in *Shipwrecked Modernity*, Kindle location 997–1464.
10. Holinshed, *Chronicles of England* (1577), vol. 4, p. 1853. Accessed at *The Holinshed Project*, http://english.nsms.ox.ac.uk/holinshed/texts.php?text1=1577_5332.
11. Knell, *A declaration of such tempestious, and outragious fluddes*, A2. Knell is paraphrasing Psalm 107.
12. Spenser, *Faerie Queene*, Bk IV, Canto xi, 30.7; 'A Pastorall Aeglogue upon the Death of Sir Phillip Sidney, Knight', l. 102.
13. Taylor, *A verry merry vvherry-ferry-voyage*, B3.
14. Abbot, John. *Iesus praefigured, or, A poëme of the holy name of Iesus in five books* (1623), p. 77.
15. *God's marvellous wonders in England*, Ch. 4, pp. 10–11. For a recent account of a beached whale on the North side of the Humber Estuary, see 'Dead Humber Estuary Whale Was "Rare" Species', BBC News, http://www.bbc.com/news/uk-england-humber-15104896 (accessed 5 November 2017).

16. Marvell, 'To his Coy Mistress', ll. 6–7.
17. Sabie, *The fissher-mans tale*, D3v.
18. Sanders, *The Cultural Geography of Early Modern Drama*, p. 51.
19. Cited in Sanders, *The Cultural Geography of Early Modern Drama*, p. 51. On Lyly's use of Virgil, see Scragg, 'Introduction' to the Revels edition, pp. 6–10.
20. Wiseman, *Writing Metamorphosis in the English Renaissance*, p. 2.
21. See Lyne, *Ovid's Changing Worlds*, pp. 28, 75.
22. For a discussion of Lyly's expansion upon academic style, particularly 'the insistent location [. . .] of alternative potentialities branching outwards from an initial proposition', see Scragg, 'Introduction', pp. 3–4.
23. Ovid, *Metamorphosis*, trans. Arthur Golding. All subsequent references to the *Metamorphosis* are to this edition and appear in the body of the essay.
24. Bellamy, *Dire Straits*, pp. 3, 40.
25. eagre, n. OED Online. Oxford University Press, http://www.oed.com.ezproxy.library.ubc.ca/view/Entry/58945?redirectedFrom=eagre&. Sanders proposes that Agar is a version of the term *eágor*, a regional dialect term for the tidal wave on the Humber Estuary (p. 51).
26. Masten, *Queer Philologies*, p. 72. In Handel's operatic adaptation of 'Acis and Galatea' (1718), the role of Acis is played by an alto castrato. In some recent productions, the part has been played by a woman. See 'Review: *Acis and Galatea*, Annex Theatre, Vancouver, Sept. 16, 2017', *Opera Canada*, http://operacanada.ca/review-acis-galatea-annex-theatre-vancouver-sept-16-2017/ (accessed 6 November 2017).
27. Phillida's objections are more pragmatic. Keeping company with boys will mean committing 'follies unseemly for my sex . . . I shall be ashamed of my long hose and short coat' (I, iii, 18–22).
28. Walsham, *The Reformation of the Landscape*, p. 20.
29. Walsham, *The Reformation of the Landscape*, p. 20.
30. Scragg, 'Speaking Pictures', pp. 301–2.
31. Kesson observes, with respect to the tree as stage prop, that the audience is never permitted 'to assume that any part of the play is quite what it seems to be' (*John Lyly and Early Modern Authorship*, pp. 118–19).
32. Van de Noort, *The Humber Wetlands*, pp. 140, 153.
33. Nardizzi, *Wooden Os*, pp. 6–12.
34. Van de Noort attributes increased problems with water to a period of cooler and wetter weather, dated to the 200 years after 1250, and to a relative regional sea-level rise:

> The former affected the whole of the Humber Wetlands, but the latter had a disproportionate impact on the floodplains, most notably those of the Rivers Hull and Ancholme, and on the Lincolnshire Marsh. [. . .] Historical evidence, including the appointment of commissioners who were to survey the riverbeds and sea defences in 1285, shows continued problems throughout the thirteenth, fourteenth and much of the fifteenth century. [. . .] These sea-level changes many not have been directly responsible for settlement desertion and depopulation, but would certainly have reduced the viability of arable farming in these low-lying areas. The resulting conversion to pasture, either by farmers themselves or under the direction of principle landowners, would have contributed to unemployment and depopulation and thus to settlement desertion. (*The Humber Wetlands*, pp. 156–7)

See also Ellis et al., *Wetland Heritage*.
35. Owen, 'The Upkeep of the Lindsey Sea Defences', pp. 23–30.

36. *The Humber Environment in Focus*, p. 29. See also 'Tide Facts: The Humber Estuary', p. 3.
37. Peat bog deposits bear the traces of long submerged forests dominated by oak but also alder, ash, willow and poplar. For a discussion of the 'impossible possibilities' that might take place in the grove, see Traub, *The Renaissance of Lesbianism*, pp. 5–6, 327–30.
38. Wiseman, *Writing Metamorphoses in the English Renaissance*, p. 8. Wiseman's source is Henry Charles Lea's *Materials Toward a History of Witchcraft* (ed. Arthur C. Howland, vol.1 [New York and London: Thomas Yoseloff, 1957] pp. 178-80), who in turn cites Migne, *Patrilogia Latina* CXXXII, 353.
39. Lyne, *Ovid's Changing Worlds*, p. 65.
40. Lyne, *Ovid's Changing Worlds*, p. 74. For further discussion of Golding's Christian translation, see Lyne, pp. 62–74.
41. Walsham, *The Reformation of the Landscape*, p. 27.
42. Ibid., p. 13. See also Lyne, p. 67.
43. St Peters, Barton-Upon-Humber is one of England's most studied churches, in part because of its Saxon architectural features. There is no evidence of a major Roman settlement at Barton, but there is evidence of 'localized centers of occupation' (Warwick Rodwell, *St Peter's Barton-upon-Humber, Lincolnshire*, p. 2). The church contains recycled Roman building materials in its fabric, but it was not built on the site of a Roman-period structure. For a detailed treatment of the church's architectural past, see Rodwell, *St Peter's Barton-upon-Humber, Lincolnshire*, pp. 4–10. See also, 'History of St Peter's Church', English Heritage, http://www.english-heritage.org.uk/visit/places/st-peters-church-barton-upon-humber/history/. Another relevant example of an English church built with Roman materials is found in Bede's account of Paulinus's conversion of Blecca, the mayor of Lincoln, in AD 629 on the South Bank of the Humber 'bending even unto the seas side'. According to Bede, Blecca marked the site of his conversion with a 'well wrowght churche of stone' which 'is nowe cast down' for 'long lack of reparations, or by the spoyle of some enemies'. Its walls 'stand yet to be seene', Bede notes, and 'at this present daie and yearly some or other miracles are wont to be shewen ther to the greate good, and comforte of them which faythe fully seeke therefore.' The church to which Bede refers may be the lost church of St Paul's in Lincoln, built on a site that apparently hosted post-Roman, Anglo-Saxon, medieval, eighteenth- and nineteenth-century churches – the last of which was torn down in 1971, revealing beneath it the flooring of a Roman forum. See the Venerable Bede, *The History of the Church of Englande*, Ch. 16, S1v–S2v. For a description of the archaeological remains on the site, see 'Site of St Paul-in-the Bail church and churchyard, Lincoln', *LINCS to the Past*, http://www.lincstothepast.com/Site-of-St-Paul-in-the-Bail-church-and-churchyard--Lincoln/239929.record?pt=S and 'The Church of St Paul-in-the-Bail', *Visit Lincoln*, https://www.visitlincoln.com/things-to-do/interest/the-church-of-st-paul-in-the-bail.
44. See Walsham, *The Reformation of the Landscape*, p. 10.
45. Traub, 'Introduction: Transversions of *Iphis and Ianthe*', p. 23, this volume.
46. On the subject of the girls' sameness, see Traub, *The Renaissance of Lesbianism*, pp. 327–30.
47. Mentz, *At the Bottom of Shakespeare's Ocean*, pp. xii. Much of my concluding argument is indebted to Mentz's sense that 'ecology won't keep us dry':

> Hopes for a dry life, an easy, pastoral sustainable relationship between nature and culture, seem as unlikely as a full season of calm seas. It's not that we don't

want it. It's not that we shouldn't work toward it. It's that we won't get it.
(pp. 96–7)

On the relationship between early modern wetscapes and our own ecological predicament, see also Duckert, *For all Waters*.

48. This idea was the basis of a panel, organised by Jeffery Jerome Cohen and sponsored by the Medieval and Early Modern Studies Institute at George Washington University, called 'Catastrophe and Periodization' presented at the International Medieval Studies Congress (Kalamazoo) in 2017.

BIBLIOGRAPHY

Abbot, John. *Iesus praefigured, or, A poëme of the holy name of Iesus in five books* (1623). STC 42.
Bellamy, Elizabeth Jane, *Dire Straits: The Perils of Writing the Early Modern English Coastline from Leland to Milton* (Toronto: University of Toronto Press, 2013).
Carter, Sarah, *Ovidian Myth and Sexual Deviance in Early Modern English Literature* (Basingstoke: Palgrave Macmillan, 2011).
Chronica Monasterii de Melsa, A Fundatione Usque Ad Annum 1396, vols 2 and 3, ed. Edward Augustus Bond (Longmans, Green, Reader & Dyer, 1868).
Dooley, Mark, 'Inversion, Metamorphosis and Sexual Difference: Female Same-Sex Desire in Ovid and Lyly', in Goran V. Stanivukovic (ed.), *Ovid and the Renaissance Body* (Toronto: University of Toronto Press, 2001), pp. 59–76.
Duckert, Lowell, *For all Waters: Finding Ourselves in Early Modern Wetscapes* (Minneapolis: University of Minnesota Press, 2017).
Ellis, S. Fenwick, H., Lillie, M. and Van de Noort, R. (eds), *Wetland Heritage of the Lincolnshire Marsh: An Archaeological Survey* (Wetlands Project, University of Hull, 2001).
God's marvellous wonders in England containing divers strange and wonderful relations that have happened since the beginning of June, this present year 1694 [etc.] (1694). Wing G960A.
Holinshed, Raphael, *Chronicles of England* (1577), vol. 4, p. 1853. Accessed through *The Holinshed Project*, http://english.nsms.ox.ac.uk/holinshed/texts.php?text1=1577_5332.
The Humber Environment in Focus (Leeds: Environment Agency, 2011).
The Humber Flood Risk Management Strategy: Planning for Rising Tides (Leeds: Environment Agency, 2008).
Kesson, Andy, *John Lyly and Early Modern Authorship* (Manchester: Manchester University Press, 2011).
Knell, Thomas, *A declaration of such tempestious, and outragious fluddes* (1570).
Lancashire, Anne Begor, 'Introduction', in John Lyly, *Gallathea and Midas*, ed. Anne Begor Lancashire (Lincoln: University of Nebraska Press, 1969).
Lyly, John, *Galatea*, ed. Leah Scragg (Manchester: Manchester University Press, 2012).
Lyne, Raphael, *Ovid's Changing Worlds: English Metamorphoses, 1567–1632* (Oxford: Oxford University Press, 2001).
Marvell, Andrew, 'To His Coy Mistress', in *The Complete Poems*, ed. Elizabeth Story Donno (London: Penguin, 1996), pp. 50–1.
Masten, Jeffrey, *Queer Philologies: Sex, Language, and Affect in Shakespeare's Time* (Philadelphia: University of Pennsylvania Press, 2016).
Mentz, Steve, *At the Bottom of Shakespeare's Ocean* (London: Continuum Books, 2009).
Mentz, Steve, *Shipwrecked Modernity: Ecologies of Globalization, 1550–1719* (Minneapolis: University of Minnesota Press, 2015).

Morton, Timothy, *The Ecological Thought* (Boston, MA: Harvard University Press, 2010).
Nardizzi, Vin, *Wooden Os: Shakespeare's Forests and England's Trees* (Toronto: University of Toronto Press, 2013).
Ovid, *Metamorphoses*, trans. Arthur Golding (1567), ed. Madeleine Forey (London: Penguin, 2002).
Owen, A. E. B., 'Coastal Erosion in East Lincolnshire', *Lincolnshire Historian* 1: 9 (1952), pp. 330–41.
Owen, A. E. B., 'The Upkeep of the Lindsey Sea Defences, 1550–1650', *Lincolnshire Historian* 2: 10 (1963), pp. 23–30.
Rodwell, Warwick, with Caroline Atkins, *St Peter's Barton-upon-Humber: A Parish Church and its Community. Vol. 1 History, Archaeology and Architecture* (Oxford: Oxbow Books, 2011).
Sabie, Francis, *The fissher-mans tale of the famous actes, life and loue of Cassander a Grecian knight* (1595) STC 21535.
Sanders, Julie, *The Cultural Geography of Early Modern Drama* (Cambridge: Cambridge University Press, 2011).
Scragg, Leah, 'Speaking Pictures: Style and Spectacle in Lylian Comedy', *English Studies* 86: 4 (2005), pp. 298–311.
Scragg, Leah, *The Metamorphosis of* Gallathea: *A Study in Creative Adaptation* (Washington, DC: University of America Press, 1982).
Spenser, Edmund, *The Faerie Queene* (London: Penguin, 1978).
Spenser, Edmund. 'A pastorall Aeglogue upon the Death of Sir Phillip Sidney, Knight' in *Astrophel: A Pastorall Elegie*. University of Oregon, Renasence Editions http://www.luminarium.org/renascence-editions/astrophel.html.
Taylor, John, *A verry merry vvherry-ferry-voyage: or Yorke for my money sometimes perilous sometimes quarrellous, performed with a paire of oares, by sea from London* (1622). STC 23812.
'Tide Facts: The Humber Estuary', TIDE Project, http://www.tide-project.eu/index.php5?node_id=Reports-and-Publications;83&lang_id=1.
Traub, Valerie, *The Renaissance of Lesbianism in Early Modern England* (Cambridge: Cambridge University Press, 2002).
Walsham, Alexandra, *The Reformation of the Landscape: Religion, Identity, and Memory in Early Modern Britain and Ireland* (Oxford: Oxford University Press, 2011).
Wiseman, Susan, *Writing Metamorphoses in the English Renaissance* (Cambridge: Cambridge University Press, reprint, 2016).
Van de Noort, Robert, *The Humber Wetlands: The Archaeology of a Dynamic Landscape* (Macclesfield, Cheshire: Windgather Press, 2004).

9

ILLEGIBLE BODIES: READING INTERSEX AND TRANSGENDER IN EARLY MODERN FRANCE (THE CASE OF ISAAC DE BENSERADE'S *IPHIS ET IANTE*)

Kathleen Perry Long

INTRODUCTION

In early modern French culture intersex individuals, designated 'hermaphrodites', were represented as a problem to be solved. Many social phenomena (marriage, inheritance, governance, the language) were dependent on the concept of two distinct genders, masculine and feminine, a dependence that was omnipresent in the culture, based as it was on a Romance language, one of a number of grammatical gender languages, in which everything is ordered according to a system of binary gender, including inanimate objects and abstract concepts.[1] Intersex reveals the flaws of this system of gender in a number of ways, calling into question the division of humanity into masculine and feminine and presenting a range of bodies and identities that do not map readily into this division but that suggest a spectrum of gender where a diversity of possibilities exists. Intersex reveals the abstraction that this division entails, and the failure of that abstraction in the face of natural variation.[2] This might explain why so much space is devoted to 'hermaphrodites' in early modern treatises on monsters, as 'monsters' in these works are all creatures that do not fit into categories.

In the early modern period, monsters were a problem for natural philosophy, as they were the creatures that defied the perceived order of nature. Since their forms could not be universalised into categories, they were designated as 'natural particulars'.[3] Intersex individuals presented a striking example of 'natural particulars', as their observable physiological characteristics varied a great deal and called into question the possibility of understanding such bodies in the context of binary gender.

As a result, intersex individuals present problems of legibility to a culture in which signs were deployed and interpreted to confer masculine or feminine gender. They present signs that designate both genders, or that do not clearly designate one gender or the other.[4] In France, early modern medical treatises and philosophical and literary works offer sustained consideration of the difficulty of knowing the intersex body, and the implications of this difficulty for the forms of knowledge that Europeans used to understand the world. Thus it should not be surprising that the question of the gender status of intersex individuals should arise across a range of works.

In a number of these early modern texts, the intersex body is associated with the transgender one, as particular signs are used to assign the male or female gender to bodies. Certain signs reappear in early modern discussions of gender distinction: hair length and condition, length of stride, strength, fairness of complexion, loud or soft, deep or shrill qualities of the voice, external genitalia, presence or absence of breasts. The signs used to designate gender themselves leave room for ambiguity, where a middle ground between loud or soft, deep or shrill, strong or weak may exist. Gender is also confirmed by clothing that marks the individual as male or female, and by the conferring of a name. In Ovid's tale of 'Iphis and Ianthe' in the *Metamorphoses* and Isaac de Benserade's retelling in his play, *Iphis et Iante*, the potential ambiguity of these signs, and their inherent instability, raises questions concerning the legibility of ambiguously gendered bodies. This legibility is related in the early modern period to doubts expressed by the heirs of Pyrrhonian scepticism[5] concerning the efficacy of signs as a means of reading that which is not readily apparent to us. Pyrrhonians saw all knowledge as necessarily embodied, in that all that we observe, from which we draw conclusions about the world and ourselves, is perceived through our corporeal senses. These senses are unstable and inconstant, being easily affected by changes in the condition of the perceiving subject and the context in which the perception takes place. While Pyrrhonian sceptics believed that humans could assent to immediate perceptions, they refused the possibility of forming opinions or drawing conclusions concerning those perceptions. In this, their concept of knowledge departed from Aristotelian, Platonic and other dogmatic epistemologies.

Although knowledge is embodied, knowledge about the body is necessarily limited to what we can perceive, and thus our knowledge of the body is also unstable and inconstant. The logical conclusion relative to gender of this understanding of knowledge is that one cannot draw conclusions about gender based on the apparent (or 'suggestive' as Sextus Empiricus calls them) signs on the body. The potential ambiguity of signs interpreted to confer gender on an intersex individual can be useful for thinking about the complexities of transgender identities in the early modern world. The tale of 'Iphis and Ianthe' in the *Metamorphoses* offers the opportunity to scrutinise the legibility of gender and the nature of the body on which it is constructed. Appearing in a number of literary and other texts, medieval and early modern, it strategically deploys the ambiguity of these signs to convey the 'moment' of transformation as a complex process, one depending as much upon interpretation of the change as upon the change itself.

Signs of Gender: Ovid's Tale of 'Iphis and Ianthe'

Ovid places the tale of 'Iphis and Ianthe' in the context of an epic that features other tales of gender transformation, that of Tiresias in Book Three and of Caenis/Caeneus in Book Twelve, for example, not to mention the tale of Salmacis and Hermaphroditus in Book Four. But the moment of Iphis's transformation is told with the greatest detail:

> Iphis walked beside her as she went, but with a longer stride than was her wont. Her face seemed of a darker hue, her strength seemed greater, her very features sharper, and her locks, all unadorned, were shorter than before. She seemed more vigorous than was her girlish wont.
>
> sequitur comes Iphis euntem,
> quam solita est, maiore gradu, nec candor in ore
> permanet, et vires augentur, et acrior ipse est
> vultus, et incomptis brevior mensura capillis,
> plusque vigoris adest, habuit quam femina.
> (*Met.* IX.786–90)

This transformation, while detailed, is perhaps not as dramatic as one might expect. Iphis's identity is already ambiguous from the beginning of the story; her name is appropriate for a boy or a girl: 'The mother rejoiced in the name; for it was of common gender and she could use it without deceit' ('gavisa est nomine mater, / quod commune foret, nec quemquam falleret illo', 709–10). The common gender in Latin is both masculine and feminine, and thus can be used to designate masculine or feminine people and things. Her beauty is presented as ambiguously gendered: 'its face would have been counted lovely whether you assigned it to a girl or a boy' ('facies, quam sive puellae, sive dares puero, fuerat formosus uterque', 712–13). That is to say, in appearance, the difference between male and female is not perceptible in at least some circumstances. Thus in name and facial appearance, Iphis can be masculine or feminine. She is given boy's clothing, and this act alone renders her masculine; the text enacts this transformation by using a masculine adjective in the place of a noun: 'The child was dressed like a boy' ('cultus erat pueri', 712). Thus a body that cannot be deciphered as male or female is inscribed as masculine by means of clothing, used as a supplement to the body.

In fact, although Iphis is born a girl ('nata est ignaro femina patre', 705), she is designated as a boy once her mother lies about her: 'the mother, with intent to deceive, bade them feed the boy' ('iussit ali mater puerum mentita', 706). Complicating the rhetorical presentation is the layering of feminine and masculine forms in these two phrases: the girl is 'surrounded' by her unknowing father ('ignaro femina patre', cited above), and the boy by his lying mother ('mater puerum mentita', cited above), in a feat of parallel structure that alternates masculine and feminine grammatical forms to heighten the sense of gender confusion of the passage. Iphis is a girl, but her father does not know this, and she is a boy, because her mother lied. The phrase 'cultus erat pueri', cited above, uses the masculine form of the verb, creating a sense of circular movement: 'the boy was dressed as a boy'. The beautiful face, whether that of a girl or a boy, is nonetheless designated by an adjective in the masculine form ('formosus'). The girl is both written and read as a boy, both by her mother and father, and by the author.

When Iphis falls in love with Ianthe, however, they are both designated as feminine by the word 'ambarum' ('both') in the phrase 'hinc amor ambarum tetigit rude pectus' ('Hence love came to both their hearts all unsuspected', 720). Iphis reads herself as a girl, even when she has been dressed in boy's clothing and raised as a boy. Thus even as she is represented and interpreted as a boy, her experience of herself, particularly in the context of her love for Ianthe, is as a girl. This oscillation in gender depending on the context and the person one is with creates a sense of ambiguity that is sustained throughout the tale.

All of the details in the description of Iphis's transformation play with perceived signs that are made legible by interpretation within a grid of gender norms, that is to say generalisations, conclusions or opinions about what this or that gender is like. In this case of extreme misogyny, and in the presence of the threat of female infanticide, the appearance of Iphis's face as a child is ambiguous, allowing her to be assigned female or male gender according to the context. The transformation of the face and body are represented by signs that may reflect diet, upbringing or training: first, the gait lengthens ('maiore gradu', 787); the brightness of complexion disappears ('nec candor in ore permanet', 787–8); strength increases ('vires augentur', 788); the face looks sharper ('acrior ipse est vultus', 788–9); and the hair is both shorter and uncombed ('incomptis brevior mensura capillis', 789). Finally, the increased strength is underscored once more ('plusque vigoris adest', 790). It is significant that the idea of strength is emphasised by means of words linked to maleness (*vir/vires/vigoris*), as if the mere naming of maleness conveys that state. The one grammatical gender designation used in this passage, 'quam solita est' ('than was her wont', 787) is feminine, as if to underscore that she was once accustomed to a feminine gait. Iphis is called 'puer' twice in this passage (lines 791 and 797).

These signs of gender are slippery at best: strength can be acquired through work or training and lost through illness or idleness; gaits can be practised and performed; skin colour can be altered by exposure to the sun; features can become sharper or softer through loss or gain of weight; hair can be left uncombed or carefully arranged. None of these signs of gender are stable. The wonder is that, having been dressed and raised as a boy, Iphis takes on these more masculine characteristics only at the moment immediately prior to marriage, that is, when her masculinity will be confirmed by holy rituals. One could imagine that, in order to pass as a boy, the girl Iphis already wore her hair in a more masculine fashion, walked more like a boy, and tried in other ways to act masculine.

Ovid does not mention aspects of the body that would more generally be used to designate gender, particularly at birth, such as genitalia. This is a striking difference between the story of Iphis and early modern medical accounts of intersex individuals, which nonetheless pick up many of the aspects of this tale.

Deferring Gender: Benserade's *Iphis et Iante*

Isaac de Benserade published his play, *Iphis et Iante*, in 1637, the same year René Descartes published his *Discourse on Method* (*Discours de la méthode*), reinterpreting sceptical methods to serve the search for a universal truth. In distinction to Descartes' quest for certainty, Benserade's play foregrounds the uncertainties of gender in the original Ovidian tale, and offers an even more ambiguous and subjective presentation of gender transformation at the end of the play than in Ovid's version. Iphis declares himself to be male, listing some of the characteristics noted by Ovid, and adding some new ones: along with greater strength and a longer step, Benserade's Iphis proclaims his tougher skin, harsher voice and flat bosom. This emphasis on the transformed individual's own voice and own interpretation of his gender echoes Ambroise Paré's suggestion that the individual in question should determine whether he or she functions as male or female.

> Miracle! I am a man, a male vigor
> Makes my members stronger, as well as my heart,
> My body becomes robust in the opposite sex,
> And I walk with a step that is larger than it used to be,
> Venus, who all alone occupied my gaze,
> Steps back in my eyes to give way to Mars;
> Neither my skin nor my voice is so delicate any more,

And my speech strikes with a stronger tone;
My breast which I hid has become all flat,
And I believe that my skin no longer has a lively glow.

Miracle! Je suis homme, une mâle vigueur
Rend mes membres plus forts aussi bien que mon coeur,
Mon corps devient robuste en un sexe contraire,
Et je marche d'un pas plus grand qu'à l'ordinaire,
Vénus, qui tout seule occupait mes regards,
Se resserre en mes yeux pour faire place à Mars;
Ni ma peau, ni ma voix n'est plus si delicate,
Et c'est d'un ton plus fort que ma parole éclate;
Mon sein que je cachais est devenu tout plat,
Et je crois que mon teint n'a plus son vif éclat.[6]

It is significant that Iphis describes his transformation himself, and positions it rhetorically as a miracle, that is, a phenomenon produced by a deity and thus to be seen in a positive light, but also as something beyond human comprehension. This rhetorical move, echoing the divine intervention of Ovid's version of the tale, thus eliminates the possibility of questioning the transformation itself, as only God understands a miracle.

The longer stride of Ovid's Iphis is repeated here, along with greater strength, a louder voice and more masculine interests. Some of these attributes could be acquired with medicines or cosmetics; for example, the inhabitants of *The Island of Hermaphrodites* use special waters (possibly tinctures) to soften and brighten their skin.[7] Others can be practised, such as the longer stride and the louder voice. Whereas in the *Metamorphoses*, none of the physiological features would definitively mark Iphis as a male, in Benserade's play Iphis emphasises his newly flattened chest. Yet, since Iphis was disguised as a boy, this chest has seemed flattened all along, and this detail raises the question of the relationship between appearance and possible corporeal reality. This description leaves out the hair, avoiding one of the more easily (and obviously) manipulated signs of gender, a detail that might have contributed a tone of irony to Ovid's description of Iphis. In fact, the focus in this account of transformation is largely on acquired characteristics such as strength, gait, warlike behaviour and a loud voice, as if acting like a man will make Iphis one. In the contrast between his former interest in love (Venus) and his newfound interest in war (Mars), he emphasises the subjective nature of this transformation; gender is as much a feeling as it is a set of physical characteristics. Finally, Iphis's celebratory announcement of his transformation reiterates Ambroise Paré's injunction that intersex individuals (whom he calls hermaphrodites) should be allowed to choose their own gender, although the legal parameters of this gender are the binary male/female options.

Social recognition of gender transformation is crucial, and this recognition is both achieved and marked by means of a range of signs. If Iphis is accepted socially as a man, he can pass as one; he is already dressed in men's clothing (since birth) and has a man's name (as well as a woman's), so he meets the required social signs of male gender signalled by Paré. But intriguingly, as Iphis announces his transformation, it is clear that his new gender identity is not evident to any of the witnesses present. His mother asks him 'Is this true, dear Iphis?' ('Est-il vrai, cher Iphis?'). Téleste and Ligde ask each other what to think about Iphis's declaration of masculinity. Iante expresses some doubt: 'if the gods have transformed your sex in some way' ('Si les dieux en ton sexe ont fait ce changement').[8] To assuage their fears, Iphis must declare:

> If you do not judge my speech to be truthful,
> I will let you see palpable effects of it,
> And my dear other half in a good way
> Will prove in nine months that Iphis is a boy.

> Si vous ne jugez pas mes discours véritables,
> Je vous en ferai voir des effets palpables,
> Et ma chère moitié d'une bonne façon
> Prouvera dans neuf mois qu'Iphis est un garçon.[9]

As we have seen, many of the signs that appear to be legible as one gender or the other can be manipulated and exposed. But examination of the body itself would violate the decorum of the stage. So, in the absence of immediately apparent gender characteristics, the only socially legible sign of gender is the begetting of children (a form of proof that is listed in Jacques Duval's treatise on hermaphrodites and childbirth, *Des hermaphrodits et accouchements des femmes*). The proof of Iphis's gender must be deferred, and so the outcome of the play remains uncertain; all of the other characters have expressed some disbelief ('Est-il vrai, cher Iphis?'), but they must suspend that disbelief for at least nine months. The delicacy of this solution is a far cry from medical accounts of determining gender.

Thus, in Benserade's play, only Iante has access to the truth of Iphis's gender, and the dissonance between the surface presentation and the underlying body leaves her 'dans l'incertitude' ('in uncertainty'), appropriately so, as this truth is about to shift. Iante would be content with this marriage to another girl, if natural law allowed it. After Iphis's transformation, she and the other characters in Benserade's play do not seek to know what the body itself says about Iphis's gender; this question is subordinated to the social demands of the situation, the need for a marriage and future heirs. In fact, Iante does not seem thrilled about the change and invokes instead her duty ('Je dois participer à ton contentement', 125). Although those around Iphis doubt, they are willing to accept his word – and yet the proof he claims will appear after nine months also hangs like a threat over his head (what if the proof is not forthcoming?). The obsession with wealth and patrilineal succession in the play (similar to most comic plays of the classical era in this regard) guarantees that this proof will be absolutely necessary to Iphis's retention of his social status and perhaps his life, as the sensational case of Marin le Marcis, whose life depended on proving that he was male, suggests.

Embodied Knowledge: The Sceptical Critique of Knowledge in the Sixteenth Century

Benserade's version of the tale of Iphis might be better understood in the broader context of philosophical debates concerning knowledge that had been taking place for at least seventy-five years prior to the publication of his play. Questions concerning the possibility of understanding gender were being raised in France at a time that saw the revival of an alternative to Aristotelian and Platonic philosophies that had dominated medieval and early modern thought. From the publication of Henri Estienne's Latin translation of Sextus Empiricus's *Hypotyposes* (or *Outlines of Pyrrhonism*) in 1562, through the debates between René Descartes and Pierre Gassendi in the 1640s, Pyrrhonian scepticism is present throughout French culture, in philosophical debates, medical works and a range of literary genres including poetry and novels. Scepticism became a predominant philosophical mode in late sixteenth- and early seventeenth-century France, with Pierre Charron (1541–1603), Jean-Pierre Camus (1584–1654), and Pierre Gassendi (1592–1655), among others, continuing Michel de Montaigne's legacy of Pyrrhonian thought. Of course, figures like Marin Mersenne (1588–1648) mounted a counterattack on Pyrrhonism, and such resistance helped to shape Descartes' own use of scepticism. These debates kept such modes of thought prominent in the intellectual circles of the day.

Regarding knowledge of the body, Pyrrhonian scepticism suggests that knowledge is in fact embodied, partial and unstable. Such knowledge is processed through the corporeal senses of sight, touch, smell, hearing and taste. Our perception is flawed, as it is dependent on a variable body that changes over time and space, and is affected by the physical environment and location relative to the thing being perceived. As a result, humans can assent or react to immediate impressions (if our house is burning, we can take actions to avoid the fire), but we cannot conclude any larger truths from these impressions.

One of the fundamental strategies of Pyrrhonian sceptical philosophy is the suspension of judgment:

> Skepticism is an ability, or mental attitude, which opposes appearances to judgments in any way whatsoever, with the result that, owing to the

equipollence of the objects and reasons thus opposed, we are brought firstly to a state of mental suspense and next to a state of 'unperturbedness' or quietude.[10]

This quietude is achieved in a non-dogmatic manner; the sceptical philosopher speaks only of what is perceived, 'without making any positive assertion regarding the external realities'.[11] The sceptics offer a range of expressions as tactics for avoiding dogmatism, using such phrases as 'I suspend judgment'[12] and 'To every argument an equal argument is opposed'.[13] Significant for a philosophical understanding of the concept of intersex is the ability to hold two opposing thoughts in one's mind at the same time. This suspension of judgment becomes a model for religious toleration, and it is thus not surprising that the moderates arguing in favour of religious toleration, the *politiques*, were often represented in satirical pamphlets as hermaphrodites.[14]

The Ten Modes or arguments of Pyrrhonian scepticism present an understanding of knowledge that is both contextual and embodied. Differences in animals create different sense-impressions of the world.[15] Sextus suggests that physiological differences might lead to different sense-impressions; for example, the difference in the configuration of the eye in various animals would suggest differences in vision. Even physiological differences within a given animal can alter sense-perceptions; jaundice can change the perception of colour, illness like a cold can affect the sense of smell, differences in tongues can lead to differences in the capacity to taste.[16]

The second of the ten arguments is that differences among humans cause different sense impressions; for example, food that may be agreeable to people of one nationality may be disagreeable to those of another. Even between humans in the same culture, one person may feel cold in an environment where another does not.[17] The third argument suggests that differences in the senses create contradictory sense-impressions: 'Honey, too, seems to some pleasant to the tongue but unpleasant to the eyes.'[18] The circumstances of an impression can change the nature of that impression: thus states of 'waking or sleeping, with conditions due to age, motion or rest, hatred or love, emptiness or fullness, drunkenness or soberness, predispositions, confidence or fear, grief or joy' can change how we perceive objects.[19] The first four modes all propose that the condition or situation of the perceiving subject alters that which is perceived.

The fifth argument suggests that the relationship (spatial or otherwise) between the subject of perception and the perceived object can affect the sense impression, stating that 'positions, distances, and locations' can affect our perception of objects. For example, 'the same tower from a distance appears round but from a near point quadrangular'.[20] The particular state of the object itself can affect how we perceive it. According to the sixth mode, admixtures can change our perception of things; for example, odours are stronger in a hot or humid environment. The seventh mode is based on the idea that the 'quantity or constitution' of an object can change our perception of it; so, some drugs are helpful in certain quantities, but too much of those drugs can harm the patient. Silver filings look black, but when melted together look white.[21] The eighth mode presents the theory that all things can only be perceived in relation to other things; this mode seems to pull all of the previous modes together, and suggests that no object can be perceived simply in itself, but is always seen (or tasted or felt or heard) in a context and in relation to other objects and to the subject.[22] The ninth mode considers the rarity or constancy of an event; the sun is not deemed more miraculous than a comet, even though it is just as impressive, because we see it every day.[23] Thus, just as variations in the perceiving subject can affect what is perceived, so different states of the object and different environments can alter perception of that object.

Social customs and laws also affect human understanding of the world. The tenth mode takes into account ethical questions, such as 'rules of conduct, habits, laws, legendary beliefs, and dogmatic conceptions'. Some examples given here are the acceptance of homosexuality in Persian culture, while it is forbidden in Rome, or the acceptance by men in Persia of what might be deemed feminine attire. This latter example suggests that signs of gender depend upon the social context in which they are deployed and interpreted, and therefore are not constant or reliable means for determining gender.[24] The conclusions that can be drawn from these modes is that knowledge is both embodied, that is to say, processed by means of the body, and that it is a result of a process, not a fixed or immutable thing. These conclusions have significant impact on representations of gender in a range of medical, philosophical and literary texts.

Another question that sceptical philosophy raises is whether the body itself can be known. In the second book of his *Outlines of Pyrrhonism*, Sextus discusses the types of signs by which we apprehend objects:

> Now the pre-evident objects . . . do not require a sign, for they are apprehended of themselves. And neither do the altogether nonevident, since of course they are not even apprehended at all. But such objects as are occasionally or naturally nonevident are apprehended by means of signs – not of course by the same signs, but by 'suggestive' signs in the case of the occasionally nonevident and by 'indicative' signs in the case of the naturally nonevident.[25]

A 'suggestive' sign is associated with the thing signified, as smoke suggests the presence of fire. 'An "indicative" sign, they say, is that which is not clearly associated with the thing signified, but signifies that whereof it is a sign by its own particular nature and constitution, just as, for instance, the bodily motions are signs of the soul.'[26] Sextus then questions the existence of the indicative sign; a sign cannot stand in for something that is not itself immediately apparent.

This last example, concerning the proof of the existence of the soul, an invisible thing, by means of the visible bodily motions, has enormous implications for the religious controversies of the day. But these questions concerning the variations of perceptions in different contexts and the variability of the body as a perceiving subject, along with the question of whether visible signs can tell us about invisible things, also have implications for gender. Masculinity and femininity are understood or read through a set of signs on or in the body. In this period, before clinical examination was a common aspect of studies of physiology, the 'proof' of gender was generally thought to be revealed on the surface of the body. This process assumes that which is evident is a sign of that which is non-evident. Because sceptics assent to that which is apparent to them but refuse to make judgments based on these appearances, a good sceptic would not assign gender based on external corporeal signs. Their solution to the problem of gender would be to suspend judgment, either keeping both genders in play or choosing neither (which amounts to two sides of the same coin). This suspension of judgment concerning gender creates the space for the existence of a third gender, or even a range of non-binary possibilities, as was occasionally recognised by some early modern philosophers, medical practitioners and literary authors.

Montaigne's Refusal: The Philosophy of Gender Ambiguity

Michel de Montaigne, seen as the transmitter of Pyrrhonian ssepticism to French philosophy and culture,[27] unites sceptical philosophy and questions of gender throughout his *Essays*.[28] At the end of his essay, 'On some Verses of Virgil', he states: 'I say that males and females are cast in the same mold; except for education and custom, the difference is not great' ('je dis que les masles et femelles sont jettez en mesme moule: sauf l'institution et l'usage, la différence n'y est pas grand').[29] Montaigne is writing in the context of the revival of Pyrrhonian scepticism, and repeats many of the examples and discussion of Sextus Empiricus's *Outlines of Pyrrhonism* in his 'Apology for Raymond Sebond'.[30] The intersection between gender and scepticism in his thought is made manifest in a striking example he gives of feminine self-supplementation in the effort to seem even more feminine:

> Just as women wear ivory teeth where their natural ones are lacking, and in place of their real complexion fabricate one of some foreign matter; as they make themselves hips of cloth and felt, and flesh of cotton, and in the sight and knowledge of everyone, embellish themselves with a false and borrowed beauty; so does science ... She gives us in payment and as presuppositions the things that she herself teaches us are invented ... As

also, for that matter, philosophy offers us not what is, or what it believes, but the most plausible and pleasant thing it forges.

> Tout ainsi que les femmes employent des dents d'yvoire où les leurs naturelles leur manquent, et, au lieu de leur vray teint en forgent un de quelque matiere estrangere; comme elles font des cuisses de drap et de feutre, et de l'embonpoinct de coton, et, au veu et sçeu d'un chacun, s'embellissent d'une beauté fauce et empruntée: ainsi faict la science . . . elle nous donne en payement et en presupposition les choses qu'elles mesmes nous aprend estre inventées . . . comme aussi au reste la philosophie nous presente, non pas ce qui est, ou ce qu'elle croit, mais ce qu'elle forge ayant plus d'apparence et de gentillesse.[31]

The feminine personifications of Science and Philosophy underscore the slippery ground upon which knowledge of gendered bodies, as an example of all knowledge, is built; they emphasise the constructed nature of these forms of knowledge, even as they present them, eliciting our sceptical response to these forms. For Montaigne, women can enhance the surface of their bodies to better perform femininity, just as our knowledge systems, devised to understand the natural world (or that of human law), embellish or reorganise any underlying reality, making it even less accessible to us. But, in Pyrrhonian scepticism, external signs are separated from any non-visible existence. Thus, when Sextus Empiricus offers his list of ten modes of scepticism, with the last mode focusing on how different cultures accept different practices, he points out that 'Aristippus considers the wearing of feminine attire a matter of indifference, though we consider it a disgraceful thing'.[32] Montaigne modifies this example in his summary of the ten modes:

> Dionysius the tyrant offered Plato a robe in the Persian style, long, damascened, and perfumed. Plato refused it, saying that having been born a man, he would not willingly wear a woman's robe; but Aristippus accepted it with this reply, that no accouterment could corrupt a chaste heart.

> Dionysius le tyran offrit à Platon une robe à la mode de Perse, longue, damasquinée et parfumée; Platon la refusa, disant qu'estant nay homme, il ne se vestiroit pas volontiers de robe de femme; mais Aristippus l'accepta, avec cette responce que nul accoutrement ne pouvoit corrompre un chaste courage.[33]

For Aristippus, clothing, as an external sign, does not affect the character of a person, which is something internal to that individual. These two versions of the tale indicate an indifference to specific cultural understandings of the relationship between clothing and gender, which is related to the Pyrrhonian rejection of indicative, visible, signs, that are interpreted as proof of the existence and nature of things that cannot be seen. So, appearances are ambiguous, appearances are indecipherable, appearances deceive and they can be manipulated to many ends. In short, they cannot communicate any universal 'truth' about gender.

But this scepticism exists in tension with institutionalised notions of gender difference promoted by both Church and State. The ascendance of the gender binary in the political sphere is made evident by discussions of the Salic law, which prevented women from exercising royal power in their own right.[34] With this exclusion of women from the public sphere and from inheriting property, particularly among the nobility, certainty of gender status becomes a crucial aspect of public identity. This is especially obvious in the violent reactions to the perceived effeminacy of Henri de Valois and his *mignons*.[35] In this context, individuals who do not fit neatly into this binary must navigate their social roles cautiously and deliberately; the stakes, it seems, are high, as the execution of 'Mary' (like Marie-Germain, an inhabitant of Vitry), for his refusal to accept the gender assigned at birth as well as for his use of devices to supplement his masculinity, makes clear: 'And she was hanged for illicit inventions to supplement the lack particular to her sex' ('Et fut pendue pour des inventions illicites à supplir au défaut de son sexe').[36] The Wars of Religion, which raged from 1559 until 1629 and which decimated the French population,[37] also raised the stakes on gender distinction, as the absence of a royal male heir fuelled conflict for many years.[38] In these circumstances, the importance of a certain clarity regarding masculinity in particular was heightened, with the possibility of generating children serving as the only certain sign of an adult male's status.[39] Thus the scepticism concerning both binary gender and the performance of gender roles opens the way for variation and 'play', but the range of this play is limited by laws concerning gender – laws enforced with a great deal of invasive scrutiny and state-sponsored violence.[40] The result is that performances of gender that do not convincingly present a male or female identity are considered subversive and even dangerous.[41]

Montaigne demonstrates his scepticism towards various aspects of gender when he presents figures like Marie-Germain in his essay, 'Of the Force of the Imagination' (discussed below) and the shepherd from Médoc, in 'Of a Monstrous Child'. Marie-Germain transforms from female to male, but the essayist seems to express some doubt about this transformation. The shepherd remains almost completely lacking any definitive signs of gender:

> I have just seen a shepherd in Médoc, thirty years old or thereabouts, who has no sign of genital parts. He has three holes by which he continually makes water. He is bearded, has desire, and likes to touch women.
>
> Je viens de voir un pastre en Medoc, de trente ans ou environ, qui n'a aucune montre des parties genitales: il a trois trous par où il rend son

eau incessamment; il est barbu, a desir, et recherche l'attouchement des femmes.[42]

The phrase 'attouchement des femmes' is much more ambiguous than the translation indicates. In a society where the sexual role dictated for men was active, for women passive, the transformation of the verb into a noun leaves an intriguing ambiguity: does the shepherd seek to touch women or to be touched by them? This ambiguity is telling, given that all of the other details, except for perhaps the beard, tell us nothing about gender: the shepherd has no genitals, only three holes through which he constantly passes water, as if his body simply leaks; he desires, but the exact nature of that desire is not clear, suspended between active and passive modes. This ambiguity mimics the suspension of judgment that sceptics upheld as the ideal philosophical practice. Similarly, the absence of the physiological signs that are most frequently used to determine gender leaves the reader without any clear evidence. Furthermore, although the beard was often read as a definitive marker of masculine gender, the well-known existence of bearded women, feminine in all other aspects, casts doubt on the universal nature of this sign.[43] The body of the shepherd remains outside of the possibility of definitive interpretation, as does that of the 'monstrous' child described in the essay; they are both merely signs of the limitations of man's knowledge and understanding of the world around him.[44]

Conferring Gender Identity: Scepticism in Medical Discourse

Ovid places gender transformation in the context of gender ambiguity, and this association resonates in the work of one medical authority, Ambroise Paré, author of numerous treatises on surgery, and of the collection conjoined to one of those treatises, *On Monsters and Marvels*, first published in 1573. Paré writes a chapter on 'Memorable Stories about Women who have Degenerated into Men', in which he tells of the transformations of Maria Pacheca into Emanuel, a young woman named Jeanne in the city of Rheims who becomes Jean, and Marie-Germain, from Vitry-le-François. He asserts that the reverse transformation cannot occur, citing the Aristotelian humoral explanation of female inferiority (they are cold and wet, whereas males are hot and dry) to support the assertion that 'we therefore never find in any true story that any man ever became a woman, because Nature tends always towards what is most perfect and not, on the contrary, to perform in such a way that what is perfect should become imperfect' ('nous ne trouvons jamais en histoire veritable que d'homme aucun soit devenu femme, pour-ce que Nature tend tousjours à ce qui est le plus parfaict, et non au contraire faire que ce qui est parfaict devienne imparfaict').[45] While this analysis of gender transformation suggests a malleable body, there are limits to this malleability: the body cannot change in such a way as to diminish the social standing of the individual concerned. Thus social demands shape the interpretation of gender and of gender transformation.

Furthermore, Emanuel, Jean and Germain do not take on their masculine identities until those identities are socially sanctioned. In the case of Paré's examples, each is rebaptised with a male name and given men's clothing. These signs are a crucial part of the construction of male identity.[46] For Iphis in Benserade's play, the ambiguous name and male clothing allow her to pass as male when she is still a woman, but create some confusion when she becomes a man. The double-gendered name does not clearly indicate gender, and the other characters realise that Iphis's appearance has been misleading all along, sending them into a tailspin of doubt.

The bodily marks of gender are presented in Paré's discussion of intersex individuals (whom he calls hermaphrodites), which precedes the chapter on gender transformations. But the corporeal clues, themselves not always clear, cannot be read in isolation from what we now would consider to be more culturally driven aspects of identity. In this way, Paré's list echoes Ovid's narration of Iphis's transformation:

> The most expert and well-informed physicians and surgeons can recognize whether hermaphrodites are more apt at performing with and using one set of organs than another, or both, or none at all. And such a thing will be recognized by the genitalia, to wit, whether the female sex organ is of proper dimensions to receive the male rod [penis] and whether the menstrues [menses] flow through it; similarly by the face and the hair, whether it is fine or coarse; whether the speech is virile or shrill; whether the teats are like those of men or of women; similarly, whether the whole disposition of the body is robust or effeminate; whether they are bold or fearful, and other actions like those of males or of females.
>
> Et telle chose se cognoistra aux parties genitales, à sçavoir si le sexe feminine est propre en ses dimensions pour recevoir la verge virile et si par iceluy fluent les menstrues; pareillement par le visage, et si les cheveux sont deliez ou gros; si la parole est virile ou gresle; si les tetins sont semblables à ceux des hommes ou des femmes; semblablement si toute l'habitude du corps est robuste ou effeminee, s'ils sont hardis ou craintifs, et autres actions semblables aux males ou aux femelles.[47]

The guidelines offered by Paré for reading the signs of gender leave room for interpretation. The size of genitalia, particularly the penis, is important, but what that size should be is not clear.[48] Similarly, the 'female sex organ' must be 'of proper dimensions', but we are not told what those dimensions should be. The 'teats' should be like those of a man or a woman, the body robust or effeminate, the speech virile (masculine) or shrill. These definitions operate in a circular manner, using terms that signal masculine or feminine qualities without clarifying what constitutes those qualities. Again, surface appearances in the form of fine or coarse hair, bold or fearful behaviour, are to be read as signalling one or the other gender.

When Paré addresses the question of whether an individual functions as male or female, he leaves this determination largely to the individual in question:

> Similarly, one must examine carefully to see whether the male rod is well-proportioned in thickness and length, and whether it can [become] erect, and whether seed issues from it, [all of] which will be done through the confession of the hermaphrodite.
>
> Semblablement faut bien examiner si la verge virile est bien proportionnee en grosseur et longueur et si elle se dresse et d'icelle sort semence, qui se fera par la confession de l'hermafrodite.[49]

This advice to leave the determination of how the penis functions to the individual in question is not a universal attitude among authors of medical treatises, but Paré's work was influential and imitated by Montaigne and other authors. In this way, there is a space created for the possibility of determining one's own gender and representing it discursively so as to establish it publicly. Benserade takes this possibility and expands upon it in *Iphis et Iante* in such a way as to suggest the power of discourse to shape gender in the context of contradictory signs.

It is instructive that this list of gender characteristics appears in the chapter on individuals of ambiguous gender, as if to indicate that the binary distinction is already problematic. Paré designates six different genders: male, female, male hermaphrodite, female hermaphrodite, male and female hermaphrodite and neuter hermaphrodite.[50] In other words, the distinction between male and female is not clear, and this lack of distinction cannot simply be reduced to a one-sex theory of gender.[51] Rather, the potential for a spectrum of gender presentations is already present in a diverse range of bodies, further complicated by surface transformations of those bodies.

In 'Memorable Stories about Women who have Degenerated into Men', Paré suggests the masculinity of Marie-turned-Germain by means of his description of the 'young man of average size, stocky, and very well put together, wearing a red, rather thick beard' ('jeune homme de taille moyenne, trappe et bien amassé, portant barbe rousse assez espesse').[52] Montaigne, in the version of the tale he offers in his essay 'Of the Force of the Imagination', is more guarded: 'He was now heavily bearded, and old, and not married' ('Il estoit à cett'heure-là fort barbu, et vieil, et point marié').[53] The essayist places this tale in the middle of his discussion of whether the imagination can truly affect bodies, or whether it merely affects our perception of them. He points out that it is no surprise that such gender transformations seem to occur fairly frequently; after all, humans are so obsessed with sexuality that it is no wonder that we imagine such events:

> It is not such a wonder, that this sort of accident is frequently encountered; because, if the imagination can do anything in these cases, it is so continually and vigorously attached to this subject that, in order not to fall back into the same thought and ardent desire, it would do better to incorporate, once and for all, this virile part in girls.
>
> Ce n'est pas tant de merveille, que cette sorte d'accident se rencontre frequent: car si l'imagination peut en telles choses, elle est si continuellement et si vigoureusement attachée à ce subject, que, pour n'avoir si souvent à rechoir en mesme pensée et aspreté de desir, elle a meilleur compte d'incorporer, une fois pour toutes, cette virile partie aux filles.[54]

In the guise of a vulgar joke about the penis, Montaigne implies that gender itself is an effect of the imagination.

Signs of Gender in Popular Culture

This play between the surface appearance and underlying gender differences is also present in a story from Claude de Tesserant's continuation of Pierre Boaistuau's *Histoires prodigieuses* (*Marvelous Tales*),[55] published in 1567 and one of the sources for Paré's treatise on monsters. In his 'Story of a Man with Woman's Hair' ('Histoire d'un homme avec des cheveux de femme'), Tesserant begins the tale with two choices of monsters: those that are born as the result of natural accidents and those that are artificially created. Among these stories, he finds those of women who suddenly become men (apparently the 'natural' transformation) and those of men who, 'to satisfy their abominable debaucheries' ('pour satisfaire à leurs abominable paillardises'),[56] transform themselves into women (the artificial creation). The obsession with beards and hair length as signs of gender in these stories reflects the prevalence of this connection in a broad range of cultural discourses, from medicine and hygiene to the theatre.[57] The beard and marriage to a woman become outward signs that the women have become men: 'Licinius Mutianus assures us that he has seen in Argos a woman named Arescusa ... become a man, wear a beard, and marry a woman, and he was called Arescon' ('Licinius Mutianus asseure avoir veu en Argos une femme nommée Arescusa ... devint homme, porta barbe, & espousa une femme, & fut appellé Arescon').[58] Tesserant also cites the case of Lucius Cossitius from Pliny's *Natural History*. He asserts that becoming a man is honourable, whereas becoming a woman is an act against nature, citing Nero and Heliogabalus, among other examples, of the monstrosity of this desire. Tesserant claims that both emperors wore wigs to disguise themselves as women, while they shaved off all of their facial and body hair.[59] In the case of Heliogabalus, the barbers removed not only these signs of gender, but, according to our author, 'everything male about him' ('tout ce qu'il avoit d'homme').[60]

As in the stories of Marie-Germain and Iphis, hair becomes a marker of gender, eliding the more troublesome (and invasive) question of genitals that might not entirely conform to the public persona. A beard marks the man; long hair marks the woman. So much so, that in an illustration of conjoined hermaphroditic twins in Paré's work,[61] also depicted in the second tale of the Tesserant version of the *Histoires prodigieuses*,[62] the male hermaphrodite has short hair, the female long, and that is the only clear distinction between the two of them. Tesserant, like Paré after him, insists that women can naturally transform into men, but men can only become women by unnatural means. Nonetheless, the emphasis on surface signs of gender calls that binary distinction into question.

Hair and beards became significant, but problematic, markers of virility and femininity in the Valois court. The *mignons*, Henri de Valois's followers, grew their hair long and curled it, much as does the man with woman's hair in the illustration to Tesserant's story. As Gary Ferguson points out, 'the hair of the *mignons*, carefully styled and curled, becomes a veritable leitmotif of the satiric literature about them'.[63] They are also depicted in the satirical novel about the Valois court, *The Island of Hermaphrodites*, as curling their hair and perfuming their beards, thus creating an appearance that plays up gender ambiguity. Women, in turn, stuffed their long hair into masculine hats, as many portraits and poems indicate.[64] In short, gender appearance was routinely manipulated in late sixteenth-century France, thus rendering many of the signs of gender listed by Ovid and Paré problematic.

Reading Ambiguously: Marin le Marcis

In Paré's accounts of gender transformation, the newly-born men are given clothing that establishes their new-found gender, along with a new name, both apparently granted by religious authorities. The situation is quite different for Marin le Marcis, the young man who was born and baptised a female, who wore men's clothing, who married a widow in adulthood, and who was then accused of violating gender norms and sentenced to death in Rouen.[65] It is clear in the surgeon Jacques Duval's account of this case, published in 1612, that the law did not permit individuals free choice to determine their gender identity, even if they tried to do so by means of clothing.

The rhetoric of Duval's account nonetheless expresses gender ambiguity in the context of a culture dependent on the strict gendering of everything into masculine and feminine. The opening lines of this account, in chapter sixty-two of his treatise, *Des Hermaphrodits*, evokes the complexity of Marin's gender:

> In this category we will also place Marin le Marcis, who having been baptized, named, dressed, raised & educated as a girl, up until the age of twenty years, after which he felt the signs of his virility, changed his clothing, and had himself called Marin instead of Marie.
>
> Sous ceste espece nous mettrons aussi Marin le Marcis, qui ayant esté baptisé, nommé, vestu, nourri & entretenu pour fille, iusques à l'aage de vingt ans: apres qu'il eut senti indices de sa virilité, changea d'habit, & se faisant appeller Marin, au lieu de Marie. [66]

Duval insistently uses the masculine form of the past participle, even as he is describing Marin's childhood as a girl, thus underscoring the dissonance between the official view of his gender and the identity that Marin wants to establish for himself and that Duval seeks to confirm in order to save Marin's life. Duval notes 'the variety that fortune wanted to exercise ... in his body' ('la variété que fortune à voulu pratiquer ...en son corps').[67] In this case, he is suggesting that an individual who has appeared to be transgender is in fact intersex.

Marin, whom Duval calls by his chosen name even in the account of his childhood, works as a chambermaid until he is twenty-one, meets Jeanne le Febvre, and reveals his 'virile member' to her. The couple fall in love, and he takes her home to meet his parents, whose only objection to the proposed marriage is the young widow's poverty and two dependent children. They apply to abjure their Protestant faith and marry within the Catholic Church, openly sharing the story of Marin's newly revealed identity.[68]

When Marin is arrested and examined, the two surgeons involved find no sign of virility in him ('ne trouver en luy aucun signe de verilité'),[69] whereupon another examination is undertaken, with the same results. While his wife says that Marin's physiology is much like that of her dead husband's, all of his former employers state that he only shows signs of being a girl. Marin is told that 'he had offended God and Justice, to have called himself a man, when no one had found any signs of that, but rather all the signs of a girl' ('il avoit offencé Dieu & la justice, de s'estre dit homme, veu qu'on n'en avoit trouvé aucuns indices, mais au contraire tous signes de fille'). Marin is convicted of taking the clothing of a man, usurping a man's name and thus violating the male sex. He is also convicted of sodomy, but as Duval's marginal note points out, this crime would require having a penis, a fact which would invalidate the conviction. According to the court documents, 'Marie' le Marcis is condemned to be burned alive; Jeanne, to be publicly beaten.[70]

Upon their appeal of this sentence, Marin is examined once more. The signs that his body presents are confusing. He is solidly built ('Il avoit le corps trappe, fourni, bien ramassé'; 'his body was solid, well-built, and compact'), with short hair, but this hair is neither wiry nor soft ('la chevelure courte, de qualité entre dure et molle'). He has a moustache ('la levre superieure noircissante, par le poil copieux & noir'), but his voice is high and feminine ('la voix claire & fort semblable à la feminine') and he has a large chest with breasts ('poitrine large, ornee de tetins gros & glanduleux en forme de mamelles'). He has a large stomach, large buttocks and thighs, and is very hairy all over, much more so than a woman supposedly would be. He has a small clitoris, and where the vulva should be, the examining surgeons find something that resembles a small penis.[71] Marin is the pendant, or conceptual opposite, of Montaigne's shepherd from Médoc: whereas that figure bore almost no signs of gender, Marin has an excess of contradictory signs, and so his body eludes interpretation. The shepherd can be seen as an example of the sceptical expression 'neither this nor that', while Marin represents the suspension of judgment, with evidence of both genders to be found on and in his body. Both bodies are illegible in the context of a culture that can only read bodies as male or female.

Nonetheless, Marin's body must be read as male, or he will die. Like Paré, Duval seeks to establish masculinity by means of the erection of the penis and ejaculation. Paré left it to the hermaphrodite himself to determine whether these elements pertained; Duval performs a horrifyingly invasive penetration of Marin's body to find the proof, even though the other surgeons and doctors present refuse to touch the body. This examination saves Marin from execution, and Duval insists that he performed it for this reason, but it proves masculinity paradoxically by treating Marin as a woman, according to the sexual dictates of the day, even while speaking and writing about him as a man.[72]

Duval criticises his colleagues for reading only the external signs and not considering what nature had hidden: 'I began to blame to myself the negligence of those, who wanted to judge by inspection of the exterieur, that which nature had kept and hidden in a more secret room' ('Je commençay blasmer à part moy la negligence de ceux, qui vouloient par l'inspection de l'exterieur, juger et decider de ce que nature avoit retenu, & reconcé en un plus secret cabinet').[73] The external signs are no longer reliable as markers of gender; for Duval, sight does not indicate an underlying truth. In this, he is the heir of the sceptical Montaigne. He goes a step further, however, in suggesting that touch or feeling is a better indicator of gender than visual cues; the body cannot be read, but felt, both by him and by Jeanne, who testifies to her experience of Marin's masculinity. In the end, however, the contradictory signs on and in Marin's body cause Duval to call him a 'gunanthrope' or womanly man.[74]

Pertinent to Benserade's representation of Iphis's transformation is Duval's insistence that the signs of gender vary according to the situation of the person being observed. As a 'gunanthrope' with both masculine and feminine characteristics, Marin can become more feminine or masculine depending on his context. When he slept in a comfortable bed, ate well, had plenty of exercise and fresh air, adequate sleep and frequent sex with his wife, he looked and acted more like a man. In prison, sleeping on a straw mat, eating bread and water, engaging in little activity, getting no fresh air, no sunshine, little sleep and no sex, he takes on the appearance of a woman. The fear engendered by the criminal trial, the constant surveillance of an unpleasant prison guard and the lack of freedom all contribute to his feminisation by changing his dominant humours from sanguine to phlegmatic or melancholic. Since he is forced to wear women's clothing throughout the trial and even afterwards for a number of years, his appearance is further feminised. Duval makes it clear that all of these external influences have feminised Marin's body.[75] By the end of his account of this trial, Duval has described an intersex individual whose body changes in response to different contexts and elicits opposing interpretations, bringing the tales of intersex and transgender individuals together in one person.

The sentence of the court mirrors this complexity, as Marin is required to live as a woman until he is twenty-five years old, without sexual contact with other people of any gender. Ten years later, Duval describes him as bearded and living as a man, in 'an even better manly state' ('meilleure habitude virile'), working as a man's tailor. He 'undertakes, performs and completes all duties pertaining to a man, he has a beard on his chin, and that which is necessary to content a woman, and to beget children by her' ('entreprend, faict, execute tous exercices à homme appartenans, porte barbe au menton, & à dequoy contenter une femme, pour engendrer en elle').[76] Duval lists some of the usual signs of masculinity, in order to affirm Marin's chosen gender. But throughout his detailed account, Duval conveys both the complexity and mobility of gender, suggesting that one's reading of this case is driven by the context in which it is found.

Iphis et Iante

The case of Marin le Marcis was decided by the Court in 1601; Jacques Duval published his account in 1612, as well as a response to Jean Riolan's dismissal of his assertion that Marin was intersex in 1614.[11] More even than Paré's work, this heated medical and legal debate transmitted sceptical ideas concerning gender to a larger public sphere. Duval's treatise also underscores the intersections between transgender and intersex identities, the signs that are used to designate individuals with these identities as male or female, and the inconstant and indecipherable nature of those signs. Given the importance of the surface characteristics of gender in all of the works analysed here, as well as their elusive nature, gender is not a stable referent in early modern France. Yet, given the centrality of cross-sex marriage and patrilineal succession to the stability of early modern French society, gender is a crucial, if inadequate, sign of the capacity to reproduce and therefore to govern and to guarantee continued governance of the realm.

Benserade's *Iphis et Iante* presents this tension by means of a perspective that cuts anamorphically (in the sense that it forces us to consider other perspectives) across what Ligde, Iphis's father, presents as a conventionally gendered marriage that will connect his family with a wealthier and more powerful one. Ligde's speech at the beginning of the play repeatedly emphasises the wealth of Iphis's potential father-in-law; the word 'bien' ('property') is invoked repeatedly as the main pretext for the marriage, and Ligde says crassly: 'Il est en bonne odeur, il a du revenu' ('He is in good repute, he has an income'). Iante and the children she will bear are presented as the conveyors of the wealth to be exchanged between men: 'Pourvu que la richesse accompagne une fille, / On la croit belle, honnête, et de bonne famille' ('Provided that wealth accompanies a girl, / She is believed to be beautiful, honorable, and from a good family').[78] For Ligde, this marriage is about his status and security as well as that of his family. But this security depends upon Iphis being male. And the crudeness of Ligde's rhetoric underscores the crassness of what is in essence a monetary exchange.

This tension between the need for gender certainty in the face of family demands and the possibility of fluid or uncertain gender remains unresolved, even at the end of the play, after the wedding night and the sexual consummation of the marriage, as Iphis promises future proof of his new gender identity in the form of children. His response to his parents' doubt promises the ultimate proof of masculinity, his ability to beget children and, given the need to provide the proof, suggests that his masculinity is still in question. Thus, at the end of the play, the family members are left confused as to Iphis's gender.

But this confusion itself creates the space for Iphis's re-invention of himself. Montaigne and Duval argue for an acceptance of gender ambiguity and variety. Their arguments are based for the most part on the diversity of bodies, which do not all present as clearly male or female. They thus address the limits of human knowledge and understanding. Benserade takes their arguments one step further in suggesting the very personal, individual and fugitive nature of gender, which can transform itself to suit the situation one is in or the person one is with. What Benserade seems to be proposing in Iphis's crucial self-description as a male is that, in this context of ambiguous and even unstable gender, gender is subjective, arising from the individual's sense of self. Furthermore, this sense of self can be performed differently for different audiences. This subjectivity is also underscored by Iphis's emphasis on feelings as a component of gender identity; he abandons thoughts of love (Venus) in favour of more warlike views (Mars). Gender is as much a feeling as it is a corporeal state in this play.

In this emphasis on the subjective nature of gender, *Iphis et Iante* seems to echo Ambroise Paré's injunction in his discussion of 'hermaphrodites' that the individual should determine whether he or she functions as a male or female.

I would argue that Benserade takes this idea even further, in allowing Iphis to create his identity discursively, redescribing himself and providing a reading that genders himself masculine for the benefit of his parents. He seems to have appropriated the literary and medical discourses of gender to this end. The unstable and illegible signs of gender that these discourses present create the possibility of self-reinvention and re-creation, a possibility that Iphis embraces. But will he recreate himself once more for Iante, who, given the choice, might have preferred the female Iphis?

NOTES

1. Recent research suggests a link between grammatical gender languages ('characterized by their nouns, which are always assigned a feminine or masculine [or sometimes neuter] gender') and higher levels of gender stereotyping in the cultures that use those languages; see Prewitt-Freilino et al., 'The Gendering of Language', p. 269.
2. In his keyword essay for the *Transgender Studies Quarterly*, 'Intersex', p. 111, Morland presents the complexities and contradictions of the term and its usage:

    Intersex was coined in 1915 by the zoologist Richard Goldschmidt to describe moths with atypical sex characteristics (Stern 1997: 156). The definition was soon extended to encompass several types of human 'hermaphroditism', but the latter word remained in circulation as a medical diagnosis throughout the twentieth century. Intersex is often popularly conflated with ambiguous genitalia – external sexual anatomy that cannot be easily described as entirely female or male, such as a larger-than-typical clitoris. However, for clinicians, an intersex diagnosis can refer also to attributes that are not apparent on the body's surface, including XXY sex chromosomes or indifference to the hormones that produce effects connotative of masculinity. What such intersex diagnoses have in common is the medicalization of a failure to classify the body as one of two sexes. That such a failure would be problematic is not obvious, nor is its medicalization; nonetheless, medical treatment of intersex is standard practice in the West.
    [. . .]
    The older protocols fostered a tenacious belief among many doctors and parents that genital surgery is a kind of preemptive psychological treatment, on the grounds that an individual's sense of gender will follow from the experience of having a dichotomously sexed anatomy. Several assumptions were implicit in this belief – that having an unambiguous and univalent gender is desirable; that it is better not to reflect consciously on the formation of one's gender; and, in turn, that early medical treatment can promote healthy gender development by averting conscious reflection on the formation of one's gender and its relationship (if any) to one's sexual anatomy.

3. See Daston and Park, 'Wonder Among the Philosophers' and 'Monstrous Particulars', in *Wonders and the Order of Nature*, pp. 111–72.
4. For this, see Epstein, 'Either/Or – Neither/Both', pp. 99–142.
5. Pyrrhonian scepticism is the belief that the search for knowledge is a continual one, as human perception, upon which our knowledge is based, is affected by a number of factors that render it unstable or uncertain. Even signs, used to designate things not readily apparent, are seen as unreliable for conveying knowledge. This form of scepticism does not deny the possibility of acquiring knowledge, but

merely questions whether one can attain certain knowledge by means of human perception or reason. In this, it opposes dogmatism, which posits the possibility of attaining universal truth. It also opposes Academic scepticism, which asserts that nothing can be known.
6. Benserade, *Iphis et Iante*, p. 124. Translations of passages from this play are my own. For an analysis of this play in the context of later seventeenth-century versions of the tale, see Leibacher-Ouvrard, 'Speculum de l'autre femme', pp. 365–77.
7. *L'Isle des hermaphrodites*, p. 62: 'J'en voyois d'autres qui usoient de certaines eaux dont on les lavoit qui avoient telle puissance qu'elles pouvoient d'un teint fort grossier en fair un delicat' ('I saw others who used certain waters with which they were washed and which had such a property that they could turn a rough complexion into a delicate one').
8. Benserade, *Iphis et Iante*, p. 124.
9. Benserade, *Iphis et Iante*, p. 126.
10. Sextus, *Outlines of Pyrrhonism*, I.4.8, pp. 6–7.
11. Sextus, *Outlines of Pyrrhonism*: 'while the dogmatizer posits the matter of his dogma as substantial truth, the skeptic enunciates his formulae so that they are virtually canceled by themselves, he should not be said to dogmatize in his enunciation of them. And, most important of all, in his enunciation of these formulae he states what appears to himself and announces his own impression in an undogmatic way, without making any positive assertion regarding the external realities', I.7.15, pp. 10–11.
12. Sextus, *Outlines of Pyrrhonism*, I.22.196, pp. 114–15.
13. Sextus, *Outlines of Pyrrhonism*, I.27.202, pp. 118–21.
14. See Kathleen Long, 'The Royal Hermaphrodite: Henri III of France', in *Hermaphrodites*, pp. 189–213.
15. Sextus, *Outlines of Pyrrhonism*, 'The *first* argument (or *trope*), as we said, is that which shows that the same impressions are not produced by the same objects owing to the differences in animals', I.14.40, pp. 26–7.
16. Sextus, *Outlines of Pyrrhonism*, I.14.44–58, pp. 26–35.
17. Sextus, *Outlines of Pyrrhonism*, I.14.80–2, pp. 48–9.
18. Sextus, *Outlines of Pyrrhonism*, I.14.92, pp. 54–5.
19. Sextus, *Outlines of Pyrrhonism*, I.14.100–1, pp. 58–61.
20. Sextus, *Outlines of Pyrrhonism*, I.14.118, pp. 68–71.
21. Sextus, *Outlines of Pyrrhonism*, I.14.125–34, pp. 72–9.
22. Sextus, *Outlines of Pyrrhonism*, I.14.135–40, pp. 78–83.
23. Sextus, *Outlines of Pyrrhonism*, I.14.141–2, pp. 82–5.
24. Sextus, *Outlines of Pyrrhonism*, I.14.145–55, pp. 84–91.
25. Sextus, *Outlines of Pyrrhonism*, II.10.97–9, pp. 212–15.
26. Sextus, *Outlines of Pyrrhonism*, II.10.100–1, pp. 214–15.
27. See Brahami, *Le scepticisme*; Elizabeth Guild, *Unsettling Montaigne*; Hubert Vincent, *Vérité du scepticisme*; Giocanti, *Penser l'irrésolution* – to name just a few.
28. Krier, *Montaigne et le genre instable*.
29. Montaigne, *Essays*, 3.5, p. 685; *Essais*, p. 897.
30. Montaigne, *Essays*, 2.12, pp. 318–457; *Essais*, pp. 436–604.
31. Montaigne, *Essays*, 2.12, p. 401; *Essais*, 2.12, p. 537.
32. Sextus, *Outlines of Pyrrhonism*, I.55, p. 61.
33. Montaigne, *Essays*, 2.12, p. 438; *Essais*, p. 581.
34. See Taylor, 'The Salic Law', pp. 358–77, and Cosandey, 'De lance en quenouille', pp. 799–820.
35. Long, *Hermaphrodites*, ch. 7, 'The Royal Hermaphrodite: Henri III of France', pp. 189–213.

36. Montaigne, *Journal de Voyage*, p. 77.
37. Knecht, *The French Religious Wars*, p. 91: 'The total of deaths during the wars has been roughly estimated at between two and four million.'
38. From 1559 until 1601, there was no legitimate royal heir to the throne of France. François II, Charles IX and Henri III did not have any legitimate children and, as a result, two families of royal blood, the Guise (Catholic) and the Bourbon (of which Louis de Condé and Henri de Navarre were both Protestant) vied for the right of succession to the throne. When Henri III named Henri de Navarre his heir, hostilities intensified. Henri de Navarre converted to Catholicism in 1593, in order to ascend to the throne of France, and eventually pacified the country (for the most part), promulgating the Edict of Nantes, the best-known of the edicts of the Wars of Religion in France, in 1598. The birth in 1601 of the future king, Louis XIII, confirmed Henri IV's place on the throne. For the relationship between the question of succession and the Wars of Religion, see Greengrass, *France in the Age of Henri IV*, 'The French Civil Wars', particularly the section on 'The Disputed Succession', pp. 37–42.
39. See Paré, *On Monsters*, p. 26; *Des monstres*, p. 24.
40. See Warner, *The Ideas of Man and Woman*.
41. See Crawford, *Perilous Performances*.
42. Montaigne, *Essays*, 2.30, p. 539; *Essais*, p. 713.
43. See Fisher, '"His Majesty the Beard"', in *Materializing Gender*, pp. 83–128.
44. See Mathieu-Castellani's analysis in her chapter 'L'essai, corps monstrueux', from *Montaigne. L'écriture de l'essai*, pp. 221–40, and Renner, 'A Monstrous Body of Writing?', pp. 1–20.
45. Paré, *On Monsters*, p. 33; *Des monstres*, p. 30.
46. Paré, *On Monsters*, pp. 31–2; *Des monstres*, pp. 29–30.
47. Paré, *On Monsters*, pp. 27–8; *Des monstres*, pp. 25–6.
48. Paré, *On Monsters*, pp. 28–9; *Des monstres*, p. 26.
49. Paré, *On Monsters*, pp. 28–9; *Des monstres*, p. 26.
50. Benkov has already noted that the juxtaposition of the chapter on hermaphrodites and the one on gender transformations which, in spite of its subject, seems to affirm gender distinction in a vehement way, 'signals the tensions in the late sixteenth- and early seventeenth-century interpretations of the body as filtered through competing discourses', 'Rereading Montaigne's Memorable Stories', p. 204. Regosin has noted 'the chiasmic potential of the man within the woman', in his essay on 'Montaigne's Memorable Stories', pp. 100–14.
51. For an introduction to this theory, see Laqueur, 'New Science, One Flesh', from *Making Sex*, pp. 63–113.
52. Paré, *On Monsters*, pp. 31–2; *Des monstres*, p. 29.
53. Montaigne, *Essays*, 1.21, p. 69; *Essais*, 1.21, p. 99.
54. Montaigne, *Essays*, 1.21, p. 69; *Essais*, 1.21, p. 99.
55. Tesserant, *Autres histoires prodigieuses*.
56. Tesserant, *Autres histoires prodigieuses*, pp. 227–8. All translations of this text are my own.
57. See Fisher, '"His majesty the beard": beards and masculinity' and '"The ornament of their sex:" hair and gender', in *Materializing Gender*, pp. 83–158.
58. Tesserant, *Autres histoires prodigieuses*, p. 228.
59. Tesserant, *Autres histoires prodigieuses*, pp. 231–2.
60. Tesserant, *Autres histoires prodigieuses*, p. 232.
61. Paré, *On Monsters*, p. 27; *Des monstres*, p. 25.
62. Tesserant, *Autres histoires prodigieuses*, p. 223.
63. Ferguson, *Queer (Re)Readings*, p. 95.

64. Ferguson, *Queer (Re)Readings*, pp. 93–9.
65. The best-known assessment of this case is undoubtedly that of Greenblatt, in his chapter, 'Fiction and Friction', in *Shakespearean Negotiations*, pp. 73–86. An interesting, but somewhat inaccurate, account of the case, is presented by Foucault, in his lecture from '22 January 1975', from *The Abnormal*, pp. 68–70 (*Les Anormaux*, pp. 63–5). For a review of the medical context in which the case of Marin le Marcis unfolds, see Donald Beecher, 'Concerning Sex Changes: The Cultural Significance of a Renaissance Medical Polemic'. While Beecher provides a useful overview of the range of medical interpretations of sex change in early modern Europe, both Duval's and Montaigne's nuanced and complex rhetoric defy the clear readings he offers. He admits that 'Montaigne might be joking' in his account of the Marie-Germain case, but asserts that Montaigne is 'misreading' Paré (992), an interpretation that misses the context in which the essayist's version of the case is presented, a sustained ironic critique of popular, scientific and historical beliefs. Similarly, Beecher oversimplifies Duval's account of Marin's case. First, he consistently names him 'Marie', whereas Duval only uses the feminine name to designate Marin during the period of time when he thought he was a woman. Then, he asserts the court 'declared her legal sex as female', whereas the court had condemned Marin to dress as a female and avoid sexual relations with persons of either gender until the age of twenty-five. Thus, Duval finds Marin ten years later living openly as a man, as clearly he had not been declared definitively female, but rather forced to live as one until the age of majority. While Duval's physical description of Marin suggests he is intersex, he nonetheless asserts that Marin is male. Marin's own testimony, cited in detail by Duval, echoes medical accounts of sex change, suggesting his awareness that this was a legitimate way of justifying his chosen gender identity. It is very possible that this is a legal strategy, rather than evidence of strong belief in the anatomical possibility of gender transformation. Most scholarly work on this case ignores the details of Duval's account in favour of the broader context of the history of medicine, but Duval's obsession with precise language, evident throughout his treatise, suggests that a close reading might be useful.
66. Duval, *Des hermaphrodits*, p. 383. All translations of Duval's work are my own.
67. Duval, *Des hermaphrodits*, p. 383. For an excellent study of this work, see Brancher, 'Le "genre" incertain', pp. 307–24.
68. Duval, *Des hermaphrodits*, pp. 386–9.
69. Duval, *Des hermaphrodits*, p. 393.
70. Duval, *Des hermaphrodits*, pp. 393–4.
71. Duval, *Des hermaphrodits*, pp. 400–1.
72. Duval, *Des hermaphrodits*, pp. 402–5.
73. Duval, *Des hermaphrodits*, p. 405.
74. Duval, *Des hermaphrodits*, p. 407.
75. Duval, *Des hermaphrodits*, pp. 416–18. See Long, *Hermaphrodites*, p. 84.
76. Duval, 'Advertissement', *Des hermaphrodits*, A7.
77. Jean Riolan, *Discours sur les hermaphrodits*, and Duval's response, *Responce au discours fait par le Sieur Riolan*. For an excellent analysis of Riolan's treatise, see Leibacher-Ouvrard, 'Imaginaire anatomique', pp. 111–24.
78. Benserade, *Iphis et Iante*, p. 42. Interestingly, the only objection Marin le Marcis's mother has to his choice of spouse is that Jeanne le Febvre is poor: 'sa mere se fust efforcee de le divertir de l'amitié de ladicte Jeanne le Febvre, disant que ce n'estoit son cas, d'autant qu'elle estoit pauvre & n'avoit aucuns moyens' ('his mother tried to distract him from his friendship with the said Jeanne le Febvre, saying that she wasn't his type, all the more so since she was poor and had no means'), Duval, *Des hermaphrodits*, p. 387.

Bibliography

Beecher, Donald, 'Concerning Sex Changes: The Cultural Significance of a Renaissance Medical Polemic', *Sixteenth Century Journal* 36, 2005, pp. 991–1016.

Benkov, Edith, 'Rereading Montaigne's Memorable Stories: Sexuality and Gender in Vitry-le-François', *Montaigne after Theory: Theory after Montaigne*, ed. Zahi Zalloua (Seattle: University of Washington Press, 2009), pp. 202–17.

Benserade, Isaac de, *Iphis et Iante*, ed. Anne Verdier (Vijon: Lampsaque, 2000).

Brahami, Frédéric, *Le scepticisme de Montaigne* (Paris: Presses Universitaires de France, 1997).

Brancher, Dominique, 'Le "genre" incertain: De l'hermaphrodisme littéraire et medical', *L'Hermaphrodite de la Renaissance aux Lumières*, ed. Marianne Closson (Paris: Garnier, 2013), pp. 307–24.

Cosandey, Fanny, 'De lance en quenouille: la place de la reine dans l'État modern (14e–17e siècles)', *Annales, Histoire, Sciences Sociales* 52, 1997, pp. 799–820.

Crawford, Katherine, *Perilous Performances: Gender and Regency in Early Modern France* (Cambridge, MA: Harvard University Press, 2004).

Daston, Lorraine and Park, K., *Wonders and the Order of Nature: 1150–1750* (New York: Zone Books, 1998).

Duval, Jacques, *Des hermaphrodits et accouchemens des femmes: et traitement qui est requis pour les relever en santé* (Rouen: David Geuffroy, 1612).

Duval, Jacques, *Responce au discours fait par le Sieur Riolan Docteur en medecine et professeur de chirurgie & pharmacie à Paris, contre l'histoire de l'Hermaphrodit de Rouen* (Rouen: Julian Courant, 1614).

Epstein, Julia, 'Either/Or – Neither/Both: Sexual Ambiguity and the Ideology of Gender', *Genders* 7, 1990, pp. 99–142.

Ferguson, Gary, *Queer (Re)Readings in the French Renaissance* (Burlington, VT: Ashgate, 2008).

Fisher, Will, *Materializing Gender in Early Modern English Literature and Culture* (Cambridge: Cambridge University Press, 2006).

Foucault, Michel, *Abnormal: Lectures at the Collège de France, 1974–1975*, trans. Graham Burchell (New York: Picador, 2003).

Foucault, Michel, *Les Anormaux: Cours au Collège de France, 1974–1975* (Paris: Gallimard/Seuil, 1999).

Giocanti, Sylvia, *Penser l'irrésolution: Montaigne, Pascal, La Mothe le Vayer: Trois itinéraires sceptiques* (Paris: Champion, 2001).

Greenblatt, Stephen, *Shakespearean Negotiations: The Circulation of Social Energy in Renaissance England* (Berkeley: University of California Press, 1988).

Greengrass, Mark, *France in the Age of Henri IV: The Struggle for Stability* (New York: Routledge, 1995).

Guild, Elizabeth, *Unsettling Montaigne: Poetics, Ethics, and Affect in the* Essais *and other Writings* (Cambridge: D. S. Brewer, 2014).

Knecht, Robert J., *The French Religious Wars: 1562–1598* (Oxford: Osprey Publishing, 2002).

Krier, Isabelle, *Montaigne et le genre instable* (Paris: Classiques Garnier, 2015).

L'Isle des hermaphrodites, ed. Claude-Gilbert Dubois (Geneva: Droz, 1996).

Laqueur, Thomas, *Making Sex: Body and Gender from the Greeks to Freud* (Cambridge, MA: Harvard University Press, 1992).

Leibacher-Ouvrard, Lise, 'Imaginaire anatomique, débordements tribadiques et excisions: Le *Discours sur les hermaphrodits* (1614) de Jean Riolan fils', *L'Hermaphrodite de la Renaissance aux Lumières*, ed. Marianne Closson (Paris: Garnier, 2013), pp. 111–24.

Leibacher-Ouvrard, Lise, 'Speculum de l'autre femme: Les avatars d'*Iphis et Ianthe* (Ovide) au XVIIe siècle', *Papers in French Seventeenth-Century Literature* 30, 2003, pp. 365–77.
Long, Kathleen, 'Hermaphrodites Newly Discovered: The Cultural Monsters of Sixteenth-Century France', in *Monster Theory*, ed. Jeffrey J. Cohen (Minneapolis: University of Minnesota Press, 1996), pp. 183–201.
Long, Kathleen, *Hermaphrodites in Renaissance Europe* (Aldershot: Ashgate, 2006; reprint, New York: Routledge, 2016).
Mathieu-Castellani, Gisèle, *Montaigne. L'écriture de l'essai* (Paris: PUF, 1988).
Montaigne, Michel de, *Essais,* ed. Pierre Villey (Paris: Presses universitaires de France, 1965).
Montaigne, Michel de, *Essays*, trans. Donald Frame (Stanford: Stanford University Press, 1965).
Montaigne, Michel de, *Journal de Voyage*, ed. Fausta Garavini (Paris: Gallimard, 1983).
Morland, Iain, 'Intersex', *Postposttranssexual: Key Concepts for a Twenty-First-Century Transgender Studies, Transgender Studies Quarterly* 1, 2014, pp. 111–15.
Ovid, *Metamorphoses*, trans. Frank Justus Miller (Cambridge, MA: Harvard University Press, Loeb Classical Library, 1984).
Paré, Ambroise, *Des monstres et prodiges*, ed. Jean Céard (Geneva: Droz, 1971).
Paré, Ambroise, *On Monsters and Marvels*, trans. Janis L. Pallister (Chicago: University of Chicago Press, 1982).
Prewitt-Freilino, Jennifer L., Caswell, T. A. and Laakso, E. K., 'The Gendering of Language: A Comparison of Gender Equality in Countries with Gendered, Natural Gender, and Genderless Languages', *Sex Roles* 66, 2012, pp. 268–81.
Regosin, Richard, 'Montaigne's Memorable Stories of Gender and Sexuality', *Montaigne Studies* 6, 1994, pp. 100–14.
Renner, Bernd, 'A Monstrous Body of Writing? Irregularity and the Implicit Unity of Montaigne's "Des Boyteux"', *French Forum* 29, 2004, pp. 1–20.
Riolan, Jean Riolan, *Discours sur les hermaphrodits, où il est démontré contre l'opinion commune, qu'il n'y a point de vrays hermaphrodits* (Paris: Ramier, 1614).
Sextus Empiricus, *Outlines of Pyrrhonism*, trans. R. G. Bury (Cambridge, MA: Harvard University Press, Loeb Classical Library, 1933).
Stern, Curt, *Richard Benedict Goldschmidt, 1878–1958* (Washington, DC: National Academy of Sciences, 1967).
Taylor, Craig, 'The Salic Law and the Valois Succession to the French Crown', *French History* 15, 2001, pp. 358–77.
Tesserant, Claude de, *Autres histoires prodigieuses*, in Pierre Boaistuau, *Quatorze histoires prodigieuses de nouveau adjoustées aux precedentes* (Paris: Chez Jean de Bordeaux, 1567).
Vincent, Hubert, *Vérité du scepticisme chez Montaigne* (Paris: L'Harmattan, 1998).
Warner, Lyndan, *The Ideas of Man and Woman in Renaissance France: Print, Rhetoric, and Law* (Farnham: Ashgate, 2011).

10

LESBIANISM IN BENSERADE'S *IPHIS ET IANTE* (1634): GALLANTRY AND THE MAKING OF HETEROSEXUALITY IN SEVENTEENTH-CENTURY FRANCE

Matthieu Dupas

In 1634, a French theatre company called the *Comédiens du Roy* presented the first performance of *Iphis et Iante*, a comedy by Isaac de Benserade. To anyone familiar with Ovid's *Metamorphoses*, the very title of the play would have announced a risky theme – lesbianism – and Benserade did nothing to domesticate it. Whereas Ovid arranged for Iphis to be safely transformed into a boy before the marriage day, Benserade has the two young girls wed and then face an awkward situation: Iante discovers that she has actually married another female, and Iphis fears her inability to satisfy the young bride. But if the gamble was risky, Benserade won his bet. To be sure, his play has not been celebrated by posterity, and in the history of French literature Benserade is considered only a second-rate writer. But the play was fairly successful at the time of its first performance, according to Paul Tallemant, a contemporary witness.[1]

The relative success of *Iphis et Iante* at its release gives pause for thought. Benserade's comedy is the only play in the repertoire of seventeenth-century French drama that addresses so straightforwardly the subject of female homo-eroticism, and it is precisely for this reason that it has been published in a modern edition[2] and has come under scrutiny in recent scholarship.[3] But how could a play that narrates a story about love between two young girls attract a large audience without creating any concern whatsoever about the topic of female homoeroticism? Unlikely as such an outcome may seem, that is exactly what appears to have taken place.

241

In the eighteenth century, *Iphis et Iante* is mentioned in dictionaries and summarily dismissed by commentators, who see no need to dwell on it. In their *Histoire du Théâtre français* (1734–49), Claude and François Parfait observe that 'since the subject of the play is well-known, it is enough to account for the way the author exposed it onstage'.[4] Indeed, the first act of the play, usually devoted to the exposition of the plot, provided very little background explanation, apparently assuming that everybody already knew the basic story.[5] Another late eighteenth-century commentator, the Chevalier Fieux de Mouhy, mentions the play as an idle curiosity which he falsely attributes to La Calprenède.[6] In his *Bibliographie du théâtre français depuis son origine* (1768), the Duc de La Vallière characterises *Iphis et Iante* as 'cold and languishing', and considers the wedding of the two young girls to be simply 'ridiculous'.[7]

But if Iphis and Iante's marriage gave rise to no scandal, it hardly follows that the depiction of the two young girls' marriage and the evocation of their wedding night played no part in the aesthetic pleasure experienced by the audience. Rather, both the reception and the aesthetics of the play pose the problem of the cultural legibility of lesbianism as represented on stage. In the discussion that follows, I would like to account for the representation of female homoerotic desire in *Iphis et Iante* in light of gallantry, the amorous culture that was dominant among social elites in seventeenth-century France, which shapes Benserade's comedic dramaturgy.

In the two last decades, gallantry has become a central category in the cultural history of seventeenth-century France.[8] For more than two centuries, critics had used the category of 'preciosity' to dismiss those learned women of the gentry who refused love, and even sometimes marriage, and who used literature to promote their non-sexual conception of love and friendship. Scholars have recently noticed that none of the individuals so described, however, would have recognised themselves under that label.[9] It appears that the same people who were long classified as 'précieux' actually characterised themselves and their writings as 'gallant'. For them, gallantry referred primarily to an art of loving and, more generally, to a way of behaving among Parisian social elites that was marked by ostensible respect for women and greater acceptance of the sensual dimensions of love.[10] By mid-century, the notion was recuperated by writers who frequented Madeleine de Scudéry's salon where this culture of love was elaborated in great detail as 'gallant'.[11] But gallantry is more than simply a literary school. Located at the crossroad of literature, fine arts and amorous behaviours among the seventeenth-century French nobility, it constitutes an aesthetics not only for art, but also for life – an 'aesthetics of existence' that enabled the social elites of the time to reinvent themselves by displacing the limits between the licit and the illicit as regards gender, love and sex.[12]

Surprisingly enough, whereas gallantry provides one opportunity to think afresh about gender and erotic relations in the context of seventeenth-century

France, scholars who have worked on the subject have failed to historicise either gender or desire. While highlighting how gender and desire were central to gallantry, they have presented the phenomenon as a distinctive expression of a transhistorical heterosexuality and the Grand Siècle as a new Golden Age of heterosexual love.[13] I suggest, in contrast, that gallantry is part of the history of sexuality as Michel Foucault understood that scholarly enterprise – that is, a history of the desiring human subject.[14] It more specifically constitutes one important step in the making of heterosexuality on the threshold of modernity. Reading *Iphis and Iante* from this viewpoint enables us to better understand the cultural significance of female homoeroticism in seventeenth-century court culture. Indeed, while taking what had until then been simply considered a form of amity, and transforming it into a field of practice soon to be called 'sexuality', *Iphis et Iante* constructs a lesbian character that is irreducible to the scandalous figure of the 'tribade', thereby anticipating the lesbian as a sexual identity specific to modernity.

A GALLANT REPRESENTATION OF LESBIANISM: BEYOND AMITY AND TRIBADISM

In order to account for the audience's enjoyment of *Iphis et Iante* in the context of what Valerie Traub has suggestively called a 'renaissance of lesbianism'[15] – not only in England, but also in France[16] – some scholars have mobilised the notion of libertinage. As Elizabeth Wahl explains, 'In his rewriting of the Ovidian myth of Iphis and Ianthe [. . .] Benserade exploits the sensuous appeal of the myth's lesbian homoeroticism within a theatrical setting for the pleasure of a libertine audience composed largely of male spectators and women of the demi-monde'.[17] A libertine reading of the play is not completely convincing, however.

Benserade entered the literary scene as a playwright who published three tragedies in quick succession – *Cléopâtre* (1636), *La Mort d'Achille et la Dispute de ses Armes* (1636), *Méléagre* (1640) – as well as two comedies – *Gustaphe ou l'Heureuse Ambition* (1637) and *Iphis et Iante* (1637). Although he did not persevere in his dramatic career,[18] he became a regular at Mme de Rambouillet's salon, where in 1653 he contributed to the outbreak of the *Querelle des Anciens et des Modernes* (the literary dispute over the respective merits of classical and modern writers) with a poem on the subject of Job. This sonnet, a paraphrase of the Biblical story that he sent to a young lady, was placed in competition with another poem, the 'Uranie' of Vincent Voiture. It led to a dispute about their relative merits, which long divided the court and its wits into two parties, styled respectively the 'Jobelins' and the 'Uranistes'.[19] Benserade has also gained fame in the history of French literature for providing lyrics for the ballets at the royal court over a span of more than twenty years. In 1674, he was eventually admitted to the Académie Française, where he wielded considerable influence. As it happens, Benserade's career is typical of those new professional writers who came from the lower nobility of the robe,[20] which administrated the modern state brought about by absolute monarchy,[21] and who proved to be instrumental to the blossoming of the gallant aesthetic throughout the seventeenth century.

Significantly, Benserade staged his comedy at the Hôtel de Bourgogne, the same theatre where Corneille presented his first comedy *Mélite ou les Fausses Lettres* a few years earlier, in 1629, at a moment when theatre was closely monitored by Cardinal de Richelieu, who wanted to make it a form of entertainment for an audience of 'honest' people. Corneille is well known for his tragicomedy *Le Cid*, also staged at the Hôtel de Bourgogne in 1637. The success of his tragicomedy, later relabelled a 'tragedy', enticed the notorious *Querelle du Cid* (1637–8), which played such an important role in establishing the Académie Française, newly created in 1634. But even before meeting success on the tragic stage, Corneille became one of the most successful playwrights of his generation by introducing onto the Paris stage *Mélite*, a comedy inspired by Terence's 'romantic' comedies, which put the love plot – a 'galanterie' in the language of the time[22] – at the forefront and described love in its sensual dimensions, while keeping sex out of view. At a time when the medieval genre of the farce was still alive, *Mélite* constituted a form of comedy which both men and women, even of high society, could attend without fear for their reputation.

To be sure, the pressure to exhibit greater decorum and propriety (*bienséance*) in the theatre increased over the course of the seventeenth century, and did not begin to weigh heavily until later in the century.[23] It is therefore likely that Benserade was afforded a greater freedom of tone than subsequent playwrights. Adopting Corneille's gallant aesthetics, however, Benserade addressed the theme of lesbianism in decorous terms, in accordance with the cultural politics of Cardinal de Richelieu. This characteristic is particularly striking in the depiction of Iphis and Iante's awkward wedding night between Acts 3 and 4: staying away from bawdiness and indecency, it gave rise (maybe for that reason) to no scandal at the time, at least as far as we know.

Perhaps influenced by the notion that a seventeenth-century play representing female homoeroticism could only be transgressive, many scholars have identified the character of Iphis as a 'tribade',[24] a figure represented in medical and libertine writings[25] as a phallic woman whose clitoris protrudes to such an extent that it enables her to penetrate a female (or male) partner.[26] But no evidence supports that view in Benserade's play. On the contrary, at different moments in the play, Iphis expresses her anxiety about her 'imperfection', with a double entendre that suggests that she is not equipped to penetrate Iante's body. This allusion comes as soon as the second act of the play, when Iphis presents herself in a positive and modest light to better please Iante. Iphis first expresses her astonishment that she managed to conquer Iante's heart:

> Love gave me so many perfect rivals,
> Yet, with my defects, I defeated them all!
>
> L'amour m'a suscité tant de parfaits rivaux,
> Et je les ai vaincus avec tous mes défauts.
> (II, iii, 67)

This gives rise to a short argument between the two girls, which has Iphis exclaim:

> And to tell you the truth, I don't think I deserve,
> Imperfect as I am, so many perfect charms.
>
> Et pour n'en point mentir, je ne mérite pas,
> Imparfait que je suis, de si parfaits appâts.
> (II, iii, 68)

It is worth recalling here that Benserade became a successful poet because of the wittiness of his rhymes. Accordingly, a double entendre in this passage contributes to the audience's delight, while avoiding bawdiness. Whereas Iante (who does not know that her lover is a girl) understands Iphis as simply mobilising the cliché of the imperfection of the lover compared to the perfect beauty of the beloved mistress, the audience understands Iphis to also implicitly be referring to her 'imperfection' as a characteristic of her body (implicitly gendered in Galenic terms), thereby revealing her anxiety that she might not be able to satisfy Iante's desire on their wedding night.

It is precisely because of such female 'imperfection' that other characters in the play seem to consider any sexual contact between the two girls as benign, if not insignificant. Ergaste, for instance, who knows that Iphis is actually a girl and who is in love with her, does not become jealous until he considers the possibility, which will be realised at the end of the play, that one of the two girls may be a boy:

> I invent in my mind a thousand objects of fear,
> Everything makes me confused, and I begin to suspect,
> That one of these two lovers may actually be a boy.
>
> Je me forge en l'esprit mille sujets de crainte,
> Tout me met dans l'ombrage, et j'entre en un soupçon
> Que l'un des deux Amants ne se trouve garçon.
> (II, i, 56)

Ergaste contemplates this possibility, which the goddess Isis will eventually make real, for the audience's ironic delectation. For him, so long as Iphis is not a boy, whatever lovemaking results from their courtship does not count, according to a cultural definition that Ergaste shares with his sister.[27] Indeed, at the end of the first act, Télétuze, Iphis's mother, shares with Ergaste's sister (who also knows Iphis's true gender) her concern about seeing her daughter pass as a boy and marry another girl. But for Ergaste's sister, the situation is not desperate. For her, the fact that Iphis and Iante have the same gender will prevent the couple from having sex, and therefore produce no perversion or monstrosity:

> The two of them bring to their union too much sympathy;
> Their marriage lacks the best part. There will be
> Shame for one, and for the other resentment,
> And of their bed Chastity will make her throne.
>
> Tous deux pour s'accorder ont trop de sympathie,
> Il manque à leur hymen la meilleure partie;
> L'une aura de la honte, et l'autre du dépit,
> La chasteté fera son trône de leur lit.
>
> (I, iii, 47)

The two characters explicitly evoke the wedding night the two girls are about to experience if the marriage takes place. In line with Iphis's argument about her own 'imperfection', Ergaste's sister asserts that in order for Iphis to be able to make love with Iante, she would need to overcome her female 'imperfection' and get 'the best part' – namely the phallus. As suggested by the allegory of Chastity making a throne out of the couple's bed, for Ergaste's sister (and, apparently, for Iphis's mother, who does not object), the erotic encounter of the two young girls is not, strictly speaking, sexual. It is precisely because this encounter is not conceived as sexual that it is possible to evoke it so freely on stage. And yet, the phrase 'too much sympathy' ('trop de sympathie') proves to be ambivalent. It signifies, on the one hand, that because Iphis and Iante have the same gender, the attraction between them will prove 'too much' and prevent the two girls from being attracted to each other and therefore from feeling sufficient desire. On the other hand, the words 'too much' ('trop'), might well work to emphasise a concentration of intense feeling. From that perspective, the excess of sympathy between the two girls may actually underline the erotic attraction between them and the sexual character of their encounter, despite the precautions taken by the playwright. Supplementing the absent phallus, such excess perhaps suggests that contrary to what the characters imply, the fact that Iphis is not a tribade is insufficient to deny the possibility that the two young girls actually enjoy sex during their wedding night. In that context, even the gracious allegory of Chastity is likely to intensify, rather than neutralise, the erotic charge of the depiction. As a whole, the passage is typical of Benserade's gallant aesthetics which addresses the question of sex while maintaining decorum. For that purpose, his aesthetics draws on the indecisiveness of what may or may not be articulated on stage, an ambiguity that eventually poses the question of what does or does not 'count' as sex.

This problem underpins the depiction of the wedding night after it takes place between Acts 3 and 4. In turning Ovid's tale into a dramatic comedy, Benserade implemented a significant temporal change in the plot: Isis's intervention is delayed and Iphis's metamorphosis occurs only after the marriage. The whole of Act 4 is then devoted to a discussion of the same-sex wedding night.

At the beginning of the act, on the morning that follows her wedding, Iphis tells her mother what happened. Asserting, on the one hand, the insignificance of their intercourse and the 'pointlessness' of her passion, she underscores, on the other, the pleasure she experienced during the night:

> What was hidden by the light of the day was uncovered by night.
> We would have wanted very much to satisfy our longing.
> And I was never so sad and so enraptured at once!
> Iante's lack of satisfaction did indeed cause me worry;
> Yet at the same time, my possession of her enraptured me!
> And although my ardour was nothing but pointless to us both,
> I forgot for a while that I was a girl,
> And I never got so much satisfaction.
> I gave myself over to my raptures;
> By kissing her, I eased the fever of my love,
> And my soul was poured out to my very lips,
> In the sweet enjoyment of those superfluous goods,
> I even forgot about the very one I was longing for most,
> I kissed her beautiful body, of which the pure whiteness
> Urged me to find for her a place within myself,
> I touched her, I kissed her, and my heart was satisfied.

> Ce que le jour cachait, la nuit l'a découvert,
> Nous eussions bien voulu contenter notre envie,
> Et je ne fus jamais si triste et si ravie,
> Son mécontentement me donnait du souci,
> Mais la possession me ravissait aussi,
> Et quoique mon ardeur nous fût fort inutile,
> J'oubliais quelque temps que j'étais une fille,
> Je ne reçus jamais tant de contentement,
> Je me laissais aller à mes ravissements,
> D'un baiser j'apaisais mon amoureuse fièvre,
> Et mon âme venait jusqu'au bord de mes lèvres,
> Dans le doux sentiment de ces biens superflus;

> J'oubliais celui même où j'aspirais le plus,
> J'embrassais ce beau corps, dont la blancheur extrême
> M'excitait à lui faire un place en moi même,
> Je touchais, je baisais, j'avais le cœur content.
>
> (V, iv, 112–13)

To be sure, Iphis forgot for a while that she was a girl, but she explicitly asserts that she could not penetrate Iante's body. In her own words, she could not attain the goal she 'was longing for most' and her 'ardour was pointless [*inutile*] to us both'. As Wahl explains, Iphis 'remains technically "innocent" of the crime of sodomy because of her inability to consummate the union'.[28] Indeed, in the patriarchal terms of the seventeenth century, in the absence of coitus, there is no sex – hence, the possibility for a comedic but decorous treatment of the episode.

Even as Benserade emphasises the 'pointlessness' of the wedding night, his rewriting of the Ovidian tale puts pleasure under scrutiny, as if things are not so simple after all. For one thing, Iphis's depiction of her wedding night underlines less her 'impotence' than the erotic 'plenitude' she experiences.[29] Although there is no coitus, there is 'possession' [*possession*]. Experiencing rapture [*ravissement*] and enjoyment [*doux sentiment*] at the same time, it seems that Iphis is aroused to the point of orgasm.[30] What is more, Iante too experiences pleasure. To be sure, Iphis tells her mother that Iante remained insensitive, and even compares her to a tree stump.[31] But she also mentions Iante's satisfaction [*contentement*], and in a soliloquy at the beginning of Act 5, after Iphis's gender identity has just been revealed, Iante herself evokes the pleasure she experienced:

> This marriage is pleasing, I find in it sufficient charms;
> And if people wouldn't make fun of it, I would not complain about it:
> I would have no regret that we had been yoked together.
>
> Ce mariage est doux, j'y trouve assez d'appâts
> Et si l'on n'en riait, je ne m'en plaindrais pas:
> Je n'aurais pas regret qu'on nous joignît ensemble.
>
> (V, i, 105)

Iante appears in these lines as an innocent young girl, apparently unaware of the gravity of the situation, and therefore expressing only slight reservations about her marriage to Iphis. For her, this marriage is subject to jokes and mockery, but elicits no inner conflict. In this manner, she guarantees that the play stays within the bounds of honesty. And yet, the words 'pleasing' [*doux*] and 'charms' [*appâts*] explicitly evoke pleasure in seventeenth-century French. For the audience – who has already heard Iphis's account of the wedding night – this exchange of pleasure might well have been at odds with the notion that the absence of penetration meant no sex.

This is the subtlety of Benserade's adaptation of Ovid: because no penetration was involved, the girls' erotic pleasure did not culturally signify as transgressive and could be freely portrayed on stage. And yet, this pleasure was significant enough to warrant devoting an entire act to discussing it, presumably to the delight of the audience. Benserade's talent consists precisely in exploiting this indecisiveness about the status of female erotic pleasure for the purpose of a comedy that, according to the cultural patterns of gallantry, celebrates, rather than restrains, the erotic dimensions of love.[32] In so doing, Benserade reveals how gallantry, while shifting the boundary between the licit and the illicit, poses a problem of definition: what kind of erotic pleasure is effectively considered sex in this new cultural context?

In *The Renaissance of Lesbianism*, Valerie Traub has coined the notion of 'the (in)significance of lesbian desire' to address the conditions of intelligibility in which female homoeroticism becomes culturally salient:[33] whereas tribadism, which generally was thought to imply penetration, is usually seen as unnatural and outrageous in the early modern era, amity, which refers to a homoerotic friendship physically expressed by caressing and kissing, is generally perceived as benign, if not insignificant, because of its reputably non-penetrative nature. There are instances, however, where female homoeroticism becomes significant, even though no sexual penetration is involved. The decorous spectacularising of Iphis and Iante's wedding night is one of them. To be sure, there is no tribadic sex represented in the play. In that sense, Iphis and Iante's lesbianism evokes amity. But insofar as the play portrays an awkward – but, for the audience, arousing – erotic encounter (which substitutes for the heterosexual intercourse typically expected on a wedding night), it represents their love as implicitly sexual. As a result of the aesthetics of gallantry, the characterisation of Iphis sits uneasily between the poles of tribadism and amity that usually shape early modern representations of lesbianism. Reading Benserade's gallant aesthetics through the lens of the history of sexuality enables a better understanding of how non-penetrative female eroticism could be considered sex in seventeenth-century France.

THE LOVE MATCH: FEMALE EROTIC AGENCY IN MATRIMONIAL NEGOTIATIONS

Although the choice of Ovid as a source for the plot, the location of the action on Crete, the decoration of the stage and the final metamorphosis evoke, at least for its first audience, the genre of the pastoral tragicomedy, the structure of the plot follows the model of Cornelian comedy. In order to compose *Mélite ou Les fausses Lettres*, Corneille took his inspiration from ancient comedy and especially from the Roman playwright Terence, considered at the time the greatest comic dramatist and whose plays were included in the *ratio studiorum* in the Jesuit colleges where Corneille received his education. Though it often turned on a love-plot, ancient comedy, however, did not dramatise love itself – it did not explore love as a space of conflict. In the seventeenth century, tragicomedy and pastoral tragicomedy were the two most fashionable theatrical genres devoted to dramatising love.[34] For that reason, some critics have labelled the six comedies Corneille wrote at the beginning of his career 'urban pastorals',[35] to emphasise that he simply transferred the amorous plot typical of pastoral literature to the urban context typical of ancient comedy. As it happens, the subgenre of gallant comedy results from Corneille's blending of the genre of the pastoral – which usually focuses on love as a space of conflict between the lovers – with the genre of the comedy – which focuses on marriage, over which fathers, usually playing the role of naysayers, exercise vigilant control.

Ancient comedy did not completely ignore love. Terence, for instance, specialised in 'romantic' comedies where love played an important part. But it is worth underlining the difference between the way Terence dramatised love and the way Corneille and his followers, including Benserade, did, when gallantry shaped the amorous behaviours of the nobility. In order to turn Ovid's tale into a comedy, Benserade constructs one dramatic action with two strands, thereby including in his play characters that do not exist in Ovid's text. At the level of the main action, two lovers will eventually get the love match they want. At the level of the secondary action, Ergaste (who knows that Iphis is a girl) is in love with her, while another girl, Mérinte, is in love with him. These two strands eventually result in only one action insofar as what happens at the level of the main action is correlated to what happens in the secondary action. It is in order to avoid having to marry Mérinte, the sister of his friend Nise (whom he does not want to offend by refusing the alliance) that Ergaste is prompted to accuse Iphis of being female. Because, in the end, Iphis will be transformed into a boy so as to be able to remain married to Iante, Ergaste will eventually agree to marry Mérinte. The plot assumes the form of the gallant comedy à la Corneille, insofar as the shift in Ergaste's amorous quest makes changing lovers a crucial part of the regular functioning of the love plot, which celebrates courtship as key to matrimonial success and happiness.

Indeed, just as in Corneille's comedies, and in contrast with romantic comedies à la Terence, the duplication of the plot goes hand in hand with a shift in the nature of the conflict that relocates the dramatic action from the confines of the family to the intricacies of the love plot itself. In Terence's comedies, love is depicted as a family matter. The male protagonist defies paternal authority by attempting to marry a girl of his choice; the dramatic conflict opposes father and son as the father attempts to constrain the vagaries of love while the girl in question never appears onstage.[36] The amorous relationship is a given, but it is not directly dramatised, let alone problematised. By contrast, in the Cornelian model of gallant comedy followed by Benserade, love itself generates the conflict resolved by the play. Indeed, the primary conflict consists in the rivalry between friends who are in love with the same young girl, while parents fail to play their traditional role of naysayers and romantic obstacles. This is the case in *Iphis et Iante*, where both Iphis's and Iante's fathers support the girls' love match, while Ergaste jeopardises the two heroines' happiness by revealing that Iphis is female.

This brief comparison between romantic comedy à la Terence and Corneille's gallant reworking of the genre points to the fact that, in the latter, love no longer disturbs patriarchal order or impedes the regular functioning of marriage over which fathers in ancient comedy once exercised vigilant control. In seventeenth-century gallant comedy, love as a space of conflict between lovers actually leads to marriage and supports the social order, since all it now takes for lovers to succeed in their amorous quest is to have their love reciprocated. In other words, the shift of comedic conflict from paternal obstacle to amorous rivalry integrates love into the economy of marriage. Love is no longer depicted as a passion that threatens marriage or that contravenes the orderly transaction of marriage legitimately defended by the hero's father. Instead, parents prove themselves unable, or unwilling, to counter their progeny's wishes, and mutual love, even passion, is presented as the *sine qua non* of marriage. There is no conflict between generations, and love does not conflict with marriage. Paving the way for marriage, love becomes part of the regular functioning of the reproduction of the 'apparatus of alliance', in Foucault's terms.[37] Supporting this apparatus is why modern comedies, according to Corneille, should end with a promise of marriage, if not the wedding itself.[38]

As Susan Lanser notes in her essay in this volume, the modernity of Benserade's play notably arises from its preoccupation with 'youth as such'.[39] This is true for Benserade's play, and more generally for the gallant comedies that focus on the conflict among lovers in the field of courtship for the purpose of marriage. But does Benserade's gallant comedy promote the interests of youth against patriarchal heternormativity? To be sure, the focus on the experience of youth opens a space wherein heterosexuality is contested. But Iphis's transformation into a boy at the end of the play suggests that such contestation must be muted eventually – a point to which I will return. What is more, the structure of the plot affirms the ultimate compatibility of the romance plot with patriarchal authority, along with the reproduction of the social order, the exchange of women among men and dynastic succession.[40] Indeed, Benserade's play shows how, in a cultural context dominated by gallantry, integrating the interests of youth into marriage negotiations results in a particular transformation of patriarchal heteronormativity – one, however, that does not actually forward the interests of a lesbian-affirmative ethos.

One result of the integration of love (as romance) into the social practice of marriage (as a contractual, economic and dynastic arrangement) is to promote mutual desire as a cultural expectation. Since desire now actively leads to marriage, lovers can succeed in their amorous quest only by having their love reciprocated. In this context where lovers, not parents, decide who will marry whom, female lovers' inclinations assume a much more prominent, indeed determinative, role. A significant characteristic of the gallant version of the love-plot, then, is that both female and male characters may both be objects and subjects of love.

In Benserade's play, however, mutuality does not go without saying. Mérinte is in love with Ergaste, who does not reciprocate her love right away. It is not until Iphis has been turned into a boy that Ergaste forsakes his love for her, or rather *him*. While the secondary action, as shown by Ergaste's journey, includes a shift in the amorous quest for at least one character, there is no shifting of purpose in Iphis's and Iante's amorous quest. Nevertheless, in both cases, the gallant scenario points to the activation of female erotic agency in the love plot, which gives love and erotic desire a new prominence in the economy of marriage. On this account, mutual love and desire are nothing more than the dramatic expression of the ideology of gallantry, which allows for female erotic autonomy and agency, thereby giving rise to new comedic models, which in turn illustrate the tenets of that ideology. The comedic but decorous representation of female homoeroticism in *Iphis et Iante* indicates that, in the context of gallantry, female erotic autonomy acquires value insofar as it comes to constitute the basis for the elaboration of love-marriage, a new social form which realigns sex, love, gender, marriage and eroticism in historically unprecedented ways. Just as companionate marriage did in England, gallantry contributed, in France, to conscripting desire to love as a matrimonial institution – what Traub has called 'domestic heterosexuality'.[41] Gallantry, in that sense, is part of the genealogy of 'sexuality' as a modern and heteronormative apparatus.[42]

From Homoeroticism to Homosexuality

In light of this genealogical perspective, it is possible to return to the question of the cultural significance of lesbian desire in Benserade's play. In *The Sexuality of History*, Lanser suggestively argues that female homoeroticism figures the 'collapse of predictable family'.[43] In the world of the play, Iphis proves herself an agentic character inasmuch as she reconfigures the alliances pursued by the four families at stake in the plot – not only those of Iphis and Iante, but also of Ergaste's and Mérinte's families. In this regard, it is worth noting that Isis's intervention at the end of the play does not sanction Iphis's and Ianthe's homoerotic desire: on the contrary, she is the *deus ex machina* through which homoerotic desire is refigured for the benefit of patriarchial reproduction. If family effectively ceases to be predictable, it is not because of Iphis and Ianthe's temporary lesbian love; it is because of the erotic agency mobilised by Iphis and Iante, either as male or female, in gallant courtship for marriage. What the goddess sanctions at the end of the play, then, is not lesbianism, but erotic agency as the force that now determines matrimonial alliances. In so doing, she ratifies a profound transformation of heterosexual patriarchy, which now relies on both male and female erotic agency and autonomy to reproduce itself. In this light, the 'lesbian' character functions as a discursive device that problematises – but also instantiates – female erotic agency.

In a context where female erotic agency is integral to the regular functioning of the exchange of women through marriage, it is no surprise that such autonomy comes under increased scrutiny. Female erotic autonomy does not go without saying in Benserade's play: first represented as an impasse under the guise of lesbian love, it must be subjected to the dictates of heterosexual patriarchy in order to persist and prove itself effective. Besides, Mérinte's indefatigable and even exasperating complaints until Ergaste consents to marry her point to social anxiety about such autonomy, as if female desire might perpetually threaten the male characters. This fear of female desire, however, is an aspect of gallant comedies in general. What Benserade's comedy specifically does is to make female pleasure a central issue, thereby pointing to a new economy of affects in relation to sex.

Indeed, the theatrical representation of Iphis's and Iante's mutual love as well as the detailed account of their wedding night in Act 4 suggests that it is not only female erotic autonomy, but also female intimacy, that come under increased scrutiny. With gallantry, love is not only crucial to successful marriage, but it paves the way for conjugal sex. From this viewpoint, although there was no penetration during the girls' wedding night, the detailed exploration of the pleasure they experienced – which will culminate in a second wedding night announced by Télétuze in the last scene – designates such pleasure, in Henry Abelove's terms, as sexual preliminaries or 'foreplay'.[44] Indeed, Iphis's and Iante's pleasure does not pertain to tribadism, nor does it pertain to amity; rather, gallantry has taken amity and transformed it into a field of practice that will be called, by the end of the eighteenth century, 'sexuality'.[45] In this light, lesbian desire not only figures the erotic agency granted to individuals in the regime of domestic heterosexuality, but also emblematises a new economy of emotions and sensations in relation to sex – specifically, a new definition of caressing and kissing as part of a teleology of sexual pleasures. In recasting what used to pertain to homoerotic friendship as nothing but a preliminary to sex as the complete expression of mutual heterosexual love, Benserade's comedy consolidates heterosexual patriarchy, premised as it is on the reproductive imperative recalled at the end of the play.[46] But conversely, in defining Iphis's pleasure in bodily contact with Iante as sexual (even though it includes no mention of penetration), the play constructs female homoeroticism as irreducible to either tribadism or amity. It thereby contributes to shaping the lesbian as a modern figure, who may be either a butch lesbian (Iphis)[47] or a femme lesbian (Iante),[48] but who either way constitutes a sexual identity. In this further articulation of sexual identities, gallantry paves the way for 'sexuality' as a specifically modern formation.

Conclusion: Erasing Lesbianism

Reading *Iphis et Iante* through the lens of the history of sexuality, then, allows us to understand what is at stake in its staging of female homoeroticism, but also in its being rendered invisible in the context of gallantry. Benserade's use of the genre of comedy highlights the connection between the aesthetics of gallantry endorsed by the seventeenth-century French nobility and the profound reorganisation of marriage, premised on heterosexual desire, that occurred at the time. His play thus shows how gallantry intensified heteronormativity on the threshold of modernity, thereby recasting a part of people's affective life that once pertained to friendship as a form of sexuality. In the context of this new erotic economy, the significance of Benserade's lesbian character proves to be highly ambivalent.

On the one hand, Benserade's lesbian embodies a conception of female homoeroticism as not sexual, which therefore may be decorously represented onstage. On the other, as the comedic plot implicitly redefines female homoeroticism as homosexuality, the lesbian character progressively appears as an outrageous figure of resistance to heteronormativity, who must therefore be removed from the realm of possibility. Isis's intervention warns the audience: once it has become obvious that lesbianism is about homosexuality rather than homoeroticism, it is no longer appropriate to represent it onstage. In the end, Iphis's transformation into a boy ratifies the obliteration of female homoerotic friendship, while performatively denying the lesbian's status as intrinsically sexual.

In its ultimate erasure of lesbianism, the play seems to anticipate the terms of its own erasure from the history of literature. Indeed, if the seventeenth-century audience applauded *Iphis et Iante*, the play's success was not recorded for posterity and, a century later, commentators seemed unable, if not reluctant, to understand Benserade's comedy. The reservations they expressed about the play turn on the fact that they found it, as we have seen, 'cold and languishing'. To be sure, Benserade's dramaturgy is not as sophisticated as Corneille's, even at the moment when the latter had not yet become the prominent tragic poet we admire today. Yet it is precisely the way that even such a brilliant dramatist as Corneille portrayed love that Voltaire objected to. In his *Commentaires sur Corneille*,[49] the philosopher constantly compared Corneille with Racine, arguing that while Racine was the first to represent true love on stage, Corneille never proved capable of breaking with gallantry, the affective form his earliest comedies introduced into the French theatre. The philosopher repeatedly uses the adjective 'cold' to dismiss Corneille's dramatic representation of love.⁵⁰ Voltaire's commentary may sound reductive, but it shows that the aesthetics of gallantry had become outdated by the eighteenth century.

As it happened, in the course of the seventeenth century, another model for love had become pervasive, whose content was more personal and whose form was less formulary: the discourse of 'love as passion', extensively elaborated by novelists such as Mme de La Fayette and by dramatists such as Racine.⁵¹ Meanwhile, gallantry had progressively become a mere form of civility or a euphemism for libertinage. Because they mobilised an amorous aesthetics that was already outdated, both Benserade's and Corneille's comedies were criticised as 'cold and languishing' by eighteenth-century commentators. By then, however, the aesthetics of gallantry had done its work: it contributed to transforming the regular functioning of the exchange of women by acknowledging and even activating female erotic agency in the making of matrimonial alliances.

In Benserade's comedy, Iphis and Iante embody such erotic agency as a startling novelty. One century later, however, the notion that women may legitimately enjoy erotic autonomy in courtship for marriage had become pervasive in literary production.⁵² In that context, the use of female homoeroticism as a way of highlighting such erotic autonomy might well have looked inadequate, especially since, by that time, the assumption of lesbianism as non-penetrative and non-sexual had apparently vanished in polite discourse. In his *Dictionnaire philosophique*, Voltaire significantly speaks about 'Socratic love' as an 'abomination' that affects the two sexes, without mentioning tribadism or amity.⁵³ Adopting cultural patterns specific to their time, eighteenth-century commentators have missed Iphis's passion, articulated as it was in an outmoded form of love on the stage and no longer recognisable outside of the comedic plot. What gallantry had momentarily opened up – a female erotic agency that might escape heterosexual marriage – the eighteenth-century elevation of domestic heterosexuality resolutely shut down.

Notes

1. Tallemant, 'Discours sommaire touchant la vie de Monsieur de Benserade':

    A peine était-il sorti du collège qu'il donna deux ou trois pièces de théâtre. J'en ai vu deux dont l'une s'appelait *Iphis et Iante*, et l'autre *Marc-Antoine*; elles eurent toutes deux assez de succès. (n.p.)

    He was fresh out of college when he presented two or three theater plays. I have seen two of them, one of which was *Iphis et Iante*, and the other one *Marc-Antoine*: both were fairly successful.' (My translation)

2. For a modern edition of the play, see Benserade, *Iphis et Iante*, preface by Verdier.
3. See the many recently published studies of the play: Harris, 'Disruptive Desires'; Biet, 'À quoi rêvent les jeunes filles'; Legault, 'An Obsession with the Absent Phallus', *Female Intimacies in Seventeenth-Century French Literature*, pp. 96–118; Leibacher-Ouvrard, 'Divergences et queeriosités' and 'Speculum de l'autre femme'.

4. Parfait, *Histoire du théâtre français*: 'Le sujet de cette pièce étant très connu, il suffit d'en rendre compte de la façon dont l'auteur l'a exposée au théatre', t. 1, p. 600 (my translation).
5. On the rewritings of Ovid's tale in the seventeenth century, see Leibacher-Ouvrard, 'Speculum de l'autre femme'.
6. Chevalier Fieux de Mouhy, *Abrégé de l'histoire du théâtre français*, p. 26.
7. Duc de La Vallière, *Bibliographie du théâtre français*, Vol. II: 'froide et languissante', p. 543.
8. Pelous, *Amour précieux, amour galant*; Denis, *Le Parnasse galant: Institution d'une catégorie littéraire au XVIIe siècle*; Habib, *Galanterie française*; Viala, *La France galante*.
9. Denis, 'Préciosite et galanterie'.
10. Pelous, *Amour précieux, amour galant*. See also Viala, *La France galante*: 'Bref, à égale distance du rigorisme religieux qui bannirait le corps, sources de pulsions sexuelles, et des libertinage libidineux, les vrais galants accordent confiance à l'humain, corps compris, à condition qu'il soit bien tempéré', p. 155. 'In short, equally distant from religious rigorism, which would banish the body, source of sexual impulses, and from libidinous libertinage, true gallants give confidence to the human, including the body, provided that it is well tempered' (my translation).
11. Viala, *La France galante*, pp. 45–8.
12. Michel Foucault, *The Use of Pleasure*.
13. See in particular Habib, *Galanterie française*.
14. Foucault, *The History of Sexuality* and Halperin, 'Introduction: In Defense of Historicism', *How to Do the History of Homosexuality*, pp. 1–23, in particular p. 9.
15. Traub, *The Renaissance of Lesbianism*.
16. Lanser, *The Sexuality of History*.
17. Wahl, *Invisible Relations*, p. 63.
18. For biographical information, see Verdier's introduction to her edition of the play, pp. 7–33.
19. *Cf.* Asselineau, *Histoire du sonnet* (1856).
20. See Viala, *Naissance de l'écrivain* (1985), pp. 183–4: Viala classifies Benserade among the 'écrivains de profession' whose social strategies consist in following the 'cursus honorum' of the nascent literary field, p. 306.
21. For the role of the nobility of the robe in the success of the aesthetics of gallantry, see also Viala, *La France galante*, 'Ralliés et Parvenus', pp. 176–91.
22. See the definitions of 'galant' and 'galanterie' in Furetière, *Dictionnaire universel* (1690): 'Galant, subst. masc. Amant qui se donne tout entier au service d'une maistresse. Il y a bien des *galants* qui recherchent cette fille en mariage.' 'A lover who gives himself entirely to the service of his mistress. Many gallant men look for this girl in marriage' (my translation). 'Galanterie, se dit aussi de l'attache qu'on à [sic] courtiser les Dames. Il se prend en bonne & en mauvaise part. Il y a une *galanterie* ouverte entre ces deux personnes; leur commerce ne passe point l'honeste *galanterie*.' 'Is said of one's dedication to courting Ladies. Is used in a good and bad sense. There is an open galanterie among those two people. Their commerce does not go beyond the limits of honest gallantry' (my translation).
23. Bray, *La formation de la doctrine classique*.
24. See Verdier, *Iphis et Iante*, 'Preface', pp. 7–33; Legault, *Female Intimacies in Seventeenth-Century French Literature*, 'Benserade: An Obsession with the Absent Phallus'; Leibacher-Ouvrard, 'Divergences et queeriosités' and 'Speculum de l'autre femme'.
25. See Leibacher-Ouvrard, 'Tribades et gynanthropes', p. 520.

26. Traub, *The Renaissance of Lesbianism*, p. 17.
27. Bonnet, *Les relations amoureuses entre les femmes*:

 > La doctrine chrétienne est restée totalement muette sur la luxure entre femmes [...] Le désintérêt de la religion chrétienne pour cette branche féminine de la luxure est cohérent. En effet, pourquoi condamnerait-elle un plaisir insignifiant ? D'ailleurs, peut on parler de plaisir quand il y manque l'instrument essentiel ? [...] En revanche, la femme qui s'habille en homme représente un danger. Un danger d'ordre social et non sexuel. (pp. 35–6)

 > The Christian doctrine has remained totally silent on lust among women. The disinterest of the Christian religion for this feminine branch of lust is coherent. Indeed, why should an insignificant pleasure be condemned? Besides, can one speak of pleasure when the essential instrument is missing? [...] On the other hand, a woman who dresses as a man is a danger. A social but non-sexual danger. (My translation)

28. Wahl, *Invisible Relationships*, p. 64.
29. Wahl, *Invisible Relationships*, emphasises the ambivalence of the play, which oscillates between a representation of female homoeroticism in Benserade's play as 'sexual plenitude' and 'impotence', p. 63.
30. *Ibid.*, p. 64.
31. Je lui baise le sein, je pâme sur sa bouche
 Mais elle s'en émeut aussi peu qu'une souche. (V, iv, 113).
32. See Pelous, *Amour précieux, amour galant*, pp. 304–454.
33. Traub, 'The (In)Significance of "Lesbian" Desire in Early Modern England', in *The Renaissance of Lesbianism in Early Modern England*, pp. 158–87.
34. Forestier, *Passions tragiques et règles classiques*.
35. Fumaroli, *Héros et orateurs*, p. 36.
36. In Terence's *Andria*, Pamphilus would like to marry Glycerium, an unseen character. The whole plot consists of him convincing his father Simo to let him marry her instead of Chremes's daughter.
37. Foucault, *The History of Sexuality*.
38. Corneille, *Writings on the Theatre*, 'Discours de l'utilité et des parties du poème dramatique':

 > Pour la comédie, Aristote ne lui impose point d'autre devoir pour conclusion que de rendre amis ceux qui étaient ennemis; ce qu'il faut entendre un peu plus généralement que les termes ne semblent porter et l'étendre à la réconciliation de toute sorte de mauvaise intelligence; comme quand un fils rentre aux bonnes grâces d'un père qu'on a vu en colère contre lui pour ses débauches, ce qui est une fin assez ordinaire aux anciennes comédies; ou que deux amants, séparés par quelque fourbe qu'on leur a faite, ou par quelque pouvoir dominant, se réunissent par l'éclaircissement de cette fourbe, ou par le consentement de ceux qui y mettaient obstacle ; ce qui arrive presque toujours dans les nôtres, qui n'ont que très rarement une autre fin que les mariages.

 > As for comedy, Aristotle only recommends that in its conclusion enemies should depart as friends – a statement that should be understood a little more broadly than the words seem to suggest, so as to include the resolving of any kind of discord, such as when a son obtains forgiveness from his father who was mad at him because of his debauchery, an ending that is quite common in ancient comedies; or when two lovers, once separated from each other by some deceit or some authority, eventually reunite by clarifying the deceit, or by obtaining the

assent of those who were opposed to it, which is almost always the case in our comedies, which rarely have any other ending than a marriage. (My translation)

39. Lanser, 'Changing the Ways of the World', this volume.
40. Rubin, 'The Traffic in Women'.
41. Traub, *The Renaissance of Lesbianism*, pp. 261–70.
42. For the notion of genealogy, see Halperin, *How to Do the History of Homosexuality*, pp. 1–23, in particular pp. 10–13.
43. Lanser, *The Sexuality of History*, p. 25.
44. See Abelove, 'Some Speculations on the History of Sexual Intercourse'.
45. Davidson, 'Sex and the Emergence of Sexuality'.
46. See the two very last lines of the play in Act 5, scene 6:

> Et ma chère moitié d'une bonne façon
> Prouvera dans neuf mois qu'Iphis est un garcon.
> (p. 124)

> In a good way will my better half
> Demonstrate that Iphis is a boy.
> (My translation)

47. Leibacher-Ouvrard, 'Speculum de l'autre femme', p. 372.
48. Wahl, *Invisible Relations*, p. 65.
49. Voltaire, *Commentaires sur Corneille*.
50. See Barbafieri, 'Corneille vu par Voltaire'.
51. See Luhman, *Love as Passion*.
52. This is true in Voltaire's tragedy, where female erotic autonomy often conflicts with female obedience to the law of the father. See Sclippa, *La loi du père et les droits du cœur*.
53. Voltaire, *Dictionnaire philosophique, portatif*, pp. 16–18.

BIBLIOGRAPHY

Abelove, Henry, 'Some Speculations on the History of Sexual Intercourse during the Long Eighteenth Century in England', *Genders* 6, 1989, pp. 125–30.
Asselineau, Charles, *Histoire du sonnet pour servir à l'histoire de la poésie française* (Alençon: Poulet-Malassis et De Broise, 1856).
Barbafieri, Carine, 'Corneille vu par Voltaire: Portrait d'un artiste en poète froid', *Dix-septième siècle* 4, 2004, pp. 605–16.
Benserade, Isaac de, *Iphis et Iante* ed. Ann Verdier (Vijon: Lampsaque, 2000).
Benserade, Isaac de, *Cléopâtre* (Paris: A. de Sommaville, 1636).
Benserade, Isaac de, *La Mort d'Achille et la dispute de ses armes* (Paris: A. de Sommaville, 1636)
Benserade, Isaac de, *Méléagre* (Paris: A. de Sommaville, 1640).
Benserade, Isaac de, *Gustaphe ou l'heureuse ambition* (Paris: A. de Sommaville, 1637).
Benserade, Isaac de, 'Sur l'Amour d'Uranie avec Phillis: Stances', in *Poésies de Benserade*, ed. Octave Uzanne (Paris: Librairie des bibliophiles, 1875), pp. 165–73.
Biet, Christian, 'À quoi rêvent les jeunes Filles: Homosexualité féminine, travestissement et tragi-comédie: Le cas d'*Iphis et Iante* de Benserade', *La femme au XVIIe siècle: Actes du colloque de Vancouver, University of British Columbia, PFSCL* 138, 2000, pp. 53–84.
Bonnet, Marie-Jo, *Les relations amoureuses entre les femmes, XVIe–XXe siècle* (Paris: Odile Jacob, 2001).
Bray, René, *La formation de la doctrine classique en France* (Paris: Nizet, 1966).

Butler, Judith, *Gender Trouble: Feminism and the Subversion of Identity* (New York: Routledge, 2011).
Corneille, Pierre, *Writings on the Theatre*, ed. H. T. Barnwell (Oxford: Basil Blackwell, 1965).
Davidson, Arnold I., 'Sex and the Emergence of Sexuality', *Critical Inquiry* 14, 1987, pp. 16–48.
Denis, Delphine, *Le Parnasse galant: Institution d'une catégorie littéraire au XVIIe siècle* (Paris: Champion, 2001).
Denis, Delphine, 'Préciosite et galanterie: Vers une nouvelle cartographie', *Les femmes au Grand Siècle. Le Baroque: musique et littérature, musique et liturgie*, PFSCL 144, II, 2002, pp. 17–39.
Fieux de Mouhy, Chevalier, *Abrégé de l'Histoire du théâtre français depuis son origine jusqu'aux premiers jours de l'année 1780* (Paris: L. Jorry, 1780).
Forestier, Georges, *Passions tragiques et règles classiques: Essai sur la tragédie française* (Paris: Presses Universitaires de France, 2003).
Foucault, Michel, *The History of Sexuality: An Introduction*, vol. 1, trans. Robert Hurley (New York: Pantheon, 1978).
Foucault, Michel, *The History of Sexuality: The Use of Pleasure*, vol. 2, trans. Robert Hurley (New York: Pantheon, 1985).
Fumaroli, Marc, *Héros et orateurs* (Geneva: Droz, 1996).
Furetière, Antoine. *Dictionnaire universel* (Rotterdam and The Hague: A. and R. Leers, 1690).
Habib, Claude, *Galanterie française* (Paris: Gallimard, 2006).
Halperin, David M., *How to Do the History of Homosexuality* (Chicago: University of Chicago Press, 2002).
Harris, Joseph, 'Disruptive Desires: Lesbian Sexuality in Isaac de Benserade's *Iphis et Iante* (1634)', *Seventeenth-Century French Studies* 24, 2002, pp. 151–63.
King, Helen, *The One-Sex Body on Trial: The Classical and Early Modern Evidence*, coll. The History of Medicine in Context (Farnham and Burlington, VT: Ashgate, 2013).
Lanser, Susan S., *The Sexuality of History: Modernity and the Sapphic, 1565–1830* (Chicago: University of Chicago Press, 2014).
Laqueur, Thomas W., *Making Sex: Body and Gender from the Greeks to Freud* (Cambridge, MA: Harvard University Press, 1990).
La Vallière, Duc de, *Bibliographie du théâtre français depuis son origine*, vol. II (Dresde: Michel Groel, 1768).
Legault, Marianne, *Female Intimacies in Seventeenth-Century French Literature* (Aldershot: Ashgate, 2012).
Leibacher-Ouvrard, Lise, 'Divergences et queeriosités: Ovide moralisé ou les mutations d'Iphis en garcon (XIIe–XVIIIe)', *French Literature Series* 34: 1, 2007, pp. 13–33.
Leibacher-Ouvrard, Lise, 'Speculum de l'autre femme: Les avatars d'*Iphis et Iante* (Ovide) au XVIIe siècle', *PFSCL* 30, 2003, pp. 365–77.
Leibacher-Ouvrard, Lise, 'Tribades et gynanthropes (1612–1614): fictions et fonctions de l'anatomie travestie', *PFSCL* 24, 1997, pp. 519–36.
Luhmann, Niklas, *Love as Passion: The Codification of Intimacy* (Stanford: Stanford University Press, 1998).
Parfait, Claude et François, *Histoire du Théâtre français* (Amsterdam: aux dépens de la Compagnie, 1734–49; Geneva: Slatkine Reprint, 1967).
Park, Katharine, *Secrets of Women: Gender, Generation, and the Origins of Human Dissection* (New York: Zone Books, 2006).
Pelous, Jean-Michel, *Amour précieux, amour galant. Essai sur la représentation de l'amour dans la littérature et la société mondaines* (Paris: Klincksieck, 1980).

Rubin, Gayle, 'The Traffic in Women: Notes on the "Political Economy" of Sex', *Toward an Anthropology of Women*, ed. Rayna Reiter, *Monthly Review* 1, 1975, pp. 157–210.
Sclippa, Norbert, *La loi du père et les droits du cœur. Essai sur les tragédies de Voltaire* (Geneva: Droz, 1993).
Tallemant, Paul, 'Discours sommaire touchant la vie de Monsieur de Benserade', in *Oeuvre de Benserade*, vol. I (Paris: Charle de Sercy, 1697), n. p.
Traub, Valerie, 'The Renaissance of Lesbianism in Early Modern England', *GLQ: A Journal of Lesbian and Gay Studies* 7: 2, 2001, pp. 245–63.
Traub, Valerie, *The Renaissance of Lesbianism in Early Modern England*, coll. Cambridge Studies in Renaissance Literature and Culture, vol. 42 (Cambridge: Cambridge University Press, 2002).
Traub, Valerie, 'The (In)Significance of "Lesbian" Desire in Early Modern England', in *The Renaissance of Lesbianism in Early Modern England* (2002), pp. 158–87.
Verdier, Anne, 'Préface', in *Iphis et Iante*, comédie d'Isaac de Benserade (Vijon: Lampsaque, 2000), pp. 7–33.
Viala, Alain, *Naissance de l'écrivain* (Paris: Les Editions de Minuit, 1985).
Viala, Alain, *La France galante: Essai historique sur une catégorie culturelle, de ses origines jusqu'à la Révolution* (Paris: Presses Universitaires de France, 2008).
Voltaire, *Commentaires sur Corneille*, in *Œuvres Complètes de Voltaires*, vols 53–5 (Oxford: Voltaire Foundation, 1975).
Voltaire, *Dictionnaire philosophique, portative* (London: Cramer, 1764).
Wahl, Elizabeth S., *Invisible Relations: Representations of Female Intimacy in the Age of Enlightenment* (Stanford: Stanford University Press, 1999).

11

CHANGING THE WAYS OF THE WORLD: SEX, YOUTH AND MODERNITY IN BENSERADE'S *IPHIS ET IANTE*

Susan S. Lanser

In *The Way of the World*, that pathbreaking book written before he became a distant reader, Franco Moretti makes a powerful two-pronged argument: that youth is the 'material sign' of modernity, and that the *Bildungsroman*, which by definition tracks a young person's development, is therefore modernity's 'symbolic form'. Moretti traces the 'century of the *Bildungsroman*' from the aesthetic harmonies of Goethe's *Wilhelm Meister* to the dissonant destinies of Eliot's *Middlemarch* as the arc of time when '*the biography of a young individual was the most meaningful viewpoint*' for understanding a 'new world'.[1] The novel's preoccupation with 'youth as such', says Moretti – youth as restlessness, yearning, self-scrutiny, risk – fosters an 'interiorization of [the] contradiction' between ambition and tradition, resistance and capitulation, autonomy and conformity that 'plunged' Europe into the permanent 'double [political and industrial] revolution' of a modernity with which it was not yet prepared to cope.[2]

It may seem perverse to explore an early seventeenth-century play by evoking the nineteenth-century novel. My goal is neither to challenge Moretti's articulation of the relationship between youth and modernity that configures the classical *Bildungsroman*, which I find brilliantly resonant, nor to collapse the distinctive temporalities of modernities early and mid-, nor to deny generic differences between novel and play. But I do want to argue that the dynamics of the *Bildungsroman* that Moretti posits as hallmarks of the 'modern' make an early appearance, under the pressure of queer desire, in Isaac de Benserade's

Iphis et Iante, first performed in Paris in 1634 and published in 1637. Such a claim, in turn, asks us to reconsider the ways in which gender and genre may converge to promote the interests of youth against orthodox elders and thus the ways in which our understandings of the vexed term modernity and its literary consequences may need to be refined. This thought experiment seems especially resonant for the present volume insofar as the project of the *Bildungsroman* is itself bound up with conversion – that is, with turning the restless young person toward an acceptable place in the social order, to which Moretti sees the English novel as mostly capitulating and the French novel as mostly resisting.[3] In a modest and early way, I suggest, *Iphis et Iante* articulates the kind of generational struggle that lies at the heart not only of the *Bildungsroman* but of the sex-gender system as it comes to be challenged. The resemblance between the historically disparate moments that I evoke in this project may help us to recognise the extent to which modernity itself is a function of temporal consciousness rather than temporal rift. Put differently, what a given moment perceives as new or modern is arguably what creates the sense of rift between historical periods, and the fact that scholars have designated multiple moments as 'modern' shifts the emphasis from external changes to the ways and contexts in which those changes are processed in cultural consciousness. Said in yet another way and to appropriate Latour, we have never been modern or we have always been modern according to whether, and where, 'we' perceive continuity or breach.

In *The Sexuality of History: Modernity and the Sapphic, 1565–1830*, I argue that the preoccupation with female same-sex affiliation in the period we designate as 'early modern' can be read as a story of modern consciousness *tout court*, not least because of the period's repeated association of the sapphic with the unprecedented, the new, the disruptive. This association encourages us, in turn, to read sexual representations for the larger-than-sexual questions they engage. In flipping the phrase 'history of sexuality' to 'sexuality of history', then, I ask not so much what seventeenth-century texts like *Iphis et Iante* can tell us about sexuality, but what the text's inscriptions of sexuality can tell us about the seventeenth century. *Iphis et Iante* figures in *The Sexuality of History* as a revision of the Ovidian story that sets sapphic desire against paternal power to challenge hierarchical norms.[4] The play appears in a chapter focused on the sapphic and the state that explores representations of female homoerotic relations both in explicitly political contexts such as the Jacobite rising in England and in family dynamics that implicitly raise larger questions of governance. Along with the Spanish playwright Cubillo de Aragón's *Añasco el de Talavera* (1635), performed only a year after Benserade's play, *Iphis et Iante* enters a public discourse that questions the necessity of masculinity as the crux-point of social organisation and that augurs a collapse of patriarchal authority. While scholars do not know why either playwright chose this subject, the plays themselves suggest that same-sex desire is more means than end.

In this essay, I press my argument for the radical potential of *Iphis et Iante* in a different direction by focusing on the struggles of young people as such. The resistance to conversion in Benserade's rescripted plot opens *Iphis et Iante* formally and thematically not only to versions of homoerotic desire but to the modernity that Moretti too ultimately dates back to the seventeenth century by means of the attention to 'the everyday that becomes interesting' in Dutch realist art.[5] As I have suggested above, I understand the vexed term 'modernity' – which Moretti, like most of its deployers, does not explicitly define – as a '*perceived* break in the regular passage of time', to quote Bruno Latour though with my own emphasis,[6] a perception that has been 'a way to differentiate past and future, north and south, progress and regress, radical and conservative', an effort to be 'free . . . from the weight of the past' that requires 'every generation' to raise 'questions anew'.[7] In this sense, modernity functions as a field of perception, a repeated self-confirming belief that certain ways of thinking and doing *are* modern, together with a set of values meant to foster practices that depart from those of a perceived past. If we accept modernity as a perception, then we can also see how the term gets attached to particular historical moments or movements when social and cultural changes become or seem intensified. *Iphis et Iante*, I argue, sets itself up as modern in this perceptual sense and implicitly as modern over and against its Ovidian source: through the same dynamics that Moretti associates with modernity, Benserade's play embeds the sapphic in a generational conflict that prefigures or even parallels the struggles that lie at the heart of the nineteenth-century *Bildungsroman*. If this play is at all representative, then queer desire may have inaugurated the changed generational relations that will solidify into the *Bildungsroman*.

Perhaps not incidentally the first dramatic production of a twenty-two-year-old whose protagonist is but twenty, *Iphis et Iante* does more than reinscribe the Ovidian tale from which it springs. Benserade's Iphis, like Ovid's, was raised as a boy because her father would have destroyed an infant daughter; she falls in love with Iante; a wedding looms; and the goddess Isis changes Iphis's sex to legitimate the union. But Benserade radically alters the temporal contours of Ovid's plot: he shifts the timing of Iphis's metamorphosis so that it follows rather than precedes the marriage, forcing Iphis to reveal her sex to Iante on their wedding night and enabling a complex dynamic of desire, despair and indecision. Through both dialogue and soliloquy, Benserade articulates Iphis's inner struggles, but he also gives interiority, indeed the representation of inner conflict, to other characters including Iante, who is wholly silent and passive in Ovid's tale. *Iphis et Iante* further expands – and further queers – its cast of characters by inventing yet another restless youth, Ergaste, who is in love with Iphis and privy to the secret of her sex. In adding as well

Ergaste's friend and confidant Nise, and Nise's sister Mérinte (in love with Ergaste), Benserade creates a cadre of young people triangulated in several plots of desire. In a more conventional Renaissance drama like those so prevalent on the Elizabethan and Golden Age stage, these plot triangulations could have yielded a 'natural' outcome, with the discovery of Iphis's sex leading her to change her habit (in both senses) and give her hand to the faithful and long-suffering Ergaste. But predictably given its source text, *Iphis et Iante* rejects those heteronormative options for the supernatural magic of sex change. At the same time, however, Benserade shifts the story's discursive emphasis from the private preservation of a secret to the public confrontation of an impasse. By revealing to all the characters the knowledge that in Ovid remains exclusive to mother, daughter and nurse – that is, exclusive to women – Benserade's play makes the sapphic a space for social struggle – indeed presenting what Joseph Harris calls 'a profound challenge to the social code'[8] – and in a seventeenth-century culture where the pressure of normative controls is displacing a logic of external sanction. That the more typical heteronormative scenario does not ensue begins to suggest the ways in which sapphic configuration might constitute the *Bildungsroman*'s avant-garde.

Benserade's audience would certainly have recognised both the fidelities and the critical differences between his version and the story inscribed in Book IX of the *Metamorphoses*. Latin versions of Ovid were abundant, French adaptations had already appeared by the fifteenth century, and new prose and verse translations were printed and reprinted between 1606 and 1628.[9] By giving agency and interiority to its young protagonists, by reconfiguring Ovid's plot to enable a same-sex marriage, by creating family dynamics that pit the imperatives of youth against the strictures of elders, and by resisting the metamorphosis to which it eventually but uneasily succumbs, *Iphis et Iante* already confronts the conflict between the desiring subject and the traditional order that Moretti is not alone in placing at modernity's crux. Reading *Iphis et Iante* through the lens of *Bildung* thus also raises questions about genre as well as temporality, asking us to consider the textual practices that might enable early modern stage performance to advance projects conventionally attached to the nineteenth-century novel.

The play's first departure from the Ovidian original is also the first sign of its investment in youth. This is not a union arranged by the patriarch – 'your father found you a bride' ('cum pater, Iphi, tibi flavam despondet Ianthen', 9: 54–5) – that both attracts and horrifies the original Iphis. The marriage in Benserade's version is propelled by Iphis herself; Iphis's father Ligde even argues that 'it is up to his young heart to love whoever pleases him' ('c'est à son jeune coeur d'aimer ce qui lui plaît'), and the parents' role is explicitly 'to love his preference' ('d'aimer son intérêt').[10] While Ovid's Telethusa prays, worries and delays the marriage, Benserade's Télétuze vehemently opposes it, chastising her daughter to 'think about what you are doing, restrain your passion [and] find a more appropriate object for your affections' ('Pense à ce que tu fais, règle ta passion, / Cherche un objet plus propre à ton affection', 44) and resists signing the marriage contract. And while Ovid's Iphis laments what Miller and Gould translate as her 'strange and monstrous' ('prodigiosa novaeque' 9: 727) desire, to the point of wishing herself dead for being the only creature of any species 'on fire' for another woman,[11] Benserade's Iphis embraces those endless fires ('feux . . . infinis', 44) and insists with queer logic that 'I am a girl, she is a girl and I must marry her' ('Je suis fille, elle est fille et je dois l'épouser', 74). Iphis's tenacity in following her sapphic desire is thus a rebuke to both the father from whom she has had to hide her sex and the mother who orchestrated the initial deception.[12] On their wedding night, Iphis will tell Iante that she has 'a heart that nature has made unlike others' ('un coeur que la nature a fait contraire aux autres', 92), an articulation of individuality that will echo through modernity – indeed arguably signify modernity – in the famous beginning of Jean-Jacques Rousseau's posthumously published *Confessions* (1782) and in the myriad reinscriptions of the Rousseauvian passage, including the one in Anne Lister's lesbian-encoded diaries.[13] Equally pertinent here is Rousseau's influence on Hegel's concept of the conflict between 'the law of the heart' and 'the way of the world', which Moretti takes up as a feature of the *Bildungsroman*, a conflict that generates the 'confinement' of certain values that are thereby only made 'more vehement'.[14]

If Ovid's Iphis despairs in her desire for Iante, Benserade's counterpart grieves her deception but not her passion or its pursuit. In two private scenes between the lovers, one before the marriage and one just after the couple has entered the bridal chamber, Iphis hints at an inadequacy that she fails to explain and wavers between disclosure and death wish. 'Let me die without speaking', she pleads, 'You are my spouse, and you will be my widow' ('permettez-moi de mourir sans parler . . . Vous êtes mon épouse, et vous serez ma veuve', 91). At the same time, she cannot bear 'dying of thirst' next to the 'fountain' of Iante's erotic charms ('meur de soif auprès d'une fontaine', 93). The uncomprehending Iante, bewildered and alarmed, can only plead for Iphis's confidence: 'I love you too much not to share / in the sad situation that is afflicting you' ('je vous aime trop, pour ne point partager / Au triste événement qui vous vient affliger', 94). The upshot of this impasse is that Iphis's sex gets revealed to Iante only in the unstaged gap between Acts IV and V and is then presented dramaturgically as fact: first in the voice of Iante, who is shocked at 'this deception' ('cette tromperie') unknown in the world ('Qui vit jamais au monde un prodige pareil?', 105), and then in parallel by Iphis, who laments that 'I've betrayed this beauty' ('J'ai trahi cette belle', 109).

Yet both Iphis in her despair and Iante in her confusion affirm the pleasures of the wedding night: Iphis 'sometimes forgot that I was a girl' ('J'oubliais quelque temps que j'étais une fille', 112) and describes in lyrically erotic language – to her still indignant mother – her ecstasy at touching Iante's 'beautiful body':

> I let myself yield to my raptures,
> With a kiss I soothed the fever of love,
> And my soul rose to the brim of my lips
> ...
> I embraced this beautiful body, whose extreme whiteness
> aroused me to make for her a space within myself,
> I touched, I kissed, my heart was satisfied.
>
> Je me laissais aller à mes ravissements,
> D'un baiser j'apaisais mon amoureuse fièvre,
> Et mon âme venait jusqu'au bord de mes lèvres,
> ...
> J'embrassais ce beau corps, dont la blancheur extrême
> M'excitait à lui faire une place en moi même,
> Je touchais, je baisais, j'avais le coeur content.
>
> (112–13)

Perhaps more surprisingly, Iante, even while grappling with the stunning wedding-night revelation and refusing stone-like to return Iphis's kisses, admits that the problem is not one of unsatisfied desire for the 'violent love ('amour violent', 92) of Iphis that she has already professed. In a moving soliloquy after the wedding night, Iante marks the gap between personal fulfilment and social norms: 'this marriage is sweet; it attracts me quite enough', she admits, and she could accept it if it were socially possible, would not upset their parents or, in a sweetly metatextual comment, would not be mocked on the stage:

> A girl, great gods! to marry another girl,
> That's enough to ... make them talk about us in the theatres.
> Such an encounter is worthy of being played on stage,
> ...
> This marriage is sweet, it attracts me quite enough
> And if no one would laugh, I wouldn't complain:
> I wouldn't be sorry that we were thus joined,
> If it did not profane the knot that binds us together,
> And our good parents didn't feel betrayed
> By this nuptial bond so holy and sacred to them;
> If a girl were to marry a girl like herself
> Without offending heaven and the natural law
> My heart would assuredly not be distressed.

Une fille, grands Dieux! en épouser une autre,
C'est bien pour . . . faire parler les théâtres de nous,
Une telle rencontre est digne qu'on la joue.

. . .

Ce mariage est doux, j'y trouve assez d'appâts
Et si l'on n'en riait, je ne m'en plaindrais pas:
Je n'aurais pas regret qu'on nous joignît ensemble,
Si l'on ne profanait le noeud qui nous assemble,
Et si nos bons parents n'abusaient à leur gré
De cet hymen qu'on tient si saint et si sacré;
Si la fille épousait une fille comme elle,
Sans offenser le ciel et la loi naturelle
Mon coeur assurément n'en serait point fâché.

(105)

Even as Iphis despairs that only her suicide can save Iante from a life of shame, she too recognises their problem as one of public relations; she would be happy enough to love Iante 'in the state I'm in' ('en l'état où je suis', 93) but feels pressed to call upon the universe to 'make her what people think she is' ('fais que je sois ce qu'on croit que je suis', 94). The pressure here is thus primarily external, and in this sense both Iphis's and Ianthe's reflections, like those Moretti attributes to the *Bildungsroman*, seek to create coherence between the intimate self and the social body. Yet one striking aspect of these musings is the absence of any concern for progeny: nowhere in their response to the revelation of Iphis's sex does either character worry about the reproductive imperative of marriage and the impossibility of their conceiving a child. The play's construction of conjugality thus sits firmly in the realm of socially sanctioned pleasure, an implicit rupture with the primacy of generation and its implications of continuity in favour of the satisfaction of personal desire. Even Ergaste does not use the argument for generative coupling in his bid for Iphis to choose him over Ianthe, other than to drop the comment that 'in making children, you'll make miracles' ('en faisant des enfants, vous ferez des miracles', 73).

Even after the marriage has been performed, Benserade's invented side-plot sustains a potential forking path that could turn the text away from a simple *dea ex machina* transformation toward heteronormative marriage. Since Iphis is textually marked simply as 'une fille en garçon' at a time when Europe's theatres are filled with such 'filles' (played in England by boys and on the continent by women), Ergaste speaks plausibly when he insists that 'clothes alone make the distinction between mistress and suitor' ('un habit seulement / Fait la distinction de maîtresse et d'amant', 55) and implies the ease with which Iphis could be his. Interestingly, it is Ergaste who first introduces the notion of metamorphosis into the play, in an apostrophic soliloquy to Iphis: 'my heart would like above all / That the heavens give you a metamorphosis / So that I could love you in a different way' ('Que le ciel fît en vous une métamorphose / Afin que je vous pusse aimer d'autre façon', 72). The metamorphosis he seeks, however, is not a change of sex but the change of sexual orientation; the problem is not that Iphis is a woman, but that 'she loves a girl more than a man' ('elle aime mieux une fille qu'un homme', 55).

As I have noted, however, a change in the direction of desire – the metamorphosis so common to early modern drama – is precisely the one that *Iphis et Iante* disavows in adhering to the Ovidian script that the play otherwise goes to such lengths to complicate. The rejection of the convenient male suitor, who would provide resolution in many a typical Renaissance play, thus reinforces the text's insistence on uniting two women according to their desire, a perversity further underscored when Ergaste, urged by Iphis's mother Télétuze to help prevent the marriage, tries to tell everyone that Iphis is really a girl in disguise and is met with ridicule for his queer and delusional longing for another boy; tellingly, it is to Ergaste alone that Benserade attaches the notion of desire that Ovid attributes to Iphis; as the yet unknowing Iante puts it, Ergaste 'burns for Iphis with a disordered flame' ('Il brûle pour Iphis d'un feu désordonné', 86).

Faithful to the Ovidian resolution, Benserade will bring the goddess to intervene, rescuing Iante from shame, Iphis from a noble suicide, and the parents from outrage and leaving Ergaste to settle for the second-best Mérinte. The quick resolution in the play's last scene gestures toward restoring a traditional order, what Moretti might recognise as a 'stable community', in which each youth 'faithfully repeats' the life pattern 'of his forebears'. But just as the *Bildungsroman* launches 'an uncertain exploration of social space',[15] *Iphis et Iante* has already cast doubt on conventional closure through its queering of the marriage plot. The hurried conversion of Iphis leaves a hefty remainder, lending weight to Ergaste's resistance to its validity: 'I don't believe any of it' ('Pour moi, je n'en crois rien', 122), he says immediately after Iphis proclaims herself metamorphosed. Both Ligde, the father, and Iante, the wife, react in grammatically conditional phrases – they will be pleased *if* the sex change has really happened, *if* the gods have obliged. Even the final sentence of the play, in which Iphis claims that he will prove his manhood in nine months ('prouvera dans neuf mois qu'Iphis est un garçon', 124), defers the validity of sex change and hangs without corroborating comment. When Iante's father Téleste proclaims in one of the play's final speeches that 'thus the Immortals change the order of things' ('ainsi les Immortels changent l'ordre des choses', 124), one might speculate that it is not only the gods who have changed the order of things but the young people who insist on following the uncharted paths of their desires.

Iphis's hasty, postmarital and as yet unverified transformation already suggests one of the strategies through which Benserade's play shifts the Ovidian focus from the single character to a preoccupation with 'youth as such'. By delaying the metamorphosis, Benserade puts the onus on the characters, and particularly on young characters, to figure out a resolution to the several impasses forged by crossed desires. But *Iphis et Iante* also uses other formal and thematic strategies to keep the play focused on youth as modernity's sign and struggle. Most obviously, Benserade multiplies his young characters. Ovid's version gives us only Iphis and Ianthe in a world of grown-ups, while in Benserade's revision, Iphis, Iante, Ergaste, Nise, Mérinte and Ergaste's unnamed sister populate the *dramatis personae* with twice as many youths as parents. The intersecting triangles formed by Ergaste's desire for Iphis, Iphis's for Iante and Mérinte's for Ergaste, complicated further by tensions between Ergaste and Nise, likewise tilt the text away from the single instance – the exceptional girl raised as a boy – toward a larger and more general focus on the struggles of youth as such.[16]

Iphis et Iante also gives verbal emphasis to generational difference, with the older people decrying the younger and the other way around. Nise speaks of 'the rights of youth', Iphis of 'young desires' and Mérinte of 'rebellious love'. Ergaste is especially vehement about the refusal of the two fathers to accept his word that Iphis is female – knowledge that Iphis's mother Télétuze has enjoined him to reveal – as if the adults have passed to the younger generation the burden of truth. Conversely, Télétuze's frustration with Iphis is generalised to youth as such; in an impassioned speech to her daughter in Act V, she admonishes:

> Today children think they're so wise
> That good advice offends their dignity,
> It's a strange case, that from a young age
> They want to shake off the yoke of their parents.
> In my day, nature was more settled,
> They knew better how to live as children unaware,
> But we weren't yet in this damnable century
> When virtues are no longer in favour.
>
> Aujourd'hui les enfants pensent être si sages,
> Qu'un salutaire avis offense leurs courages,
> C'est un étrange cas, que dès leurs jeunes ans
> Ils veulent secouer le joug de leurs parents.
> De mon temps, la nature était bien mieux réglée,
> On savait mieux conduire une enfance aveuglée,
> Aussi n'étions-nous pas en ce siècle maudit,
> Où toutes les vertus ne sont plus en crédit.
>
> (112)

And later in this scene she laments, 'My god! How little joy our children give us' ('Mon Dieu! Que les enfants nous donnent peu de joie', 114).

For Moretti, the representation of '"youthful" attributes of mobility and inner restlessness' that characterises the *Bildungsroman* is not only the sign but the consequence of new conditions.[17] He thus makes much of the novel's ability to represent interiority and thereby to articulate the struggles between autonomy and socialisation of *Bildungsroman* protagonists. The technologies of interiority are arguably more challenging for the stage than for the novel, but both the soliloquy and the private confidence provide conventional stage vehicles for articulating consciousness or exploring doubts. As Dorrit Cohn writes in *Transparent Minds*, although the stage soliloquy can certainly engage in 'self-conscious posing', its similarity to the modernist interior monologue bears recognition; the 'twin denominators common to all thought-quotations, regardless of their content and style', she notes, are 'the reference to the thinking self in the first person, and to the narrated moment (which is also the moment of locution) in the present tense'.[18] Underscoring 'the somewhat loose analogy that some critics have perceived between interiority in Shakespearean soliloquy and in novelistic free indirect discourse', Daniel Pollack-Pelzner reminds us that emergent *Bildungsromane* such as *Pride and Prejudice* also make blatant use of soliloquy; he recalls Elizabeth Bennet's famous 'moment of recognition' after reading Darcy's letter, rendered in a form ('How despicably I have acted!') that closely resembles the Shakespearean.[19]

Benserade makes substantial use of soliloquies in *Iphis et Iante*, almost always for purposes of self-revelation and self-questioning. Significantly, these soliloquies are distributed to all three of the young principals and none whatever is assigned to a character of the older generation, not even to Iphis's anguished mother Télétuze. Moreover, much of the play is taken up with confidences in which a single character bares his or her soul to another, the kind of conversation Moretti describes as necessary to 'the formation of the individual, once located within everyday life'.[20] Indeed, of the play's twenty-six scenes, only ten include more than two characters; another ten are intimate conversations usually between two young persons and another six scenes are soliloquys. Structurally speaking, then, these events already inscribe alienation and separation, both of individuals from individuals and youth from age. The soliloquies also provide the primary sites where conflicts between personal desire and social conformity are pondered. And if Moretti is onto something when he sees modern youth as 'perennially dissatisfied and restless', we see intimations of this restlessness likewise in Benserade's play. The tropes Moretti associates with 'youth as such' help to explain why Iphis is represented as miserable only after she gets the marriage she wants – and yet not only miserable, since she admits that she was at once 'never so sad and so enchanted' ('je ne fus jamais si triste et si ravie', 112). Ergaste is likewise set up for restless compromise in marrying his second choice; his agreement to wed Mérinte is expressed in passive and rather tepid terms: 'Since Love has changed the object of my concern, If Mérinte wants me, I want her too' ('Puisqu'Amour a changé l'objet de mon souci, / Si Mérinte me veut, je la veux bien aussi', 123). Ergaste's doubt that Iphis has had a sex change, and the lingering homeroticism of his desire, open the marital aftermath to the restlessness of his compromise. Such strategies shape Benserade's play toward ends that the Ovidian account does not consider, and the power of same-sex desire to propel a sharp opposition between the social and the personal is only incompletely resolved by the required metamorphosis.

Moretti makes much of capitalism as causality for modernity's focus on youth. His logic is that the 'new and destabilising forces' of both status and market forge fissures in conventional generational pathways especially for the 'class in the middle'.[21] Walter Cohen articulates a similar argument, however, for the early modern stage; in *Drama of a Nation: Public Theatre in Renaissance England and Spain*, Cohen attributes the 'remarkable features of kinship' between the 'theatrical institutions, dramatic genres, [and] individual plays' of Golden Age Spain and Elizabethan England – both of which, of course, are known for the ubiquity of metamorphic cross-dressing – to a 'concurrence of social and political forces, most notable among them the early growth of capitalism' in an absolutist state.[22] That same constellation, he notes, appears in France 'between about 1600 and 1625, roughly duplicat[ing] [the conditions] in Madrid and London a quarter of a century earlier'.[23] The destabilisation wrought by early French capitalism, in uneasy relationship to increased French absolutism, may well have encouraged the generational fissure in Benserade's reading of Ovid's tale. The seventeenth century is certainly also an age of conversion in the religious sense; we should not forget that the beloved Henri IV, a Hueguenot, legendarily decided that Paris was well worth a mass and became a Catholic to take the throne, nor that even the Catholic Richelieu, to whom Isaac Benserade is said to be related, made his alliances with the Protestants during the thirty years' war, nor that Benserade's father was almost certainly a Huguenot who turned the family Catholic in Isaac's youth. Jacques Schérer has described early seventeenth-century French theatre as a 'dazzling' world where a 'flowering of radically new works attests to the enthusiasm and the talent of young authors' and where 'the rules of propriety (*les bienséances*) did not yet exist'.[24] These factors suggest that *Iphis et Iante* inhabits a moment, and a context, in which some of the features Moretti associates with the nineteenth century are visible. At the same, it is worth being mindful of Margreta de Grazia's caution, in an essay brilliantly questioning the modernity of Hamlet's most famous soliloquy, that 'we resist the impulse to make the early modern look modern before its time; that we instead slow down and fan out its streamlined drive.'[25]

What, insights, then – about gender, genre and temporality – might reading *Iphis et Iante* through the lens of the *Bildungsroman* reasonably provide? I am not claiming that *Iphis et Iante* is a theatrical *Bildungsroman* nor that it engages the identical social and personal challenges of the later genre. But I do want to suggest that an insistence on the novel's novelty may obscure similar and shifting engagements across genres, whereby problems confronted in one literary kind at a particular historical time or place are taken up later, perhaps through different literary techniques. It is worth remembering Frances Ferguson's astute claim that 'free indirect style is the novel's one and only contribution to literature';[26] if so, then both the various technologies for representing inner struggle and the thematisation of youth may have no necessary connection to the novel or, arguably, to the nineteenth century.

Indeed, I would propose that the early modern stage serves as the repressed underside of Moretti's own study. *The Way of the World* opens with a reference to *Hamlet* that Moretti then works to dismiss: he reminds us that Hamlet is thirty years old, far from young by Renaissance standards, and that '*our* culture, in choosing Hamlet as its first symbolic hero, has "forgotten" his age, or rather has had to alter it, and picture the Prince of Denmark as a young man.'[27] Even more ironically, Moretti's title, *The Way of the World*, is not only a catchphrase, which Moretti evokes through Mephisto's speech in Goethe's *Faust* – 'Das ist der Lauf der Welt' – and thus links to the era of the *Bildungsroman* and to *Wilhelm Meister*; its original source is William Congreve's famous comedy of 1700, *The Way of the World*. That Congreve and his play go wholly unmentioned in Moretti's book strikes me as a kind of objective correlative for his leap to the historical originality of the *Bildungsroman*'s engagements with the interiority of restless and conflicted youth.

It may thus be useful to consider that *Iphis et Iante* is not the only early modern text that confronts the dynamic of 'youth as such' by means of same-sex desire. Cubillo de Aragón's lesbian-inflected play (*c.* 1635) *Añasco el de Talavera* offers its own version of generational turmoil and ends up giving its homodesiring protagonist Dionísia extraordinary power over her male suitors, over the female cousin she loves and, most tellingly, over her own father, in an upheaval of hierarchy tantamount to a dictatorship of daughterhood. Cubillo's play verges on tragedy; the critical balance between the self and the social comes at high cost to both. *Bildung* too can readily turn tragic, as it does in such novels as *Le Rouge et le noir*, *Illusions perdues*, *L'éducation sentimentale* and *Jude the Obscure* that demolish the potential for reconciling restless youth with the social order. In that light, we might consider the sharp emphasis on youth in *Romeo and Juliet* and the way in which this tragedy rests on a desire that departs insistently from the age-old Capulet–Montague hostility in favour of protagonists who are repeatedly characterised as young. H. Edward Cain has argued that *Romeo and Juliet* is ultimately a tragedy born of the 'inability of crabbed age and youth to understand each other'. He exposes the play's abundant references to young and old; to the parents' inability 'to plumb the depths of youthful minds'; conversely, to the lack of interest of the young protagonists 'in the quarrels of their elders'; and to the dying Mercutio's 'plague o' both [their] houses' as recognising the futility of 'permit[ing] old men's grudges to end young men's lives'.[28] It is plausible to consider *Romeo and Juliet* as another late sixteenth-century play preoccupied with 'youth as such', or what Will Stockton calls 'the fierce urgency of now'[29] and Carla Freccero as 'the driving negativity of teen spirit'. We can add an interesting layer to this preoccupation if we also consider the arguments advanced in recent decades for *Romeo and Juliet* as affirming queer desires.[30]

Yet with a directness not exceeded by any of Shakespeare's plays, *Iphis et Iante* shows us how sexuality can become not simply the product but the producer of history, bringing questions of nature, gender, desire and the ends of marriage into a contested space. It is feasible to read Benserade's play as a call for a different kind of metamorphosis with different agency. When Iphis is transformed, Iante's father pronounces that 'thus the Immortals change the order of things / They have certainly made metamorphoses before' ('Ainsi les Immortels changent l'ordre des choses / Ils ont bien fait jadis d'autres métamorphoses', 124). But arguably it is Iphis herself who has 'changed the order of things' through her persistence in fulfilling the homoerotic address of her desire. In *The Sexuality of History*, I argue that rather than seeing modernity as the instantiation of heterosexual difference as scholars have tended to do, we might understand modernity equally as the instantiation of the sapphic within a logic of possibility. *Iphis et Iante* makes that case, I argue, despite its last-minute capitulation to cross-sex marriage – a capitulation that also, of course, characterises the *Bildungsroman* in its comic mode.

We might wonder, then, what literary engagements could have ensued had Benserade's play – and other sapphic texts of this period – enjoyed a more robust afterlife. *Iphis et Iante* was published only once, in 1637; it is absent from the collected *Oeuvres* of Monsieur Benserade published in 1698 and, as far as I can tell, was never translated into another language. The only book-length study of Benserade's works, published in 1940 and focused on his *ballets de cour*, gives the play a scant two pages.[31] In this regard, *Iphis et Iante* continues an early modern pattern whereby sapphic representations fall into silence, with scant index of their reception – especially when something more than condemnation or prurience is at stake. Perhaps the literary story of modernity would have been different if texts like Benserade's had remained in circulation. Only in the twenty-first century has *Iphis et Iante* gained some modest visibility: there are now two paperback editions and the *Comédie française* performed the play in 2013. At that time, *Les Echos* called it a 'forgotten classic', an 'astonishing' play about 'mariage pour tous' – marriage for all – in the seventeenth century. In this sense, Benserade's play begins to intimate something more radical than the compromise effected by the *Bildungsroman*: the necessity that conversion be relocated from the deviant individual to society itself.[32] Although *Iphis et Iante* did not have an immediate afterlife to which modern scholars are privy, reading the *Bildungsroman* through Benserade's play suggests that the struggles of 'youth as such' with the ways of the world may have been queerer than Moretti imagines.

Benserade himself never quite let go of his engagement with sapphic subjects. Iphis reappears four decades later in his *Metamorphoses d'Ovide en rondeaux* (1676), an illustrated volume of verses commenting on popular Ovidian figures. In his entry on Iphis, Benserade proclaims that a disastrous ménage would have ensued had Iphis remained a girl: 'A boy was created from a maiden / And without this stroke which quelled the storm / You'd have seen a very bad household' ('D'une Pucelle en firent un garçon; / Et sans ce coup qui termina l'orage, / On alloit voir un fort mauvais ménage').[33] In contrast to the 1634 play, the Iphis of this later poem is motivated by social fear rather than personal desire: because Iante was 'renowned', Iphis 'did not dare' say no to the match; both the erotic attraction between the couple and Iphis's agency in pressing for the marriage are here denied. And in his long (forty-quatrain) posthumously published poem 'Sur l'amour d'Uranie avec Philis', a cross between a diatribe and a lament, the poet could be speaking through the voice of an Ergaste, complaining to the 'faithless Uranie' that she prefers a woman to himself and confounded that the 'strange' love between the two women, a 'folle idée', has 'so long endured' (avait tant duré)'. Uranie, he proclaims, should prefer himself to the 'beautiful, adorable, charming' Philis simply because he is a man and he loves her. Not only doesn't he allow the female couple erotic pleasure, he denigrates their kisses as 'timid', like those of mother to son; conversely, he shames Uranie for failing to do what Iphis did for Iante's sake – 'devenir garçon' ('become boy') – here using the story of Iphis as evidence that a woman cannot confer the 'solid pleasures' of a man. The poem bluntly designates women as nothing in themselves, worthless without men: 'you are mere parts / you are nothing at all ... you are but shadows / Without strength and without power. / You are zeros, and we are the numbers / that give you worth' ('Vous n'estes que parties, / Vous n'estes rien du tout. ... vous n'estes que des ombres / Sans force et sans pouvoir. / Vous estes les zéros, et nous sommes les nombres / Qui vous faison valoir').[34]

Among highly recognised seventeenth-century French writers, Benserade was an exceptional man of no rank, and as I noted earlier, his father probably converted the family to Catholicism in Isaac's youth but without changing his son's Protestant first name. The nineteenth-century scholar Paul de Musset commented that 'No one ever saw someone raise himself with so little tax', and that he was 'almost the only man of low origin who would have walked beside the great members of Louis XIV's court'.[35] With Morettian logic, we might see

Benserade's own life as a movement from restless youth to ensconced insider and infer that, at least where primary female–female alliances are concerned, this older Benserade has lost the rebellious questioning of his younger self and capitulated to the status quo. We can be grateful, then, for the slice of time in which a young playwright glimpsed the possibility of changing the ways of the world.

NOTES

1. Moretti, *The Way of the World*, pp. 5, 227 (emphasis in original).
2. Ibid., pp. 227–8, 4–6.
3. I thank David Halperin for suggesting 'thought experiment' in response to the first version of this piece, presented at the University of Michigan in 2016.
4. See Lanser, *The Sexuality of History*, pp. 79–83.
5. Moretti makes this observation in the 2000 preface (p. vii) to the re-edition of his 1987 book.
6. Latour, *We Have Never Been Modern*, p. 10 (my emphasis).
7. Latour, *Reset Modernity!*, pp. 1–3.
8. Harris, 'Disruptive Desires', p. 156. I share with Harris a positive reading of the sapphic in this play. I thus also disagree with Marianne Legault ('*Iphis et Iante*'), who reads the play as a much more negative intervention.
9. Translations of the *Metamorphoses* were published in France in 1539; versions were published respectively in 1539 (*Les XV livres de la Metamorphose D'ovide*), in 1597 (*Olympe, ou Metamorphose d'Ovide*), in 1603 (Raymond et Charles de Massac, *Les métamorphoses d'Ovide, mises en vers françois*), and in 1606 (Nicolas Renouard's *Les Métamorphoses d'Ovide traduites en prose françois*). Renouard's version, the most popular, was reprinted in 1614, 1617, 1619 and 1628; the Massac translation was also reissued in 1617. For a fuller discussion of Ovid's place in the period, see Taylor, *The Lives of Ovid in Seventeenth-Century French Culture*. Rather surprisingly, though, Taylor barely notices any of Benserade's multiple engagements with Ovid and does not even mention his *Iphis et Iante*.
10. Benserade, *Iphis et Iante: Comédie* (1637), ed. Verdier, p. 39. Further references will be to the Verdier edition and will appear in the body of the text. Translations are my own and do not attempt to replicate the alexandrine couplets that constitute the verse form of the original. The gender mixing that I enact in this discussion, in which I speak of Iphis as female but translate Ligde's references to Iphis through male pronouns, reminds us of the 'transversion' in which the text itself is engaged.
11. Given my argument here about the sapphic and the modern, it may not be irrelevant that Ovid describes Iphis's desire not only as monstrous or freakish but as *nova* – i.e. new.
12. In another emphasis on the modern, Ligde even tells Télétuze that her opposition to the marriage is no longer 'à la mode' (p. 39).
13. Rousseau begins his *Confessions* with the assertion that 'je sens mon coeur, et je connais les hommes. Je ne suis fait comme aucun de ceux que j'ai vus; j'ose croire n'être fait comme aucun de ceux qui existent' ('I know my own heart, and I know men. I am not made like anyone that I have seen, I daresay not like anyone in existence'). Anne Lister will quote this passage in her diary entry of 20 August 1823; see *I Know My Own Heart*, p. 283.
14. Moretti, *Way of the World*, p. 85.
15. Ibid., p. 4.
16. It is worth comparing Benserade's *Iphis et Iante* to an immediate predecessor,

Henry Bellamy's Latin play *Iphis*, a college production probably written in the 1620s and extant only in presentation manuscript. Like Benserade, Bellamy creates the kind of love triangle popular in Renaissance theatre by adding a young Nisus who is in love with Ianthe, who spurns him for an effeminate Iphis. It is thus Nisus, not Iphis or Ianthe, who takes the primary part of unhappy youth. But it would be a stretch to see Bellamy's as a play focused on generational struggle: the contest between Lygdus and Telethusa over Lygdus's decision to kill a girl child and the concealed sex of the baby Iphis together occupy the entirety of the first two acts; Telethusa supports and Téleste cheerfully entertains Nisus's wish to wed Ianthe; and as the love triangle and sex change unfold, Iphis and Ianthe have astonishingly small roles as speaking voices: in a play of over 1,150 Latin lines, Iphis's and Ianthe's parts together comprise barely 100 lines. It is striking that both Bellamy and Benserade create a character named Nisus (perhaps after Virgil's hero, passionately attached to Euryalus), though Bellamy's Nisus and Benserade's Nise differ in both character and plot; it is not impossible, though quite improbable that Benserade knew about Bellamy's play.
17. Moretti, *Way of the World*, p. 5.
18. Cohn, *Transparent Minds*, p. 13.
19. Daniel Pollack-Pelzner, 'Jane Austen, the Prose Shakespeare', p. 771. The quotation from *Pride and Prejudice* appears in Chapter 36 of Austen's novel.
20. Moretti, *Way of the World*, p. 49.
21. Ibid., p. 5.
22. Cohen, *Drama of a Nation*, p. 311.
23. Ibid., p. 105.
24. Jacques Schérer, *Théâtre du XVIIe siècle*, vol. I, pp. xxiv, xix, translation mine.
25. De Grazia, 'Soliloquies and Wages in the Age of Emergent Consciousness', pp. 86–7.
26. Ferguson, 'Jane Austen, *Emma*, and the Impact of Form', p. 159.
27. Moretti, *Way of the World*, p. 3.
28. Cain, 'Crabbed Age and Youth in *Romeo and Juliet*', pp. 187–90 *passim*.
29. See Stockton, 'The Fierce Urgency of Now', both for Stockton's own arguments and for his iteration of diverse grounds for 'queering' *Romeo and Juliet*.
30. Freccero, 'Romeo and Juliet Love Death', p. 302.
31. See Silin, *Benserade and his Ballets de Cour*, pp. 29–31. Of the sexual tone of the play, Silin writes, 'Sometimes the pleasantries border on the obscene, but on the whole, though the subject might have suggested a coarse treatment of the homosexual possibilities, the comic element is remarkably clean and the jokes are innocuous' (p. 31).
32. I'm led to recall Nancy Armstrong's well known and controversial claim that the novel shows 'the modern individual' to be 'first and foremost a woman'. As I have written elsewhere (see Lanser, 'The Novel Body Politic'), the 'individualism' accorded to women seems to me much more circumscribed than Armstrong acknowledges. It is not accidental that despite his own inclusion of *Pride and Prejudice* and *Jane Eyre* in *The Way of the World*, Moretti considers the *Bildungsroman* a masculine genre. Writing for the second edition, he ruminates that 'wide cultural formation, professional mobility, full social freedom – for a long time, the west European middle-class man held a virtual monopoly on these, which made him a sort of structural *sine qua non* of the genre' (p. ix). If we were to bring Moretti and Armstrong together, though, we could be conjuring a rather queer modern individual, perhaps an Iphis who entertains rebellion without conversion in the name of desire and who thus also stands against the necessity of the patriarchal subject.

33. Benserade, *Metamorphoses en rondeaux*, p. 319.
34. Benserade, 'Sur l'Amour d'Uranie avec Phillis: Stances', pp. 165–73.
35. Musset, *Extravagants et originaux du XVIIe siècle*, p. 342, translation mine.

BIBLIOGRAPHY

Bellamy, Henry, *Iphis: Text, Translation, Notes*, eds Jay M. Freyman, William E. Mahaney and Walter K. Sherwin (Salzburg: Institut für Anglistik und Amerikanistik, 1986).
Benserade, Isaac de, *Iphis et Iante: comédie* [1637], ed. Anne Verdier (Vijon: Editions Lampasque, 2000).
Benserade, Isaac de, *Metamorphoses en rondeaux* (Paris: Imprimerie Royale, 1676).
Benserade, Isaac de, *Les oeuvres de Monsieur de Bensserade, première partie* (Paris: Charles de Sercy, 1698).
Benserade, Isaac de, *Poésies de Benserade*, ed. Octave Uzanne (Paris: Librairie des bibliophiles, 1875).
Cain, H. Edward, 'Crabbed Age and Youth in *Romeo and Juliet*', *Shakespeare Association Bulletin* 9: 4, 1934, pp. 186–91.
Cohen, Walter, *Drama of a Nation: Public Theater in Renaissance England and Spain* (Ithaca, NY: Cornell University Press, 1985).
Cohn, Dorrit, *Transparent Minds: Narrative Modes for Presenting Consciousness in Fiction* (Princeton: Princeton University Press, 1978).
Cubillo de Aragón, Álvaro, *Añasco el de Talavera: Comedia famosa* (Madrid, n.d.).
De Grazia, Margreta, 'Soliloquies and Wages in the Age of Emergent Consciousness', *Textual Practice* 9: 1, 1995, pp. 67–92.
Ferguson, Frances, 'Jane Austen, *Emma*, and the Impact of Form', *Modern Language Quarterly* 61, 2000, pp. 157–80.
Freccero, Carla, 'Romeo and Juliet Love Death', in Madhavi Menon (ed.), *Shakesqueer: A Queer Companion to the Complete Works of Shakespeare* (Durham, NC: Duke University Press, 2011), pp. 302–7.
Harris, Joseph, 'Disruptive Desires: Lesbian Sexuality in Isaac De Benserade's *Iphis et Iante* [1634]', *Seventeenth Century French Studies*, 24, 2002, pp. 151–63.
Lanser, Susan S., 'The Novel Body Politic', in Paula Backscheider and Catherine Ingrassia (eds), *The Eighteenth-Century Novel: Companion to Literature and Culture* (Oxford: Blackwell, 2005), pp. 481–503.
Lanser, Susan S., *The Sexuality of History: Modernity and the Sapphic, 1565–1830* (Chicago: University of Chicago Press, 2014).
Latour, Bruno, ed., *Reset Modernity!* (Cambridge, MA: MIT Press, 2016).
Latour, Bruno, *We Have Never Been Modern*, trans. Catherine Porter (Cambridge, MA: Harvard University Press, 1993).
Legault, Marianne, '*Iphis et Iante:* Traumatisme de l'incomplétude lesbienne au Grand Siècle', *Dalhousie French Studies* 81, 2007, pp. 83–93.
Lister, Anne, *I Know My Own Heart: The Diaries of Anne Lister 1791–1840*, ed. Helena Whitbread (London: Virago, 1988).
Moretti, Franco, *The Way of the World: The Bildungsroman in European Culture* (London: Verso, 1987; reprinted 2000).
Musset, Paul de, *Extravagants et originaux du XVIIe siècle* (Paris: Charpentier, 1873).
Ovid, *Metamorphoses, English and Latin*, trans. Frank Justus Miller (Cambridge, MA: Harvard University Press, 1977).
Pollack-Pelzner, Daniel, 'Jane Austen, the Prose Shakespeare', *SEL: Studies in English Literature* 53: 4, 2013, pp. 763–92.
Rousseau, Jean-Jacques, *Confessions* (Paris: Cazin, 1782).

Schérer, Jacques, *Théâtre du XVIIe siècle* (Paris: Gallimard, 1975).
Silin, Charles I., *Benserade and His Ballets de Cour* (Baltimore: Johns Hopkins, 1940).
Stockton, Will, 'The Fierce Urgency of Now: Queer Theory, Presentism, and *Romeo and Juliet*', in Valerie Traub (ed.), *The Oxford Handbook of Shakespeare and Embodiment* (Oxford: Oxford University Press, 2016), pp. 287–301.
Taylor, Helena, *The Lives of Ovid in Seventeenth-Century French Culture* (Oxford: Oxford University Press, 2017).

APPENDICES: TRANSLATIONS AND IMAGES OF 'IPHIS AND IANTHE'

Appendix A: 'Iphis and Ianthe' in the *Ovide moralisé* 9: 2763–3398
Translated by Miranda Griffin, Blake Gutt and Peggy McCracken

In Crete, there was great talk of the transformation of Biblis into a fountain, and there would have been yet more, had it not been for another marvel which happened there. News of this other marvel spread far and wide: it concerned Iphis, a maiden who was transformed into a young man. This surpassed the fame of the fountain of which I speak. In those days, between Phaestia and Crete lived a baron who was both rich and noble. I think his name was Ligdus – he was known by many people, but his name was little known. He was a valiant, loyal man, with no spot of villainy or pride. He had a pregnant wife. When she was close to delivering her child, he left his land, but first he bade his wife farewell. As he left, he said to her, 'Lady, I ask two things: one, that you be delivered easily and without great pain; the other, that you have a male heir, for there is too much trouble in a woman – I know of no heavier burden. Women lack strength and valour, and many men have come to grief because of women. That is why I pray to God that you do not have a daughter, which would grieve me. But if you do have a daughter after all, make sure that I don't see her. Have her killed straightaway. I'm very sorry to have to say this'. [2763–98]

At these words, both Ligdus and the lady wept copiously. Telethusa quickly sought to persuade her husband, and begged him to put her mind at ease. But her efforts were in vain. He would not turn away from his desire to be rid of a daughter, and this disturbed her greatly. When she had carried her pregnancy to term and it was nearly time for her to give birth, she reflected on the harsh sentence that Ligdus had given her when he dictated that her child should be killed if she were female. The noble lady was compassionate and she was very afraid. One night, while sleeping, Telethusa had a vision of the goddess Isis and her retinue standing by her bedside. It seemed to her that the goddess had a garland of golden wheat on her head, and two crescent horns on her forehead. She wore a crown and held a sceptre and she had the bearing of a queen. Anubis, who bays and howls like a dog, was in her retinue. With her was the holy priestess Bubastis, who sang the mass and made sacrifices, as well as multi-coloured Apis and the cantor, who signalled for silence and began the hymn – all the others responded, instruments resounded. Also in this company were Osiris who never answers prayers and the serpent from a foreign land that brings sleeping oblivion. [2799–838]

Telethusa awoke and saw Isis with this retinue. The goddess addressed her very gently: 'Telethusa, fair, good sister, leave your worries and cares and do not be dismayed, I beg you. Do not obey the commandment of your lord but, whether you have a boy or a girl, let it live without fear. Ignore the father's judgment and nurture the child as a good mother should. I am a caring, merciful and compassionate goddess. You have called on me, as you should. We will ensure that my help is valuable to you: you will have succour from me.' [2839–55]

Isis left the bedchamber. Joyfully, Telethusa rose and piously lifted her hands and face to the heavens and prayed to God that her vision be true. Unbeknownst to the father, at the end of her pregnancy the lady had a daughter. She pretended that she had a son and sent the baby to a wet nurse. Ligdus believed her, never suspecting any deception. No one else in the world knew the secret, except the woman who suckled the girl. Her father, who had been hoping for a male heir, was overjoyed. He used his wealth to make offerings and gifts to the gods, as he had promised. He named his child after her grandfather. The girl's grandfather, did I say? He was called Iphis and she was called Iphis (but Ligdus thought she was a 'he'). The mother rejoiced since the name was suitable for both male and female. She was pleased that her daughter had this name, which could be given to a woman, since it meant that she could truly speak her name without revealing the deception. Thus the lie is hidden. [2856–85]

The girl wore boy's clothes, which suited her very well. Her face was such that whoever saw her would say that she could be either a girl or a boy. She was beautiful; he was handsome. The fair maid was thirteen when Ligdus, whom I mentioned earlier, arranged her marriage and promised her a wife, the most beautiful in the land. Her name was Ianthe, and she was born in Phaestia. Her father was called Telestes: he was an Athenian of great renown. Iphis and Ianthe were equal in age and beauty; they had the same upbringing and they had the same temperament. This was the reason for their attachment, and they loved each other equally, but they had different hopes and expectations for the marriage which was to come. [2886-907]

Ianthe, the daughter of Telestes, loved Iphis, and truly believed that he was the man she should have and do with as a wife does with a husband. Iphis returned her love, but she despaired and did not think that she could ever take pleasure with her beloved, nor that they could be united. This intensified and redoubled the love which inflamed the maiden Iphis for fair Ianthe. Iphis often lamented and moaned, weeping softly. 'Alas!' she said, 'What shall I do, what is the best way to proceed? What will become of me? Who has ever seen anyone put her intention and hope in such a foolish desire? I am not worthy of such love. Had the gods been kind to me, they would have kept me from this folly; had they wanted to destroy me with the insanity of love, why couldn't I have directed my desires towards a more fitting beloved? What cow seeks another cow; what mare approaches another mare? Ewes desire rams, and the cow's affection is for the bull. Thus each female seeks a male of her own kind. No female would ever plan or wish to be joined to another female in a lustful manner. But that's exactly what I want, so unwisely! I wish I'd never been born to have such foolish hope.' [2908-45]

'All misfortune comes from Crete. Pasiphae was born in Crete: her heart was inflamed with love for the bull, but – alas! – my love surpasses hers in its folly and insanity. That which I call love I should call madness! I'm so insane that even Pasiphae loved more in accordance with her own kind than I do. As I understand it, she loved the bull, joining a female to a male. She cunningly deceived him with fraud and ingenuity, but nothing can make two women a fitting pair. My desire can't be fulfilled; I can't become a man, nor can she who awaits me. Unhappy Iphis, where does your heart lead, when it embraces such love? It inflames and binds you and there is no way that you can bring your desire to fulfilment. No one can advise you how to do this! You must take care and be vigilant to rid yourself of this madness and passion! Don't deceive yourself, you madwoman! Pay attention to what you were born for. Be reasonable, and seek what is appropriate and suitable for you to have. Forget this love, which plunges you into foolish hope. It harms you and holds you back, for you are not, by nature, worthy to be joined to such a creature. Your sex destroys your hope.' [2946-83]

'I can confidently come and go as I please with Ianthe since there is nothing to stop me from being with her – no forbidding father or strict nurse. I fear no obstacle, not even a jealous husband. I can embrace her whenever I wish. She herself, just like any beloved, wishes for this and doesn't refuse me; and yet I cannot act on it. I can go no further than dalliance, for nothing can help me realise my foolish thoughts. I can't bring my hope to a successful climax. The gods are good to me since it pleases them to give me most of what I desire. My father and lord, as well as my beloved, do not disapprove of what I want: as far as I can tell, the only one who disapproves is Nature, who opposes us all. She vetoes everything that we desire and is much more powerful than all of us put together.' [2984–3006]

'The longed-for marriage day draws near, and fair Ianthe will be mine. But what good is this joy to me? Surrounded by water, we will die of thirst. For I will not be able to do with her what a husband should do with a wife. Hymen and Juno, what business would you have at our nuptials? Whoever heard of a marriage without a husband? We will both be married and yet both without husbands!' [3007–18]

Fair Iphis lamented and languished in this way, and the other maiden was no less assailed by love. She railed against time, which dallied and moved too slowly, and she thought that she would never see the hour of her marriage arrive. Ianthe prayed that the marriage day would come quickly, but Iphis' mother invented obstacles and hindrances, and sought problems and postponements to delay the wedding. For example, she claimed to the families that Iphis had been suddenly taken ill and he couldn't face the celebrations or demands of a wedding. In this way, she deceived them and unstintingly delayed as long as she could. [3019–36]

When she could no longer delay, the marriage could not be avoided, and with only one day remaining until the wedding, Telethusa and her daughter, their hair unfastened, went to the temple of Isis. Devoutly, Telethusa kissed the altar. She humbly called on the goddess, praying, 'Isis, with fear and terror, this humble, sorrowing sinner calls upon you. Isis, it was you who pleaded for my daughter's life when I saw your signs. I saw your beautiful retinue; I saw their burning torches and heard their resounding instruments. I saw the sceptre you held when you came to comfort me and commanded that I should not kill my daughter, but nurture her instead. I know what you said to me then, and I know well that you promised me your help and succour without fail. Now is our hour of need. Help us, I beg you! Following your counsel, my daughter has lived in hope until now. Now I beg you that you proceed straightaway and without delay to save her and care for her. For I cannot keep the secret any longer if you will not intervene.' Telethusa wept piteously as she spoke. It seemed to her that Isis, as a sign of consolation, appeared to her in the same semblance, the same manner and the same vestments as she had seen all those years before. She had two crescent horns on her forehead. The instruments resounded and Telethusa saw the temple doors and altar tremble. [3037–3079]

Telethusa left the church, happy with the sign she saw. Iphis, her daughter, followed her, with a longer stride than she used to take. Her face became less white than it had been; her strength and boldness grew; her hair became shorter. Her body, which used to be slender, became much more vigorous than before, more vigorous than a woman's would be. Her stature and being, and her feminine nature had completely changed and become masculine. Iphis the daughter had become a son – this was certain and sure! It was the clear truth, without a word of a lie! Telethusa made generous offerings, gifts and sacrifices at the temples. Everyone, high and low, knew that Iphis the daughter had become a son. [3080–103]

When the next day dawned, the boy Iphis left to take Ianthe as his wife. There was great joy, and everyone sang. All the gods of marriage – Hymenaeus, Juno and Venus – attended joyfully, as they should. Nothing and no one was missing from the festivities. Iphis was happy and full of joy. He took Ianthe as his own. [3104–12]

Now I wish to tell you the historical explanation of this fable, which could be true according to a historical reading. It could be – and indeed it was the case without doubt – that long ago a woman seemed to be a man in her clothing and behaviour. Everyone who saw her in this clothing believed her to be a man, and her mother encouraged this belief, testifying to its truth. There may have been some maiden who saw her looking noble, attractive and fine in her men's clothing, and truly believed that she was a man. She hungered to have her in love and marriage. That other foolish and silly woman agreed to take her as wife, even though she had nothing like a penis or any other member to serve this purpose. Nevertheless she desired, against all that is right and natural, to fulfil her affection and lust in a carnal way, despite this impediment about which the other, her beloved wife and true lover, knew nothing. [3113–38]

This one, who was attempting such foolish love, lamented and languished until, through the cunning art and advice of a witch (a hideous old crone), she fulfilled her evil desire. She married the woman whom the laws of marriage forbade her from having. In order to fulfil her duty to her wife, she deceived her with a false member. When the maiden realised what was happening, the trick could no longer be concealed, but was fully revealed: everyone talked about it, and the woman was thoroughly shamed, as she so richly deserved. May no one desire to undertake such an act, for it is most damnable and vile. [3139–57]

It seems to me that I could give this tale a better meaning, through allegory, and gloss the text differently: this is the preferred meaning. The renown should be great – and indeed it was – of Sovereign Wisdom, when, especially for mankind, He deigned to humble Himself, joining with mankind in love. He is the living, true fountain, the source of all goodness, the fountain which brings the dead back to life. He replenished the earth when He descended from heaven to seek and take on our humanity. He suffered much pain for our sins, and for us He was hung on the cross and His blood spilled to bring us from death into life. God showed us great generosity, and we should give Him great thanks, when He was willing to spill His blood for us and redeem us all, the dead and the living. But it seems to me that God, the Heavenly Father, gave us an even greater gift – greater than any other – when, out of grace and pity, He desired, through worthy love, to give heavenly joy to the sinful soul and make her dwell in glorious eternity. [3158–89]

Now I shall tell you the truth that I understand in the allegory of the tale you have just heard. Ligdus, the spiritual father, is God, loyal and true. He had a wise wife, Telethusa: this is Holy Church, whom God filled abundantly with new life. God, the spiritual father, the loyal, true judge, gave a harsh, strict verdict against feminine nature – that is, against the sinful soul, who sins and does not cease from sinning. She sought worldly pleasures: flirtations, riches, dalliances, mockery, frivolity and extravagance. She was so weak and careless, so lazy and wretched that she could not undertake to do any good at all, nor withstand any bad; and she did not care to mend her ways. God therefore condemned her to die. God condemned her to eternal mortal damnation. But Holy Church, our mother, judged this sentence to be too harsh: it condemned her daughter to martyrdom. Her daughter is the soul, which was regenerated in the font of baptism, born from the body of the Church, and submitted to her authority. [3190–223]

When she contravened the vow that she had made at her baptism, the idle soul dedicated her heart to folly, vanity and empty pleasures. She gave herself over to mortal sin, and then the soul was condemned to death by the verdict of God the Father. Nevertheless, our good Mother nurtured her in the pious hope that she would gain true penitence, which should lend her aid and succour and revise the verdict. Divine Mercy, espoused by God the Father, is our compassionate Mother. She does not lightly suffer that those who are the sons of God, predestined to attain the kingdom of great spiritual joy, should be condemned to everlasting death as soon as they commit a mortal sin. Instead she endures and bides her time patiently, waiting to be vindicated by them. In order to bring them to repentance, she provides them with time and space, and showers them with her grace. She awakens them from the shadows of malice, where they foolishly slept, and illuminates them with her divine splendour, so that they might perceive their bad deeds, offences and foolish errors, and come to true repentance and correct confession. [3224–59]

Isis and her retinue can denote true repentance, confession and penitence, which is accorded to the sinful soul by Divine Mercy, so that she can live in good hope, avoiding the harsh sentence the righteous judge pronounces on the soul which gives itself over to sin. This is the queen, the lady, who saves and redeems the sinful soul from eternal death so that she can gain glory in her court. The sinful, guilty soul abandons sin for fear of eternal damnation. Confession wears on her head a hat or a crown made of golden wheat, which constantly pricks and needles the soul to repent for the errors and grievous crimes she has committed. In her repentance, she is forced to lament and complain bitterly to purge all the vileness of her disgusting corruption. Without further dishonouring or besmirching herself, and without undertaking further sin, the soul must pierce her conscience with sharp repentance. [3260–88]

In addition, I believe that Confession must have two glowing horns on her forehead: one illuminates all the sins the soul used to commit so that she may recognise and acknowledge them; the other lights the correct path that the soul should take so that she can attain and savour heavenly joy. In her right hand, she carries a chastising staff, for it is right that the soul should submit after making her confession and abandoning folly for penitence and the avoidance of the sins that she used to commit. The soul should sacrifice herself to atone for her malice. Like a guard dog constantly on the alert, the soul should always be vigilant, on guard lest the devil take her unawares and cause her to fall back into sin. The soul should also ensure that the devil, who is always watching and spying on her, does not corrupt her with fraud and deception. She should bay against the devil through pious prayer, to chase away the rapacious wolf. This wolf can be chased away through prayer. The soul should also paint and colour herself with good and charitable works, and sing to our Lord devout hymns of praise, celebrating honour. To avoid vainglory, which captivates many fools, she should carry out her penitence, pray and be abstinent in private, keeping her right hand closed so that the left hand does not know about it. [3289–330]

Whoever does this can be certain that God will not remember the evil or felony that he has committed throughout his life. Instead, He will certainly commute the sentence given to those on the left, which the soul feared. He will give him heavenly glory, joyful immortality and eternal rejoicing, if evil does not claim him; but he cannot hope for these before he atones for the sins of his wretched life. [3331–44]

When the soul, with great contrition, comes to confession to purge and erase her sins, and she enters into the state of grace and embarks on the path to salvation, she often elevates herself to a higher way of thinking through contemplation and redirects her understanding towards the great joy of glorious eternity. It seems to the soul that she attains this joy and that she possesses it, or that she should have it. She delights in the memory and in the sweet pleasurable thought of this spiritual joy that she contemplates and considers. Then she reconsiders and examines her conscience, remembering the folly, the vanity, the sins and the offences that she committed, and she pronounces herself weak, vile and unworthy of paradise. There is so much folly in her that in all of her life she could never atone for the sins that she has committed. How can she, so sinful and so guilty, be worthy of this great eternal joy which she has lost through ignorance? She will never deserve the great pleasure for which she longs, unless God extends His pity to her; but she knows that she can never serve God enough to deserve such good. Then she weeps and laments and humbles herself, repenting of her foolishness, seized by fear and trembling. This intensifies and redoubles her love, for joy which seems a little hopeless is desired all the more. And the more the soul is fearful, the more she is ardent and desiring because she hasn't completely abandoned hope. So she suffers, works, undergoes fasts and privations, afflictions and penitence, and prays for divine grace, that she should be given time and space to live in an altered state. When God sees the soul's repentance, her good works and her good intentions, He wishes to give her sweet repose. [3345–98]

Appendix B: 'Iphis and Iante' in John Gower's *Confessio Amantis*, IV.451–515
Translated by Karma Lochrie

451   During a quarrel Ligdus the king
       Spoke to Thelacuse his wife,
       Who was at that time great with child;
       He swore it would not be prevented
455   That if she should bear a daughter,
       It should be immediately destroyed
       And slain, for which the queen was sorrowful.
       So it came to pass by chance,
       When she was about to give birth,
460   Isis, the goddess of childbirth,
       By night in a secret visit

APPENDIX B

      Came to aid Thelacuse's distress,
      Until that lady was normal-sized again,
      And had soon given birth to a daughter.
465 Which child the goddess bade her by all means
      That she keep, and that they should say
      It was a son; and thus Iphis
      They named him, and in this way
      The father was made to believe [Iphis was a boy].
470 And thus in the chamber with the queen,
      This Iphis was afterwards withdrawn,
      And clothed and arrayed in such a manner
      Just as a king's son should be dressed.
      Afterwards, as fortune would have it,
475 When it [Iphis] was ten years of age,
      He was betrothed in marriage
      To wed a duke's daughter,
      Who was called Iante, and often abed
      These children lay, she and she,
480 Who were equal in age.
      So that within a period of years,
      Together as they were playmates,
      Lying abed one night,
      Nature, which causes every person
485 Upon her law to wonder,
      Compels them, so that they use
      Thing [things] that was to them entirely unknown;
      At which moment Cupid immediately
      Took pity on their great love,
490 And caused [love] to be set above nature [*kinde*],
      So that her law may be observed,
      And they, for their passion, excused.
      For love hates nothing more
      Than things which stand against the teaching
495 Of what nature [*nature*] naturally [*in kinde*] has established.
      Therefore Cupid has so invested
      His grace upon this situation,
      That he in accordance with nature,
      When he saw the best moment,
500 As they each had kissed one another,
      Transforms Iphis into a man,
      From which moment he [Iphis] won the natural [*kinde*] love
      Of his passionate young wife Iante.

And afterwards they led a happy life,
505 Which was no offence to nature [*kinde*].
Genius:
'And thus to draw an example from this,
It seems love is benevolent
To those who are persevering
With diligent heart to pursue
510 The thing that is to love due.
Wherefore, my son, in this matter
You might take example of this,
That through your great diligence
You might attain the rewards
515 Of love, as long as there is no Sloth.'

APPENDIX C: 'IPHIS AND IANTHE' IN CHRISTINE DE PIZAN'S *LA MUTACION DE FORTUNE*, LL. 1094–1158
TRANSLATED BY MIRANDA GRIFFIN

Ovid also tells us about a king of Lydia,[1] who hated women so much that he ordered his wife, the queen, who was pregnant and preparing to give birth, that, if she had a daughter, she should have her burned or killed in secret, on pain of death – for he did not wish to have a daughter. But, if the child were a son, she should protect him and ensure that no harm came to him.

The queen gave birth to a daughter, but she certainly did not give her up for a cruel or bitter death: her maternal nature prevented her from doing so. Instead, she brought her up as her son, and made sure that the news spread that she had given birth to a fine son; the king believed this. The girl had an attractive face and body; she was called Iphis, which was a name that could be used either for a daughter or a son.

She was soon grown up and shapely, but hidden beneath boy's clothes. Her mother denied any suggestion that she was a girl, fearing that her father would exile her. Her father wished to arrange her marriage. Her mother said that it was too soon: after a long while the marriage was arranged and she could no longer object. Then the queen was terrified; she hated her life, for she could see nowhere to turn, no path to take, to ensure that her daughter was concealed. Now she believed that she would truly be shamed; she did not know how to deny the fact any longer. She wept softly, in secret.

She went to the goddess Vesta,[2] kneeling before her in the temple, where she soaked the stone floor with her tears. She made offerings and oblations to the goddess; lit candles; said prayers; burned incense and wax; made vows. She

---

1 In Christine's telling, Ovid's humble Ligdus becomes an unnamed king of 'Lide'.
2 In the *Metamorphoses* and the *Ovide moralisé*, the goddess to whom Iphis' mother prays is Isis.

sacrificed heifers and cattle. On her bare knees, she beat her breast. She begged and pleaded with the goddess that she come to help her in her hour of need, when death threatened her. She prayed with such devotion that the goddess took pity on her: she demonstrated this to her by sending her a sign. The queen was somewhat comforted, and leapt from the temple door.

Iphis' wedding was prepared, hastened by the king; there was much joy and feasting. It came about in this way: the goddess performed a great miracle, for that night she brought great happiness to the queen and Iphis her daughter, who became a son, thanks to the ingenious goddess Vesta, who undid her woman's body and made him a son.

Appendix D: 'Iphis and Ianthe' in Arthur Golding's *Metamorphosis* (1567) Bk. 9, pp. 121–3

The xv. bookes of P. Ouidius Naso, entytuled Metamorphosis, translated oute of Latin into English meeter, by Arthur Golding Gentleman, a worke very pleasaunt and delectable. London: Willyam Seres. Huntington Library. STC 18956.

> The fame of this same wondrous thing perhappes had filled all
> The hundred Townes of *Candye* had a greater not befall
> More néerer home by *Iphys* meanes transformed late before.
> For in the shyre of *Phestos* hard by *Gnossus* dwelt of yore
> A yeoman of the meaner sort that Lyctus had too name.
> His stocke was simple, and his welth according too the same.
> Howbéet his lyfe so vpryght was, as noman could it blame.
> He came vntoo his wyfe then big and ready downe too lye,
> And sayd: twoo things I wish thée. T'one, that when thou out shalt crye,
> Thou mayst dispatch with little payne: the other that thou haue
> A Boay. For Gyrles too bring them vp a greater cost doo craue.
> And I haue no abilitie. And therefore if thou bring
> A wench (it goes ageinst my heart too thinke vppon the thing)
> Although ageinst my will, I charge it streyght destroyed bée.
> The bond of nature néedes must beare in this behalf with mée.
> This sed, both wept excéedingly, as well the husband who
> Did giue commaundement, as the wyfe that was commaunded too.
> Yit *Telethusa* earnestly at *Lyct* her husband lay,
> (Although in vayne) too haue good hope, and of himselfe more stay.
> But he was full determined. Within a whyle, the day
> Approched that the frute was rype, and shée did looke too lay
> Her belly euery mynute: when at midnyght in her rest
> Stood by her (or did séeme too stand) the Goddesse *Isis*, drest
> And trayned with the solemne pomp of all her rytes. Twoo hornes

Uppon her forehead lyke the moone, with eares of rypened cornes
Stood glistring as the burnisht gold. Moreouer shée did weare
A rich and stately diademe. Attendant on her were
The barking bug *Anubis*, and the saint of *Bubast*, and
The pydecote *Apis*, and the God that giues too vnderstand
By fingar holden too his lippes that men should silence kéepe,
And *Lybian* wormes whose stinging dooth enforce continuall sléepe,
And thou *Osyris* whom the folk of Aegypt euer séeke,
And neuer can haue sought inough, and Rittlerattles eke.
Then euen as though that *Telethuse* had fully béene awake,
And séene theis things with open eyes, thus *Isis* too her spake.
My seruant *Telethusa*, cease this care, and breake the charge
Of *Lyct*. And when *Lucina* shall haue let thy frute at large,
Bring vp the same what ere it bée I am a Goddesse who
Delyghts in helping folke at néede. I hither come too doo
Thée good. thou shalt not haue a cause hereafter too complayne
Of seruing of a Goddesse that is thanklesse for thy payne.
When Isis had this comfort giuen, shée went her way agayne.
    A ioyfull wyght rose *Telethuse*, and lifting too the sky
      Her hardened hands, did pray hir dreame myght woorke
        effectually.
Her throwes increast, and forth alone anon the burthen came,
A wench was borne too *Lyctus* who knew nothing of the same.
The mother making him beléeue it was a boay, did bring
It vp, and none but shée and nurce were priuie too the thing.
The father thanking God did giue the chyld the Graundsyres name,
The which was *Iphys*. Ioyfull was the moother of the same,
Bycause the name did serue alike too man and woman bothe,
And so the lye through godly guile forth vnperceyued gothe.
The garments of it were a boayes. The face of it was such
As eyther in a boay or gyrle of beawtie vttered much.
When *Iphys* was of thirtéene yéeres, her father did insure
The browne *Iänthee* vntoo her, a wench of looke demure,
Commended for her fauor and her person more than all
The Maydes of *Phestos*: *Telest*, men her fathers name did call.
He dwelt in *Dyctis*. They were bothe of age and fauor léeke,
And vnder both one schoolemayster they did for nurture séeke.
And hereuppon the hartes of both, the dart of Loue did stréeke.
And wounded both of them aléeke. But vnlike was theyr hope.
Both longed for the wedding day toogither for too cope.
For whom *Iänthee* thinkes too bée a man, shée hopes too sée
Her husband. *Iphys* loues whereof shée thinkes shée may not bée

Partaker, and the selfe same thing augmenteth still her flame.
Herself a Mayden with a Mayd (ryght straunge) in loue became.
> Shée scarce could stay her teares. What end remaynes for mée
> (quod shée)
>> How straunge a loue? how vncoth? how prodigious reygnes in
>> mée?
If that the Gods did fauor mée, they should destroy mée quyght.
Or if they would not mée destroy, at least wyse yit they myght
Haue giuen mée such a maladie as myght with nature stond,
Or nature were acquainted with. A Cow is neuer fond
Uppon a Cow, nor Mare on Mare. The Ram delyghts the Eawe,
The Stag the Hynde, the Cocke the Hen. But neuer man could shew,
That female yit was tane in loue with female kynd. O would
Too God I neuer had béene borne. Yit least that *Candy* should
Not bring foorth all that monstruous were, the daughter of the Sonne
Did loue a Bull. Howbéet there was a Male too dote vppon.
My loue is furiouser than hers, if truthe confessed bée.
For shée was fond of such a lust as myght bée compast. Shée
Was serued by a Bull beguyld by Art in Cow of trée.
And one there was for her with whom aduowtrie to commit.
If all the conning in the worlde and slyghts of suttle wit
Were héere, or if that *Daedalus* himselfe with vncowth wing
Of Wax should hither fly againe, what comfort should he bring?
Could he with all his conning crafts now make a boay of mée?
Or could he O *Iänthee* chaunge the natiue shape of thée?
Nay rather *Iphys* settle thou thy mynd and call thy witts
Abowt thee: shake thou of theis flames that foolishly by fitts
With out all reason reigne. Thou séest what Nature hathe thée made
(Onlesse thow wilt deceyue thy selfe.) So farre foorth wysely wade,
As ryght and reason may support, and loue as women ought
Hope is the thing that bréedes desyre, hope féedes the amorous thought.
This hope thy sex denieth thée. Not watching doth restreyne
Thée from embracing of the thing wherof thou art so fayne.
Nor yit the Husbands iealowsie, nor rowghnesse of her Syre,
Nor yit the coynesse of the Wench dooth hinder thy desyre.
And yit thou canst not her enioy. No though that God and man
Should labor too their vttermost and doo the best they can
In thy behalfe, they could not make a happy wyght of thée.
I cannot wish the thing but that I haue it. Frank and frée
The Goddes haue giuen mée what they could. As I will, so will hée
That must become my fathrinlaw. so willes my father too.
But nature stronger than them all consenteth not theretoo.

This hindreth mée, and nothing else. Behold the blisfull tyme,
The day of Mariage is at hand. *Iänthee* shalbée myne,
And yit I shall not her enioy. Amid the water wée
Shall thirst. O *Iuno* president of mariage, why with thée
Comes *Hymen* too this wedding where no brydegroome you shall sée,
But bothe are Brydes that must that day toogither coupled bée?
   This spoken, shée did hold hir peace. And now the toother mayd
   Did burne as whote in loue as shée. And earnestly shee prayd
The brydale day myght come with spéede. The thing for which shée longd
Dame *Telethusa* fearing sore, from day too day prolongd
The tyme, oft feyning siknesse, oft pretending shée had séene
Ill tokens of successe. at length all shifts consumed béene.
The wedding day so oft delayd was now at hand. The day
Before it, taking from her head the kerchéef quyght away,
And from her daughters head likewyse, with scattred heare she layd
Her handes vpon the Altar, and with humble voyce thus prayd.
   O Isis who doost haunt the towne of *Paretonie*, and
   The féeldes by *Maraeotis* lake, and *Pharos* which dooth stand
By *Alexandria*, and the *Nyle* diuided intoo seuen
Great channels, comfort thou my feare, and send mée help from heauen,
Thyself O Goddesse, euen thyself, and theis thy relikes I
Did once behold and knew them all: as well thy company
As eke thy sounding rattles, and thy cressets burning by,
And myndfully I marked what commaundement thou didst giue.
That I escape vnpunished, that this same wench dooth liue,
Thy counsell and thy hest it is. Haue mercy now on twayne,
And help vs. With that word the teares ran downe her chéekes amayne.
The Goddesse séemed for too moue her Altar: and in déede
She moued it. The temple doores did tremble like a réede.
And hornes in likenesse too the Moone about the Church did shyne.
And Rattles made a raughtish noyse. At this same luckie signe,
Although not wholy carelesse, yit ryght glad shée went away.
And *Iphys* followed after her with larger pace than ay
Shée was accustomd. And her face continued not so whyght.
Her strength encreased, and her looke more sharper was too syght.
Her heare grew shorter, and shée had a much more liuely spryght,
Than when shée was a wench. For thou O *Iphys* who ryght now
A modther wert, art now a boay. With offrings both of yow
Too Church retyre, and there reioyce with fayth vnfearfull. They
With offrings went too Church ageine, and there theyr vowes did pay.
They also set a table vp, which this bréef méeter had.

The vovves that Iphys vovvd a vvench he hath performd a Lad.
Next morrow ouer all the world did shine with lightsome flame,
When *Iuno*, and Dame *Venus*, and Sir *Hymen* ioyntly came
Too *Iphys* mariage, who as then transformed too a boay
Did take *Iänthee* too his wyfe, and so her loue enioy

Appendix E: 'Iphis and Ianthe', in George Sandys' *Ovid's Metamorphosis* (1632) Bk. 9, pp. 315–18

George Sandys. *Ovid's Metamorphosis Englished, Mythologiz'd, and Represented in figures. An Essay to the Translation of Virgil's Aeneis. By G. S.* Iohn Lichfield: Oxford. University of British Columbia

The fame of this so wonderfull a fate
Had filled *Creets*[l] hundred Cities; if of late
The change of *Iphis*, generally knowne,
Had not produc't a wonder of their owne.
For *Phaestus*, neere to *Gnossus*, fostered
One, *Lygdus*, of vn-noted parents bred:
How'euer, free. Nor did his wealth exceed
His parentage: yet both in word and deed
Sincerely iust, and of a blameless life.
Who thus bespake his now downe-lying wife.
Two things I wish: that you your belly lay
With little paine; and that it proue a boy.
A daughter is too chargeable, and we
Too poore to match her.[m] If a girle it be,
I charge, what I abhorre (ô Pietie
Forgiue me!) that, as soone as borne, it die.
This hauing vtter'd; the Commanded wept
And the Commander; teares no measure kept.
Yet *Telethusa* still with fruitless praire,
Desires he would not in the Gods despaire.
But he too constant. Now her time was come,
And the ripe burden stretcht her heauie womb:
When [a]*Inachis*, with all her sacred band;
In dead of night, or stood, or seem'd to stand
Besides her bed. Her browes a crowne adornes,

Editors' note: The following notes are Sandys' own and appear in the margins of the edition alongside the text. We have retained the original's notation scheme.
[l] Her father lately of Creet.
[m] It was vsuall among the Grecians to expose, or make those children away, which they would not, or were not able to foster.
[a] *Io* the daughter of *Inachus*; after deified by the *AEgyptians*, and called *Isis*.

ᵇWith eares of shining corne, and *Cynthian* hornes.
   Barking ᶜ*Anubis,* and ᵈ*Bubastis* bright,
   Black ᵉ*Apis* spotted variously with white,
   ᶠHe whose mouth-sealing finger silence taught,
   ᵍ*Tymbrells,* ʰ*Osiris* neuer enough sought,
   ⁱAnd forreine serpents, whose dire touch constraine
   A deadly slumber, consummate her traine.
   Then (as if seene awake) the Goddesse said:
   My *Telethusa,* be not thus dismaid;
   Reject these cares, thy husband disobay:
   And when ᵏ*Lucina* shall thy belly lay,
   Foster what ere it be. A Deity
   Auxiliary to Distresse am I;
   Ready to helpe, and easily implor'd:
   Nor shall it grieue thee that thou hast ador'd
   Vngratefull *Isis*. This admonished,
   Shee leaues the roome. When, rising in her bed,
   Her hands to heauen glad *Telethusa* threw
   And humbly prayes her vision may proue true.
   Increasing throwes at length a girle disclos'd.
   Both by the father and the world suppos'd
   To be a boy; so closely hid: and knowne
   But to the mother, and the nurse alone.
   ˡHe paies his vowes, and of his Fathers name
   It *Iphis* calls; which much rejoyc't the dame,
   To each sex common; nor deceaues thereby:
   Who still with pious fraud conceales her lie.
   A boy in show; whose lookes should you assigne
   To boy or girle, loue would in either shine.
   At thirteene yeares her Father her affide
   To yellow-trest *Ianthe*: she the pride
   Of *Phaestian* virgins for vnequald faire:
   Telestes daughter, and his onely heire,

ᵇ   Taken also for the Moone, as the moone for *Ceres*.
ᶜ   *Mercury*, worshipped by the *AEgyptians* in the forme of a dog.
ᵈ   *Diana*; so named of *Bubastis*, a citty in *AEgypt*, where she had her Temple.
ᵉ   An Oxe, adored by the *AEgyptians*.
ᶠ   *Harpocrates*, the God of Silence.
ᵍ   *Sistrum*: a lowd instrument peculiar to the *Aegyptians*.
ʰ   The husband of *Isis*: see the comment. [*Editor's note*: Sandys is referring to his own commentary (pp. 306–8), not reproduced here.]
ⁱ   *Aspes,* which the *Aegyptians* worshipped.
ᵏ   The Goddesse of Childbirth.
ˡ   *Lygdus*

Like young, like beautifull, together bred,
Inform'd alike, alike accomplished:
Like darts at once their simple bosoms strike;
Alike their wounds; their hopes, ô far vnlike!
The day they expect. *Ianthe* thought time ran
Too slow; and takes her *Iphis* for a man.
Poore *Iphis* loues, despaires; despaire eiects
Farre fiercer flames: a maid, a maid affects.
    What will become of me (she weeping said)
Whom new, vnknowne, prodigious loues invade!
If pittifull, the Gods should haue destroy'd
Or else haue giuen what might haue beene injoy'd:
No Cow a Cow, no Mare a Mare pursues:
But Harts their gentle Hindes, and Rammes their Ewes.
So Birds together paire. Of all that moue,
No Female suffers for a Female loue.
O would I had no being! Yet, that all
Abhord by Nature should in *Creet* befall;
[a]*Sol's* lust-incensed daughter lou'd a Bull:
They male and female. Mine, ô farre more full
Of vncouth fury! for she pleas'd her blood;
And stood his errour in a Cow of wood
Shee, for her craft, had an adulterer.
Should all the world their daring wits confer:
Should *Daedalus* his waxen wings renue,
And hither fly; what could his cunning doe!
Can art convert a virgin to a boy?
Or fit *Ianthe* for a maidens ioy?
No, fixe thy minde; compose thy vast desires:
O quench these ill aduis'd and foolish fires!
Thinke of thy sex,[b] or euen thy selfe abuse:
What may be, seeke; and loue as femals vse.
Hope wings desire; hope *Cupids* flight sustaines:
In thee thy Sexe this deads. No watch restraines
Our deare imbrace, nor husbands jealousies,
Nor rigorous Sires; nor she her selfe denies:
Yet not to be inioy'd. Nor canst thou bee
Happy in her; though men and Gods agree!
Now also all to my desires accord:

---

[a] *Pasiphae*
[b] As well as others, by seeing what thou art not.

What they can giue, the easie Gods afford;
What me, my father, hers, her selfe, would please,
Displeaseth Nature; stronger then all these.
Shee, shee forbids. That day begins to shine;
Long wisht! wherein *Ianthe* must be mine:
And yet not mine. Of mortalls most accurst!
I starue at feasts, and in the riuer thirst.
^c*Iuno*, ô *Hymen*, wherefore are you come?
We both are Brides: but where is the Bride-groome?
    Here ended. Nor lesse burnes the other Maid;
Who, *Hymen*, for thy swift apparance pray'd.
Yet *Telethusa* feares what she affects;
Protracting time: oft want of health objects;
Ill-boading dreames, and auguries oft faines:
But now no colour for excuse remaines.
Their nuptiall rites, put off with such delay;
Were to be solemniz'd the following day.
When she vnbinds, hers, and her daughters haire;
And holding by the Altar form'd this praire:
Isis; who ^a*Paraetonium*, ^b*Pharos* Ile,
Smooth ^c*Mareotis*, and seuen-channeld ^d*Nile*,
Chear'st with thy presence: thy poore suppliants heare:
O helpe in these extreames, and cure our feare!
Thee Goddesse, thee of old; these ensignes, I
Haue seene, and know: thy lamps, attendancie,
And sounding ^eTimbrells: and haue thee obayd.
To me, impunitie; life, to this maid,
Thy sauing counsell gaue: to both renue
Thy timely pitty. Teares her words pursue.
The Goddesse shakes her Altar; when the gate
Shooke on the hinges: hornes that imitate
The waxing Moones, through all the Temple flung
A sacred splendor: noyse-full Timbrells rung.
The Mother, glad of this successefull signe,
Though not secure, returnes from *Isis* shrine.
Whom *Iphis* followes with a larger pace

---

^c Invoked at Nuptials.
^a A citty in *Aegypt*, consecrated to *Isis*.
^b Adioyning now to *Alexandria*.
^c A Lake not far distant.
^d The only river of *Aegypt*.
^e Sistra.

Then vsuall; nor had so white a face.
Her strength augments; her looke more bold appeares;
Her shortning curles scarce hang beneath her eares;
By farre more full of courage, rapt with ioy:
For thou, of late a Wench, art now a Boy.
Gifts to the Temple beare, and[f] *Iö* sing!
Sing Ioy! Their gifts they to the Temple bring;
And adde a title; in one verse display'd:
What *Iphis* vow'd a Wench, a Boy he pay'd.
The Morning Night dismasks with welcome flame:
[g]When *Iuno*, *Venus*, and free *Hymen* came
To grace their marriage; who, with gifts diuine,
Iphis the Boy, to his *Ianthe* ioyne.

Appendix F: Select Images of 'Iphis and Ianthe' to 1700

We include four illuminations that accompany the 'Iphis and Ianthe' story in two fourteenth-century manuscripts of the *Ovide moralisé*. The first set of images, from the Rouen Bibliothèque Municipale manuscript 04, includes the birth of Iphis; Telethusa and Iphis praying to Isis; and the marriage of Iphis and Ianthe. The fourth image is from Bibliothèque National de France Arsenal manuscript 5069, another representation of the birth of Iphis.[1]

We also include images from Bernard Salomon's Cycle of 178 woodcuts (1557) produced to accompany simplified editions of *The Metamorphoses* in French and Italian (Figures F.5–F.8). Salomon chose to illustrate two scenes: the first, a moment prior to the birth of Iphis, in which Telethusa lies in bed, and the second in which Iphis and Telethusa pray to Isis. The same scenes would be selected by subsequent illustrators: the work of Virgil Solis (1632) and Petrus Vander Borcht (1591) is, for example, clearly indebted to Salomon's (Figures F.9–F.12 and Figs F.13–F.14). Crispijn van de Passe would combine the two scenes into one image (1607) and Francis Clein would use only the second scene in his illustration of various moments from Book 9 for Sandy's 1632 English translation (Figures F.17, F.18).

What is most remarkable about the print illustrations is just how similar they are to each other. In the case of the first scene, most of the images show Isis (recognisable by the moon-shaped horns above her head) and her train. The scene is often identified as featuring Lyctus (Latin for Ligdus) even though it seems clear that the figure who stands aside is Harpocrates, the god of silence

---

[f] An acclamatio in triumphs.
[g] Deities propitious to marriage.
[1] For information on these manuscripts and on illuminations of the *Ovide moralisé* more generally, see Françoise Clier-Colombani, *Images et imaginaire dans l'Ovide moralisé* (Paris: Droz, 2017).

(*Metamorphoses* 9: 692). The exceptions here are Pietrus de Jode's (1606) and van de Passe's (1607) interpretations which modify the scene to match the inscription (Figures F.15, F.17). Here Isis and her god and animal companions have vanished and Lyctus appears to be passing his instruction on to a nurse while Telethusa languishes behind him. While late seventeenth-century prints return Isis to the scene (Figures F.19–F.21), none of the early modern images follow the medieval manuscripts by illustrating the actual birth of Iphis.

Solis and Vander Borcht follow Salomon in their illustrations of the temple scene, as does Clein in his composition (Figures F.6, F.8, F.10, F.12, F.14, F.18). In these images the figures of Telethusa and Iphis kneel before the figure of Isis. Also notable in these illustrations are the two figures walking away. Both look female, suggesting that the transversion has yet to begin or is only partially underway. However, de Jode and van de Passe modify this scene so as to complete the transformation and illustrate Iphis as a boy (Figures F.16, F.17). Küsel's (1681) and Kraus's (1694) illustrations of the scene remove the transition altogether (Figures F.22, F.23). Both of these were likely conceived as illustrations of other scenes. The marriage of Iphis and Ianthe, treated in the Rouen manuscript, does not appear to have interested early modern illustrators.[2]

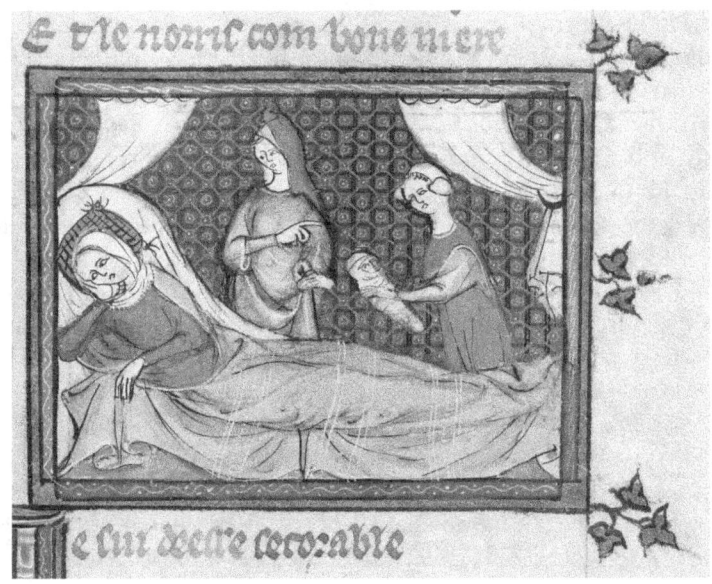

Figure F.1   'Birth of Iphis' (detail). *Ovide moralisé* (14c.). Rouen Bibliothèque Municipale ms. 04, fol. 243.

[2] For information on illustrations of Ovid generally see Paul Bafolsky, *Ovid and the Metamorphoses of Modern Art from Botticelli to Picasso* (New Haven, CT: Yale University Press, 2014).

Figure F.2 'Telethusa and Iphis Pray to Isis' (detail). *Ovide moralisé* (14c.). Rouen Bibliothèque Municipale ms. 04, fol. 244v.

Figure F.3 'Marriage of Iphis and Ianthe' (detail). *Ovide moralisé* (14c.). Rouen Bibliothèque Municipale ms. 04, fol. 244v.

APPENDIX F

Figure F.4 'Birth of Iphis' (detail). *Ovide moralisé* (14c.).
Bibliothèque Nationale de France. Bibliothèque de l'Arsenal, ms. 5069, fol. 131.

Figure F.5 Bernard Salomon. 'Lygde & Teletuse'. *La métamorphose d'Ovide figureé* (Lyon, 1557), 60(r). Bibliothèque Nationale de France.

Figure F.6   Bernard Salomon. 'La fille Iphis en fils'. *La métamorphose d'Ovide figureé* (Lyon, 1557), 60(v). Bibliothèque Nationale de France.

132 LIBRO

Teletusa fa credere al marito che la
sua figliuola è maschio. 120

Fu sempre della Donna vsanza vecchia
Monstrare il falso al credulo marito.
Nella fè della sua Lyddo si specchia
Si, che senza dishnor riman tradito.
Vccider giura, & farlo s'apparecchia,
S'altro che maschio è del suo corpo vscito.
Con tutto ciò la moglie, fuor di duolo,
Creder gli fa che maschio è il suo figliuolo.

Figure F.7   Bernard Salomon. 'Teletusa fa credere al marito che la sua figliuola è maschio'. Gabriele Simeoni, *Del Metamorphoseo abbreviato, con la rinovatione d'alcune stanze, libro decimoquinto, con figurator* (Lyon, 1559), p. 132, plate 120. Warburg Institute.

Figure F.8 Bernard Salomon. 'La figliuola di Lyddo conuertita in maschio'. Gabriele Simeoni, *Del Metamorphoseo abbreviato, con la rinovatione d'alcune stanze, libro decimoquinto, con figurator* (Lyon, 1559), p. 133, plate 121. Warburg Institute.

Lyctus & Telethusa vxor. IX.

PHæstos oppidū est in ísula Creta, vbi Lyctus generosi animi ac præstantis fidei homo degens, ab vxore sua Telethusa iam grauida & partui vicina, petiit, vt si puellam pareret, eam stati interficeret, sin puerum, sobolem patriæ conseruaret. Cúmque ambo cōiuges pro futuro casu dedissent lachrymas, mater filiam enixa, manus ei afferre uiolentas non potuit. Isis autem Dea lugéti puerperæ adfuit, & ipsa infantem (patre filij opinione decepto) pro puero enutriuit.

Figure F.9 Virgil Solis. 'Lyctus & Telethusa uxor'. Johan Spreng, *Metamorphoses Ovidii, argumentis quidem soluta oration . . . una cum singularum transformationum Iconibus, a Vergilio Solis, eximo picture, delineates* (1570), p. 115. Bibliothèque Nationale de France.

Iphis puella in marem. V.

Vm Iphis puella iam ad maturam peruenisset ætatem, parens eam, falsus à coniuge, marem existimans, virginem formosissimam ex Theleste genitam ipsi despondit. Variis autem animi fluctibus, cùm æstuaret Iphis mater, valdéque metueret, ne Iphis puella cum infamia reperiretur, Dea Isis rursus auxilio Telethusæ rebus deploratis adfuit, & instantibus iam nuptiis, vt matrimonium fieret legitimum, Iphin puellam in puerũ transfigurauit.

Figure F.10 Virgil Solis. 'Iphis puella in marem'. Johan Spreng, *Metamorphoses Ovidii, argumentis quidem soluta oration . . . una cum singularum transformationum Iconibus, a Vergilio Solis, eximo picture, delineates* (1570), p. 116. Bibliothèque Nationale de France.

LIBER IX. 383

terficeret, ſin puerum, ſobolem patriæ conſerua-
ret. Cumq; ambo coniuges pro futuro caſu dediſ-
ſent lacrymas, mater filiam enixa, manus ei
afferre violentas non potuit: Iſis autem Dea lu-
genti puerperæ adfuit, & ipſa infantem (patre filij opinione decepto) pro puero enutriuit.

*F*Ama noui centum *ᵃ* Cretæas forſitan vrbes
Impleſſet monſtri: ſi non miracula nuper
Iphide * mutato Crete propiora tuliſſet.
Proxima Gnoſſiaco nam quondam Phæſtia regno
Progenuit tellus ignotum nomine * Lyctum
Ingenua de plebe virum: nec cenſus in illo
Nobilitate ſua maior: ſed vita, fidesq́;
Inculpata fuit: grauidæ qui coniugis aures
Vocibus his monuit, cùm iam prope partus adeſſet:
Quæ voueā duo ſunt, minimo vt ᵇreleuēre dolore,

ᵃ Cretam: vn-
de Miletus in
Aſiam profu-
gerat.
* mutata libr.
tres Ciof.
* Ligdū Naug.
& m. ſc.

ᵇ Vteri ſcili et
onere, h. e. pa-
rias.

Figure F.11   Anonymous (after Virgil Solis). 'Telethusa and Isis'. *Pub. Ovidii Nasonis
Metamorphoseon libri XV, ex postrema Jocobi Micylli recognitione, et recensione nova
Gregorii Bersmarni, cum eiusdem notationibus* . . . (Leipzig: Joannes Steinman, 1582),
p. 383. Warburg Institute.

386   METAMORPH.

a Pactarum nuptiarum.
* virum m. sc. & impr.
*qua m.sc. Sed notarunt aliq, hunc poëtam frequenter vti hac generis ἐναλλαγή.
* tenens m. sc. & pler. impr.
* Parcere m. s. perper.
b Naturæ consentaneŭ, conueniens naturæ : h. e. non virginis amorem, sed viri.
c Me perijsse, Comica locutione.
d Pasiphaë.

Coniugium, *a* pactǽq, expectant tempora tedæ,
Quemq, virum putat esse,*suũ fore credit Ianthe.
Iphis amat : * quo posse frui desperat : & auget
Hoc ipsum flammas : ardetq, in virgine virgo :
Vixq,*tenet lacrymas, Quis me manet exit? inqt:
Cognita quàm nulli, quam prodigiosa, nouǽq,
Cura tenet Veneris ? si Dij mihi parcere vellent,
*Perdere debuerant : si non & perdere vellent :
b Naturale malum saltem, & de more dedissent.
Nec vaccam vacca, nec equas amor vrit equarum.
Vrit oues aries: sequitur sua femina ceruum:
Sic & aues coëunt : interq, animalia cuncta
Femina femineo correpta cupidine nulla est.
Vellem *c* nulla forem. ne non tamen omnia Crete
Monstra ferat, taurum dilexit *d* filia Solis :
Femina nempe marem. meus est furiosior illo,

Si

Figure F.12   Anonymous (after Virgil Solis). 'Iphis Disguised as a Youth Prays to Become a Youth'. *Pub. Ovidii Nasonis Metamorphoseon libri XV, ex postrema Jocobi Micylli recognitione, et recensione nova Gregorii Bersmarni, cum eiusdem notationibus . . .* (Leipzig: Joannes Steinman, 1582), p. 386. Warburg Institute.

Figure F.13 Petrus Vander Borcht. 'Lyctus et Telethusa Uxor. IX'. Lactantius Placidus, *P. Ovidii Nasonis Metamorphoses: argumentis brevioribus / ex Luctatio Grammatico [i.e. Lactantius Placidus] collecti expositae; una cum vivis singularum transformationum iconibus in aes incisis* (Antwerp: Ex Officina Plantiniana apud viduam & J. Moretum, 1591), p. 235. Warburg Institute.

Figure F.14 Petrus Vander Borcht. 'Iphis Puella in Marem. X'. Lactantius Placidus, *P. Ovidii Nasonis Metamorphoses: argumentis brevioribus / ex Luctatio Grammatico [i.e. Lactantius Placidus] collecti expositae; una cum vivis singularum transformationum iconibus in aes incisis* (Antwerp: Ex Officina Plantiniana apud viduam & J. Moretum, 1591), p. 237. Warburg Institute.

OVIDIAN TRANSVERSIONS

Figure F.15   Pietrus de Jode. 'The order of Lyctus to Telethusa about the child'. Antonio Tempesta. *Metamorphoseon sive Transformationum Ovidianarum libri quindecim, aeneis formis ab Antonio Tempesta Florentino incise* . . . (Antwerp, 1606), plate 89. Warburg Institute.

APPENDIX F

Figure F.16 Pietrus de Jode. 'Telethusa Praying to Change Iphis to a Man'. Antonio Tempesta. *Metamorphoseon sive Transformationum Ovidianarum libri quindecim, aeneis formis ab Antonio Tempesta Florentino incise* . . . (Antwerp, 1606), plate 90. Warburg Institute.

Figure F.17 Crispijn van de Pass, the Elder. 'Lyctus, Telethusa, Iphis'. *P. Ovid Nasonis XV Metamorphoseon librorum figurae elegantissime a Crispiano Passaeo laminis aeneis incisae* (Cologne: Passaeus; Arnhemia: Janssonius, 1607), plate 84. Herzog August Bibliothek, Wolfenbüttel.

APPENDIX F

Figure F.18 Francis Clein (engraved by P. Lombart and S. Savery). George Sandys. *Ovids Metamorphosis: Englished, mythologiz'd, and represented in figures* (Oxford: 1632), p. 301. University of British Columbia.

302   LES METAMORPHOSES
      FABLE DOUZIÉME.

ARGUMENT.

Iphis qui avoit toûjours été fille, & qui pourtant avoit toûjours été élevée comme garçon, change de sexe, & épouse Iante.

*F*Ama novi centum Cretæas forsitan urbes
  Implesset monstri, si non miracula nuper
Iphide mutatâ Crete propiora tulisset.
Proxima Gnossiaco nam quondam Phæstia regno
Progenuit tellus, ignoto nomine Ligdum
Ingenuâ de plebe virum : nec census in illo
Nobilitate sua major : sed vita fidesque
Inculpata fuit. gravidæ qui conjugis aures
Vocibus his movit, cum jam prope partus adesset :
Quæ voveam duo sunt ; minimo ut relevere labore,
Utque marem parias. onerosior altera sors est :
Et vires fortuna negat. quod abominor ergo
Edita forte tuo fuerit si fœmina partu,
(Invitus mando, pietas, ignosce) necetur.
Dixerat : & lacrymis vultum lavere profusis,
Tam qui mandabat, quam cui mandata dabantur :
                                    Sed

LE bruit de ce prodige eut bien-tôt rempli d'admiration & d'étonnement les cent villes de l'Isle de Crete, si le changement d'Iphis en garçon qui arriva en même tems, n'eut déja preoccupé les esprits. Un certain habitant de Pheste homme d'assez basse condition, & qui n'avoit pas plus de bien que de noblesse ; mais qui étoit un exemple de probité, voiant que sa femme étoit grosse, & qu'elle étoit prête d'accoucher, lui parla en cette maniere. Je demande deux choses aux Dieux, l'une que vous accouchiez sans douleur, & l'autre que vous accouchiez d'un fils, parce que si vous avez une fille, c'est un fardeau que vous nous donnez. En effet l'education & la garde d'une fille est ordinairement difficile ; & après tout, nous n'avons pas assez de bien pour la pourvoir honnêtement. Enfin je crains sur toutes choses de me voir pére d'un enfant qui me feroit toûjours de la peine. Si vous accouchez donc d'une fille, faites la mourir en naissant. C'est malgré-moi que je vous fais un commandement si inhumain, & j'en demande pardon à la nature que j'offense par ce discours. Il n'eut pas sitôt parlé que par une tendresse naturelle, ils repandirent tous deux des larmes, aussi bien celui qui donnoit cét ordre, que celle qui le recevoit.
                                    Tou-

APPENDIX F

Figure F.20   Johann Wilhelm Baur. 'Iphis Puella in Marem'. *Bellissimum Ovidii theatrum* . . . (Nuremberg: P. Fürstii, 1687; first published in Vienna in 1641). Warburg Institute.

Figure F.21 Melchior Küsel I (after Johann Wilhelm Baur). 'Lyctus and Telethusa uxor'. *Metamorphosis oder Ovidii der Poeten Wunderliche Verenderung* (Augsburg, 1681), p. 89. Warburg Institute.

APPENDIX F

Figure F.22   Melchior Küsel I (after Johann Wilhelm Baur). 'Iphis puella in marem'. *Metamorphosis oder Ovidii der Poeten Wunderliche Verenderung* (Augsburg, 1681), p. 90. Warburg Institute. *Note*: This image is described as an illustration of 'Baucis and Philemon' (Bk. 8 of *Metamorphoses*) in Baur (see Figure F.20).

Figure F.23 Johann Ulrich Kraus. 'Iphis Changed from a Girl into a Youth by the Grace of Isis'. *Die Verwandlungen des Ovidii in zweyhundert und sechs und zwanzig Kupffern* (Augsburg: Kraus, 1694). p. 82, plate 159. Warburg Institute.

INDEX

Note: Page numbers in *italics* indicate figures and page numbers followed by n indicate end-of-chapter notes. Page numbers followed by *app* refer to the appendices.

Abelove, Henry, 253
'Acis and Galatea' (trans. Golding), 191, 197–8, 199, 200, 201, 203
affective engagement, 173, 175, 179, 184, 185
agency, 252–3, 255, 264
alchemy, 151–5, 157, 158, 160, 164–6, 180–1
allegory, 43–5, 54–7, 71, 73–8, 107, 111
amity, 249; *see also* friendship
amor impossibilis, 82
anamorphosis, 44, 234
ancient comedy, 249–50
Anguillara, Giovanni Andrea dell', 125, 127
archipelagoes, 133–4
  Isolario (Sonetti), 134, 136–40
archipelogic, 140
Aristotle, 151
Arnulf of Orléans, 2
Ascham, Roger, 173, 175
asterisk, 17, 61, 118–20, 121; *see also* trans*
asterisk-like compass, 138–40
astronomy, 155–6, 158, 180, 181
atlases, 137

Bacchus, 122–4
Barkan, Leonard, 20
Baur, Johann Wilhelm, 'Iphis Puella in Marem', 317*app*

beards, 230
Bellamy, Elizabeth Jane, 197
Bellamy, Henry, 276n
Benserade, Isaac de, 243–4, 274–5; *see also*
  Iphis et Iante (Benserade)
Bersuire, Pierre, 3, 46
Bevington, David, 163
Bibliographie du théâtre français depuis son origine (La Vallière), 242
Bildungsroman, 261–2, 263, 265, 267, 268, 270, 271–2
bilingualism, 123–4
'Birth of Iphis', 298*app*, 301*app*
Blount, Thomas, 126
Blumenfeld-Kosinski, Renate, 45
Boaistuau, Pierre, 229
body, 1, 2, 19, 213, 214, 215, 216
  Galatea (aka *Gallathea*) (Lyly), 6, 14, 19, 22, 177, 180–1
  Metamorphoses (Ovid), 43
  Ovide moralisé, 53, 55, 56, 57, 65, 66, 75, 80, 81
  Pyrrhonian scepticism, 220, 222, 223
  Worlde of Wordes, A (Florio), 122, 126, 140
  see also gender; intersex; transformation

321

Book of Ovyde Named Methamorphose, The (Caxton), 88–9
boy actors, 11, 163, 174, 176–7
boys' playing companies, 163
Brinsley, John, 173
bronze sculpture (Rodin), 23–4
Bullokar, John, 120
Buondelmonti, Cristoforo, 134
   Liber insularum archipelagi, 134, 135

Cain, H. Edward, 272
capitalism, 271
Cartwright, Kent, 162
case, 128–9
Catholic church, 3
Caxton, William, 3, 88–9, 160
Ceyx and Alcyone, 112–13
Chess, Simone, 11
Christian allegory, 56
Christianity, 21, 43–4, 54–5, 73–8, 204–5
Christine de Pizan, 99–101; *see also La Mutacion de Fortune* (Christine de Pizan)
church, 3, 203, 204, 205, 225
   St Peter's Church, Barton-Upon Humber, 206, 210n
Circe, 109
Clein, Francis, *Ovid's Metamorphosis* (Sandys), 315*app*
clothing, 224
coastal squeeze, 201–2
Cohen, Walter, 271
Cohn, Dorrit, 270
comedy, 249–51, 254
compass-as-asterisk, 138–40
Confessio Amantis (Confessions of the Lover) (Gower), 46, 81, 84–6
   comparison to Caxton, 89
   comparison to Ovid, 83–4, 92
   ignorance, 88, 89
   kinde love, 591
   Latin gloss, 86–9, 95n
   Ligdus, 84
   nature, 90–2
   riddles, 85–6, 88–9, 90–2, 93
   text, 286–8*app*
   thing (member apostate), 89, 93
   transformation, 92, 93–4
Confession, 73–5
Congreve, William, 272
Conley, Tom, 137, 138
conversion, 20
   religious, 21, 22–3, 43–4
copia, 158
Corneille, Pierre, 244, 249–50, 251, 254
cross-dressing, 5, 11, 50–4, 80
Cubillo de Aragón, 272

De Grazia, Margreta, 271
de Jode, Pietrus, 'Telethusa Praying', 312*app*, 313*app*
death, 64–5, 66
Dedalus, 14, 48–9, 82
Des Hermaphrodites (Duval), 230–3
desire, 9, 10
   monstrous, 80, 82, 265
   natural, 46–9
   prodigious, 12–13, 82
   unnatural, 47–9
   see also under Galatea (aka *Gallathea*) (Lyly); *Iphis et Iante* (Benserade); *Ovide moralisé* (anon.)
Dictionarie (Rider), 119–20
dictionaries, 6, 12–13, 17, 18, 119–21; *see also Worlde of Wordes, A* (Florio)
disknowledge, 152–4, 155–6, 160, 163, 165–6
Drama of a nation (Cohen), 271
Duval, Jacques, 230–3

Early Modern Conversions Project, 19, 20, 21, 23, 32n
education *see* humanist pedagogy
Elizabeth I, 150, 157, 164, 165
embodied knowledge, 214, 220–3
embodiment-as-process, 21
English Expositor (Bullokar), 120
Enke, A. Finn, 17
Enterline, Lynn, 162–3, 175
environmental metamorphosis, 201–2
epistemology, 15, 22–3, 133
Erasmus, Desiderius, 158
erotic agency, 252–3, 255
erotic desire *see* desire
eroticism, 11; *see also* female homoeroticism

'Fable Douzième', 316*app*
fables, 50, 102
false knowledge, 151; *see also* disknowledge
false member (*member apostis*), 51–2, 53, 71, 72, 111
feelings, 234
female erotic agency, 252–3, 255
female homoeroticism, 241, 244–9, 252–4, 255; *see also* lesbianism
Ferguson, Gary, 230
Fieux de Mouhy, Chevalier, 242
floods, 192, 194–5, 196–7, 206–7
Flora's Fortune (Sabie), 195–6
Florio, John, 121
   earlier works, 123
   see also Worlde of Wordes, A (Florio)
forests, 199–200, 202
Foucault, Michel, 243, 251
Fox, Cora, 165

France
  capitalism, 271
  gallantry, 243–4
  intersex individuals, 214
  mignons, 230
  Pyrrhonian scepticism, 220–3
  Wars of Religion, 225
friendship, 157–8; *see also* amity

Galatea (aka *Gallathea*) (Lyly), 6, 14, 19, 22
  affection, 176, 182–3
  alchemy, 151–5, 157, 158, 160, 164–6, 180–1
  boy actors *see* boy actors
  coastal squeeze, 201–2
  church, 203, 204, 205
  criticism, 26n
  desire, 10, 11, 182
  disguise, 177–8
  disknowledge, 152, 154–5, 160, 163, 164, 165–6
  false knowledge, 151; *see also* disknowledge
  flooding, 192, 194–5, 196–7, 206–7
  forests, 199–200
  humanist pedagogy, 158–61, 162–3, 172–7
  Humber Estuary, 191–4, 196, 198–201, 207
  imitation, 178
  love, 156, 159–60, 173, 174, 176, 184, 185, 191, 203, 204
  masculinity, 175, 177–8, 181, 183
  masterly models, 153, 181–5
  mystery, 154–5, 156, 159, 164
  pastoral, 195–6, 201
  prologue, 150–1
  subordination, 177–81
  transformation/metamorphosis, 156–60, 164–66, 176–7, 179, 180–1, 184–5, 191, 202–3, 205–6
  transubstantiation, 203
  Virgil, 196
  see also 'Iphis and Ianthe' (Ovid); *Ovid's Metamorphoses* (Golding): 'Acis and Galatea'
gallant comedy, 250–1, 254
gallantry, 242–9, 250, 253, 254, 255
Garland *see* John of Garland
Gates of Hell sculpture (Rodin), 23–4
gender, 213–14
  dictionaries, 121
  grammatical gender, 66, 215–16
  Worlde of Wordes, A (Florio), 122, 124–7
  see also body, intersex; transgender
gender ambiguity, 223–6, 227, 234; *see also* intersex; transgender
gender binary, 225
gender change *see* transformation

gender distinction, 214, 217, 222, 223, 229–30
gender identity, 234–5
  medical discourse, 226–9
gender translation, 126–7
generational struggle, 262, 263–5, 268–70, 271, 272–3
geography, 16
Girl Meets Boy (Smith), 80
gloss, *Confessio Amantis* (Gower), 86–9, 95n
Golding, Arthur, 3, 12, 48; *see also Ovid's Metamorphoses* (Golding)
Gower, John, 46, 81; *see also Confessio Amantis (Confessions of the Lover)* (Gower)
grafting, 123–4
grammatical case, 128–9
Greek islands, 133–4
  Isolario (Sonetti), 134, 136–40
Green, Ian, 161
Gurr, Andrew, 163

hair, 229–30
Hamlet, 272
Harris, Joseph, 264
Hayward, Eva, 61, 119
Henri IV, 230, 271
hermaphrodites, *Island of Hermaphrodites, The*, 218, 230; *see also* intersex; transgender
hermaphroditic twins, 230
heterosexuality, 243, 253
Hiere Island, 138
His Farewell to Militarie Profession (Riche), 5
Histoire du Théâtre français (Parfait), 242
historical sentence, 56–7
history, euhemerist interpretations, 43, 44–6, 49–54, 71–3, 110–11
history, sexuality of, 45–6, 56, 262, 273
history of sexuality, 11, 20, 243, 262
Holinshed, Raphael, 194
homoerotic love, 173; *see also* female homoeroticism; lesbianism
homosexuality, 222, 253–4; *see also* lesbianism
hope, 70–1
  foolish, 62, 64, 66, 69, 73, 77–8
humanist pedagogy, 158–64, 172–7, 179–80, 184, 185
Humber Estuary, 191–6, 198–201, 202, 207
Hunter, G. K., 164
Hutson, Lorna, 158

Icarus, 134
ignorance, 88; *see also* sexual ignorance
'imitatio', 174, 175, 178
inherited knowledge, 106–8
Integumenta Ovidii (John of Garland), 2

interiority, 270–1
intersex, 213–15, 218, 227, 235n
    Marin le Marcis, 230–3
intersex studies, 92
intertextuality, 27–8n
Iphis (Bellamy), 276n
Iphis and Iantha (anon), 4, 14
'Iphis and Ianthe' (Ovid)
    adaptations, 4
    animals in, 46
    bronze sculpture, 23–4
    classicists' readings of, 28n
    critical neglect of medieval and early modern versions, 1–2, 7–9
    Early Modern Conversions Project, 19
    gender, 216–17
    gender translation, 126–7
    grammatical gender, 215–16
    intertextuality, 27–8n
    Isis, 159–60, 203, 205
    lament, 1, 4, 10, 11–12, 13
    lesbian and queer interpretations, 9–14
    Ligdus, 104
    love, 12–13, 82, 83
    in medieval texts, 4, 88–9
    miracles, 5, 82
    opportunistic engagements with, 4
    stageplays, 6–7
    synopsis, 1, 81–3
    Telethusa, 1, 81, 205
    transformation of gender or sex, 83, 105, 156, 159–60, 165, 191, 203, 204–5, 215–17
    translations, 5–6, 15–16
    wedding night, 106
'Iphis and Iante' in *Ovide moralisé see Ovide moralisé*
'Iphis Changed from Girls into a Youth' (Kraus), 320*app*
'Iphis Disguised as a Youth' (anon), 308*app*, 309*app*
Iphis et Iante (Benserade), 6, 7, 10, 22, 234–5
    as *Bildungsroman*, 261–3, 265, 270–2
    desire, 252–3, 263–4, 265, 268–9, 271
    domestic heterosexuality, 254, 255
    eighteenth century commentators, 242, 254
    Ergaste, 250, 263, 267–9, 271
    female erotic agency, 253, 255
    female homoeroticism, 241, 244–9, 252–4, 255
    gallantry, 242, 251, 255
    gender ambiguity, 219, 227
    generational struggle, 262, 263–5, 268–70, 271
    heteronormativity, 254
    libertinage, 243
    Ligde (Lidgus), 219, 234, 264, 268
    love, 250, 251–2, 254–5
    Mérinte, 246, 250, 264, 268
    modernity, 243, 261–3
    Nise, 264, 268
    prayer, 68
    publications, 273
    relation to medical texts, 234–5
    sexual pleasure, 245, 248–9, 266–7
    sexuality of history, 262–3, 273
    social pressures, 266–7
    soliloquies, 266–7, 270–1
    Télétuze (Telethusa), 246, 253, 268, 269
    transformation/metamorphosis, 217–20, 247, 263, 267–8, 268–9
    wedding night, 247, 265
'Iphis puella in marem' (Kusel), 319*app*
'Iphis Puella in Marem' (Baur), 317*app*
'Iphis puella in marem' (Solis), 307*app*
'Iphis Puella in Marem. X' (Vander Borcht), 311*app*
Isis and Osirus, 105, 130
Island of Hermaphrodites, The, 218
isolarii (island books), 134
Isolario (Sonetti), 134, 136–40

James, Heather, 14, 48, 126–7
John of Garland, 2
Jove, 123

Kay, Sarah, 44
Kilgour, Maggie, 13
kinde love, 91
Knell, Thomas, 194
knowledge
    embodied, 214, 220–3
    false, 151
    inherited, 106–8
    knowledge relations, 69–70
    presumptive, 84
    see also disknowledge
Kraus, Johann Ulrich, 'Iphis Changed from Girls into a Youth', 320*app*
Kusel, Melchior
    'Iphis puella in manem', 319*app*
    'Lyctus and Telethusa uxor', 318*app*

'La figliola di Lyddo conuertita in maschio' (Solomon), 304*app*
'La fille Iphis en fils' (Solomon), 303*app*
La Mutacion de Fortune (Christine de Pizan), 99–113
    Ceyx and Alcyone, 101
    Circe, 109
    inherited knowledge, 106–8
    Ligdus, 104, 107
    relations to *Metamorphoses* and *Ovide moralisé*, 102–6, 112

sensual memory, 108–9
sentience, 111–12
skin, 112–13
text, 288–9*app*
Tiresias, 110
touch, 102–3, 108, 109, 113
transformation, 100, 102–3, 104, 105–6, 110, 113
translation, 101
La Vallière, Duc de, 242
L'Advision Christine (Christine de Pizan), 113
Lanser, Susan, 10, 20, 45, 251, 252, 273
Latin gloss, *Confessio Amantis* (Gower), 86–9, 95n
Latour, Bruno, 263
Le metamorfosi di Ovidio (Anguillara), 125, 127
lesbianism, 9–10, 82, 242, 243–9, 253–4; *see also* female homoeroticism; sapphism
Lestringant, Frank, 138
Liber insularum archipelagi (Buondelmonti), 134, *135*
libertinage, 243
Ligdus
  Confessio Amnatis (Gower), 84
  Iphis et Iante (Benserade), 219, 234, 264, 268
  La Mutacion de Fortune (Christine de Pizan), 104, 107
  Metamorphoses (Ovid), 104
  Ovide moralise (anon), 60, 67, 71, 104, 111
Lincolnshire, 191–6, 200–1; *see also* Humber Estuary
love
  amor impossibilis, 82
  Confessio Amantis (Confessions of the Lover) (Gower), 90–3
  Galatea (Lyly), 176, 184, 185, 203, 204
  humanist pedagogy, 173–4, 175
  Iphis et Iante (Benserade), 250, 251–2
  as passion, 255
'Lyctus, Telethusa, Iphis' (van de Pass), 314*app*
'Lyctus & Telethusa uxor' (Solis), 306*app*
'Lyctus and Telethusa uxor' (Kusel), 318*app*
'Lyctus et Telethusa Uxor. IX' (Vander Borcht), 310*app*
'Lyde & Teletuse' (Solomon), 302*app*
Lyly, John, 6, 150–1, 161–2, 163–5; *see also Galatea* (Lyly)
Lyne, Raphael, 16, 176, 204

'making much of', 22, 157, 182–3, 202
Marin le Marcis, 230–3, 238n
'Marriage of Iphis and Ianthe', 300*app*
Masten, Jeffrey, 11, 13, 119
masterly models, 181–5

medical discourse, 226–9
medical writers, 4
Mélite (Corneille), 244, 249
member apostis (false member), 51–2, 53, 71, 72, 111
memory, 108–9, 110
Mentz, Steve, 206
metamorphic plots, 10
metamorphic stories, 20
Metamorphoses (Ovid)
  adaptations, 4
  archipelagoes, 133–4
  Circe, 109
  divine interventions, 43
  etiologies, 8
  form, 7–8
  influence on medieval and early modern literature, 7, 8
  influence on Shakespeare, 14, 20
  Latin commentaries, 2
  Ligdus, 104
  Tiresias, 110
  translations, 3, 160–1, 196–8, 203, 204–5
  use in schools, 2–3, 159–61, 175
  see also 'Acis and Galatea' (trans. Golding); 'Iphis and Iante' (Ovid); *Ovide moralisé* (anon)
Marie-Germain, 225–6
Metamorphoses d'Ovide en rondeaux (Benserade), 274
metamorphosis, 203
  environmental, 192, 194–5, 196, 201–2
  Galatea (Lyly), 21, 157; *see also Galatea*: transformation/metamorphosis
  Iphis et Iante (Benserade), 247, 263, 267–8
  Ovide moralisé (anon), 44
  see also anamorphosis; transformation; transversion
Meteorologica (Aristotle), 151
mignons, 230
Mills, Robert, 11, 52, 85, 100, 105
Minerva, 123
miracles, 5, 12–13, 82
modernity, 261, 262, 263, 269, 271, 273
monsters, 12–13, 213, 229
Montaigne, Michel de, 223–6, 228–9
moralisation, 56; *see also Ovide moralisé*
Moretti, Franco, 261, 270, 271, 272
Mulcaster, Richard, 173–4, 179–80, 183
multiplicity, 130
mystery, 154–5, 156, 159, 164

'Narcissus and Echo' (Ovid), 19
Nardizzi, Vin, 201
narration, 56
natural particulars, 213–14

325

nature, 107–8, 199
natured love, 90–2
Newcomb, Lori Humphrey, 20
Newman, Karen, 16
novels *see* Bildungsroman

Oakley-Brown, Liz, 16
obedience, 172, 177, 179–80; *see also* subordination
On Monsters and Marvels (Paré), 226–7
'On some Verses of Virgil' (Montaigne), 223
'On the Force of the Imagination' (Montaigne), 228–9
ontology, 22
Ovid *see* Metamorphoses (Ovid)
Ovide moralisé (anon.), 2–3, 16
  adaptations, 46
  allegories, 43–5, 54–7, 71, 73–8, 107, 111
  animals, 47–8, 49, 65–6, 74
  'Birth of Iphis', 298*app*, 301*app*
  Caxton's translation, 160
  Ceyx and Alcyone, 113
  Christine de Pizan, 101
  Circe, 109
  death, 60, 62, 64–7, 71, 73, 75, 76
  desire, 46–9, 55, 64, 65–6
  euhemerist/historical interpretations, 43, 44–6, 49–54, 71–3, 110–11
  grammar, 50, 62–71
  Isis, 67
  in *La Mutacion de Fortune* (Christine de Pizan), 103–6
  lament, 63–4
  Ligdus, 60, 67, 71, 104, 111
  'Marriage of Iphis and Ianthe', 300*app*
  religion, 43, 44, 45–6, 54–6, 71, 73–8
  salvation, 74, 76
  sexual instrument, 52–3, 55, 89
  soul, 43, 44, 54–5, 56–7, 71, 73–7
  synopsis, 60
  'Telethusa and Iphis Pray to Isis', 299*app*
  temporality, 61–71
  text, 279–86*app*
  Tiresias, 111–12
  transformation, 68–78, 105
  wedding night, 106
Ovidian subculture, 2
Ovidius moralizatus (Bersuire), 3, 46
Ovid's Metamorphoses (Golding), 127–8, 131, 132, 160, 196–8, 201, 203–4, 207
  'Acis and Galatea', 191, 197–8, 199, 200, 201, 203, 207
  'Iphis and Ianthe' text, 289–93*app*
Ovid's Metamorphosis Englished (Sandys), 5–6, 293–7*app*
  illustration, 315*app*
Owen, A. E. B., 210

Paré, Ambroise, 217, 218, 226–8, 232, 234
  Marie-Germain, 228–9
Parfait, Claude and François, 242
partakers, 131, 132
parts, 131–2
Pasiphaë, 47–8, 49, 56, 82
passion, love as, 255
pastoral tragicomedy, 249–50
pastures, 200–1
perceptions *see* sense impressions
Phillips, Edward, 6
Pinet, Simon, 134, 137
Pintabone, Diane, 12
Piozzi, Hester Thrale, 6
Pizan *see* Christine de Pizan
plays *see* stageplays
Plutarch, 130
Pollack-Pelzner, Daniel, 270
popular culture, 229–30
preciosity, 242
prodigiosus, 12
prodigious, 12–13, 82
Pyrrhonian scepticism, 214, 220–3, 224–5, 235–6n

Queer Philologies (Masten), 11
queer studies, 30n

Racine, Jean, 254
Rackin, Phyllis, 14
reading, 102–3, 108, 113
religion, 271; *see also* Christianity
religious conversion, 21, 22–3, 43–4
Renaissance of Lesbianism, The (Traub), 249
retentive memory, 108–9
R.H., Gent. 123–4
Rich, Barnabe, 4, 5
riddles, 13
  Confessio Amantis (Gower), 85–6, 88–9, 90–2, 93
Riolan, Jean, 233
Romeo and Juliet, 272–3
Rousseau, Jean-Jacques, 265

S*X, 119, 142n
Sabie, Francis, 195–6
St Peter's Church, Barton-Upon Humber, 206, 210n
Saker, Austin (Narbonus), 4, 5
Salic law, 225
salvation, 54–5, 56
Sandys, George, 3
  Ovid's Metamorphosis Englished, 5–6, 293–7*app*, 315*app*
sapphism, 10, 20, 262, 263, 264, 265, 273–4
Saxton, Christopher, 192

scattering, 130–3, 140
scepticism *see* Pyrrhonian scepticism
Schérer, Jacques, 271
Scholemaster, The (Ascham), 173
Scragg, Leah, 164, 199
sculpture (Rodin), 23–4
sea level rises, 192, 201–2; *see also* floods
Semele, 123–4
sense impressions, 221–2
senses, 214
sensual memory, 108–9
sentence, 56–7, 111–12
  meilloir sentence, 53, 71
  sentence historial, 45
sex change, 5, 9; *see also* transformation, metamorphosis
Sextus Empiricus, 221, 222–3, 224
sexual desire *see* desire
sexual ignorance, 85–6, 88, 89, 93
sexual instruments, 48, 52
  false member (*member apostis*), 51–2, 53, 71, 72, 111
sexuality, 253–4
  history of, 11, 20, 243, 262
  of history, 45–6, 56, 262, 273
Sexuality of History, The (Lanser), 252, 262
Shakespeare, William, 14, 20, 22, 161
Shannon, Laurie, 46, 157–8
skin, 112–13
Smith, Ali, 80, 93
social pressures, 266–7
soliloquies, 270–1
Solis, Virgil
  'Iphis puella in marem', 307*app*
  'Lyctus & Telethusa uxor', 306*app*
Soloman, Bernard, 297*app*
  woodcuts, 302*app*, 303*app*, 304*app*, 305*app*
Sonetti, Bartolomeo dalli, 134, 136
  Isolario, 134, 136–40
spatiality, 16–18
Sporades, 133
stageplays, 6–7; *see also Galatea* (Lyly); *Iphis et Iante* (Benserade)
'Story of a Man with Woman's Hair' (Tesserant), 229
Stryker, Susan, 118
subordination, 177–81
supplementarity, 44, 52–3, 55–6, 57

Telethusa
  "Iphis and Iante" (Ovid), 1, 81
  Iphis et Iante (Benserade) *see Iphis et Iante* (Benserade): Télétuze
  La Mutacion de Fortune (Christine de Pizan), 104–5

Ovide moralisé (anon), 60, 68, 69, 70, 71, 75, 111
Ovid's Metamorphoses (Golding), 131, 205
'Telethusa and Iphis Pray to Isis', 299*app*
'Telethusa Praying' (de Jode), 312*app*, 313*app*
'Teletusa fa credere al marito che la sua figliola è maschio' (Solomon), 305*app*
temporality, 16–18, 21–2, 61
  Ovide moralisé (anon), 71–8
  see also trans* time
Terence, 244, 249, 250, 251
Tesserant, Claude de, 229–30
tide, Humber Estuary, 202
time *see* temporality; trans* time
Tiresias, 110, 111–12
'to make much of', 22, 157, 182–3
Tolias, George, 134
Tompkins, Avery, 118
touch, 102–3, 108, 109, 113
tragicomedy, 249–50
trans, 15, 16, 17–18, 119
trans-, 17–18, 119
trans*, 17–18, 31n, 61, 67–8, 118, 119, 126, 141–2n
trans*studies, 141; *see also* transgender studies
trans*survival, 60
trans* time, 62
  Iphis's lament, 62–8
  see also Ovide moralise; temporality
trans*version, 126, 130–3; *see also* transversion
transformation, 17
  'Acis and Galatea' (trans. Golding), 197–8
  Christine de Pizan, 100–1
  Confessio Amantis (Confessions of the Lover) (Gower), 92, 93–4
  Galatea (Lyly), 158–9, 166, 176–7, 179, 180–1, 184–5, 191, 203
  'Iphis and Iante' (Ovid), 83, 105, 215–17
  Iphis et Iante (Benserade), 217–20, 247, 267–8, 268–9
  La Mutacion de Fortune (Christine de Pizan), 100, 102–3, 104, 105–6, 110, 113
  medical discourse, 226–8
  Ovide moralisé (anon), 68–78, 105
  Tiresias, 110
  Worlde of Wordes, A (Florio), 125–6, 127, 128–9
  see also metamorphosis
transgender studies, 92
  keywords, 118, 141
Transgender Studies Quarterly (TSQ*), 118
transgender theory, 11, 61
trans-gendering, 124–9; *see also* transgender; trans*gender
translation, 3, 5–6, 15–16, 88–9, 126–7

327

trans-narrative, 126
transversion, 15, 18, 20–3, 126; *see also* trans*version
Traub, Valerie, 10, 82, 126, 137, 243
tribadism, 244, 249
Tylus, Jane, 16

untoward behaviour, 172, 177, 184

Valentine, David, 61
van de Pass, Crispijn
   'Lyctus, Telethusa, Iphis', 314*app*
Vander Borcht, Petrus
   'Iphis Puella in Marem. X', 311*app*
   'Lyctus et Telethusa Uxor. IX', 310*app*
Venus, 184, 185
version, 18
Voltaire, 254–5

Wahl, Elizabeth, 243, 248
Walsham, Alexandra, 199
Wars of Religion, 225
Way of the World, The (Moretti), 261, 270, 271, 272
wedding night, 106
Weinstein, Jami, 61, 119
Wetherbee, Winthrop, 88, 90–1
widowhood, 103
Wills, David, 53
Winter's Tale (Shakespeare), 20
Wiseman, Susan, 16, 196, 203
women, 225
Wooford, Susanne, 130
world atlases, 137
Worlde of Wordes, A (Florio), 12, 121–3, 140
   Bacchus, 123, 124
   scattering, 130–3, 140
   trans-gendering, 124–9

'youth as such', 251, 261, 268, 269, 270–1, 272–3, 274; *see also* generational struggle

EU representative:
Easy Access System Europe
Mustamäe tee 50, 10621 Tallinn, Estonia
Gpsr.requests@easproject.com